Harry Dunham

CONSTRUCTION PROJECT ADMINISTRATION

CONSTRUCTION PROJECT ADMINISTRATION

EDWARD R. FISK, P.E.

JOHN WILEY & SONS
NEW YORK CHICHESTER BRISBANE TORONTO

Library of Congress Cataloging in Publication Data:

Fisk, Edward R   1924-
    Construction project administration.

    Includes index.
    1. Construction industry—Management.   I. Title
TH438.F57   658.4'04   77-16455
ISBN 0-471-02312-4

Printed in the United States of America

10 9 8 7 6 5 4

PREFACE

The main objective of this book is to provide students of construction management and on-site representatives, engineers, and inspectors with ready access to a single source of information that will help them prepare for the responsibilities they will confront on every modern construction project. The book's value, however, is not limited to just this audience. Every supervisory or management-level employee of the owner, the architectural or engineering firm, the contractor, or the construction management firm can benefit from its contents.

The book covers the major elements of construction project administration that the on-site representative is likely to encounter.

I wish to extend my appreciation and thanks to Mr. Paul Askelson of CalTrans, Mr. James Acsai of NAVFAC, and Mr. Paul Lindstrom of Smith-Emery Company Laboratories who provided material used in this book. I especially want to thank Mr. Donald Scarbrough of Winn & Associates of Dallas, Texas, who carefully reviewed and critiqued the chapter on CPM scheduling and contributed ideas to it.

Edward R. Fisk

CONTENTS

Chapter 4
RECORDS AND REPORTS   45

Files and Records — Construction Progress Record — Inspector's Diary or
Construction Log — Discrepancy Reports — Documentation of Dangerous
Safety Hazard Warnings — Miscellaneous Records — Labor Standards
Review Records — Job Conferences — Contractor Submittals —
Construction Photographs — Photographic Equipment and Materials

Chapter 5
SPECIFICATIONS AND DRAWINGS   73

What is a Specification? — Conflicts Between the Drawings and
Specifications — Content and Component Parts of a Specification — What
do the Specifications Mean to the Inspector? — CSI Specifications
"Format": Its Meaning and Importance — State Highway Department
Formats — Non-Standard Construction Specification Formats in Use —
Specifications versus Special Provisions Concept

Chapter 6
ANALYSIS AND FUNCTION OF THE
SPECIFICATIONS   91

General Conditions of the Construction Contract — Using the General
Conditions — Supplementary General Conditions — Technical Provisions
of the Specifications — Addenda to the Specifications — Standard
Specifications — Master Specifications — Special Material and Product
Standards — Building Codes, Regulations, Ordinances, and Permits —
Types of Drawings Comprising the Construction Contract — Order of
Precedence of Contract Documents

Chapter 7
CONSTRUCTION LAWS AND LABOR RELATIONS   115

Compliance With Laws and Regulations — Public versus Private Contracts
— Traffic Requirements During Construction — Code Enforcement Agency
Requirements — Work Within or Adjacent to Navigable Waterways — Fair
Subcontracting Laws — Federal Labor Laws — Labor Relations

CONSTRUCTION PROJECT ADMINISTRATION

1
DESIGN/ CONSTRUCTION PROCESS

THROUGHOUT THE ages humans have been building to meet the needs of their habitation on this earth. Then, just as now, the planning and building of each such project involved the collective efforts of many different skills and types of specialized knowledge. At first the methods were primitive but effective. As the products of modern technology replaced the older, outdated tools of these early builders, the methods of construction and the types of skills and specialized knowledge required to complete a construction project have had to change to keep pace.

PROJECT PARTICIPANTS

Whether the project is a building, bridge, dam, pipeline, sewage treatment plant, water supply system, or any one of numerous other types of projects, it requires the skills and services of a project team comprised of three principal participants:

The owner
The designer
The builder

Each of the above will normally involve other participants as a part of the team effort, either as a consultant, a quality control and assurance representative, a subcontractor, or as a supplier of materials and equipment.

In practice, the owner usually enters into a contract with an architect/engineer to plan and design a project to satisfy the owner's particular needs. The owner participates during the design period to set criteria for design, cost, and time limits for completion and to provide decision-making inputs to the architect/engineer. Upon completion of the planning and design process, the project is ready for construction, and the advertising or selection process to obtain a qualified construction contractor begins.

After selection of a qualified construction contractor, the owner enters into a contract directly with the contractor, who will then be fully responsible directly to the owner or his designated representative for building the project in accordance with the plans, specifications and local laws. He has the further responsibility for the integrity of the new structure that he has built—in effect, he must guarantee his work. Although the architect/engineer is obligated to make field visitations to the construction site during the progress of the work, such periodic visits are for the purpose of observing materials and completed work to evaluate their *general* compliance with plans, specifications, and design and planning concepts only. They should not be interpreted as including full-time inspection for quality control and assurance.

Thus, on the typical project there are only two prime contracts with the owner: one with the architect/engineer for the design and planning of the project; the other with a single construction contractor or occasionally several principal construction contractors to build the project.

As is frequently the case on a modern complex project, numerous special types of construction are involved, and the contractor who entered into an agreement with the owner to build a project finds that the work can better be accomplished by subcontracting with a specialty contractor to do this portion of the work. Such subcontracts are agreements between the principal or "general" contractor and the subcontractor only, and involve no contractual relationship between any subcontractor and the owner. Under the owner's contract for construction, the general contractor is fully responsible for the entire work, whether or not he has utilized subcontractors to accomplish any portion of it. The traditional contractual arrangement is illustrated in Figure 1.

Figure 1.1 does not take into account the relationship between an owner with his own in-house engineering staff, such as many public agencies, and the construction contractor. However, by combining the functions of *owner* and *architect/engineer* in the diagram, the relationships would be similar.

Construction Administration

Construction administration and contract administration should not be confused. Contract administration refers to those functions that the owner or the registered professional engineer or architect of record performs himself. Construction administration involves only those functions of contract administration that, if not performed by the owner or the architect/engineer, will often be delegated by him to his resident project representative (resident engineer or resident inspector). Such functions, when performed by the resident project representative, must be performed under the responsible charge of the architect, engineer, or other representative of the owner responsible for contract administration. The limits of responsibility and authority of the resident project representative are, therefore,

TRADITIONAL

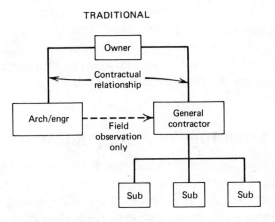

- Separate designer
- Single general contractor
- Numerous subcontractors
- Fixed price, unit price, guaranteed maximum,
  or cost plus a fixed fee construction contract
- Negotiated professional fee for design service

Figure 1.1 *Traditional construction contract relationships.*

only those tasks specifically delegated to him by the architect or engineer of record or other owner's representative responsible for administration of the construction contract—even if the resident project representative is himself a registered professional engineer or architect.

Control of Quality in Construction

Without definition, the term "quality control" in construction can have several meanings. To be sure, the actual quality of construction depends largely upon the control of the construction itself, thus involving the contractor to a great extent. What constitutes "quality control" and "quality assurance" appears to be the subject of dispute by some. For example, checking the placement of reinforcing steel in concrete formwork may be considered as quality control if the contractor does it, and as quality assurance if the owner does it; yet the physical act of checking this work is exactly the same in either case.

Whether the subject be called "quality control" or "quality assurance," the function performed is essentially that which has been recognized over the years as being construction inspection and testing of materials and workmanship to see that the work meets the requirements of the drawings and specifications. Inspection takes many forms, and its responsibilities vary somewhat depending upon the intended inspection objective. As an example, an inspector in the employ of the local building official is principally concerned with the safety and integrity of the structure being built, and whether it meets the local building code requirements. Quality of workmanship or esthetics is largely beyond his responsibility, and, because his salary is paid by the public, quality of workmanship is, to a great extent, left up to the owner to control, using his own or the contractor's or the designer's personnel. On the other hand, inspection by the owner's representative is intended to include concern not only for the structural integrity and safety of the structure, but also for the quality of workmanship, selection of materials being used, esthetic values and similar matters involving compliance with the provisions of the contract plans and specifications.

ORGANIZATIONAL STRUCTURE OF A CONSTRUCTION PROJECT

There is no single organization chart that will remotely approximate the organizational structure of the field forces of the owner, the design organization, or the contractor on all projects. Before the internal structure of any of the principals to a construction contract can be examined, some understanding of the several basic types of contractual relationships must be gained. Of the several types of relationships freqently encountered in construction, four of the principal types of contractual relationships are:

1. Traditional architect/engineer contract
2. Design/construction manager contract
3. Professional construction manager contract
4. Design-build (turnkey construction) contract

Under the provisions of the *traditional architect/engineer* contract illustrated in Figure 1.1, the owner engages the services of an architect/engineer to perform planning and design services, including preparation of plans, specifications, and estimates. Professional services of the architect/engineer during the construction are generally limited to performance of intermittent field visitations and certain contract administration functions such as review of the contractor's payment requests, review of shop drawings, evaluation of contractor claims, interpretation of plans and specifications during construction, change order requests, and final inspection.

A *design/construction manager* contract, illustrated in Figure 1.2, is quite similar to the traditional A/E contract with the exception that the architect/engineer's project manager is fully responsible to the owner during both the design and planning phases as well as the entire construction phase to provide for all project needs. This includes all scheduling, cost control, quality control, long-lead purchasing, letting of single or multiple contracts, and coordination of the work. His responsibilities do not terminate until final acceptance of the completed project by the owner.

These responsibilities include the examination of cost-saving alternatives during both the design and construction phases of the project, and the authority to require the design or construction changes necessary to accomplish the owner's objectives.

A *professional construction management* contract is based upon the relatively new concept pioneered by the General Services Administration of the federal government, and is extensively used by that agency for the construction of public buildings. While the functions performed by the professional construction manager may be no different than those of the design/construction manager, his responsibilities and contractual status are

DESIGN/CONSTRUCTION MANAGER

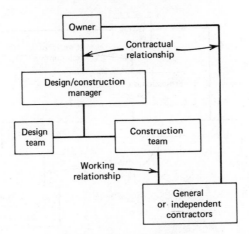

- Single firm responsible for both
  design and construction management
- Fixed price, or negotiated individual
  construction contracts or subcontracts
- Fixed price, or cost plus a fee design
  construction contract

Figure 1.2 *Contractual relationships under a design construction manager type contract.*

significantly different. Under the professional construction manager concept, illustrated in Figure 1.3, the owner engages the construction manager under a separate contract in addition to his conventional architect/engineer and construction contractor contracts. Thus, instead of only two contracts for a project, the owner has actually executed three. In keeping with the principles of this concept, the professional construction manager performs no design or construction with his own forces, but acts solely in the capacity of an owner's representative on the project. In many cases, he is responsible for reviewing the architect/engineer's payment requests in addition to those of the contractor. In any case, he is responsible for total project time and cost control as well as quality control and as such provides supervision and control over those functions of the architect/engineer and the contractor that relate to these important subject areas.

One important distinction is that a ''construction manager'' under this concept is an organization, not an individual. Thus the construction manager firm may provide a staff of both field and office personnel, including estimators, schedulers, accountants, superintendents, field engineers, quality control personnel, and others.

A *design-build* contract, illustrated in Figure 1.4, popularly called ''turnkey construction,'' is based upon the owner entering into an agreement with a single firm to produce all planning, design, and construction with his own in-house capabilities. Such design-build firms are generally licensed as both architect/engineer's *and* as general construction contractors in those states that require it, and offer a complete ''package'' deal to the owner.

PROFESSIONAL CONSTRUCTION MANAGER

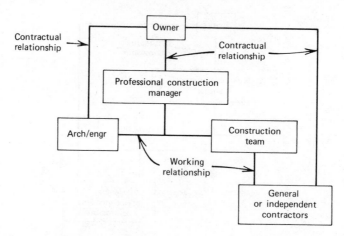

- Three party team of owner, designer, and construction manager
- Fixed price or negotiated individual construction contracts directly with owner
- Construction manager may act as owner's agent to extent delegated
- Negotiated professional fee for construction management services
- Negotiated professional fee for design services

Figure 1.3   Contractual relationships under a professional construction manager contract.

Its principal advantages, where its use is permitted, are the elimination of contractor claims against the owner resulting from errors in the plans or specifications and the ability to begin construction on each separate phase of a project as it is completed, without waiting for overall project design completion—the "fast-track" concept. It is in the design-build industry that fast-track construction was born.

There is one disadvantage in the system where public funds are involved in construction. Under most laws, a construction contractor must be obtained through a competitive bidding process, and the lowest bidder gets the job. Usually design firms and construction management organizations are selected on the basis of their individual expertise and previous experience in the type of work to be designed. Under this concept it is felt that the greatest savings and cost benefits to the owner will be obtained by careful planning during the design stage, and that the occasional cost savings that might result from competitively bidding the design responsibilities would be more than lost in the resultant higher construction cost that all too often follows a set of plans and specifications that had to be prepared in a hurry without checking.

Staff Assignments for Construction Quality Control

The staff requirements for the construction management and quality control activities of a construction project vary from job to job and from one employer to another. Although there seems to be a lack of uniformity in the structuring of many owners' or architect/engineers' field forces during construction, the average contractor organization seems extremely well organized in this area. This is probably to be expected, as the

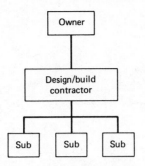

- Combined designer and construction contractor
- Numerous subcontractors
- Fixed price, guaranteed maximum or cost
  plus fixed fee designed/build contract
- No separate fee for design services

Figure 1.4   Design-build contract relation-ships (turkey construction).

contractor is performing his primary function at the site, while the owner or architect/engineer is often on less familiar ground during the construction phase.

In an effort to attempt to compare job assignments and titles of positions of comparable authority from one organization to the next, the numerous titles of the same job emphasize the difficulty of determining position by title alone. Figure 1.5 is a chart of the normal functional relationships under a design/construction management contract and will be used to illustrate the problem.

An example of supervisory job titles of comparable authority is shown in the following tabulation, which is based upon actual job titles used by some contractor and architect and engineer offices to designate the various levels of supervisory and management personnel utilized during the construction phase of a project. The levels indicated are those used in the illustration in Figure 1.5.

Level	Owner or Architect/Engineer	Contractor
Project Management Level	Project Manager Project Engineer Project Architect	Project Manager General Superintendent Construction Manager
Construction Management Level	Resident Engineer Resident Architect Construction Coordinator Resident Manager	Construction Manager Project Engineer Superintendent
Functional Management Level	Resident Project Representative Full-Time Project Representative Resident Engineer Resident Inspector Inspector Quality Control Supv.	Project Engineer Superintendent CQC Representative

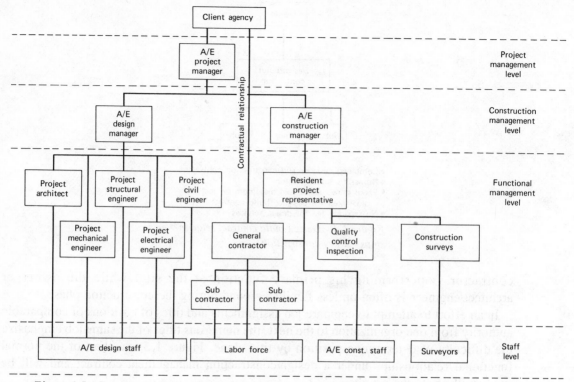

Figure 1.5 *Functional relationships under a design construction manager contract.*

All of the above levels share in the responsibility of administering various provisions of the construction contract for their respective employers. In addition to the foregoing list of full-time personnel on the project site, numerous tasks remain to be performed by specialty inspectors and representatives of the various local government agencies having jurisdiction over the project. These include the following public and private specialty and code enforcement inspectors:

1. Local building department (code enforcement)
2. Soils inspectors
3. Inspectors of other agencies whose facilities are involved
4. Utility company inspectors
5. Specialty inspectors (concrete, masonry, welding, etc.)
6. Manufacturer's representatives (special equipment or materials)
7. OSHA safety inspectors

Each of the specialty and code enforcement inspectors is responsible only for his particular specialty task; thus, the overall responsibility for project administration and quality control falls on the shoulders of the resident project representative of the owner or design firm or the contractor's quality control (CQC) representative.

Full-Time versus Part-Time Project Representative

Not all construction projects subject to inspection by the owner or the design firm will require a full-time inspector. It is not infrequent for a single construction inspector to be assigned the responsibility of resident project representative for several projects at the same time. Usually, this is a method used to provide quality assurance inspections on smaller projects whose budget or complexity of construction do not justify the financial burden of a full-time resident project representative. The difference in responsibility is slight, as the administrative responsibilities are identical to those of the full-time resident project representative on a single large project. As for the inspections performed, the inspector merely schedules his time so as to be at each of the projects at key times during construction. Generally, he is on call and can respond to a specific field problem on short notice.

PROFESSIONAL CONSTRUCTION MANAGEMENT

The term ''construction manager'' is one of the most misunderstood titles of modern day construction and defies an accurate definition acceptable to everyone. Definitions have ranged all the way from applying the term to the resident project representative to the other extreme of being a third prime contract with the owner (the other two prime contracts being that of the architect/engineer and that of the general construction contractor). In the latter case, the construction manager is the owner's agent and his duties require him to supervise some of the functions of both the design firm and the contractor. The American Society of Civil Engineers refers to this function as ''professional construction management'' to distinguish it from the type of construction management practiced by the design/construction management firms. Both the American Institute of Architects and the Associated General Contractors of America simply refer to this type of contract as ''construction management.''

Each of the major professional and technical organizations seems to agree in principle on the concept that the construction manager should be a firm that has no direct connection with either the architect/engineer firm that designs the project or the general contracting firm that constructs it. Even where a general contractor acts as construction manager, the Associated General Contractors recommends that they enter into contract under a professional services agreement, and that the firm does not use any of its own construction forces to build the project. The principal difference between the professional services agreement proposed by the Associated General Contractors and, say, that of the American Institute of Architects is that the AGC contract provides for quoting a guaranteed maximum project cost after the construction management team has developed the drawings and specifications to a point where the scope of the project is clearly defined. Under the AIA contract form, no price guarantees are made.

Engineering Definition of Professional Construction Management

The *Professional Construction Management Committee* of the American Society of Civil Engineers defines a professional construction manager as a firm or organization specializing in the practice of construction management or practicing it on a particular project as a part of a project management team consisting of the owner, a design organization, and the construction manager (usually referred to as the CM). As the construction professional on the project management team, the CM provides the following services or portions of such services, as appropriate:

1. Works with the owner and design organization from the beginning of design through completion of construction; provides leadership to construction team on all matters that relate to construction; makes recommendations on construction technology, schedules, and construction economies.
2. Proposes construction alternatives to be studied by the project management team during the planning phase, and predicts the effect of these alternatives on the project cost and schedule; once the project budget, schedule, and quality requirements have been established, the CM monitors the subsequent development of the project to see that those targets are not exceeded without the knowledge of the owner.
3. Advises on and coordinates procurement of material and equipment and the work of all the construction contractors; monitors and inspects for conformance to design requirements; provides current cost and progress information as the work proceeds; and performs other construction-related services as required by the owner.
4. In keeping with the nonadversary relationship of the team members, the CM does not normally perform significant design or construction work with his own forces.

The typical functional relationships associated with a professional construction management contract are best shown in Figure 1.6, which was prepared by the General Services Administration, Public Buildings Service of the federal government.

"Fast-Track" Construction

Frequently, a construction management contract is encountered that requires the letting and administering of multiple construction contracts for the same project, with each let at different times during the life of the project. Such staggered letting of construction contracts on the same project is referred to as "fast-track" contracting, and its principal objective is to shorten construction time for the overall project by starting some of the work as soon as it has been designed. (Chapter 10) Many times, such contracts also require purchase of special equipment or materials long before a contract has been let to install them. This is referred to as long-lead procurement, and such early purchases, along with the accompanying expediting and scheduling, is one of the functions required to be performed by the CM team. The resident project representative is a vital link in the successful operation of a construction management contract, and he will be called upon to assist in many of the tasks described.

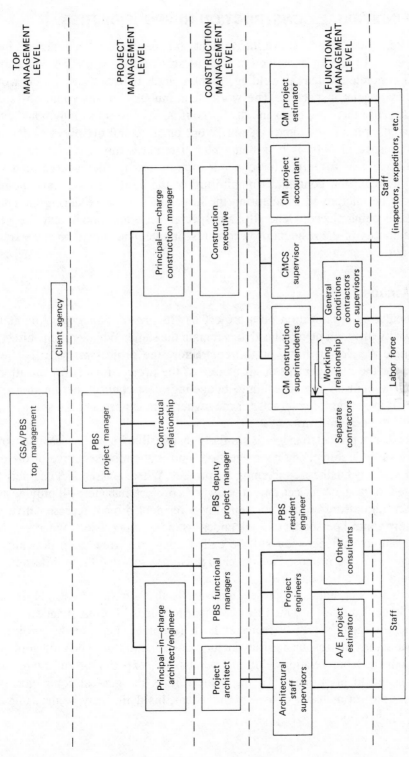

Figure 1.6 Functional relationships under a General Services Administration professional construction management contract.

DEFINITIONS OF INDIVIDUAL CONSTRUCTION RESPONSIBILITIES

Local building codes often require intermittent and sometimes "continuous" inspection on certain critical types of construction such as structural concrete, structural masonry, prestressed concrete, structural welding, high-strength bolting, and similar work to be performed by special inspectors. The word "continuous" in this context is sometimes confusing because there are cases in which "continuous" is not synonymous with "constant" without a reasonable interpretation. Work on structural masonry or concrete work that can be inspected only as it is being placed requires the *constant* presence of the inspector. Placement of forms for concrete or reinforcing for concrete can fairly be interpreted as requiring continuous monitoring of the work so as to miss nothing, yet would hardly be interpreted as requiring the inspector's presence during the entire time that the steel is being placed. Generally, any special inspector coming onto the job will be under the authority of the resident project representative, and should be advised to follow his instructions.

Project Manager

Every participating organization on a project has its *project manager*. Although sometimes known by different names, his duties remain the same. Whether in the direct employ of the owner, the design firm, or the contractor, the project manager is the person responsible for the management of all phases of the project for his organization. For a design firm, he controls the scheduling, budgeting, cost control coordination of design and construction, letting of contracts for the owner, and is normally the sole contact with his client for the design firm.

For the owner, a project manager is similarly responsible for all phases of a project, but may participate in architect/engineer selection, and is the representative of the owner in connection with any business concerning the project. Where an architect/engineer firm has been engaged for design services only, the owner's project manager will provide construction contract administration and may employ a resident project representative or other on-site quality control personnel to work under his direct supervision. Wherever this is the case, the architect/engineer may still be called upon to review shop drawings for the owner, and wherever a proposed design change is contemplated the architect/engineer of record should always be consulted.

In a contractor's organization project manager is also a frequently used title, although many very large firms still use the title of "superintendent" for this function. As the title implies, the contractor's project manager is in complete charge of his project for the general contractor. His responsibilities include coordination of subcontractors, scheduling, cost control, labor relations, billing, purchasing, expediting, and numerous other functions related to his project. To the owner, *he* is the general contractor. Whether referred to as project manager or as superintendent, his duties may be the same in many contractor organizations.

Quality Control Representative

Under the provisions of the construction contracts of numerous federal agencies, in particular the Corps of Engineers, Naval Facilities Engineering Command, National Aeronautics and Space Administration, and others, an inspection concept known as "contractor quality control" (CQC) is being implemented. Under this system, the contractor must organize and maintain an inspection system within his own organization to assure that the work performed by his own and his subcontractor forces conforms to contract requirements, and to make available to the government adequate records of such inspections. Under the majority of such plans, as implemented by their respective agencies, a government representative is stationed on site to provide quality assurance inspections. In some cases, the design firm may be engaged to provide quality assurance inspection in addition to contractor quality control. In such cases, the design firm may have a full-time resident project representative and supporting staff on site to perform this function.

Resident Project Representative; Resident Engineer; Resident Inspector; Resident Manager

These titles usually refer to an on-site full-time project representative to whom has been delegated the authority and responsibility of administering the field operations of a construction project as the representative of the owner or the design firm. On some occasions the inspection needs of a particular project may require that the resident project representative be a qualified, registered professional engineer; in other cases, a highly qualified nonregistered engineer may be desired. Wherever a nonregistered engineer is permissible, it is often equally acceptable to use an experienced construction inspector for this purpose. The American Institute of Architects in their documents describe this individual as the "full-time project representative" while the National Society of Professional Engineers uses the term "resident project representative." In this book the term "resident project representative" will be used to stand collectively for resident engineer, resident inspector, full-time project representative, and resident manager.

Inspector; Field Engineer; Quality Control Supervisor

These titles usually refer to a staff-level, on-site representative of the owner, design firm, or contractor who has the responsibility of observing the work being performed, and of reporting any variations from the plans and specifications or other contract documents. In addition, the inspector should call to the attention of his supervisor unforeseen field conditions in time for remedial measures to be taken without creating delays in the work or changes in existing work to correct a problem. The inspector is the on-site eyes and ears of his employer, and although not empowered to make field changes that depart from the plans and specifications, he should be capable of evaluating field problems and submitting competent recommendations to his supervisor. On projects using a resident project representative, the inspector will normally work under his direct supervision.

Except for the responsibility for construction field administration, which is one of the principal functions of the resident project representative, the inspector's job is identical in all respects to that of the resident project representative. Inspection of construction is an occupation that requires a highly qualified person with a good working knowledge of construction practices, construction materials, specifications, and construction contract provisions. It is not in itself a job title, as the inspector may be a registered professional engineer or architect, a field engineer, a quality control specialist, or a host of other classifications. In this book the term "inspector" will be used to stand collectively for field engineer, inspector, quality control supervisor, or in some cases the resident project representative, where the duties referred to apply to all field representatives on site, whether full- or part-time.

Bibliography

"Professional Construction Management," by Donald S. Barrie and Boyd C. Paulson, Jr., Vol. 102 No. CO3, Sept 1976, *Journal of the Construction Division,* Proceedings of the American Society of Civil Engineers, pages 427 and 428.

"Standard Form of Agreement Between Owner and Construction Manager," AIA Document No. B801, Dec 1973 Edition, American Institute of Architects, Washington, D.C.

"Standard Form of Agreement Between Owner and Construction Manager (Guaranteed Maximum Price Option)" AGC Document No. 8, Sept 1974 Edition, Associated General Contractors of America, Washington, D.C.

NAVFAC Construction Quality Control Manual, NAVFAC P-445, March 1975, Department of the Navy, Naval Facilities Engineering Command, Alexandria, VA.

2
INSPECTOR RESPONSIBILITY AND AUTHORITY

THE INSPECTOR AS A MEMBER OF THE CONSTRUCTION TEAM

The effective management of a construction operation can only be achieved through a well-coordinated team effort. The inspector is a vital member of that team, for without him there will normally be no direct involvement in the construction of the project by the architect/engineer or the owner. The inspector is the eyes and the ears of the architect or engineer and the owner and his authority and responsibility on the project are largely based upon that concept. To be sure, one architect or engineer may delegate more or less authority to the inspector than another architect or engineer; however, that is a matter of employer-employee relations between the inspector and his employer. In addition, many federal construction contracts require a resident inspector in the employ of the contractor under the principle of "contractor quality control" (CQC). Generally, in the absence of specific instructions to the contrary, the guidelines in this chapter are considered by many members of the construction industry as the normal standards.

WHY AN INSPECTOR AT ALL?

It is not enough to leave the assurance of quality workmanship and materials entirely in the hands of the contractor. The architect/engineer or other design firm who was responsible for the determination of site conditions and for the preparation of the plans and specifications should be retained during the construction phase to provide field administration and quality control for the owner, the safety of the public, and the professional reputation of both the design firm and the contractor. Many architects and engineers seem to believe that if their design is adequate and the plans and specifications are carefully prepared, the field construction will take care of itself. Experience has proven this to be far from true.

Although a design firm acting as the agent of the owner during the construction phase of a project does not guarantee the work of the contractor, nor does he in any way relieve the contractor of any of his responsibilities under the terms of the construction contract, the design firm through its field inspection forces must endeavor to guard the owner against defects and deficiencies in the work. When, in the judgment of the designer, the plans and specifications are not being properly followed, and he has been unable to obtain compliance by the contractor, the owner should be notified so that appropriate measures can be taken. Inspection should be performed during the progress of the work; inspection after completion defeats the purpose of providing quality control and assurance on the job, as many potential difficulties must be detected during construction; otherwise, they may be permanently covered. The result would be a latent defect that may not be discovered for years; then, when it is discovered, it may be too late, as it may have been instrumental in contributing to a structural failure or other disaster.

Often, the word "supervision" has been used in the past in connection with field inspection. It is a legally dangerous term, and as such its use has long been discouraged by all technical and professional societies of the construction industry. In the recent revision of the General Conditions of the Contract for Construction by the American Institute of Architects, with the help of the Associated General Contractors of America, the American Subcontractor's Association, the Associated Specialty Contractors, and the National Society of Professional Engineers, the general contractor is allowed greater management control while the architect's involvement during the construction phase is lessened. The new version of the AIA General Conditions states that the architect "will not be responsible for and will not have control of construction means, methods, techniques, or procedures, or for safety precautions." Therefore, the resident inspector, as the resident project representative for the design firm and the owner should not direct, supervise, or assume control over the means, methods, techniques, sequences, or procedures of construction except as specifically called for in the project specifications. Instead, the resident project representative should exercise his authority on behalf of the owner so that such activities will result in a project substantially in accordance with the requirements of the contract documents.

Construction administration and construction quality control by the contractor or quality assurance by the design firm or owner should include continuous on-site inspection during all structural construction of a building by one or more competent, technically qualified and experienced inspectors. If employed directly by the owner or by the design firm, all such inspectors should be under the architect/engineer's supervision and direction and should report any discrepancies directly to the architect/engineer. If there is a staff of several inspectors on a project, all other inspectors should be under the direct supervision of the resident project representative, and all communications between them and the owner or design firm should be through the resident project representative. It is the responsibility of these other inspectors to see that all details of the engineer's or architect's design drawings, shop drawings, bar placing drawings, and similar documents that have been approved by the engineer or architect are constructed in strict accordance with their respective requirements. In addition, each inspector must see that all the requirements of the specifications have been met and that all workmanship and construction practices are equal to or in excess of the standards called for in the contruction contract documents. The inspector should also make certain, as the job progresses, that the mechanical and electrical installations are constructed in accordance with the approved drawings, and that nonstructural items do not adversely interfere with structural elements. Supervision by the architect/engineer and by the inspector are really quite different, particularly in one very important respect. The inspector should have no authority to change plans or specifications, nor to make his own interpretations, even though he may be a qualified engineer with both design and construction experience. If any question of interpretation arises, or if there is a disagreement on a technical matter between the inspector and the contractor, or if there appears to be any possibility of error or deviation from good construction practice that is noticed by the inspector, it should immediately be brought to the attention of the architect/engineer's project manager for decision. Inspection by the contractor under a CQC Contract should follow similar procedures. On the other hand, supervision by the architect/engineer or his designated project manager, as distinct from that of the resident project representative (resident inspector), may include the authority to modify the plans and specifications consistent with the contract provisions between the owner and the design firm and between the owner and the contractor, if job conditions indicate that a change would be in the interest of improvement of the structure or if such a change were otherwise justified and consistent with sound design principles followed in the original design.

AUTHORITY AND RESPONSIBILITY OF THE RESIDENT PROJECT REPRESENTATIVE

Certain specific authority must be given to the resident project representative so that he can function effectively. In addition, the contractor should be made fully aware of the authority of the resident project representative. Although a number of documents have been published that set forth a recommended scope of an inspector's authority and responsibility, the following is recommended because it represents a set of standards that have been established as the result of evaluating the answers to numerous pertinent questions contained in questionnaires that have been circulated by the *Task Committee on Inspection* of the Construction Division of the American Society of Civil Engineers to a nationwide cross-section of contractors, owners and owner representatives, engineers, federal, state, and local governmental agencies, independent inspection agencies, and others.

Responsibility*

As the resident project representative for a design firm or the owner, the resident inspector is responsible for seeing that the work he is inspecting is being constructed in accordance with the requirements of the plans and specifications. This, however, does not give him the right to unnecessarily or willfully disrupt the operations of the contractor. In the performance of his assigned duties, the resident project representative, who is referred to in the following guidelines simply as the "inspector," would normally assume the following responsibilities:

1. He must become thoroughly familiar with the plans and specifications as they apply to the work he is to inspect, and he should review them frequently. The inspector must be capable of immediately recognizing if the work he is inspecting conforms to the contract requirements.
2. If any material or portion of the work does not conform to the requirements, the inspector should so notify the contractor, tell him why it does not conform, and record it in his daily diary or log. Should the contractor ignore the notice and continue the operation, then the inspector should promptly advise the architect/engineer or owner.
3. As a member of the construction team, the inspector must perform his duties in a manner that will promote the progress of the work. He should be familiar with the construction schedule and should know how the work that he is inspecting fits into the overall schedule. Completion of the work within the contract time is of importance to the owner also.
4. The inspector must studiously avoid any inspection, testing, or other activity that could be construed as a responsibility of the contractor; otherwise, he may prejudice the owner's position in the event of a dispute or claim. This applies particularly to the contractor's quality control program for testing and inspecting his materials and workmanship, as a part of his contractual responsibility.
5. When the inspector is assigned to any operation, he should cover it as long as the work is proceeding or see to it that another inspector takes over, should he have to leave. This applies particularly to work that will not be viewed again, such as driving piles, laying pipe in a trench, and placing concrete.
6. The inspector's daily report should include a recording of the day's happenings, the contractor's activity on the work he is inspecting, instructions given the contractor, and any agreements made. The inspector must remember that in the event of contract disputes, his daily reports and diary or log book assume legal importance.
7. In the matter of on-site testing, tests should be performed expeditiously and carefully; test samples carefully handled and protected; and test failures reported to the

*"Recommended Standards for the Responsibility, Authority, and Behavior of the Inspector," by the Committee on Inspection of the Construction Division, Vol. 101, No. CO2, June 1975, *Journal of the Construction Division,* Proceedings of the American Society of Civil Engineers, pages 360 to 363, inclusive. Reproduced by permission.

contractor without delay. It is a needless waste of time and money when a contractor is informed of an unsatisfactory result of a test that was performed two or three days previously.

8. Inspections and tests should be promptly made and timely:
    a. Materials should be checked as soon after they are delivered as possible. An inspector who rejects materials after it has been placed in its permanent position is not working in the best interest of the owner.
    b. Preparatory work such as clean-up inside the forms, fine grading of footing areas, winter protection for concrete, and so on should be promptly checked to minimize delay to subsequent operations.
    c. Work should be inspected as it progresses. For example, postponing the inspection of the placing of reinforcing steel and other embedded items until they are 100 percent complete does nothing but delay progress.
    d. An inspector has the responsibility to be available at all times to provide prompt inspection, and a decision on acceptance when required. A contractor should not be required to delay his work while the inspector is locating the architect/engineer's or owner's project manager to make a decision. Of course, by the same token, the contractor is expected to give adequate notice to the inspector when he (the contractor) will be ready for inspection on an operation.

9. If any specific tolerance governing the contractor's work is found to be unrealistic, it is the responsibility of the inspector to so report it to the architect/engineer or owner.

10. Too literal an interpretation of the specifications can cause problems if it is not applicable to the particular situation. In such instances, the inspector must review the conditions and seek guidance from the project manager, if necessary.

11. Whenever possible, problems should be anticipated in advance of their occurrence. The contractor's superintendent or foreman may seem to be unaware of a sleeve or other embedded item that must be set in the forms. It is incumbent upon the inspector to point this out to the superintendent or foreman. By this advance notice, the inspector contributes to maintaining the progress of the work.

12. Unacceptable work should be recognized in its early stages and reported to the contractor before it develops into an expensive and time-consuming operation. The notification should be confirmed in writing where necessary. For example, if the contractor is using the wrong form lining, stockpiling unacceptable backfill material, or placing undersize rip-rap material, he should be informed of this at the first opportunity. An inspector who has thoroughly familiarized himself with the contract requirements can recognize these situations almost immediately.

13. Occasionally a problem may arise that the inspector is unable to handle by himself. He should report this to the architect/engineer or owner for prompt action. Unresolved problems can sometimes develop into critical situations and claims.

14. Rather than make a hasty decision, the inspector should thoroughly investigate the situation and its possible consequences. Many embarrassing situations develop from decisions made prematurely. For example, a request by the contractor to be

permitted to begin placing concrete at one end of a long footing while his men are completing the reinforcing at the far end should be given consideration and not be automatically denied. If necessary, the inspector should seek advice from the architect/engineer or owner's engineering staff.

15. When work is to be corrected by the contractor, the inspector should follow it up daily. Otherwise corrections may be forgotten or the work soon covered over.
16. The inspector should stand behind any decision he makes on the contractor's work. An untrue denial by the inspector can cause immeasurable damage to the relations between the contractor and inspection personnel.
17. In the course of his work, the inspector must be capable of differentiating between those items that are essential and those that are not, as defined by the architect/engineer or owner's engineering staff.
18. The inspector should be safety minded. If he observes a dangerous condition on the job, it is his responsibility to call it to the attention of the contraction and then note it in his daily diary or log book. The mere physical presence of the owner's representative on the site makes it his responsibility to report a recognizable unsafe condition.
19. The inspector has a responsibility to be alert and observant. He should report to the architect/engineer or owner on any situation that he thinks may cause delay in the completion of the project.

Authority*

The inspector must be delegated certain authority if he is to perform his duties properly. His close working relations with the contractor demand it. The inspector should use his given authority when the situation demands it. He should not, on the other hand, abuse it. Also, the contractor is entitled to know when his work is not proceeding in an acceptable manner.

1. The inspector should have the authority to approve materials and workmanship that meet the contract requirements and he should give his approval promptly, where necessary.
2. The inspector should *not* be given the authority to order the contractor to stop his operation. When a contractor is ordered to immediately halt an active operation it becomes a costly item to him, particularly if expensive equipment and material such as concrete are involved. If the stop order is not justifiable by the terms of the contract, the contractor has just cause to demand reimbursement for the damage he has suffered. Because of the nature of his duties, the inspector cannot be familiar with all the details of the contract nor with all the other contractual relationships. Authority for the issuance of a stop order should be left to the judgment of the architect/engineer's or owner's project manager. (See Chapter 9 for possible exception to the rule.)
3. The inspector should not have the authority to approve deviations from the contract requirements.

4. The inspector should not require the contractor to furnish more than that required by the plans and specifications.
5. The inspector should not under any circumstances attempt to direct the contractor's work; otherwise, the contractor may be relieved of his responsibility under the contract.
6. Instructions should be given to the contractor's superintendent or foremen, not to his workmen nor to his subcontractors.

Although most documents that define the inspector's responsibility and authority are the result of studies and recommendations by professional societies such as the American Society of Civil Engineers (ASCE), the National Society of Professional Engineers (NSPE), and the American Institute of Architects (AIA), in at least one state such requirements have been incorporated into law for certain types of work.

Exhibit "A" to Standard Form of Agreement
Between Owner and Engineer for Professional Services
(NSPE 1910-1-A, 1974 Edition)

Duties, Responsibilities and Limitations of the Authority of Resident Project Representative

A. General.

Resident Project Representative is ENGINEER's Agent and shall act as directed by and under the supervision of ENGINEER. He shall confer with ENGINEER regarding his actions. His dealings in matters pertaining to the on-site Work will in general be only with ENGINEER and CONTRACTOR. His dealings with subcontractors will only be through or with the full knowledge of CONTRACTOR or his superintendent. He shall generally communicate with OWNER only through or as directed by ENGINEER.

B. Duties and Responsibilities.

Resident Project Representative shall:

1. Schedules: Review the progress schedule, schedule of Shop Drawing submissions, schedule of values and other schedules prepared by CONTRACTOR and consult with ENGINEER concerning their acceptability.

2. Conferences: Attend preconstruction conferences. Arrange a schedule of progress meetings and other job conferences as required in consultation with ENGINEER and notify in advance those expected to attend. Attend meetings, and maintain and circulate copies of minutes thereof.

3. Liaison:

a. Serve as ENGINEER's liaison with CONTRACTOR, working principally through CONTRACTOR's superintendent and assist him in understanding the intent of the Contract Documents. Assist ENGINEER in serving as OWNER's liaison with CONTRACTOR when CONTRACTOR's operations affect OWNER's on-site operations.
b. As requested by ENGINEER, assist in obtaining from OWNER additional details or information, when required at the job site for proper execution of the Work.
c. In the interest of preserving the proper channels of communication, advise ENGINEER of any direct communication between OWNER and CONTRACTOR.

4. Shop Drawings and Samples:

a. Receive and record date of receipt of Shop Drawings and samples which have been approved by ENGINEER.
b. Receive samples which are furnished at the site by CONTRACTOR for ENGINEER's approval, and notify ENGINEER of their availability for examination.
c. Advise ENGINEER and CONTRACTOR or his superintendent immediately of the commencement of any Work requiring a Shop Drawing or sample submission if the submission has not been approved by ENGINEER.

5. Review of Work, Rejection of Defective Work, Inspections and Tests:

a. Conduct on-site observations of the Work in progress to assist ENGINEER in determining that the Project is proceeding in accordance with the Contract Documents and that completed Work will conform to the Contract Documents.
b. Report to ENGINEER whenever he believes that any Work is unsatisfactory, faulty or defective or does not conform to the Contract Documents, or has been damaged, or does not meet the requirements of any inspections, tests or approvals required to be made; and advise ENGINEER when he believes Work should be corrected or rejected or should be uncovered for observation, or requires special testing or inspection.
c. Verify that tests, equipment and systems startups and operating and maintenance instructions are conducted as required by the Contract Documents and in presence of the required personnel; and that CONTRACTOR maintains adequate records thereof; observe, record and report to ENGINEER appropriate details relative to the test procedures and startups.
d. Accompany OWNER and visiting inspectors representing public or other agencies having jurisdiction over the Project, record the outcome of these inspections and report to ENGINEER.

NSPE Publication No. 1910-1-A
1974 Edition

6. *Interpretation of Contract Documents:* Transmit to CONTRACTOR clarification and interpretation of the Contract Documents as issued by ENGINEER.

7. *Modifications:* Consider and evaluate CONTRACTOR's suggestions for modifications in Drawings or Specifications and report them with recommendations to ENGINEER.

8. *Records:*

   a. Maintain at the job site orderly files for correspondence, reports of job conferences, Shop Drawings and sample submissions, reproductions of original Contract Documents including all addenda, change orders, field orders, additional Drawings issued subsequent to the execution of the Contract, ENGINEER's clarifications and interpretations of the Contract Documents, progress reports and other Project-related documents.

   b. Keep a diary or log book, recording hours on the job site, weather conditions, data relative to questions of extras or deductions, list of principal visitors, daily activities, decisions, observations in general and specific observations in more detail as in the case of observing test procedures. Send copies to ENGINEER.

   c. Record names, addresses and telephone numbers of all CONTRACTORS, subcontractors and major suppliers of equipment and materials.

   d. Advise ENGINEER whenever CONTRACTOR is not currently maintaining an up-to-date copy of Record Drawings at the site.

9. *Reports:*

   a. Furnish ENGINEER periodic reports as required of progress of the Work and of CONTRACTOR's compliance with the approved progress schedule, schedule of Shop Drawing submissions and other schedules.

   b. Consult with ENGINEER in advance of scheduled major tests, inspections or start of important phases of the Work.

10. *Payment Requisitions:* Review Applications for Payment with CONTRACTOR for compliance with the established procedure for their submission and forward them with recommendations to ENGINEER, noting particularly their relation to the schedule of values, work completed and materials and equipment delivered at the site.

11. *Guarantees, Certificates, Maintenance and Operation Manuals:* During the course of the Work verify that guarantees, certificates, maintenance and operation manuals and other data required to be assembled and furnished by CONTRACTOR are applicable to the items actually installed; and deliver these data to ENGINEER for his review and forwarding to OWNER prior to final acceptance of the Project.

12. *Completion:*

    a. Before ENGINEER issues a Certificate of Substantial Completion, submit to CONTRACTOR a list of observed items requiring correction.

    b. Conduct final inspection in the company of ENGINEER, OWNER and CONTRACTOR and prepare a final list of items to be corrected.

    c. Verify that all items on final list have been corrected and make recommendations to ENGINEER concerning acceptance.

C. **Limitations of Authority.**

   Except upon written instructions of ENGINEER, Resident Project Representative:

   1. Shall not authorize any deviation from the Contract Documents or approve any substitute materials or equipment.

   2. Shall not undertake any of the responsibilities of CONTRACTOR, subcontractors or CONTRACTOR's superintendent.

   3. Shall not expedite Work for the CONTRACTOR.

   4. Shall not advise on or issue directions relative to any aspect of the means, methods, techniques, sequences or procedures of construction unless such is specifically called for in the Contract Documents.

   5. Shall not advise on or issue directions as to safety precautions and programs in connection with the Work.

   6. Shall not authorize OWNER to occupy the Project in whole or in part.

   7. Shall not participate in specialized field or laboratory tests or inspections conducted by others.

   8. Shall not assist CONTRACTOR in maintaining up-to-date copy of Record Drawings.

Figure 2.1 NSPE Document: Duties, responsibilities, and limitations of the authority of the resident project representative. Copyright National Society of Professional Engineers.

THE AMERICAN INSTITUTE OF ARCHITECTS

AIA Document B352

Duties, Responsibilities and Limitations of Authority Of Full-Time Project Representative

Recommended as an Exhibit to the Owner-Architect
Agreement When a Full-Time Project Representative is Employed

1. EXPLAIN CONTRACT DOCUMENTS

Assist the Contractor's superintendent in understanding the intent of the Contract Documents.

2. OBSERVATIONS

Conduct on-site observations and spot checks of the Work in progress as a basis for determining conformance of Work, materials and equipment with the Contract Documents. Report any defective Work to the Architect.

3. ADDITIONAL INFORMATION

Obtain from the Architect additional details or information if, and when, required at the site for proper execution of the Work. Become acquainted with standard or reference specifications referred to in the Specifications.

4. CONTRACTOR'S SUGGESTIONS

Consider and evaluate suggestions or recommendations which may be submitted by the Contractor to the Architect and report them with recommendations to the Architect for final decision.

5. CONSTRUCTION SCHEDULE

Be alert to the construction schedule and to conditions which may cause delay in completion, and report same to the Architect.

6. LIAISON

Maintain liaison with the Contractor and all subcontractors on the Project only through the Contractor's superintendent.

7. CONFERENCES

Attend and report to the Architect on conferences held at the Project site as directed by the Architect.

8. TESTS

Advise the Architect's office in advance of the schedules of tests and observe that tests at the Project site which are required by the Contract Documents are actually conducted; observe, record and report to the Architect all details relative to the test procedures.

9. INSPECTIONS BY OTHERS

If inspectors representing local, state or federal agencies having jurisdiction over the Project visit the site, accompany such inspectors during their trips through the Project, record and report to the Architect's office the results of these inspections.

10. RECORDS

10.1 Maintain orderly files at the site for (1) correspondence, (2) reports of site conferences, (3) shop drawings and (4) reproductions of original Contract Documents including all Addenda, Change Orders and supplementary Drawings issued subsequent to the award of the Contract.

10.2 Keep a daily diary or log book, recording hours on the site, weather conditions, list of visiting officials and jurisdiction, daily activities, decisions, observations in general, and specific observations in more detail as in the case of observing test procedures.

10.3 Record names, addresses and telephone numbers of all contractors and subcontractors.

11. SHOP DRAWINGS

The Contractor is not authorized to install any materials and equipment for which shop drawings are required unless such drawings have been approved in accordance with the General Conditions by the Contractor and the Architect.

1

Figure 2.2   AIA Document: Duties, responsibilities, and limitations of the authority of the full-time project representative. This Document has been reproduced with the permission of the American Institute of Architects. Further reproduction, in part or in whole is not au-

12. SAMPLES

Receive samples which are required to be furnished at the site; record date received and from whom, and notify the Architect of their readiness for examination; record Architect's approval or rejection; and maintain custody of approved samples.

13. CONTRACTOR'S APPLICATIONS FOR PAYMENT

Review the Applications for Payment submitted by the Contractor and forward them with recommendations to the Architect for disposition.

14. LIST OF ITEMS FOR CORRECTION

After Substantial Completion, check each item as it is corrected.

15. OWNER'S OCCUPANCY OF THE PROJECT

If the Owner occupies the Project or any portion thereof prior to final completion of the Work by the Contractor, be especially alert to possibilities of claims for damage to Work completed prior to occupancy.

16. OWNER'S EXISTING OPERATION

In the case of additions to or renovations of an existing facility which must be maintained in operation during construction, be alert to conditions which could have an effect on the Owner's existing operation.

17. REJECTION OF WORK

If a situation arises during construction which in your view requires that Work be rejected, report such situation immediately to the Architect.

18. LIMITATIONS OF AUTHORITY

Unless specific exceptions are established by written instructions issued by the Architect:

18.1 Do not authorize deviations from the Contract Documents.

18.2 Do not personally conduct any tests.

18.3 Do not enter into the area of responsibility of the Contractor's superintendent.

18.4 Do not expedite the Work for the Contractor.

18.5 Do not advise on, or issue directions relative to, any aspect of construction means, methods, techniques, sequences or procedures, or for safety precautions and programs in connection with the Work.

18.6 Do not authorize or suggest that the Owner occupy the Project, in whole or in part, prior to Substantial Completion.

18.7 Do not issue a Certificate for Payment.

thorized. Because AIA documents are revised periodically, users should ascertain from AIA the current edition of the document reproduced above.

3
RESIDENT INSPECTION OFFICE RESPONSIBILITIES

SETTING UP A FIELD OFFICE

The basic requirements concerning the setting up of a field office for the resident project representative (resident inspector) will have been established in the contract documents long before he reports to the project site. It is normally the project specifications that call for a field office for the resident project representative, and these same provisions often include requirements for field office furnishings, utilities, janitorial services, sanitary facilities, and telephone. If, however, the specifier fails to call for field office facilities in the specifications for a project that requires the services of a full-time resident project representative, the contractor that provided such extras at no extra cost would soon be out of business; after all, unless the contractor was aware of the requirement for such facilities at the time he bid on the job, he would not have allowed money in his bid for this purpose, and it would be unfair to expect it of him.

Many agencies that are involved in frequent construction contracts already own their own trailer-type offices, and will normally have one moved to the construction site at the beginning of the work. Thus, the contractor has no reason to even suspect that the omission of field office facilities from the specifications was an oversight.

What is to be done if a field office is needed but was not specified? Perhaps the resident project representative can prevail upon the contractor to provide a prefabricated structure for the inspector's use, but the inspector and his employer should be aware that this often takes the form of a tool shed structure that uses flap covers over side openings instead of windows. Under the circumstances the field office would be unlikely to be provided with power or lights either, so if it rains the inspector might be faced with three choices: Leave the flaps open and get the plans wet; close the flaps and sit in the dark waiting for the rain to stop; or close the shed and stay outside in the rain. Thus, if the inspector has been hired prior to advertising the job for bids, it might be in his best interests to ask the design firm or the owner to assure that proper facilities will be provided for the inspector in the specifications. It is not too late even if the job is already out for bids, for as long as the bids have not been opened, an addendum to the specifications may still be issued that can provide for these facilities. One other alternative presents itself. Generally, a contractor will provide a field office trailer for his own use. It is usually not too difficult to obtain permission to set up a corner for the resident project representative's own trailer—it sure beats sitting in the rain.

In past years, most construction field offices were prefabricated wood structures that were difficult to keep clean and were generally always too hot in the summer and too cold in the winter. Now almost all construction contractors are using the trailer-type office that is either available for purchase or can be rented on a month-to-month basis. Most of the

Figure 3.1   Large construction field office trailer.

Figure 3.2 *Typical contractor's field office trailer.*

larger trailers have inside toilets, are air conditioned and heated, and are fairly easy to keep clean.

Where the specifications do call for a resident project representative's field office, it is not uncommon for a contractor to offer to "share" his field office with the resident inspector by partitioning it across the middle, setting aside one end for the contractor and the other end for the architect/engineer. If the specifications will support the resident project representative in his request for a separate trailer for his office, he should not settle for a shared unit, as it is not a preferable arrangement. There can be numerous responses in support of the separate-but-equal trailer concept, and some of them are mentioned later in the book. One of the principal reasons is security for both architect/engineer or owner and the contractor and their respective records and property and the ability to hold confidential meetings in a separate unit. In a joint-use trailer office there are no secrets—when someone wants a private conversation, whether it be the contractor or the architect/engineer, you will notice a desire to go for a walk around the site.

FAMILIARIZATION WITH CONSTRUCTION DOCUMENTS

Upon being engaged to provide resident inspection on a project, the inspector should obtain a complete set of all contract documents including all contract drawings, standard drawings, specifications and specification addenda, and copies of all reference specifications, standards, or test requirements cited. Sufficient time should be spent carefully studying ALL of these documents, until the inspector is thoroughly familiar with all phases and details of the project as shown on the plans and specifications. This type of review should ideally take place in the office of the design organization so that the inspector can obtain first-hand responses to his questions from the design staff. This enables a better understanding of the project by the inspector, and, as a result, a smoother-run project. The inspector should mark all areas containing key provisions, and each area where special care must be taken. Cross-references should be carefully noted so that the affected sections in the specifications can be flagged to indicate locations where the different trades must interface, or the work of different contractors must be coordinated. It is also wise to mark those areas where special tests or inspections are specified and where samples are required.

At the same time the inspector must study the contract General Conditions ("boilerplate") of the specifications, as these provisions set the stage for almost all of the construction administration functions that he will be required to perform. It is an especially good idea to set up a chart showing all the tests required, the type of test required, the reference standard, the frequency of testing, and the specification section reference where they were called for (Figure 3.8). This should be done prior to starting the work at the site.

Early in the project, a complete list should be compiled in chronological order that shows the date that every milestone event on the project is to take place. This should include meetings, submittals, tests, delivery dates for equipment, contractor partial payment requests, scheduling of surveys, final date for submittal of "or equal" items, and all other "milestone" events.

EQUIPPING THE FIELD OFFICE

Field office equipment and supply requirements will vary from one job to the next, but on many public agency projects or larger private ventures such as high rise buildings, hospitals, schools, and similar projects where the field management of the construction is more organized and formal, the resident project representative's field office facilities may include any or all of the following:

1. Several desks and chairs
2. One or more plan tables and drafting stools
3. A plan rack or "stick file"
4. A four- or five-drawer filing cabinet
5. Telephone service (not coin-operated)
6. Bookcase
7. Inside toilet and lavatory (or adjacent portable unit)

8. Water, power, and lights
9. Heating and cooling facilities, as required
10. Janitorial services to clean the facility

Most of the above might normally be specified to be furnished by the contractor and thus would be included in his bid price. In addition to the items provided by the contractor, the inspector's employer would be expected to provide such additional items as a typewriter, adding machine (tape type), a small calculating machine, a postal scale, and reproduction equipment, and all expendable office supplies.

On smaller projects, the facilities provided would be scaled down accordingly. The items listed above might reasonably be expected to be provided on a project involving a construction cost of somewhere over a million dollars and involving over a full year of construction time.

Ordering Supplies and Equipment

It is generally too late if the inspector reports to the field office empty handed, only to find that the wheels of the construction process are already in motion. Before the resident project representative leaves the home office to take up residence in the new field office, he would draw as many office supplies and equipment as he can reasonably anticipate a future need for. The full list might conceivably include many, if not all, of the following items:

1. Report forms
2. Field books for diary (field log)
3. Stationery
4. Transmittal forms
5. Envelopes (all sizes)
6. Blank bond typing paper
7. Columnar pads (for estimating)
8. Loose leaf notebooks (8½ x 11 three-ring type)
9. Pens, pencils, felt-tip pens, high-lighter pens
10. Rejection or Non-Conforming tags
11. Minimum of two weeks supply of film for all cameras

In addition to the other supplies and equipment previously listed, the inspector should provide himself with all of the normal personal protective equipment required under OSHA for the types of work and environmental field conditions that he is likely to encounter.

ESTABLISHMENT OF COMMUNICATIONS

Although this is one area where the contractor almost always excels with regard to maintaining contact with members of his own field staff, some design firms and owners are beginning to realize the value to them in both time and money in investing in some

PROJECT No. 1553-04
SPECIFIED SUBMITTALS & EVENTS: CHRONOLOGICAL

Submittal or Event Item	By	Reference
PRE BID		
1. Bidders Qualifications	NASA	IB
2. Pre Work Conference	NASA	SP
BID OPENING + 10 DAYS		
1. Pre Award Survey	NASA	IB
WITHIN 5 DAYS AFTER NOTICE TO PROCEED		
1. Commence Work (Also Resident Engr on site)	Contr/A&E	IB 22
WITHIN 14 DAYS AFTER NOTICE TO PROCEED		
1. Working Schedule	Contr	IB 29; SP 5.1
WITHIN 15 DAYS AFTER NOTICE TO PROCEED		
1. CPM Job Schedule	Contr	IB 26
2. Shop Drawing & Equipment List Schedule	Contr	IB 23
3. Shop Drawing & Equipment List—1st Submittal	Contr	IB 33
4. Quality Control Program—1st Submittal	Contr	IB 70
5. Notify Contr Officer of Struct Steel Deliv Locn	Contr	SP 13.1
6. AC Water Pipe Materials List	Contr	TS 579
WITHIN 30 DAYS AFTER NOTICE TO PROCEED		
1. Receive & Review Schedule of Submittals	NASA/A&E	IB 23
2. Report Status of Subcontr & Purchase Orders	Contr	IB 56
3. Schedule of Submittals (Final)	Contr	SP 9.2
4. Electrical Shop Dwgs & Lists	Contr	TS 587
WITHIN 45 DAYS AFTER NOTICE TO PROCEED		
1. Quality Control Program Submittal (Final)	Contr/A&E	SP 4.5
WITHIN 60 DAYS AFTER NOTICE TO PROCEED		
1. Plumbing: Proposed Matls List	Contr	TS 407
2. Electrical: Proposed Matls List	Contr	TS 470
3. Low Press Comp Air: Proposed Matls List	Contr	TS 480
4. Fire Protec Equipt: Prop. Matls List & Shop Dwgs	Contr	TS 507
5. Ventil. System: Proposed Matls List	Contr	TS 554
30 DAYS BEFORE COMPLETION		
1. Equipment Manuals	Contr	IB 24; SP 9.5

means of direct communication with the resident project representative at all times. The types of personal communications devices that offer the most value to the architect/engineer, owner, or contractor for maintaining contact with the field office include the following:

1. Field office telephones (not coin operated)
2. "Beepers" or personal tone-signal radio paging devices
3. Automobile radiotelephones
4. Walkie-talkie radios
5. Voice pagers

Each of the above pieces of communications equipment has its own particular best

Page 2 - Specified Submittals and Events - Chronological

Submittal or Event Item	By	Reference
BEFORE COMPLETION (NO SPECIFIED TIMETABLE)		
1. Dwg. Change Incorporation (As-Built Dwgs)	Contr	IB 33; SP 1.5
NO SPECIFIED TIME FROM NOTICE OR AWARD		
1. Report of Subcontractors over $10,000 Update annually	Contr	IB 54
2. 5 Days after award of subcontract: Statement to NASA of Subcontr and data	Contr	IB 53
3. 30 Days before starting specific phase of work: Detailed quality control plan	Contr	IB 71
4. Prior to fabrication (General items): Shop Dwg Approvals	Contr	SP 1.1
5. Return of Contr Submittals (Appr/Not Appr)	A&E	SP 1.6
6. Plan for tracking & processing contr Submittals	A&E	A&E Contract
7. Concrete affidavits from Weighmaster Before Concrete Placement	Contr	TS 176; 102
8. Conc Matls Test Reports: As Work Progresses	Contr	TS 182; 185
9. Design Mix for Concrete: 15 Days before Start of Specified Work	Contr	TS 183
10. Hardware Samples	Contr	TS 344
Contract Cost Breakdown & Payroll Reports		IB 78
PERIODIC		
1. Monthly: Reports on Tests and Inspections	Contr	SP 4.7
2. Monthly: Progress Payment Certification	A&E	A&E Contract
3. Monthly: Quality Control Meetings	Contr/A&E	A&E Contract
4. Twice Monthly: Const Schedule & Progress Mtg	Contr/A&E	A&E Contract
5. Weekly: Construction Status Reports	A&E	A&E Contract

Figure 3.3 *List of project milestones.*

application and limitation, and it is seldom that all of them will ever be used on any one project.

Field Office Telephone

The field office telephone is by far the most common device, and regardless of whether any other communications devices are provided, every field office should be provided with a telephone (not a pay phone). The design firm or owner should be careful in specifying its telephone needs, as it could find itself in the rather unique position of being furnished a telephone that only connects to a private phone system. It may be necessary in some cases to specify that the contractor must have a field telephone in his own field office and must also provide the resident project representative's field office with a telephone on a separate line, and connected to an established telephone exchange. If the contractor is connected to a private phone system, the resident project representative's telephone should also be capable of being connected to the contractor's private phone system in addition to the established telephone system. The contractor should allow the design firm, the owner, or their authorized representatives or employees free and unlimited use of the field office telephone for all calls that do not involve published toll charges. Any toll charges received should be billed to the owner by the contractor at the rates actually charged him by the telephone company.

Tone Signal Radio Pager

The use of the "beeper" can be invaluable in maintaining contact with an inspector who is frequently at some remote location at the construction site where the field office phone cannot be heard. In areas where such service is available, every inspector should have one. There are several services available in most urban areas, and some companies actually provide a service that covers several counties. With the tone-signal pagers, or "beepers" as they are usually called, the party wishing to contact the inspector simply telephones his employer's office or other predetermined message center. The message center in turn telephones the paging service and says "Please page 2543" or whatever the paging unit number happens to be. Some areas are on computerized systems in which the pager number is keyed directly from a push button telephone. Upon hearing a beeping sound from his pager, the inspector simply turns off the signal and heads for the nearest telephone to call his message center. With a beeper, there is no way of communicating a message or determining the source of the call; thus, all calls must be returned to a central message center to find out who called and what the message was.

Automobile Radiotelephone

The value of an automobile radiotelephone is often somewhat over-rated as far as a resident inspector is concerned. After all, if the inspector is at the site he will seldom be in his vehicle and thus will not be able to receive the call directly. Connecting the radiotelephone to the auto horn is a ruse sometimes employed; however, this necessitates leaving the radio "on" at all times, even when the car is unattended. This can be quite a drain on the battery, although with modern solid-state equipment it is not as bad as it used to be. Even then, an inspector cannot know that a message was received until he returns to his vehicle—which may be too late in case of an urgent message. Contrast this with the use of a beeper, which can let the inspector know immediately that he is to call his office, regardless of where he may be at the time. There are other situations, however, where a radiotelephone *can* be of great service in construction. For a roving inspector who must serve the needs of numerous project sites, and spends a great deal of time on the road, or for the inspector of a project such as a long pipeline, highway, or canal, a radio telephone can be an extremely useful tool.

There is a significant distinction between a *radiotelephone* and a *two-way radio*. Both are in effect "two-way radios"; however, the terminology *radiotelephone* is reserved for those types of two-way radios that operate on assigned radiotelephone frequencies and have special equipment to make them compatible with standard land telephone equipment. The resident project representative should forget C-B radio for this purpose, as it is

Figure 3.4 *Radiotelephone. Photo supplied by Motorola Communications and Electronics, Inc.*

not sufficiently reliable unless served by repeater stations at strategic locations—and that *really* gets costly.

Walkie-Talkie Radios

A walkie-talkie radio is a device that is best suited to on-site communications. Projects that involve a crew of several persons at remote locations within a large construction site, and operations that involve the issuance of instructions over relatively short distances will find that the walkie-talkie radios are a great time saver. They can eliminate the sometimes misunderstood hand signals, and a clear line of sight need not be maintained to communicate within reasonable distances.

Figure 3.5 Typical industrial walkie-talkie. Photo supplied by Motorola Communications and Electronics, Inc.

Voice Pagers

Voice pagers are quite useful in some situations; however, their limitations should be evaluated before considering replacing all the beepers with voice pagers. To be sure, a central message center is not needed, and a short voice message such as a telephone number can be transmitted directly. On the other hand, if the construction area is noisy the message cannot be clearly heard, and without the convenience of a central message center the call could be lost—or at least difficult to confirm. Also, there is no privacy, and all messages received can be heard by anyone standing close to the receiver. If turned low, the inspector may not hear his own message. Of course, most voice pagers can be switched over to a tone signal if message security is wanted at some special time. Yet, unless the caller and the receiver knew that the audio was going to be turned off at any given time, how would either party know enough to call a central message center? In any

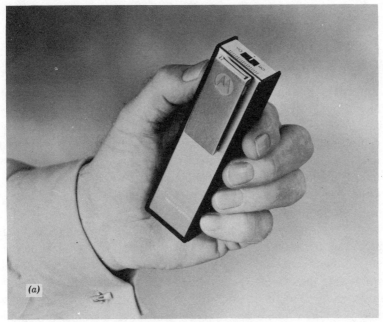

Figure 3.6 *Radio paging devices. Photo supplied by Motorola Communications and Electronics, Inc.*

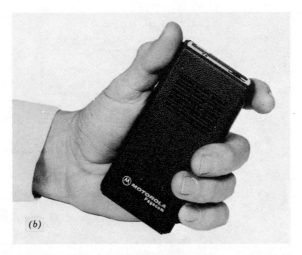

Figure 3.6 *Radio paging devices. Photo supplied by Motorola Communications and Electronics, Inc.*

case, to prevent misuse and abuse it would be in the best interests of the inspector and his employer to have all messages sent through a message center anyway.

HANDLING OF JOB-RELATED INFORMATION

The establishment of "communications" on a project does not stop with the procurement of communications hardware. Field communications is a term that must also be applied to the procedures for handling and transmitting job-related information from one party to the other, the determination of who is authorized to receive and give project information, and the routing instructions for the transmittal of all communications, records, and submittals. At the beginning of a job, one of the first and most important things to be determined is the establishment of the authorized line of communications and authority, and the method of handling such information.

Generally, it has been found preferable to establish the resident project representative as the only direct link between the contractor and the design organization even though the matters being communicated may be intended for the project manager of either the owner or a separate firm. In this way, all transmittals will be received first by the resident project representative, who will log them into his record book, and only then transmit them to the project manager. In the office of the design organization a similar procedure is followed. All transmittals at that end should be received only by the project manager; if intended for other members of the design staff, they should be distributed through the project manager. In this way, there is always a single point of communication at each end: the resident project representative in the field and the project manager at the design office.

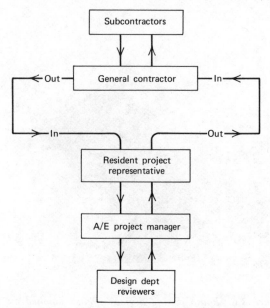

Figure 3.7   *Lines of communication in construction.*

All requests for deviations, change order claims, shop drawing submittals, and similar transmittals should be refused by the project manager if not transmitted to him through the resident project representative. Otherwise the records would be incomplete, and often coordination is lacking since the information may have bypassed the project manager or resident project representative, with a resulting conflict or confusion in the field administration of the work. Similarly, submittals from subcontractors or materials suppliers should never be received by the resident project representative directly, except through the hands of the general contractor. After all, it is his obligation to receive *and approve* all such transmittals before being considered for approval by the design firm. Officially, the subcontractor does not even exist, as far as the owner is concerned, because the owner entered into contract with the general contractor only, and thus no contractual relationship exists between the owner and any subcontractors or material suppliers.

STAFFING RESPONSIBILITIES

Staffing a field inspection office is generally not the responsibility of the resident project representative, but is normally done by the design firm, the owner, or in the case of a CQC contract, the contractor. However, the resident project representative should understand the types of persons required on some representative types of projects, because he will usually have the responsibility of supervising their activities.

Generally, on a project large enough to support a full-time resident project representative, the personnel needs of the project may vary from a single field representative of the owner or design firm under the responsible charge of a professional engineer or architect and backed up by occasional temporary special inspectors to assure building code compliance, to a moderate sized staff of three to five persons on a slightly larger project. Included as a part of this larger staff would be the resident project representative, a full-time field inspector, possibly a field office assistant with estimating background, and a clerk-typist.

CONSTRUCTION SAFETY

Although it is clearly understood that the resident project representative's involvement in construction safety is limited (See Chapter 8), and that the general contractor has the principal responsibility for all construction safety, compliance, there are certain considerations that should be kept in mind by each inspector on the site. The degree of the inspector's involvement may vary somewhat, depending upon the terms of the specific contract provisions and the actual circumstances surrounding each case of a potential hazard.

As a protection for the owner and the design firm, a contract for inspection may require the inspector to monitor the contractor's safety program to assure that an effective safety program is being provided (not uncommon in federal contracts). The inspector may be required to be involved in meetings with the contractor to discuss safety measures, and where project safety has been made one of the inspector's duties to observe, he should obtain personal assurance that safe practices are being followed. Some of the matters of concern in this type of responsibility are:

1. Review of the contractor's accident prevention program that is required by the local OSHA compliance agency.
2. A code of safe practices developed by the contractor and checked by the inspector for each project.
3. Various permits that may be required prior to starting specific work items, such as excavation, trench shoring, falsework, scaffolding, crane certifications, and similar requirements to be verified before allowing the contractor to begin.
4. Other safety items that may be pertinent to the contract such as blasting operations, personal protective gear required, backup alarms for equipment, rollover protection guards on equipment, traffic control, and similar protective requirements to be confirmed.
5. The reporting of fatal accidents or disabling accidents to be reported to the local safety compliance agency as required.

A more detailed account of the inspector's responsibilities with relation to the handling of hazardous conditions, and the effect of various construction contract provisions on the administration of safety requirements is explored in greater detail in Chapter 8.

DEVELOPMENT OF AN INSPECTION PLAN

It is desirable for each inspector to take a systematic approach to the quality control or quality assurance functions that he is required to provide for the project. Even if no formal plan is required to be submitted to the owner as a part of the quality control provisions of the contract, such as in a federal CQC (Contractor Quality Control) operation, it is an excellent inspection tool, and the resident project representative is urged to plan ahead by developing an outline of all the inspections that must be made, a check list of points to look for, and a list of the type and frequency of all tests that are required.

An inspection plan for submittal to the owner agency might reasonably be expected to cover all or some of the following items:

1. Establishment of detailed inspection procedures.
2. Outline of acceptance/rejection procedures.
3. Preparation of a chart showing all tests required, when they are needed, the frequency of sampling and testing, the material being tested, and who is obligated to perform the tests.
4. Establishment of who will be responsible for calling the laboratory for pickup of samples for testing, who will call for special inspectors when needed, and to whom will such outside people be directly responsible on the project.
5. Identification of who must physically prepare samples for testing—the contractor or the inspector; determination of whether the contractor will provide a laborer to assist the inspector in obtaining samples and transporting samples for testing.

TESTING PLAN

S – SAMPLED
T – TESTED

SPEC SECTION AND PARAGRAPH	ITEM OF WORK	TESTS REQUIRED (ASTM, ACI, COMMERCIAL STDS, ETC.)	SAMPLED BY	TESTED BY	ON SITE	OFF SITE	FREQUENCY OF TESTING
2B – EARTHWORK							
6.7.1	Sieve Analysis	ASTM C36	ABC Lab	ABC Lab		S/T	One passing test per source
6.8.2	Standard Moist.–Density	ASTM D1557 (Mod.)	ABC Lab	ABC Lab	S	S/T	One each source
6.8.4	In-place density	ASTM D1556	ABC Lab	ABC Lab	S/T		Min. 20 (Random)
3A – CONCRETE							
19.2	Mix Design	ASTM C192; C39	ABC Lab	ABC Lab		S/T	One per ea. req'd strength /agg. size
19.3.1	Test Cylinders	ASTM C31	Inspector	ABC Lab	S	T	See note (1)
19.3.2	Slump	ASTM C143	Inspector	Inspector	S/T		One per batch
19.3.3	Air	ASTM C231	ABC Lab	ABC Lab	S/T		One/set cylinders
4A – MASONRY							
10.4.1	Efflorescence	See Spec Par. 10.4.1.1	ABC Lab	ABC Lab		S/T	One passing Test
10.4.2	Mortar and Grout	See Spec Par. 10.4.2	Inspector	ABC Lab	S	T	See note (2)
10.4.3	Drying Shrinkage	ASTM C426 (See Spec)	ABC Lab	ABC Lab		S/T	One passing
10.4.4	Air dry Condition	ASTM C427	ABC Lab	ABC Lab	S/T		One Test per delivery

CONTRACTOR'S EXPLANATORY NOTES
(1) 6 CYL/DAY/50 C.Y.   TEST: 3 AT 7 DAYS; 3 AT 28 DAYS
(2) ONE EA. DESIGN MIX.   MIN. 3 EA/DAY.   TEST: 1 EA AT 7 DAYS; 2 EA. AT 28 DAYS

Figure 3.8   *Testing schedule of a quality control or inspection plan.*

6. Establishment of ground rules for acceptable timing of work operations after sampling and testing; mandatory scheduling must be provided to assure not only time to make samples and tests, but also to make corrections needed before work may be allowed to continue.

Often, on a federal project involving a CQC operation, if an architect/engineer firm is selected to provide quality assurance, it is required to submit a formal *construction surveillance and inspection plan* prior to beginning the work. Under such a program, the architect/engineer must provide a resident project representative and an appropriate field staff at the construction site, plus home office support as required. Implementation of such a program requires the architect/engineer, the construction manager, and the resident project representative to meet the contractor prior to the commencement of each phase of the work and define the responsibilities of each party under the contract. At that time the contractor should be asked to submit and explain his established systems for quality control and his accident prevention program. These programs should then be reviewed by the architect/engineer or owner and his resident project representative, and the programs compared with the specific requirements of the contract. Suggestions, if warranted, should be made by the resident project representative at that time.

OTHER JOB RESPONSIBILITIES

In addition to the items previously covered, there are numerous other field responsibilities that the resident project representative must expect to cope with. The inspector's responsibilities in connection with the tasks described are only highlighted in this chapter, as the technical details of administering each of the listed subjects is covered more thoroughly in the chapters that follow. Naturally, much of the resident project representative's work will have to be done in the field office. Unfortunately, in today's complex society, the resultant paper-work required means that a good portion of the resident project representative's time must be spent writing and recording data. Administration of a construction project is no longer as simple as it was in days past, when all that was needed was a thorough knowledge of construction—today, the paperwork is just as vital as the inspections themselves.

Construction Planning and Scheduling

A resident project representative on a sizable project will most certainly become involved in construction scheduling, or at least in an evaluation of the construction schedules prepared by the contractor. Unless the inspector has a basic understanding of the principles involved, he will be hard-pressed to fulfill all of his administrative responsibilities. The two principal types of schedules that the inspector will be likely to encounter are bar charts and network diagrams.

In a network diagram, the inspector should be capable of recognizing logical and illogical construction of a schedule. In addition, the inspector must check for realistic scheduling times, compatible delivery dates for equipment and materials, critical path operations, float (slack) times, and other related items of a network schedule. In addition, he must make frequent comparisons to see if the actual construction events are following the network diagram. In addition, the inspector should check to see that updated network data are provided as required.

Contractor's Plant and Equipment

Although it is rare that the inspector will be required to check the contractor's equipment, it is an occasional requirement under the provisions of some public agency contracts. If equipment inspection is required, all that is normally expected of the inspector is a check of each piece of major equipment and a determination of whether it has the necessary safety devices and that such devices are all in good working order. This includes devices such as safety cages, backup bells, guards over moving parts, and similar items. In addition, the equipment check should include an evaluation of whether the exhaust emissions are excessive, and that there are no cracked windshields or bad tires on automotive or other heavy motorized equipment.

Measurements for Progress Payments

One of the traditional responsibilities of the resident project representative is the review of the contractor's monthly partial payment request to see that the quantities of materials and equipment delivered to the site or used in the work agree with the quantities for which the contractor has requested payment. It should be kept in mind that on a lump-sum project, the resident project representative must still make monthly pay estimates of the contractor's work. However, the accuracy of the measurements are not as critical as they would be on a unit price contract, because such differences will be made up in the end. This is not meant to suggest that the inspector can afford to be careless about quantities on a lump-sum job; as it is highly undesirable to allow the owner to pay for more work than has actually been accomplished as of the date of the payment request. Such overruns would completely defeat the purpose of the normal 5 to 10 percent retention that is usually held by the owner until the end of the project. If no retention money is held, a policy considered for federal projects, then even on lump-sum projects the cumulative monthly progress payments must be carefully controlled so as to avoid overpayment.

On a unit price contract, a precise measurement must be made of all construction quantities, and generally a system of measurement is spelled out in the specifications under the heading of "Measurement and Payment," so that there can be no argument as to where, how, and when the measurements for pay purposes must be made. Errors in measurement or overlooked items under a unit price contract can cost the owner an immense sum of money. Because of this fact, many measurements for such contracts are performed by the design firm utilizing the services of a survey crew to determine pay quantities of pipe; to cross-section a borrow area to determine the exact quantities of earth excavated; and similar measurements.

The subject of measurement and payment during construction is covered in detail in Chapter 14, where numerous methods are described and some of the typical pitfalls will be discussed.

Filing of Notices and Certificates

Although the filing of the legal notices is primarily the responsibility of the owner, the resident project representative may find that job delegated to him as an owner's representative. The notices and certificates themselves will normally have been prepared when the resident project representative receives them; however, some knowledge of the process involved should be understood.

Such notices include the filing of the "Notice to Proceed" as well as the "Certificate of Completion" or "Certificate of Substantial Completion" at the close of construction. In addition, the inspector may be involved with the serving or filing of other forms of construction documents such as a "Field Order" and "Deficiency Notice" as well as special notices calling attention to imminent safety hazards that require immediate correction to remove a hazard to life or health.

Evaluation of Construction Materials and Methods

The inspector is frequently called upon to evaluate construction materials and methods. His responsibilities should be clear, however, and although his expertise is necessary for the good of the project, any such recommendations should be made *only* to the responsible architect or engineer, in writing, who will be the final authority as to what action to take. It is to be hoped that the architect or engineer will also recognize the value of following a formal transmittal procedure and, after reaching a decision, will submit all instructions or responses directly through his resident project representative instead of mailing or delivering them directly to the contractor.

The work on a project may also involve the preparation of work statements, estimates, and data to contractor-requested changes. The procedures are similar to those specified for evaluations of materials and methods. A fuller discussion of the handling of contractor submittals is covered under "Contractor Submittals" in Chapter 4.

Record Drawings

A large portion of the work on many projects includes the posting of "as-built" information on a set of prints at the construction site. This is sometimes followed by a requirement that all such records of changes be drafted onto a set of reproducibles of the contract drawings. This is intended to provide the owner with a permanent record of each feature of a project as it was actually constructed. The normal construction contract usually calls for the *contractor* to make a set of "record drawings" by marking a set of prints with all changes from the original drawings as bid, including all change orders, alignment changes, depth changes of underground pipes and utilities, and all other items that are not the same as they were originally drawn.

The term "as-built" drawings is usually discouraged because of the legal implications involved when the architect or engineer signs a certificate that says that everything shown on the drawings is exactly as constructed—this could come back to haunt him years later. The drafting of such data onto a set of transparencies is often required, but the resident inspector should be particularly careful when making commitments that the condition of the contract that requires the preparation of record drawings does not of itself mean that they will be drafted on reproducibles. It merely means that all changes will be marked (usually with colored pencil) on a set of record prints at the site. If work on the transparencies is required, it will be performed as a separate contract item by copying from the record drawings.

Many field people have been very lax in assuring that all record drawings are kept up to date, and unfortunately the oversight may not be discovered for several years if no further work is constructed in the same area. It is a vital concern and should not be overlooked. The most common procedure is for the contractor to prepare the record drawings as the project progresses, by clearly and legibly marking a set of prints that at the end of the project are turned over to the architect/engineer or the owner's engineers for checking. After approval by the architect/engineer or owner, these record data are normally turned over to the owner, or if the contract calls for it, drafted on a set of tracings and then turned over to the owner.

4
RECORDS AND REPORTS

I N THE EARLIER years of construction, all that seemed to be needed to assure quality construction was the assignment of a full-time resident project representative who possessed many years of experience and a track record of successful projects. The philosophy was based upon the premise that the resident project representative would assure that the owner received his money's worth by applying the knowledge learned through the years of construction experience. No detailed records were kept; in fact, many decisions were made in the field that should have been made by the architect or engineer, and many "deals" were made involving construction tradeoffs, without any documentation.

Unfortunately, too many of the old-time inspectors are still operating in this manner. In a recent case involving the installation of an underground pipeline with a special joint detail that was causing some trouble, an inspector "solved" the field problems (or thought he had), and upon completing the project proudly moved on to another project where he extolled the virtues of his technique of handling the previous job. Shortly after completion, unknown to the inspector, most of the joints were found to leak. Unfortunately, no daily reports were filed nor did the inspector maintain a daily diary or log. A couple of years later a lawsuit followed in which the contractor wanted to recover his additional costs, claiming that the engineer's design was wrong, that the manufacturer's product was deficient, and that the inspector had directed him to make changes that cost the contractor additional money without solving the problem. The case is still in court.

The engineer of record was placed in a very vulnerable position as a direct result of the failure of the inspector to maintain adequate records. If daily reports had been made out and submitted to the engineer regularly, it is quite probably that the engineer may have had the opportunity to review the problem and take corrective action at an early date, possibly preventing the occurrence of the problem altogether.

It was vital to the engineer's and owner's defense that they be capable of documenting the day-by-day events that led up to the problem, as well as the substance of conversations that took place between the inspector and the contractor, and what commitments, if any, were made by either party. Of prime importance was the issue of whether the inspector had actually warned the contractor of the possibility of leakage in the joint. This inspector had previous experience in the installation of the same kind of pipe and pipe joints on a previous job, and had noted its tendency to leak if installed in a certain manner.

The inspector was located and interviewed by the engineers who had originally designed the job over two years before. Upon careful questioning, the inspector admitted that he had recorded nothing, but claimed he could remember each incident fairly well. Subsequent questioning disproved this, and the engineer's office was left with little defense except the memory of a witness who could be easily discredited.

An interesting fact should be recognized by all inspectors. Any project could become involved in litigation, and it could be several years after the incident before testimony of the inspector as a witness is requested. Any record that the inspector makes in writing, which is recorded in a form that will retain its credibility, may be referred to by the inspector while he is on the witness stand. This is an allowable method of refreshing a witness's memory. There are some limitations, however, and one of them is that the notes recorded by the inspector must be made on the same day that the incident or conversation took place. It is *not* acceptable to write notes on scratch paper, then at a later date transcribe them into the inspector's diary or log book.

Such notes are not evidence in themselves, except for records made by certain types of public officials in the course of their official duties. Thus, these notes may not be entered as evidence, but can only be referred to in court by the party who wrote them—and then only as a device to refresh his memory.

It cannot be emphasized too strongly that the modern construction job is beset with numerous potential disputes or legal problems. *Any inspector who fails to keep adequate records is not performing a competent job,* and should be replaced. Instead of providing the services to the owner that the latter is paying for, such an inspector is simply adding to the overhead cost of the project, or worse, because the owner is lulled into the feeling that with an inspector on the job his interests are going to be adequately protected. Had he known in time, the owner could have taken corrective action.

FILES AND RECORDS

It is the resident project representative's responsibility to determine what the specific needs of his employer are with regard to the type of construction records that must be established and maintained for a specific project. One principal exception is the conduct

SMITH—EMERY COMPANY — PILE RECORD

JOB: PIERSON MFG. CO.   DATE: 6/3/76

LOCATION: 2800 SYLMAR ST., NORWALK   INSPECTOR: R. CAMP

DESCRIPTION: 1976 ADDITION

Pile number	Type	Size	Length	Cutoff	Length in ground	Tip elev.	Remarks
3-3	PRECAST	14 x 14	40'	6'	34'	248	
3-4	"	"	40'	5'	35'	247	
3-5	"	"	40'	6'	34'	248	
3-6	"	"	40'	4'	36'	246	
C-1	PRECAST	14 x 14	45'	3'	42'	240	
C-2	"	"	45'	3'	42'	240	
C-3	"	"	45'	4'	41'	241	
C-4	"	"	45'	2'	43'	239	
D-1	PRECAST	12 x 12	40'	0	40'	242	

Figure 4.1 Inspector's notes of pile driving operations.

and administration of federal agency projects in which the government agency often provides a very specific list of all types of records, reports, and other documentation that is required, plus some specific requirements concerning the form in which such records must be maintained. Often the printed forms themselves are provided.

Many local public agencies, as well as some of the larger private architect/engineer firms have preprinted forms to assist the inspector in the recording of pertinent job information, and many have procedures established for the handling, distribution, and storage of job records as well.

Without regard for whether an architect/engineer, public agency, owner, or other interested party has established such record keeping as a policy matter, each inspector, not just the resident inspector, should *always* maintain a daily diary in which notes and records of daily activities and conversations are kept. Included in such a diary should be abstracts of all oral commitments made to or by the contractor, field problems encountered during construction, how such problems were resolved, notices issued to the contractor, and similar information. It should be remembered, however, that the daily diary (or log as it is sometimes called) is *not* a substitute for the daily construction report, which describes the construction progress and normally receives wider distribution. The information recorded in the inspector's diary or log is generally of a privileged nature, and is intended for the use of the inspector and his employer only.

Construction Records

The following is a list of the principal types of construction records that the inspector should maintain on every project:

1. *Progress of the Work:* A daily construction report containing a description of the work commenced, new work started, status of work in progress, manpower and equipment at the site, weather, and visitors to the site. If no work was performed at all, a daily report should still be filed, stating "no work" (Figure 4.3).
2. *Telephone Calls:* All telephone calls made or received should be logged and a note made indicating the identities of the parties as well as a brief phrase indicating the nature or purpose of the call.
3. *Tests of Materials:* A record should be kept of all material samples sent out to the testing laboratory for testing, as well as those tests performed at the site. The report should include space for later inclusion of the test results, as well as the location in the structure where the particular material was to be installed.
4. *Diary or Log:* A daily diary or log book should be maintained by each inspector. This book is a *quasi-legal document* and should be neatly and accurately recorded. An entry should be made every day, whether or not work was performed. The detailed contents and form of the log will be described later in this chapter (Figure 4.5).
5. *Log of Submittals:* All material being transmitted to the architect/engineer through the resident inspector should be logged in and out, as described later in this chapter (Figure 4.8).

Construction Field Office Files

All field office files should be kept up to date and should be maintained for ready reference at the job site during the entire construction phase of the project. Upon completion of the work the files should be turned over to the architect/engineer, who will retain some and forward others to the owner for retention. The field office files should include the following categories:

1. *Correspondence:* Copies of all correspondence concerning the project that have been sent to the resident project representative should be maintained and filed by date.
2. *Job Drawings:* Drawings of clarification or change, or drawings that contain supplemental information should be filed at the field office, in addition to a complete set of all contract drawings as bid.
3. *Shop Drawing Submittals:* The resident inspector should maintain a drawing log and should maintain a shop drawing file of submittals that have received final review and approval (Figure 4.8).
4. *Requisitions:* Copies of all approved requisitions for payment should be kept at the site for field reference and as a guide for initial review of the next month's partial pay requisition from the contractor.
5. *Reports:* Copies of all reports of all types should be filed by date.
6. *Samples:* All approved samples showing material and/or workmanship should be kept at the job site as a basis of comparison, and should be appropriately tagged and logged.
7. *Operating Tests:* The resident project representative is responsible for seeing that all required tests are performed at the proper time. The files should include the results of all such testing.
8. *Deviation Requests:* Whenever a request for deviation is received, a copy should be maintained along with the disposition of the request.

CONSTRUCTION PROGRESS RECORD

The most commonly accepted form of construction progress record is in the form of a daily construction report, which is filled in by the resident project representative or, if applicable, by the contractor's CQC representative on a daily basis even if no work was performed at the site that day. Usually, such reports are executed in carbon copies or by the use of forms printed on NCR paper that will provide the necessary number of copies.

The daily report is highly necessary as a progress record, and the use of this report in combination with an inspector's daily diary or log allows two types of information to be recorded in separate documents. In this manner, the more privileged type information can be restricted to recording in the diary, while the true work progress can be recorded on the daily construction report where it will receive wider distribution.

The content of a daily construction report should include the following listed information (however, the inspector should remember that as long as he is keeping a separate daily diary or log, the daily construction report should contain items relating to work progress, not conversations or other transactions):

SMITH-EMERY COMPANY

CHEMISTS · TESTING · INSPECTION · ENGINEERS
781 EAST WASHINGTON BOULEVARD
LOS ANGELES, CALIFORNIA 90021
TELEPHONE: 213 749-3411

FORM P-16 5-68 P&G

ALL REPORTS ARE SUBMITTED AS THE CONFIDENTIAL PROPERTY OF CLIENTS. AUTHORIZATION FOR PUBLICATION OF OUR REPORTS, CONCLUSIONS, OR EXTRACTS FROM OR REGARDING THEM IS RESERVED PENDING OUR WRITTEN APPROVAL AS A MUTUAL PROTECTION TO CLIENTS, THE PUBLIC AND OURSELVES.

REPORT OF COMPRESSION TESTS

FILE NO.: 106220

JOB: HOWE BUSINESS CENTER

ADDRESS: 10112 EAST DATE AVENUE
SANTA FE SPRINGS, CALIFORNIA

OWNER: J. HOWE

CONTRACTOR: FORUM CONTRACTORS

LOCATION IN STRUCTURE: COLUMN E-6

DATE: APRIL 27, 1976

APPL. NO.:

FILE NO.:

MATERIAL:
CONCRETE .... ☒
MASONRY MORTAR ☐
GUNITE .... ☐
LIGHTWEIGHT FILL ☐
OTHER

CEMENT, BRAND .... COLTON TYPE II
ADMIXTURE .... POZZOLITH 300N
SAND SOURCE .... CONROCK, SAN GABRIEL VALLEY
ROCK SOURCE .... CONROCK, SAN GABRIEL VALLEY
MIX NO. 76SE-640
TIME IN MIXER, MIN. 40
SLUMP, IN. 3.0
MADE BY .... J. STERLING
DATE MADE 3/29/76
DATE RECEIVED 3/30/76
DIAMETER, IN. 6.0
AREA, SQ. IN. 28.27
SPEC. P.S.I. AT 28 DAYS 4000

LABORATORY NUMBER:	C-52931	C-52932	C-52933			
MARK:	36-A	36-B	36-C			
DATE TESTED	4/05/76	4/26/76	4/26/76			
MAXIMUM LOAD, LBS.	90,000	137,500	141,000			
COMPRESSIVE STRENGTH, P.S.I.	3185	4865	4985			
AGE TESTED, DAYS	7	28	28			
WEIGHT AS TESTED (P.C.F.)						

☒ 28 DAY TEST COMPLIES WITH SPECIFICATIONS.
☐ 28 DAY TEST FAILS TO COMPLY WITH SPECIFICATIONS.
☐ NO STRENGTH REQUIREMENT INDICATED.

REPORTED TO:
(1) OWNER
(1) ARCHITECT
(1) STRUCTURAL ENGINEER
(2) CONTRACTOR
(1) BUILDING DEPARTMENT

RESPECTFULLY SUBMITTED
SMITH-EMERY COMPANY

BY *George Battey*

K S

Figure 4.2   Laboratory test report.

50

vtn DAILY CONSTRUCTION REPORT

REPORT NO. ___132___

DATE ___11 Dec 1975___

DAY	S	M	T	W	TH	F	S
					X		

PROJECT __SHUTTLE APPROACH AND LANDING TEST FACILITY__

JOB NO. __NAS 10-8841__   VTN 1553-04

CLIENT __Kennedy Space Center__

CONTRACTOR __Santa Fe Engineers__

PROJECT MANAGER __E.R. Fisk__

WEATHER

BRITE SUN	CLEAR	OVERCAST	FOG	RAIN
	X			

TEMP.

TO 32	32-55	55-70	70-85	85 UP
			X	

WIND

STILL	MODER.	HIGH
X		

HUMIDITY

DRY	MODER	HUMID
X		

AVERAGE FIELD FORCE

Name of Contractor	Non-manual	Manual	Remarks
Santa Fe	2	0	Supervision & Q.C.
Amelco	1	3	Ducts
Samrod	1	6	Forms
A.K. Plumbing	1	7	Underground Pipe
Allied Steel	2	13	Steel Erection
Asphalt Const Co.	2	28	Paving
VISITORS Hunts Process Co.	0	2	Sawing Concrete

Time	Name	Representing	Remarks
0800	Ferguson, R.	KSC	Jobsite Visitation
"	Brannon, W.	"	" "

EQUIPMENT AT THE SITE 1-Paving Machine 1-Gradall 2-Self Loaders 3-Skip Loaders
1-5550 Backhoe 1-4000 gal Water Truck 1-5 yd Dump Truck 2-12F Motor Graders
1-15 T Hydro-Crane 2-8 yd Dump Trucks 2-580B Backhoe 1-680 Skip Loader
1-5 T Crane 2-5 T Flatbeds 1-90 T Crane 3-Concrete Saws

CONSTRUCTION ACTIVITIES ___ SANTA FE: Supervision
and Quality Control. AMELCO: Roughed in conduit thru grade beam on line #6.

SAMROD: Finished forming of grade beam on line #6. Has bulkhead between
columns "D" & "E". A.K. PLUMBING: Laid fire line and water line pipe in
trench to fuel oxidizer. Roughing in floor sinks and vent pipe in compressor
room of shops. ALLIED STEEL: Set truss and braces for column line "E".

ASPHALT CONST CO: Finished paving of mating device pad and at intersection
of main tow-way and mating tow-way. HUNTS PROCESS: Have tow-way joints cut
from south end to YF-12 tow-way.

Continued P.C.C. Paving operation. South radius into hangar
tow-way only remaining pull to be made. Structural steel crew set truss
column "E" line. Meeting in p.m. with Ferguson, KSC, and Thomas, Base Fire
Officer, regarding three fire alarm system transmittals. Will have to write
letters for added info to cover specification requirements.

G.H. Hall - Construction Inspector

DISTRIBUTION: 1. Proj. Mgr.
2. Const. Dept.
3. Inspector
4. Client
5. File

PAGE _1_ OF _1_ PAGES

BY _R.P. Blackwell_   TITLE __Res. Engineer__

VTN-280 (3-73)

Figure 4.3 *Daily Construction Report form.*

1. Project name and job number
2. Client's name (name of project owner)
3. Contractor's name (general contractor only)
4. Name of the project manager for the design organization
5. Report number and date of report (use consecutive numbering
6. Day of the week
7. Weather conditions (wind, humidity, temperature, sun, clouds, etc.)
8. Average field force, both supervisory and non-supervisory
   a. Name of each contractor or subcontractor on the job that day
   b. Number of manual workers (journeymen and apprentices) at the site
   c. Number of nonmanual workers (superintendents and foremen) at the site
9. Visitors at the site; include names, employers, and time in and out
10. List identity, size, and type of all major pieces of construction equipment at the site each day. Indicate if idle, and reason, if applicable.
11. Log all work commenced; status of all work in progress; and all new work started. Identify location of the work as well as its description, and which contractor or subcontractor is performing it.
12. SIGN the daily report with your full name, title, and date.

On large projects, Item Nos. 1 through 4 are often preprinted on the daily construction report form to avoid needless duplication of effort by field personnel.

INSPECTOR'S DIARY OR CONSTRUCTION LOG

Often called by different names, the construction log or inspector's diary is in reality the same document. The requirements for maintaining an unimpeachable legal record in the form of an inspector's diary are indicated in the following list. While variations may occur without destroying the credibility of the document, the recommendations provided here should assure the greatest degree of reliability.

It should be remembered that it is frequently necessary to consult an inspector's diary in order to give testimony during a court trial. The book itself is not generally admissible as evidence, but can only be used by the person who made the original entires in order to refresh his memory while giving testimony on the witness stand. It is because of this that certain basic record keeping rules are considered mandatory in order to preserve the integrity of the record.

Frequently, the log is referred to as the *inspector's* diary. Mention is also made of the "privileged" nature of some of its contents. This is *not* meant to imply that it is a private document to be seen and possessed by the inspector alone. On the contrary, the record normally belongs to the design firm or owner, and while it is wise for the inspector to retain a copy of its contents, the diary must normally be turned in with the job records when full or at the end of the construction project. During the progress of the work, it may be advisable to submit the daily diary at regular intervals to the project manager of the design firm or owner so as to allow inspection of its contents. In this manner the project

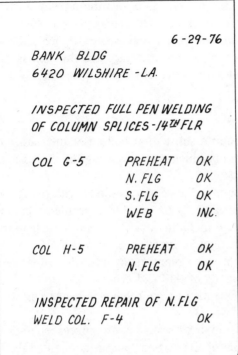

Figure 4.4 *Inspector's record of welded joints. Courtesy of Smith-Emery Company, Los Angeles.*

manager can be advised of all of the transactions that have been taking place in the field. Normally, he may want to make copies of its pages at that time; however, that does not preclude the requirement that the filled books be turned in to the project manager at the end of the job when they are often stored in the vault with other permanent job records.

The diary or log requirements can be grouped into two significant categories: format and content. Each is equally important in its own way:

Format of the Diary or Log:

1. Use only a hard cover, stitched-binding field book such as used by surveyors for their notekeeping.
2. Pages should be consecutively numbered in ink, and NO numbers should be skipped.
3. No erasures should be made. In case of error, simply cross out the incorrect information and enter the correct data next to it.
4. No pages should be torn out of the book at any time. If a page is to be voided, place a large "X" through the page, and mark "void."
5. Every day should be reported, and every calender date should be accounted for. If there is no work performed on a given date, the date should be entered on the page followed by the words "no work" or similar wording. It is still desirable to record

the weather on "no work" days, as it may have later bearing on *why* no work was performed in a case involving a claim for liquidated damages.

6. All entries *must be made on the same date that they occur.* If notes are kept on separate scratch paper and later transcribed into the diary and this fact is disclosed during a trial, the credibility of the entire diary comes into question.

Content of the Diary or Log:

1. Telephone calls made or received, and a substantial outline of the nature of such calls, including any statements or commitments made during the call. Identify the parties calling.
2. Record any work or material in place that does not correspond with the drawings or specifications, as well as the action taken. List any other problems or abnormal occurrences that arose during each day, including notations of any particular lack of activity on the part of the contractor. Note corrective actions taken.
3. Record time and the name of the contractor's representative to whom field orders are delivered, and the nature of the contents of the field order.
4. Note unforeseen conditions observed by the inspector that may cause a slowdown by the contractor.
5. Where a contractor is performing extra work because of an unforeseen underground obstruction, make a careful field count of all personnel and equipment at the site and how they are occupied. Log the number and craft of each person idled by such work, as well as any idle equipment *that would otherwise be capable of working.*
6. Record the content of all substantive conversations held with the contractor at the site, as well as any tradeoffs, deals, or commitments made by either party.
7. Record all field errors made by *any* party at the site. Identify in detail and indicate probable effect.
8. Show name of the job at the head of every page.
9. SIGN every diary entry and indicate job title immediately under the last line of entry on each day's report. This will preclude claims that additional wording was added later.

DISCREPANCY REPORTS

Although not generally a contract requirement or even common practice among most architect/engineer offices, a highly desirable practice would be the establishment of a feedback system from the inspection forces to the design firm's or owner's specifications and design departments. It can minimize the repeated errors or field problems that often occur because of the traditional failure of communication between the construction forces and the designers of the project. (Figure 4.6.).

Whenever any corrective change is necessary in field construction that will result in a variance from the specifications and drawings as originally issued, a complete detailed report should be filed with the design firm, listing the following items so that the approp-

FULLERTON RESERVOIR

CONTRACT 1.D

DATE 5-17-60 WEATHER SUNNY TEMP.: MIN. 75 MAX. 82

To JOHN M. TOUPS
District Engineer

7:30 AM ARRIVED AT RES. SITE TO MEET SURVEYORS

8:00 LEFT RES. SITE TO PICK UP DWGS @ FULLERTON OFC.

10:15 MR. LINEHAN OF L.A. TESTING PHONED AND SAYS WALKER HAS ENGAGED THEM TO DO THE MIX DESIGNS. WALKER TOLD THEM THAT ON THE 3000 PSI CONC. HE CONTACTED THE CITY WATER DEPT. AND WAS GIVEN THE OK TO USE LAGUNA SPEC. CONC. MIX DESIGN, WHICH CONTAINS AN ADMIXTURE OF PLASTIMENT. I STATED THAT OUR SPECS ONLY ALLOWED USE OF AN AIR ENTRAINING ADMIXTURE SO LAGUNA RES. MIX DESIGN WAS NOT ACCEPTABLE.

I PHONED BLUME AND CHECKED ① WHETHER ANYONE IN HIS OFFICE HAD ACTUALLY AUTHORIZED USE OF THE LAGUNA MIX. THEY HAD NOT; AND ② WHETHER WE WOULD WAIVE CONTINUOUS INSPEC. AT BATCH PLANT AND ACCEPT CERTIFICATES AS WAS DONE AT LAGUNA. BLUME SAID "YES" LETS WAIVE, BUT CALL FOR OCCASIONAL SPOT CHECK AT PLANT.

I CALLED LINEHAN BACK AND STATED THAT CONTINUOUS PLANT INSPEC. NOT REQ'D BUT WE AGREED TO HAVE AN INITIAL PLANT INSPECTION BEFORE THE FIRST BATCH IS RUN.

BLUME STATED THAT IF WE WERE HAVING TROUBLE WITH THE CONC. WE SHOULD GO TO CONTINUOUS INSPECTION.

IT WAS ALSO CONCLUDED FROM THE SPECS THAT ALTHOUGH CONTR. PAYS FOR MIX DESIGN, CITY WILL PAY FOR AGGREGATE TESTING.

3:00 PM STRUCK SAND VIEN IN EXCAVATED AREA (SEE DAILY REPORT OF THIS DATE) MATERIAL WILL REQUIRE REMOVAL AND REPLACEMENT WITH COHESIVE MATERIAL

3:30 LEFT RES. SITE.

[SIGNED] E. B. Fisk
Resident Engineer

Send duplicate to District Office daily

Figure 4.5   Sample diary page.

REPORT OF FIELD CHANGE

SPECIAL INSPECTION
REPORT No. __2__
PAGE __1__ OF __1__ PAGES
DATE __4-29-76__
CROSS. REFERENCE TO
DAILY REPORT No. __3-24-76__

PROJECT __CHAMPLAIN RESERVOIR No. 3__

PROJECT NUMBER __763-1__

INSTRUCTIONS:

Whenever any corrective change is necessary in field construction which is at variance with the specifications and drawings as originally issued, a complete detailed report shall be filed, listing the following items, so that specifications or drawings storage data can be corrected:

1. Identify the problem: Indicate why originally specified construction was not used.
2. The Solution: Describe, in detail, the recommended change or changes that were made, as applicable.
3. Indicate whether this is an isolated case or a general condition which could be improved by changing future specifications or drawings.
4. Submit sketches as necessary.

REFERENCE DATA

SPECIFICATION SECTION No. __3B__ PAGE No. __2__ PARAGRAPH No. __2.01__

DRAWING No. _____ ENTITLED _____

SKETCH NO. _____ DATED _____ ENTITLED _____

DESCRIPTION

1. DETAILED IDENTIFICATION OF THE PROBLEM __BLEEDING ALONG ALL VERTICAL JOINTS OF STEEL PANEL WALL FORMS. ALL VERTICAL JOINTS IN FINISHED WALL SURFACES SHOW EXTENSIVE EXPOSED AGGREGATE AT ALL VERTICAL WALL JOINTS. EXAMINATION OF STEEL PANEL FORMS SHOWS TYPICAL 1/32" ± GAPS AT ALL VERTICAL JOINTS, BUT TIGHT JOINTS AT ALL HORIZONTAL JOINTS. FASTENING DOGS SEEM UNABLE TO DRAW JOINTS TIGHTLY TOGETHER TO ELIMINATE LOSS OF CEMENT PASTE.__

2. DETAILED SOLUTION PROPOSED OR ACCOMPLISHED __PREASSEMBLE ALL PANEL UNITS WHILE CLEAN. REPLACE DOGS WITH BOLTED JOINTS AND DRAW TIGHT BEFORE FIRST USE. CALK ANY DEFECTS IN JOINTS. NO JOINTS SHOULD BE TIGHTENED AFTER USE WITHOUT DISASSEMBLING AND CLEANING JOINT EDGES OF PANELS. TAPE ANY JOINTS WHICH CANNOT BE DRAWN TIGHT. OTHER ALTERNATIVE: GO TO WOOD FORMS OR REQUIRE USE OF FULL FACE FORMS ONLY WHERE STEEL PANEL FORMS ARE USED. SPECIFICATIONS SHOULD BE REVISED ACCORDINGLY.__

3. IS THE PROBLEM AN ISOLATED CASE OR GENERAL? __GENERAL__

4. SUBMIT SKETCHES AS NECESSARY __PHOTOS ATTACHED__ (Attach extra sheets if necessary)

DISTRIBUTION:
1. Spec. Dept.
2. Const. Dept.
3. Inspector
4. Proj Mgr

BY _____ TITLE __RES. ENGR.__

Figure 4.6 *Report of field change.*

riate sections of the specifications or the drawings can be examined to see if the difficulty experienced in the field is one that could possibly be repetitive, and whether it can be prevented in the future by taking corrective action involving changes in design or specifications policies. The report should be in sufficient detail to allow the to understand the problem, make a determination, and issue instructions to the inspector.

1. Identify the problem: Indicate why originally specified construction is not recommended.
2. The solution: Describe in detail the recommended change or changes that are suggested.
3. Indicate whether the case appears to be an isolated one or whether it appears to be a general condition that could be improved by changing specifications or drawings.

Whether it will facilitate an understanding of the problem or its solution, the resident inspector is encouraged to submit sketches along with the field change report.

At this point the inspector should be cautioned. *The foregoing instructions are not meant to imply that the inspector is to take any corrective action that will result in a variation from the plans and specifications without the approval of the architect or engineer of record.* By definition the architect or engineer of record is that individual whose signature appears on the plans as evidence that he, either personally or as a representative of a design firm, public agency, or owner, bears legal responsibility for such plans. The authority of the inspector to take field action without consulting the architect or engineer of record is limited to cases when such action would not result in a variance from the approved plans and specifications. Otherwise, all such actions must be preapproved by the architect or engineer of record. A possible exception might be during emergency conditions, wherein a field decision must be made immediately. Even then, it is wise to telephone ahead to describe the condition and the solution recommended, followed by a written report to the architect/engineer. In any case, if forced into a decision-making role, the inspector should inform the contractor that he is not authorized to make such a determination, but that the inspector will not prevent the contractor from taking unilateral emergency action based upon the contractor's own judgment, provided that the contractor fully understands that his actions are subject to confirmation and approval by the architect/engineer, and furthermore, that in case of disapproval, the contractor may be required to take corrective action to remove portions of the work affected by the emergency at the contractor's own expense.

DOCUMENTATION OF DANGEROUS SAFETY HAZARD WARNINGS

In Chapter 8 the procedures for the handling of serious contractor safety violations are described. In addition to the action described there, certain additional precautions should be taken to document the action taken by the inspector and the contractor. This is vitally important for the resident project representative because failure to do so could result in serious charges being unfairly lodged against the design firm or owner for failure to take affirmative action in case of a death or serious injury resulting from the hazard.

It is recommended that, in each case involving an "imminent hazard," the resident inspector take the following steps *after seeing that persons in the immediate area of the hazard are removed from danger*:

1. Notify the contractor's superintendent or foreman.
2. Issue written notice to the contractor to take immediate action to correct the hazard, and record this action in the inspector's diary or log, including the exact time of day that the notice was given. Also, inform the contractor that unless immediate action is taken to correct or remove the hazard, the matter will be immediately referred to the OSHA compliance officer serving that area.
3. Upon failure or refusal of the contractor to take immediate steps to correct or remove an "imminent hazard," note the exact time of day and telephone the OSHA compliance officer and make a full oral report. After completing the call, enter into the diary or log that the contractor either failed or refused to effect immediate correction of the hazard; describe all steps taken to alleviate the hazard, including orders given to remove personnel from the danger area; record all field orders (written and oral) given to the contractor; record the exact time of day that (1) persons were ordered out of the danger area, (2) correction order was issued to the contractor, and (3) the OSHA compliance officer was notified.
4. Upon completion of the foregoing, write a full report to the design firm or owner, including a summary of all pertinent data recorded in the diary or field log. See that the report is delivered immediately.
5. Upon mailing the field report to the design firm or owner, telephone the firm or owner to advise of the forthcoming report; describe the incident briefly; indicate the action taken; and record the call in the diary or log.

MISCELLANEOUS RECORDS

There are numerous types of individual records that are important to log and retain for future reference. Many of the records that must be maintained are primarily of a technical, not an administrative nature. Thus, no detailed coverage will be attempted here. However, as a reminder, the following will serve as a partial list of some of the many technical records that must be maintained on a job, as applicable; once compiled, the handling of these records then becomes an administrative matter:

1. Manufacturer's certificates for a product
2. Laboratory test certificates (Figure 4.2)
3. Concrete transit-mix delivery tickets (Figure 4.7)
4. Records of pile driving (Figure 4.1)
5. Record of inspection of structural welding (Figure 4.4)
6. Sewer infiltration test reports
7. Fabricating plant inspection reports
8. Special inspector reports
9. Weld radiographs

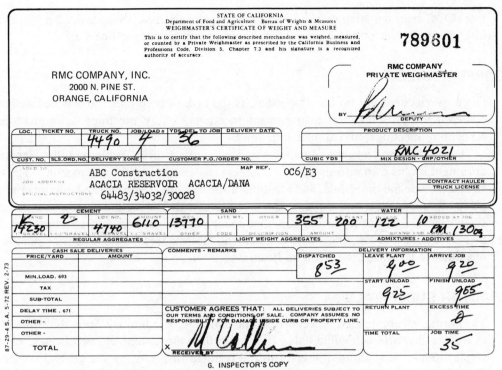

Figure 4.7 *Transit-mixed concrete delivery ticket.*

10. Acceptance certificates by public agency inspectors
11. Discrepancy reports
12. Deviation requests and action taken
13. Concrete mix designs

LABOR STANDARDS REVIEW RECORDS

On military construction contracts, the Armed Services Procurement Regulations require that regular checks be made of the contractor's employees to assure compliance with contract labor standards. Checks must be made for the following items:

1. Employee interviews to determine classifications and rate of pay, including fringe benefits. All such data must be recorded on "Labor Standards Interview" form DD 1567.
2. On-site checks of the type and classification for all work performed at the site, and the number of workers in each category.
3. Payroll reviews of prime contractor's and subcontractor's payroll submittals.
4. Comparison of the above information with available data recorded on the "Daily Report to Inspector" and the CQC Report to assure consistency.

Normally, tasks 1 and 2, above, are the responsibility of the on-site project representative (CQC representative or resident project representative), while tasks 3 and 4 are the tasks normally performed by the federal agency construction office staff.

JOB CONFERENCES

Often overlooked, but no less important, is the task of recording the proceedings of job conferences. This includes management meetings, safety meetings, coordination and scheduling meetings, and similar functions.

The resident project representative should attend all such functions, fully prepared to document for his own information the business transacted at each such meeting. The notes should include the time, date, and location of the meeting; the name and employer of each person in attendance; and the time the meeting ended. During the meeting careful notes should be taken so as to have a complete record of the substance of all important statements made at the meeting. Where statements are made by more than one person, the identities of all speakers should be listed.

CONTRACTOR SUBMITTALS

The normal recommended procedure for the handling of submittals from the contractor is to require that *all* such submittals, e.g., shop drawings, samples, certificates, or other similar items, be submitted directly to the resident inspector by the general contractor. Thus, if a submittal is mailed directly to the design firm or owner it should be returned unopened, with the request that it be transmitted through the resident project representative's field office. Similarly, if a submittal is made to the resident project representative directly from a subcontractor, it should be returned to the subcontractor unopened, with the request that it be transmitted through the general contractor. Such practices are not created out of a love of red tape, but rather to make use of a proven system that can prevent disputes or even field errors resulting from lack of communication between the parties to the contract.

Each such submittal, upon receipt by the resident project representative, should be logged in before forwarding to the office of the design firm or owner. All such material should be forwarded to the design firm or owner without action by the resident project representative, unless specifically directed to do so in any particular case. As far as contractor submittals are concerned, the resident project representative simply serves as a central receiving point and recorder for such information. As long as all submittals follow this orderly procedure, there should be no excuse for loss or delay in a transmittal. If all such material is properly logged in and out, claims by the contractor of excessive holding time by the design firm or owner, or claims of submittals that were in fact never made, can be quickly and effectively confirmed at the site.

There is often some confusion during the setting up of a contractor submittal log sheet to decide whether to assign transmittal numbers on the basis of the order *received* or on the order *returned* to the contractor. Most offices seem to find that less confusion results from assigning a transmittal number immediately upon *receipt* of a submittal. In the illustrated

CONTRACTOR SUBMITTAL LOG

ROUTING LEGEND
a. Proj. Manager e. Mechanical
b. Architectural f. Electrical
c. Civil g. Water/Sanitary
d. Structural h. Const. Services

Project _FAIRFIELD PUMP STATION_
Job No. _1415-54_
Proj. Mgr. _H.G.P._

DATE IN	Ref. Spec. Sec.	Ref. Dwg. No.	DESCRIPTION	No. Copies	REFERRED TO: (Indicate numerical sequence)								ACTION TAKEN	REMARKS	DATE OUT	TRANS-MITTAL NO.
					a	b	c	d	e	f	g	h				
6-21-73	3A		CONC. MIX DESIGN	5	1		2					3	REVISE & RESUBMIT	See also subm. dated 6-13-73	7-11-73	13
6-22-73		14	SHORING DETAILS S-1 & 5-2	4	1							2	APPROVED		6-27-73	6
7-2-73	15F		RESIDUAL CHLORINE	6	1							2	REVISE & RESUBMIT		7-11-73	11
7-2-73		8	BUTTERFLY VALVES	7	2					1		3	APPROVED AS NOTED	REQ. MIN OF 30 TURNS TO OPEN OR CLOSE	7-11-73	9
7-2-73	3A		WATERSTOP CERTIFICATES	6	2	1						3	REVISE & RESUBMIT		7-11-73	12
7-6-73		17	PROPOSED FOOTING CHANGE FOR RESERVOIR		2	1						3	APPROVED	APPROVAL SUBJECT TO NO ADD'L COST TO OWNER	7-10-73	8
7-6-73	3C	10	MANHOLE ACCESS VAULTS		2					1		3	APPROVED AS NOTED		7-30-73	16
7-16-73	15E		CHECK VALVES P1307 & P1306; PERMEABLE MATLS	6	2					1		3	APPROVED	2ND SUBMITTAL	7-23-76	14
7-18-73	3A		WATERSTOP CATALOG	3	2	1						3	APPROVED	HELD FOR 3 ADD'L COPIES	8-31-73	18
7-20-73	3A		CONC. MIX DESIGN		2	1						3	APPROVED	3RD SUBMITTAL	7-23-73	15
7-24-73	15B	8	VAULT PIPING PIPE FITTINGS CATALOG	6	1							2	APPROVED REVISE & RESUBMIT		8-3-73	17
7-26-73		11	ROOF VENTS	6	1							2	APPROVED AS NOTED		8-13-73	19
8-3-73	15E		CONTROL VALVES	6	1				2			3	DISAPPROVED	TO INSTR. & CONTROL ENGR	8-15-73	21

Contractor Submittal Log provides a permanent record of all submittals by the contractor of shop drawings, samples, and other requested data received during construction. Transmittal No. indicated should not be assigned until submitted material is being returned to the Contractor.

Figure 4.8   Sample contractor submittal log.

submittal log, spaces are provided for indicating the action taken on each submittal as well. While this may seem an unnecessary bit of added work, as such information can also be found by searching for a copy of the transmittal itself, the time saved from making searches of the files and wading through the many drawing sheets that may form a part of each such transmittal may soon make it all seem worthwhile.

In the log, it is important that the "action taken" wording conform exactly to the term used on the submittal being returned to the contractor.

CONSTRUCTION PHOTOGRAPHS

More and more reliance is being placed upon the use of photography to document construction progress, damages, technical details, types of materials, methods of installation, evidence of site conditions before starting work, and similar tasks. Basically, it is the resident project representative who will probably be called upon to do the photography.

Thus, it is to his benefit to understand the types of photographs normally used in construction, as well as the purpose of each:

1. *Public relations photography:* Selection of subject matter as well as the composition of the picture and the lighting are selected on the basis of artistic composition. The photograph is intended to appeal to the layman and show what an impressive structure is being built. An example is a view of a high rise building under construction; the photographer will use an extra wide angle lens, accent the perspective, and may even use a red filter to create striking lighting effects, which can make the steel-framed structure stand out in silhouette against some very dramatic clouds. No technical details can normally be noted, but it does produce a beautiful photograph.

2. *Progress photography:* Selection of the subject matter is based upon the need to show as much detail of the construction as possible. Photo composition is secondary, as the primary intent is to disclose the quantity and kind of work that was completed since the last progress photographs were taken. In addition, some photos are intended simply to document kinds of materials used and the method of installation. Thus, the photographer may sacrifice beauty and composition in his photograph to assure legibility of a material label or identifying mark in a finished photograph. It is considered undesirable to strive for striking lighting effects in progress photographs as they all too often obscure details in shadow areas of the picture.

Figure 4.9 Typical public relations photograph of construction.

Figure 4.10   *Typical construction progress photograph.*

3. *Time-lapse photography:* The subject of job progress photography would not be complete without some mention of "time-lapse" or interval photography. Simply stated it is just a means of using automatic equipment to take photographs at regular intervals from the same point each time. This is normally accomplished with professional equipment, using an electric motor-driven camera connected to an electric interval timer or "intervalometer." Such equipment can be used either with still cameras or with a movie camera, and by setting the delay interval between subsequent pictures to anywhere from seconds to days, a unique sequence of construction events can be recorded to show the exact nature and amount of construction work completed as of any given day or other interval. When adapted to a movie camera, this technique can also be used to simulate a speeded-up construction operation. Time-lapse photography can also be accomplished manually, using inexpensive equipment, provided that a camera can be fixed on a tripod and allowed to remain in this position during the entire sequence time. Operation of the camera can be done manually, but must be faithfully operated on a predetermined schedule each day.

Identification of Photographs

While the record data required for a public relations photograph may be minimal, the progress photograph must be considered as potential evidence in case of later claims or disputes. To be of the greatest value, certain information should be recorded on the back of each progress photograph taken:

1. Date, month, and year (sometimes time of day, also)
2. Direction camera was pointed
3. Identification of subject, with special comment if viewer's attention is directed to a specific detail
4. Photograph number (all photos should be numbered in sequence)
5. Name or initials of the photographer

Photographs as a Defense Against Claims

A camera is an important and often vital tool of the inspector, whether in the employ of the design firm, the owner, or the contractor. It is often his only means of establishing a condition of fact at any given occasion prior to its being permanently covered. The camera could well be the tool that might save the resident project representative, the design firm, the owner, or the contractor from charges that might be based upon one person's word against another had it not been for a photographic record.

Some pipeline contractors who regularly construct large underground pipelines beneath city streets in residential and business areas send a photographic crew to the site before the start of any work to photograph all of the curbs, sidewalks, and frontage of every residence and business place along the pipeline route. Every foot of frontage is photographed as a permanent record of the condition that existed prior to the beginning of construction as evidence against frivolous damage claims filed after work is completed. It is remarkable that so many honest people can have a crack in their sidewalk or curb and never notice it until a contractor starts tearing up the street in front of the house. For some reason, the home owner is invariably convinced that all such cracks or other damage were caused by the new construction. The resident project representative or the CQC representative of the contractor should be able to find a lesson in this example that will allow him to protect himself and the design firm, the owner or the contractor from the hazards of frivolous claims.

PHOTOGRAPHIC EQUIPMENT AND MATERIALS

Types of Equipment Used

Where the resident inspector is expected to take the progress photographs, he is generally asked to use either a 35mm single-lens reflex camera with interchangeable lenses, or possibly a Polaroid film pack camera. Usually the use of the Polaroid camera is limited to photographing field problem areas so that they may be immediately available to discuss

Figure 4.11 *Typical cameras used for construction.*

with the architect/engineer. Some firms will allow the use of a Polaroid for progress photography, but its disadvantages outweigh its advantages. There is no negative possible with color pack Polaroid film, thus copying of an original photograph must be done by rephotographing the print itself—seldom an ideal process. Also, if the architect/engineer wishes to retain copies of the prints and forward other print copies to the owner, both the versatility of a negative film plus the higher quality of the photographs taken with the 35mm camera will pay off.

If the contract calls for a professional photographer to provide the required photographic coverage, he will usually use a 2¼ square format camera or a 35mm camera (if you let him). Where possible to control it, there is still no substitute that will equal the results obtained from the traditional 4 x 5 sheet film cameras in the hands of a qualified professional.

Camera Handling

Although the subject of photographic technique is somewhat beyond the scope of this book, some helpful hints are offered that may assist the newcomer in resolving some of the problems of recording his project progress on film.

Exposure times are important, as an error in estimating the light conditions can lead to the loss of a picture, and in construction you will seldom get a second chance to repeat the scene. Because of this it is recommended that the inspector either have a camera with a built-in light meter or obtain a separate light meter that can be used to determine the proper shutter speed and lens aperture. This is especially important in the case of color films, as an error of as little as one shutter speed or one f-stop can result in an unsuccessful photograph.

Many cameras on the market have built-in meters, and some are coupled to the shutter mechanism for either manual or full automatic operation. This means that no matter what the subject matter is, the camera's light meter will read the average light conditions and, if it is the fully automatic type of coupling, it will actually set the controls for you. Just point and shoot. It sounds great at first; however, it has serious disadvantages. If you are standing in a shaded area, but the subject you want to show on the photograph is in bright sunlight, the meter will determine its "average exposure" from the light conditions surrounding the camera, thus making the details in the shaded area around the camera show up as properly exposed in the finished print, while the subject you actually wanted to show would be greatly overexposed—exactly the opposite of what was desired. The author recommends that a coupled meter is excellent, but do not get a fully automatic camera unless the automatic feature can be locked out and the exposure controls operated manually if desired.

In the handling of the camera in bright sunlight, it should always be remembered that the camera should be held or pointed in such a way as to avoid having the direct rays of the sun strike the lens surface. A sun shade is highly desirable to help prevent this. Occasionally, it might be necessary to aim the camera toward the sun in order to get a particular view at a particular time. In such cases, shade the lens as much as possible and hope for the best. The photograph will not generally be spoiled, but the glare on the lens surfaces creates a condition that results in a loss of brilliance in the photograph and results in extremely low contrast pictures, with accompanying loss of shadow detail. As they used to say about the old "box cameras," the safest way to get consistently good pictures is to try to keep the sun at your back at all times. It is still good, safe advice.

Selection of Equipment

In the choice of cameras, do not be misled by cameras with extremely "fast" lenses, because the measure of the quality of a camera, or of a lens either for that matter, is not in the speed of the lens, but in its quality. While the added lens speed may allow the taking of pictures under extremely low light conditions, it is not worth it if the results are not sharp and clear, or if the sharpness falls off at the edges.

A camera with an f3.5 lens is quite adequate for most field uses, and can generally be obtained at a reasonable cost. Also, as the ability of the average person to estimate distances accurately is somewhat less than that person is usually willing to admit, it is essential that the camera selected either have a rangefinder or be a reflex type camera that allows the inspector to see exactly what he is photographing and how sharp he has adjusted the focus.

If the inspector plans to select a 35mm camera for work progress photography, it is desirable to obtain one that allows the use of interchangeable lenses, if the somewhat added cost of this feature is not objectionable. Many of the subjects that the inspector must photograph will involve the inclusion of wide viewing areas, which, if a normal 50mm lens is used (standard on 35mm cameras), he may find that he must either back up too far, or find that there is insufficient space to back up any farther. A wide angle lens of 28mm or 35mm is ideal for such conditions, as it will allow the inspector to cover adequately the entire project area when necessary. Occasionally, a closeup detail may be needed of a portion of the work that is inaccessible to the photographer without turning into a human fly and walking up the side of a tall building.

A long focal length lens (telephoto) can allow the same effect as being up close. A 135mm lens is an ideal telephoto for this purpose, as they are usually priced within reason. If the inspector plans to have only one lens, however, a 50mm or a 35mm focal length lens is ideal. If two lenses are to be used, both the 50mm and the 35mm lens are a good combination, although a 28mm would be a good substitute for the 35mm.

Although the ideal camera might seem to be a Nikon, Canon, or Leica in the hands of a qualified expert, the average needs of a construction project do not require such sophistication or skill. Many low- and medium-priced cameras are on the market that are more than adequate to do the job for which they are needed.

If interchangeable lenses are to be accommodated, as suggested before, the camera shopper would do well to check the currently available models of single-lens reflex cameras. With a camera of this type, instead of a separate viewfinder, the photographer is actually looking through the camera taking lens. This allows a larger image for viewing and, in addition, requires no allowance for parallax when taking extreme closeup pictures.

Some points to look for in a single-lens reflex camera are:

- Built-in metering through the lens
- If automatic metering, be sure it can also be operated manually

(c)

Figure 4.12 *(35mm lens) (50mm lens) (135mm lens) The same subject photographed with three different lenses.*

- Automatic diaphragm—otherwise failure to remember to close down the diaphragm after viewing has ruined many pictures
- Shutter synchronization for flash X and M settings
- Match needle or coupled meter to shutter or diaphragm
- Double exposure prevention (saves many irreplaceable pictures)
- Focal plane shutter (less costly for interchangeable lenses)
- Split image focusing (a great help, particularly with wide angle lenses)
- If you are an eyeglass wearer, be sure that you can either get your eye close enough to the viewfinder with your glasses on to see the entire screen area, or that supplementary correction lenses to replace your regular glasses are available to attach to the camera.

If the cost of even the lowest price prism reflex camera is above your budget, then consider one of the many available 35mm rangefinder type cameras, as the majority of this type currently on the market fall within the medium- to low-price range, and the purchaser has a wide choice of many excellent, high-quality buys.

Although some inspectors may be tempted to cover construction with a twin-lens reflex camera, some words of caution are in order. Only one twin-lens reflex camera on the market allows for interchangeability of lenses, and its price is considerably above the range referred to here. Other twin-lens reflex cameras offer supplementary lenses to convert the existing lens to wide angle or telephoto, but these, too, are very costly. There is only one twin-lens reflex camera known to the author that falls in the medium- to low-price range. It is the Yashica Mat 2¼ x 2¼ Model 124G. However, the cost of film (120) size) and processing is considerably higher in the long run.

Several Polaroid models are available that accept Polaroid colorpack films. If cost is a major factor, cameras accepting the Type 88 color pack are considerably less costly to operate than the slightly larger Type 108 color pack series. Either is equally acceptable for quality, however. For the more experienced photographer, the Polaroid 195 camera is recommended, but it should be noted that it is not automatic as are all the others, and requires the use of a separate light meter.

Selection of Film

Although black-and-white photographs were quite acceptable for progress pictures twenty years ago, there is hardly any reason for not going to color pictures today. The added value of color in allowing more critical photo interpretation is unquestioned.

The choice of color films, then, is primarily one of answering the question, "Do you want slides or color prints?" Generally, slides cost less initially, because there are no prints to make—all that you get back is the original film that was in the camera. In case of color print film, however, you receive both a color negative (the film that was in the camera) and color prints that were made from those negatives—thus, the added cost. For construction, color *prints* are recommended. From the color negatives, slides can still be made if needed; color prints and enlargements can be made; and even black-and-white prints can be made if desired. Thus, it is a truly versatile film. On the other hand, if prints are wanted from a slide, the processor must first rephotograph the slide to make a negative, then make prints in the ordinary way. This is a considerably more costly process than if color print film had been used in the first place.

For general usage in construction, the following 35mm color films are recommended:

1. Kodak Vericolor II Professional Film, Type S (VPS 135)—Color Prints
2. Kodak Ektachrome 200 Film (Daylight) (ED 135)—Color Slides

Film and Camera Storage

Security is always a problem on a construction site, and in particular such items as cameras, pocket calculators, and similar pocket-size items of considerable value are always in jeopardy. Cameras should be locked up; however, this usually presents a problem. They are sensitive to temperature, particularly when they have film inside. Usually, the only available secure areas at a construction site are locked file cabinets in the field office (a rarity), or the locked trunk of the inspector's automobile. If the field office is cooled in the summer and heated in the winter, the file cabinet is best. The auto trunk is a high risk area for film and cameras unless special precautions are taken to prevent damage from the high heat concentrations usually present there. One method of protecting the camera and film in an automobile trunk in hot weather is to keep the camera and film in one of the popular styrofoam beverage containers designed to keep a sixpack cool on a picnic. In any case, it should be left in the trunk as little as possible. In winter months, there is little substitute for a heated field office, as nothing you can do to your auto trunk is likely to keep the camera and film from freezing when the temperature drops to these ranges.

If a camera is taken out of a heated enclosure into a very cold atmosphere, be sure to let the camera adjust to the cold air for a while before attempting to take pictures; otherwise, the condensation that may form will cause problems.

Color films require storage in cool, stable temperatures if the color balance is to be maintained. Try to keep them about 65 to 70° F at all times, if possible. Polaroid film can be an even greater problem in the field. It has been the author's experience that Polaroid color film under hot weather conditions requires special care and handling. The camera and film are better kept in an air conditioned vehicle until the actual moment that the picture is to be taken. Upon making the exposure, the camera should be immediately transported back to the air conditioned car before pulling the film tab. Once inside, the tab can be pulled and the film process begun in the usual manner with no adjustment in exposure. If the Polaroid camera with film inside is allowed to be carried outside in hot weather for any length of time, the quality of the pictures will suffer greatly. In cold weather a special ''cold clip'' is provided by the manufacturer, in which the inspector can place the newly exposed film immediately after removal from the camera, and place the entire assembly inside his shirt under the armpit to keep the temperature at optimum for processing. As with hot temperature photography, the ideal arrangement is to keep the camera in a controlled temperature inside the inspector's automobile until the actual time of exposure.

SPECIFICATIONS AND DRAWINGS

WHAT IS A SPECIFICATION?

The specifications are a part of the contract documents that define the qualitative requirements of a project that is to be built. The dictionary defines them as "a detailed description of requirements, dimensions, materials, etc., as of a proposed building, machine, bridge, etc.," and further as "the act of making specific."

The role of the drawings is to define the geometry of a project, including dimensions, form, and details. The specifications are intended to complement this by defining the nature of the materials that are to be used and the description of the workmanship and procedures to be followed in constructing the project.

All too often an inspector, just like many tradesmen, expects the drawings to provide *all* the information required, incorrectly assuming that the specifications are only needed by the lawyers in case of dispute. To be sure, the specifications may be needed in cases of dispute, but if properly used and referred to throughout the construction work can also serve to minimize disputes. Even more important to the resident project representative and the contractor is the fact that the specifications are the only documents that will spell out the obligations for administration of the project during its construction. By far the majority of the administrative tasks that the resident project representative will be required to perform are covered by the specific terms of the *General Conditions* of the contract and by nothing else. Even years of past experience cannot serve as a substitute, as the rules of the game change from project to project. What may have been proper on a previous job may be wrong on the next, and only the specifications will tell it as it should be.

CONFLICTS BETWEEN THE DRAWINGS AND SPECIFICATIONS

It should be brought out here that neglecting the specifications can lead to serious problems. In case something is shown or noted one way on the drawings and described differently in the specifications, which will govern? The answer to that question is easy. The specifications will normally take precedence unless it says *in the specifications* that the plans will govern. Thus, it is still the specifications that set the controlling criteria. Normally it is easy to determine the relative importance of one document over another, as most specifications specify the relative order of importance of the different parts of the contract documents in the General Conditions of the construction contract. However, it should be of interest that in the absence of such a specific provision, the courts have repeatedly held that the provisions of the specifications will take precedence over the drawings in case of a conflict between the two. [Appeal *of Florida Builders, Inc., ASBCA No. 9013, 69-2 BCA 8014 (1969)]*

Therefore, if the specifications are the most important single document, the inspector can hardly perform his job in a competent manner unless he becomes as familiar with the specifications as he is with the construction drawings.

In some cases, the same data are covered in both the drawings and the specifications—not a great arrangement, but it happens often enough. The problem here is that frequently one document is changed during design and the other is overlooked. This generally creates the problem referred to above. The unfortunate situation is that usually, where such a problem exists, it is the drawings that were updated to receive the latest changes or corrections, and the specifications may in fact be outdated and incorrect. The basic philosophy still controls, however, and the inspector has no authority to force the contractor to provide that which is shown on the drawings when his bid may have been based upon the article contained in the specifications. In case of any such conflict, the contractor is obligated to notify the owner's representative before continuing. However, it is well for the inspector to monitor carefully any such possibilities himself, as the contractor may honestly miss recognizing the presence of a conflict. It would also be possible for a dishonest contractor to merely *claim* to miss the conflict so as to furnish the cheaper of the two items, knowing full well that if the design firm wants it changed after the contractor has already built it in accordance with the specifications, in all likelihood he will be able to claim successfully extra compensation for such additional work.

It should be remembered that some items will appear only in the specifications and not on the drawings; others will appear only on the drawings and not be mentioned in the specifications. This is not necessarily an oversight, nor is it to be considered as a flaw in the specifications or drawings. Many architectural and engineering firms as a matter of policy prefer not to repeat data on both documents. This is done intentionally as a means of preventing conflicts due to late changes that may be made to one document alone and not to the other. The resident project representative should make certain that the foreman doing the work uses his specifications also, as it will minimize construction problems and conflicts.

CONTENT AND COMPONENT PARTS OF A SPECIFICATION

Content of the Specifications

In addition to the well-known *technical* provisions contained in the specifications, it should be clear that the term "specifications" is not necessarily limited to the technical portions alone. Generally, everything that is bound into the specifications document is referred to as the "specifications." This may include the notice of invitation to bid on the project; the bidding documents and forms, including the bid bond where required; contract (agreement) forms, including performance and payment bonds where required and non-collusion affidavits where required; the conditions of the contract, often referred to simply as the "boiler-plate" because it provides a protective shield around the contract by anticipating most of the areas of discussion or dispute that might arise, and provides for an orderly way of resolving each such case; and finally, the technical provisions. If the term "contract documents" is used, then it legitimately includes everything, including the drawings, and sometimes includes a book of "standard specifications" by reference, as well. Usually, some of the "boiler-plate" documents will specify a list of all items that are to be officially classed as a part of the "contract documents."

Another often misunderstood characteristic of a set of specifications is that the size of a specification is in no way directly related to either the size or cost of a project, but is actually more influenced by how many different trades or materials are involved in the work. Thus a public restroom building in a park with only one room and a single set of plumbing fixtures may require as thick a set of specifications as a two-story building. On the other hand, a highway construction job costing 10 times the price of either of the two described buildings may involve a specification of only three or four sections and possibly as few as eight or ten pages of technical provisions.

Most contractors, inspectors, or other construction administrators have, at some time or another, questioned the wisdom of the specification writer. If it will give the inspector any peace of mind, the author readily believes that all specifications writers are not necessarily knowledgeable in some of the subjects about which they write (sometimes an understatement). In a recent ASCE (American Society of Civil Engineers) questionnaire circulated on a national basis by its *National Task Committee on Specifications* to engineers, contractors, public agencies, owner-developers, suppliers, and attorneys, the general response from the contractors was that a specifications writer should have field construction experience before becoming a specifications writer. Every construction worker has undoubtedly run into specifications at some time during his career where it seemed obvious that the specifications writer did not possess this attribute. Part of the problem lies in the procedures often used by architects and engineers in selecting personnel for, and budgeting time and costs for, the production of specifications. All the standardized specification formats in the world cannot cure that problem. If each of the items specified is properly covered, the resident project representative or CQC representative will have the tools for and sufficient authority to assure the owner of quality in construction. Neglect these important considerations and the inspector is deprived of one of his primary tools.

Component Parts of a Specification

Generally, most specifications can be divided into three main elements, or "parts." Although these parts are not necessarily arranged on each job in the same order in which the inspector will encounter them, the various design firms or public agencies responsible will generally keep the content of the specifications within the classifications shown in Figure 5.1.

In addition to the classifications indicated in Figure 5.1, all public-funded projects require a listing of minimum wage rates. This is normally listed in the specifications.

If a public project has federal funding as well as being subject to state labor code requirements, then in addition to the requirements for state wage rates, a complete copy of the applicable federal wage rates must also be bound into the specification, and the

---

PART I — BIDDING AND CONTRACTUAL DOCUMENTS

Notice Inviting Bids	(mostly public works)
Instructions to Bidders	
Proposal (or Bid) Forms	
Proposal	
Bid Sheets	
Contractor Certificates	(mostly public works)
List of Subcontractors	(Calif. public works)
Bid Bond Form	(mostly public works)
Non-Collusion Affidavits	(mostly public works)
Agreement and Bonds	
Agreement (contract)	
Performance Bond Form	(mostly public works)
Payment Bond Form (labor & materials)	(mostly public works)

PART II — CONDITIONS OF THE CONTRACT

General Conditions (the "boilerplate")
Supplementary General Conditions (special for the project)
(In some specifications the supplementary general
conditions are referred to as "Special Conditions")

PART III — DETAIL (TECHNICAL) SPECIFICATIONS

(From this point on, the architect/engineer provides
technical sections covering the various parts of the
project.)

Figure 5.1   *Three-part specifications format.*

contractor is obligated to pay the higher of the two rates if there is a difference. The federal wage rates are normally reproduced directly from the Federal Register, which lists wage rates all over the nation. Every Friday, new listings appear in the Federal Register, which list all wage rate schedules or changes. Any specifications containing federal wage rates should also have the sheets containing the current modifications to the general wage rate determination.

The Instructions to Bidders is usually a preprinted document and is normally considered as one of the contract documents. Thus, the provisions of the Instructions to Bidders are as binding upon the bidder and the contractor as are the provisions of the technical specifications. Failure to comply with its terms can render a contractor's bid as "informal," which may be used as justification for rejecting it. The general subject area usually covered by an "Instructions to Bidders" document includes the following:

Form of bid and signature
Interpretation of drawings and specifications
Preparation of the proposal
List of documents to be submitted with the bid
Bonding requirements
What is expected of the successful bidder
Insurance policies required
Basis for selection of the successful bidder

The General Conditions or "boilerplate" as it is often called is the most overlooked, yet one of the most important documents in the specifications to the resident inspector. It is this document that establishes the ground rules for administration of the construction phase of the project. The subject matter generally covered in General Conditions is fairly consistent from job to job wherever "standard" preprinted documents of a governmental agency or AIA, NSPE, ASCE/AGC, or similar organizations are used. Whenever an architect or engineer or a public agency elects to prepare its own General Conditions, it frequently lacks many of the essentials and, worse yet, has never been "proved" in court. The general subjects covered in most "standard" General Conditions documents include:

Legal definitions of terms used in the contract
Correlation and intent of the documents
Time and order of the work
Assignment of contracts
Subcontracts
Where to serve legal notices
Authority of the architect/engineer
Change orders and extra work
Extensions of time for delays
Right of the owner to terminate the contract
Right of the contractor to terminate the contract
Right of the owner to take over work

Obligations of the contractor
Supervision by the contractor
Handling of claims and protests
Lines, grades, and surveys; who performs and who pays
Defective work or materials
Materials and workmanship
Provisions to allow access to all parts of the work
Inspection and tests; how administered and who pays
Coordination with other contractors at the site or nearby
Suspension of all or part of the work
Liquidated damages for delay
Stop notice procedures
Right of owner to withhold payment
Provisions for public safety
Changed conditions (sometimes called unforseen conditions)
Estimates and progress payments
Final payment and termination of liability
Protection and insurance
Disputes; settlement by arbitration

Part III of the specifications, as outlined in Figure 5.1, refers to that portion of the specifications that the layman usually thinks of when you speak of "specifications." In this portion of the document are the detailed technical provisions that relate to the installation or construction of the various parts of the work and to the materials used in the work. There are several ways of logically dividing these sections into subject areas so as to lend some sort of order to the final document. Most of the systems, however, generally group specifications sections into trade-related functions as a means of easy grouping. This sometimes prompts the complaint from contractors that the sections do not accurately represent the responsibility areas of the various trades. Actually, there is usually no attempt made to conform exactly to trade jurisdictions, as they vary significantly from one part of the nation to the other; in fact, in some cases jurisdictional differences may be evident from one adjacent county to the other within the same state.

It should be recognized that on any project there are usually a few technical requirements that would apply to *all* sections equally. In such cases, it has been found desirable to provide a section of the technical specifications, usually at the front of the technical portion, that may be entitled "General Requirements" and that spells out the various requirements of a *technical* nature that apply generally to the entire project. This section should not be confused with any of the text of Part II—Conditions of the Contract; there the "General Conditions" and "Supplementary General Conditions" are matters of a legal/contractual nature—*not technical provisions*. A common error made by general contractors in their dealings with their subcontractors is to hand them a single technical specifications section relating to their trade, without copies of either the General Requirements or the General and Supplementary General Conditions of the Contract. This has often created serious problems in the conduct of the work, as all of the "boilerplate" sections apply to all of the work of each subcontractor as well.

WHAT DO THE SPECIFICATIONS MEAN TO THE INSPECTOR?

The specifications, in short, are one of the inspector's vital tools. Without them, he cannot possibly do his job in a competent manner. To be able to use these tools effectively, however, the inspector should have an idea of the relative importance of each of the various component parts of the contract documents. The following is a condensed listing of some of the contract document components and their relative importance. For a more complete listing, refer to Chapter 6.

Agreement governs over specifications
Specifications govern over drawings*
Detail specifications govern over general specifications

Each month on the larger projects the contractor normally applies for and receives monthly partial payments (progress payments) for work completed thus far. The amount of each payment must be in direct proportion to the amount of work completed during the preceding month. It is the responsibility of the resident project representative to check the quantities of such work completed, estimate its value, and review the monthly payment request of the contractor prior to submitting it to the design firm's project manager or sometimes the owner, along with a recommendation for payment, if justified. In the handling of such matters, the terms of the General Conditions must be strictly followed, as the procedures for handling such payment claims must follow an orderly, prearranged plan. There are no provisions for allowing terms or creating restrictions that were not written into the original contract.

In short, the entire policy for the administration and conduct of the work at the jobsite is established under the terms and conditions of the General and Supplementary General Conditions of the construction contract. The remaining portions of the specifications more properly relate to quality control or quality assurance functions, which are a subsidiary function of the resident project representative.

CSI SPECIFICATIONS "FORMAT"—ITS MEANING AND IMPORTANCE

Briefly mentioned in earlier paragraphs was the fact that the technical portions of the specifications were generally structured in whatever manner suited the architect or engineer who prepared them. In the past years, this problem was even worse, and a contractor would indeed have to be versatile to be required to work from one type of contract documents on one job and at the same time be constructing another similar project nearby from another set of documents that bore no resemblance to the first.

In recent years, an organization called the Construction Specifications Institute (CSI)

*[Appeal of *Florida Builders, Inc.,* ASBCA No. 9013, 69-2 BCA 8014 (1969)]

tackled the task of attempting to inject some degree of uniformity and standardization into the general arrangement and method of writing construction specifications. To this end they have been enormously successful, although it can be seen that the "format" or arrangement and classification system they have devised was created by architects and engineers whose experience was limited to the construction of buildings, and the resulting format shows very little influence of engineers engaged in heavy engineering and similar types of construction. The CSI Format was indeed intended for buildings, but once entrenched nothing seemed to be able to change or even alter the system when it became desirable to extend it to other types of engineered construction as well. Thus, when the system is used for certain types of heavy engineering projects, some serious formatting conflicts present themselves. In any case, it *did* create order where none existed before by setting forth a list of 16 standardized "Divisions," which were supposed to work for everything, and with a little imagination it could indeed by adapted to many, though not all, nonbuilding construction projects, even though it may be somewhat cumbersome and awkward in certain types of work.

CSI 16-Division Format

The CSI 16-Division Format was adopted by the AGC (Associated General Contractors), the AIA (American Institute of Architects), the NSPE (National Society of Professional Engineers), and others in the United States and Canada in the form of a document entitled "Uniform System for Building Specifications." NOTE that word "building" again—no mention of heavy engineering projects. Nevertheless, it is widely used for both building and some engineering work, and is popularly known as the CSI Format. This system has been officially adopted for *all* work by the U.S. Army, Corps of Engineers; the U.S. Navy (NAVFAC); National Aeronautics and Space Administration (NASA); the State of New York for public works projects; and by numerous other public and private agencies. Eventually, all the manufacturers followed suit, and now most, if not all, building materials are identified with the CSI classification number for filing purposes, which corresponds to the CSI Division number under which each such product is intended to be grouped. Thus, most of the time, if you pick up a specification it will be under CSI Format, and even without a table of contents you should be able to find the section you are searching for. As an example, you should automatically turn to Division 3 if you are looking for concrete, or Division 16 if you are looking for electrical work (Figure 5.2).

From a civil or mechanical engineer's standpoint there are still some problems to be solved in devising a uniformly adaptable specification "Division" list. Whenever this fact is recognized and the matter studied objectively from the standpoint of those professionals who construct building as well as heavy engineering works or systems, the industry may yet see an ideal system. Nevertheless, the CSI Format is here to stay, and all inspectors should learn to use it. Memorize all 16 Division titles, as they never change, even from one job to the next.

1.	General Requirements
2.	Site Work and Utilities (includes all civil work)
3.	Concrete
4.	Masonry
5.	Metals
6.	Wood and Plastics
7.	Thermal and Moisture Protection
8.	Doors and Windows
9.	Finishes
10.	Specialties
11.	Equipment
12.	Furnishings
13.	Special Construction
14.	Conveying Systems
15.	Mechanical
16.	Electrical

> Note that whenever a job does not use a certain Division, it is simply skipped. . .but the numbers of the remaining Divisions still never change.

Figure 5.2   List of CSI 16-Divisions.

CSI Division/Section Concept

Whenever the term Division/Section Concept is heard with regard to the CSI Format, it is an expression of the relationship of the fixed-title Divisions to the subclassifications under each Division called "Sections." Although Division titles *never* change from job to job (although some Divisions may be omitted from a project if they are not applicable) the titles of the Sections that are grouped under them are adapted to the specific needs of each individual project. In Figure 5.3 all 16 fixed-Division titles may be used under each appropriate Division. In addition to the short list illustrated, the CSI also publishes a document that provides a ready index of section titles to fit the CSI 16-Division Format.

CSI Three-Part Section Format

One of the most valuable contributions of the CSI to the work of the contractor and the inspector is the development of the three-part *section format*. Under this arrangement, each *section* is divided into three parts, each containing one type of information only. With this system, less items are overlooked simply because the specifications for a particular product were sandwiched between some unlikely paragraphs dealing with the installation of some totally unrelated item—which just happened to be located there because some architect or engineer happened to think of it while he was writing that portion of the section.

In the three-part section format, all technical sections of the specification are divided

CSI FORMAT

DIVISION 1—GENERAL REQUIREMENTS
01010 SUMMARY OF WORK
01100 ALTERNATIVES
01150 MEASUREMENT & PAYMENT
01200 PROJECT MEETINGS
01300 SUBMITTALS
01400 QUALITY CONTROL
01500 TEMPORARY FACILITIES &
      CONTROLS
01600 MATERIAL & EQUIPMENT
01700 PROJECT CLOSEOUT

DIVISION 2—SITE WORK
02010 SUBSURFACE EXPLORATION
02100 CLEARING
02110 DEMOLITION
02200 EARTHWORK
02250 SOIL TREATMENT
02300 PILE FOUNDATIONS
02350 CAISSONS
02400 SHORING
02500 SITE DRAINAGE
02550 SITE UTILITIES
02600 PAVING & SURFACING
02700 SITE IMPROVEMENTS
02800 LANDSCAPING
02850 RAILROAD WORK
02900 MARINE WORK
02950 TUNNELING

DIVISION 3—CONCRETE
03100 CONCRETE FORMWORK
03150 FORMS
03200 CONCRETE REINFORCEMENT
03250 CONCRETE ACCESSORIES
03300 CAST-IN-PLACE CONCRETE
03350 SPECIALLY FINISHED
      (ARCHITECTURAL) CONCRETE
03360 SPECIALLY PLACED CONCRETE
03400 PRECAST CONCRETE
03500 CEMENTITIOUS DECKS
03600 GROUT

DIVISION 4—MASONRY
04100 MORTAR
04150 MASONRY ACCESSORIES
04200 UNIT MASONRY
04400 STONE
04500 MASONRY RESTORATION &
      CLEANING
04550 REFRACTORIES

DIVISION 5—METALS
05100 STRUCTURAL METAL FRAMING
05200 METAL JOISTS
05300 METAL DECKING
05400 LIGHTGAGE METAL FRAMING
05500 METAL FABRICATIONS
05700 ORNAMENTAL METAL
05800 EXPANSION CONTROL

DIVISION 6—WOOD & PLASTICS
06100 ROUGH CARPENTRY
06130 HEAVY TIMBER CONSTRUCTION
06150 TRESTLES
06170 PREFABRICATED STRUCTURAL
      WOOD
06200 FINISH CARPENTRY
06300 WOOD TREATMENT
06400 ARCHITECTURAL WOODWORK
06500 PREFABRICATED STRUCTURAL
      PLASTICS
06600 PLASTIC FABRICATIONS

**DIVISION 7—THERMAL & MOISTURE
PROTECTION**
07100 WATERPROOFING

07150 DAMPPROOFING
07200 INSULATION
07300 SHINGLES & ROOFING TILES
07400 PREFORMED ROOFING & SIDING
07500 MEMBRANE ROOFING
07570 TRAFFIC TOPPING
07600 FLASHING & SHEET METAL
07800 ROOF ACCESSORIES
07900 SEALANTS

DIVISION 8—DOORS & WINDOWS
08100 METAL DOORS & FRAMES
08200 WOOD & PLASTIC DOORS
08300 SPECIAL DOORS
08400 ENTRANCES & STOREFRONTS
08500 METAL WINDOWS
08600 WOOD & PLASTIC WINDOWS
08650 SPECIAL WINDOWS
08700 HARDWARE & SPECIALTIES
08800 GLAZING
08900 WINDOW WALLS/CURTAIN WALLS

DIVISION 9—FINISHES
09100 LATH & PLASTER
09250 GYPSUM WALLBOARD
09300 TILE
09400 TERRAZZO
09500 ACOUSTICAL TREATMENT
09540 CEILING SUSPENSION SYSTEMS
09550 WOOD FLOORING
09650 RESILIENT FLOORING
09680 CARPETING
09700 SPECIAL FLOORING
09760 FLOOR TREATMENT
09800 SPECIAL COATINGS
09900 PAINTING
09950 WALL COVERING

DIVISION 10—SPECIALTIES
10100 CHALKBOARDS & TACKBOARDS
10150 COMPARTMENTS & CUBICLES
10200 LOUVERS & VENTS
10240 GRILLES & SCREENS
10260 WALL & CORNER GUARDS
10270 ACCESS FLOORING
10280 SPECIALTY MODULES
10290 PEST CONTROL
10300 FIREPLACES
10350 FLAGPOLES
10400 IDENTIFYING DEVICES
10450 PEDESTRIAN CONTROL DEVICES
10500 LOCKERS
10530 PROTECTIVE COVERS
10550 POSTAL SPECIALTIES
10600 PARTITIONS
10650 SCALES
10670 STORAGE SHELVING
10700 SUNCONTROLDEVICES(EXTERIOR)
10750 TELEPHONE ENCLOSURES
10800 TOILET & BATH ACCESSORIES
10900 WARDROBE SPECIALTIES

DIVISION 11—EQUIPMENT
11050 BUILT-IN MAINTENANCE
      EQUIPMENT
11100 BANK & VAULT EQUIPMENT
11150 COMMERCIAL EQUIPMENT
11170 CHECKROOM EQUIPMENT
11180 DARKROOM EQUIPMENT
11200 ECCLESIASTICAL EQUIPMENT
11300 EDUCATIONAL EQUIPMENT
11400 FOOD SERVICE EQUIPMENT
11480 VENDING EQUIPMENT
11500 ATHLETIC EQUIPMENT
11550 INDUSTRIAL EQUIPMENT
11600 LABORATORY EQUIPMENT
11630 LAUNDRY EQUIPMENT
11650 LIBRARY EQUIPMENT

11700 MEDICAL EQUIPMENT
11800 MORTUARY EQUIPMENT
11830 MUSICAL EQUIPMENT
11850 PARKING EQUIPMENT
11860 WASTE HANDLING EQUIPMENT
11870 LOADING DOCK EQUIPMENT
11880 DETENTION EQUIPMENT
11900 RESIDENTIAL EQUIPMENT
11970 THEATER & STAGE EQUIPMENT
11990 REGISTRATION EQUIPMENT

DIVISION 12—FURNISHINGS
12100 ARTWORK
12300 CABINETS & STORAGE
12500 WINDOW TREATMENT
12550 FABRICS
12600 FURNITURE
12670 RUGS & MATS
12700 SEATING
12800 FURNISHING ACCESSORIES

DIVISION 13—SPECIAL CONSTRUCTION
13010 AIR SUPPORTED STRUCTURES
13050 INTEGRATED ASSEMBLIES
13100 AUDIOMETRIC ROOM
13250 CLEAN ROOM
13350 HYPERBARIC ROOM
13400 INCINERATORS
13440 INSTRUMENTATION
13450 INSULATED ROOM
13500 INTEGRATED CEILING
13540 NUCLEAR REACTORS
13550 OBSERVATORY
13600 PREFABRICATED STRUCTURES
13700 SPECIAL PURPOSE ROOMS &
      BUILDINGS
13750 RADIATION PROTECTION
13770 SOUND & VIBRATION CONTROL
13800 VAULTS
13850 SWIMMING POOLS

DIVISION 14—CONVEYING SYSTEMS
14100 DUMBWAITERS
14200 ELEVATORS
14300 HOISTS & CRANES
14400 LIFTS
14500 MATERIAL HANDLING SYSTEMS
14570 TURNTABLES
14600 MOVING STAIRS & WALKS
14700 TUBE SYSTEMS
14800 POWERED SCAFFOLDING

DIVISION 15—MECHANICAL
15010 GENERAL PROVISIONS
15050 BASIC MATERIALS & METHODS
15180 INSULATION
15200 WATER SUPPLY & TREATMENT
15300 WASTE WATER DISPOSAL &
      TREATMENT
15400 PLUMBING
15500 FIRE PROTECTION
15600 POWER OR HEAT GENERATION
15650 REFRIGERATION
15700 LIQUID HEAT TRANSFER
15800 AIR DISTRIBUTION
15900 CONTROLS & INSTRUMENTATION

DIVISION 16—ELECTRICAL
16010 GENERAL PROVISIONS
16100 BASIC MATERIALS & METHODS
16200 POWER GENERATION
16300 POWER TRANSMISSION
16400 SERVICE & DISTRIBUTION
16500 LIGHTING
16600 SPECIAL SYSTEMS
16700 COMMUNICATIONS
16850 HEATING & COOLING
16900 CONTROLS & INSTRUMENTATION

Figure 5.3   *CSI Format showing some recommended section titles under each division. This document has been reproduced with the permission of the Construction Specifications Institute, 1150 Seventeenth Street, N.W., Washington, D.C. 20036. Further reproduction is not authorized.*

into three distinct parts, always in the same order: (1) General, (2) Products, and (3) Execution.

PART I — GENERAL

Scope; Related Work; Submittals; Inspection
Requirements; Testing; Certificates; etc.

PART II — PRODUCTS

Technical specifications for all materials,
equipment, fabricated items, etc.; In no case
is it proper to show any installation requirements in this part, or specify quality of
workmanship in this part.

PART III — EXECUTION

Qualitative standards relating to workmanship,
etc.; covers installation, erection, construction,
etc.; In no case is it proper to cover any
product, materials, equipment, or fabricated
item requirements in this part.

Figure 5.4 Three-part section format.

If followed faithfully, as most users of the system will do, it makes the reading of the specifications a simple, orderly process and eliminates many an error due to oversight.

STATE HIGHWAY DEPARTMENT FORMATS

Long before the coming of the CSI Format, the various state highway departments established formats of their own in response to the needs of the type of construction in which they were engaged. Most states have settled on a uniform format based upon the AASHTO (American Association of State Highway and Transportation Officials) model.

The basic similarity between all state highway specifications is the fact that they all use a published, bound book of "standard specifications." This book covers in detail all general contract conditions as well as the technical specifications for all types of construction that could be reasonably anticipated in any highway department project. The subject matter covered is not as narrow as one might at first expect, and to add complications to the specification, it frequently covers several alternative methods of completing the work.

To adapt these standard specifications to a specific project requires an additional document, for the standard specifications themselves cover far too broad a subject area. Furthermore, they do not indicate whether a specific method should be used on a particular project. This adaptation is accomplished by the preparation of a small specification called the "Special Provisions." This document clearly defines the changes to the Standard Specifications or any additions or deletions from the Standard Specifications that might be necessary to adapt it to the specific project being constructed. For the sake of uniformity, the Special Provisions follow a "standard" format adopted by each using agency, so that all users throughout that state will produce a document that is in the same format, and all contractors will have prior knowledge of the basic requirements and conditions for highway construction in their state.

In the previous cases referred to, when "specifications" were mentioned, the term was interpreted to include all documents, general conditions, and technical provisions. On a state highway project, this definition must be revised. Here the "specifications" are the Standard Specifications, and the document issued for the specific project contains only supplementary material. The usual title for the book containing the documents plus the special technical conditions is "Special Provisions."

AASHTO Standard Format for Highway Construction Specifications

The majority of the state highway departments of the United States closely follow the standards of the American Association of State Highway and Transportation Officials (AASHTO).

Rather than refer to the basic or "general" standards of the AASHTO, the example used here as an AASHTO-type specification will be the Road and Bridge Standards of the Virginia Department of Highways and Transportation. Just as used in all other states, the Virginia standard specifications cover all potential types of highway and bridge construction that may be encountered, along with all of the possible acceptable alternatives. These must be supplemented by a book of Special Provisions to adapt the Standard Specifications to a particular project. In addition, as a means of keeping the Standard Specifications up to date, the State of Virginia also issues Supplemental Specifications, which are modifications sheets needed to update the Standard Specifications. These are normally bound into the set of Standard Provisions.

As with other state highway specifications, the arrangement of the subject matter in the technical portions of the Special Provisions closely parallels that of the contents of the book of Standard Specifications, wwherever possible. The Virginia Road and Bridge Specifications are initially divided into seven main divisions.

I   General Provisions (sections 101-110; contractual relationsips)
II   Materials (sections 200-258; for the work of Div. II through VII)
III   Roadway Construction (sections 301-321; execution only)
IV   Bridges and Structures (sections 401-426; execution only)
V   Incidental Construction (sections 501-519; execution only)
VI   Roadside Development (sections 601-610; execution only)
VII Signing (sections 702 and 703; execution only)

In similar fashion, the Florida Department of Transportation Standard Specifications for Road and Bridge Construction are divided into four main divisions.

I   General Requirements and Covenants (sections 1-9; contractual relationships)
II Construction Details (sections 100-715; execution only)
III Materials (sections 901-995; for the work of Div. III)
IV Contract Forms (printed under separate cover)

As in both the California and the Virginia Standard Specifications, the Florida Standard Specifications divisions are further broken down into sections related to the majority of construction materials and methods expected to be encountered in normal road and bridge construction. Anything needed for a project that is not contained in the standard specifications is specified in the Special Provisions.

What most state highway specifications have in common with the CSI Format (long before the formation of the CSI) is the strict separation of materials and execution in their specifications. Thus, in all execution portions of a state highway specification, the materials are covered by reference to the detailed specifications in the division provided for that purpose.

Numbering of the special provisions technical sections in the Virginia highway specifications uses a fixed number system that retains the numbers used in the original book of Standard Specifications, unlike the California example described later, in which a fixed numbering system is used that is wholly independent from the numbering system used in its standard specifications.

California Department of Transportation Format

The California Department of Transportation or "CalTrans" standard specifications are a departure from the AASHTO Standard, having predated AASHTO. They were designed to meet the specific needs of the construction industry in California for street, highway, and bridge construction projects and as such were adopted by many cities and counties throughout that state that administer similar projects at local levels. As with the AASHTO standard specification format, they must be supplemented by a book of Special Provisions. The format used in these special provisions has been standardized, and a uniform format with fixed-number sections and standard section titles has been adopted.

The arrangement of a typical California Department of Transportation "Special Provisions" document is shown in Figure 5.5. The list of subjects covered, as well as the standardized title of each section remains unchanged from one project to the next.

NONSTANDARD CONSTRUCTION SPECIFICATION FORMATS IN USE

There are several types of approaches to the problem of separating a project specification into seemingly logical units of construction. The two most common concepts are:

1. Separation into trade-group and material classifications, as in the CSI Format.
2. Separation by construction features, wherein each significant feature of a project is

NOTICE INVITING BIDS

SPECIAL PROVISIONS

Section 1 — Specifications and Plans (definitions)
Section 2 — Proposal Requirements and Conditions
Section 3 — Award and Execution of Contract
Section 4 — Begining of Work; Time of Completion;
              and Liquidated Damages
Section 5 — General (includes updates to Standard Specifications)
Section 6 — (Content varies)
Section 7 — Legal Relations and Responsibility
Section 8 — Miscellaneous (technical data)
Section 9 — Description of the Work (definition of scope)
Section 10 — Construction Details (technical provisions)

PROPOSAL AND CONTRACT

Proposal and Bid Sheets
Bid Bond
List of Subcontractors
Agreement
Performance Bond
Payment Bond

Figure 5.5 *California format for Special Provisions.*

described completely within a single section, including all the materials and methods involved to complete the specified structure or feature.

Depending upon the nature of a specific project, each concept may have something good to be said of it, and each could serve to special advantage if used properly. If ever the two systems would be mixed in the same specification, however, the job of field administration can become chaotic! The problems resulting from such an unwise choice include the inability reasonably to control payments to the contractor for the various portions of the work, difficulty in defining interfaces in construction, duplication of specification provisions in different parts of the work—often with varying and conflicting requirements. An inspector who gets assigned to a project like this should be prepared for a lion-sized job of maintaining cost control, especially if it turns out to be a unit-price job.

A graphic example of the complicated relationships involved can be determined from Figure 5.6, which takes the various features (or units) of construction of a recreational park project as an example, and superimposes them in matrix form with the various trade-group and material classifications that apply to the same work.

Item	Unit of Construction	CSI Division Categories														
		2	3	4	5	6	7	8	9	10	11	12	13	14	15	16
A	Site Grading	x														
B	Site Utility Lines	x	x		x										x	
C	Storm Drain System	x	x		x											
D	Valve Chamber	x	x	x	x		x		x		x				x	x
E	Streets & Parking	x	x		x				x						x	x
F	Snack Bar Building	x	x	x	x	x	x	x	x	x	x				x	x
G	Rest Room Building	x	x	x	x	x	x	x	x	x	x				x	x
H	Administration Bldg.	x	x	x	x	x	x	x	x	x	x				x	x
I	Landscaping & Irrig.	x	x												x	

Figure 5.6 *Comparison of trade group vs. units of construction formatting.*

It becomes obvious from the chart that any project that included all these various features (or units) would be most benefitted by using the CSI Format, which is based upon the separation of the specification technical provisions into sections corresponding to the *vertical* columns in the chart in Figure 5-6. Thus, there would be only one concrete section; one metals section; one electrical section; and so forth, no matter how many separate structures or units of construction were included in the project.

On the other hand, if a project only involved street paving and parking lots; street lighting and signals; landscaping and irrigation; and a storm drain system, as many municipal improvement projects do, it might be perfectly practical to divide the specifications into sections describing features (or units) of construction, corresponding to the *horizontal* lines on the chart in Figure 5.6. This is primarily because the materials of construction and the trades used in this case are peculiar to the unit being built, and the material specification for one of these units is not equally applicable to any of the other sections.

SPECIFICATIONS VERSUS SPECIAL PROVISIONS CONCEPT

This subject has been slightly touched on in earlier paragraphs, but it is of great importance for the inspector to know the relative importance of the documents he must use in the field and to understand the very important difference between these two concepts.

Specifications

The *specifications* concept is based upon the issuance of a single, all-inclusive project specifications book containing all of the contract provisions that apply to the job, although *references* to outside sources are permissible. The effect of such outside references in this

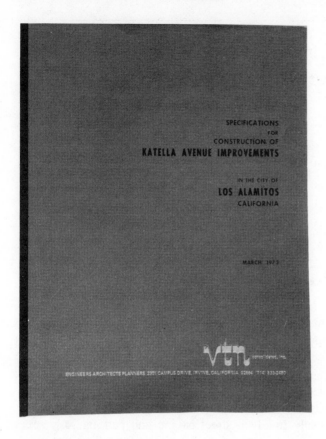
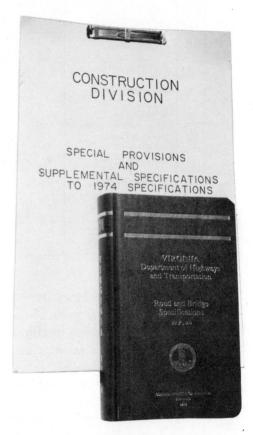

Figure 5.7 *Comparison of job specifications at left, with standard specifications plus special provisions at right, for similar projects.*

type of specifications, however, is to bind the contractor only to the extent of the specific reference specification named. Thus, if a project specification states that "portland cement shall be Type II cement as specified in Section 90 of the Standard Specifications," it limits the control of the cited reference to the *portland cement specifications only* and does not bind the contractor to any other provisions of that same section, such as the grading of aggregates for concrete, and so forth.

Special Provisions

The *special provisions* concept is based upon the idea that a previously published book of Standard Specifications is the actual detailed specification for all applicable work on the project, and that the Special Provisions are merely a supplemental document to provide for those items on a particular project that the design engineer wanted changed from the provisions of the Standard Specifications, or where he made a specific selection of options provided in the Standard Specifications. Thus, for example, while it has been already established that the entire concrete section of the Standard Specifications will control the project (insofar as it is applicable, of course) the reference in the Special Provisions that "portland cement shall be Type II cement as specified in Section 90 of the Standard Specifications" merely controls the choice of option as to the *type of cement* required for the work. The total provisions of the rest of "Section 90" still apply to the concrete work. The exact specification phrase used in the project *specifications* can have a vastly different meaning when used in a *special provisions* document.

Bibliography

E. R. Fisk, "Specifications—Design Professionals Forgotten Challenge," *Journal of the Construction Division,* ASCE Vol. 102, No. C02, Proc. Paper 12171, June 1976, pp. 303–306; presented at the November 3–7, 1976, ASCE National Convention and Expo, held at Denver, Colorado (Preprint No. 2522).

CSI Manual of Practice, Volume Two, "Formats: Specifications and Manuals," by the Construction Specifications Institute, Inc., Washington, D.C.

6

ANALYSIS AND FUNCTION OF THE SPECIFICATIONS

GENERAL CONDITIONS OF THE CONSTRUCTION CONTRACT

The *general conditions,* sometimes called the *general provisions,* specify the manner and the procedures for implementing the provisions of the construction contract according to the accepted practices within the construction industry. These conditions are intended to govern and regulate the requirements of the formal contract or agreement. They do not serve as a waiver of any legal rights that either party to the contract may otherwise possess. The general conditions of the contract are intended to regulate the functions of either party only to the extent that his activities may affect the contractual rights of the other party or the proper execution of the work.

Although the general conditions of most construction contracts vary somewhat from one set to another, depending upon the requirements of the agency that originated the document, the following list taken from the "General Conditions" of the "Contract Documents for Construction of Federally-Assisted Water and Sewer Projects," Document No. 11, may well be considered as somewhat typical of many:

1. Definitions (terms used in the contract documents)
2. Additional Instructions and Detail Drawings (legal status of such)
3. Schedules, Reports, and Records (submittals by the contractor)
4. Drawings and Specifications (intent, order of precedence, conflicts)
5. Shop Drawings (contractor's obligations, procedures for handling
6. Materials, Services, and Facilities (responsibility for)
7. Inspection and Testing

8. Substitutions (handling of ''or equal'' products)
9. Patents (payment of royalties, hold harmless provisions)
10. Surveys, Permits, Regulations (who furnishes and who pays)
11. Protection of Work, Property, Persons (responsibility for)
12. Supervision by the Contractor (requirements for)
13. Changes in the Work (change orders)
14. Changes in Contract Price (as the result of change orders)
15. Time for Completion and Liquidated Damages
16. Correction of Work (correction of rejected work)
17. Subsurface Conditions (discovery of unforseen conditions)
18. Suspension of Work, Termination, and Delay
19. Payments To Contractor (procedures)
20. Acceptance of Final Payment as Release
21. Insurance (P.L. & P.D., workmen's compensation, builder's risk, fire)
22. Contract security (performance and payment bonds)
23. Assignments (no assignment of contract)
24. Indemnification (hol harmless)
25. Separate Contracts (owner's right to have)
26. Subcontracting (must be modified in some states)
27. Engineer's Authority
28. Land and Rights-of-Way (obligations to provide)
29. Guaranty (work and materials)
30. Arbitration (agreement to arbitrate future disputes)
31. Taxes (who pays)

Other standard sets of general conditions have been developed by various segments of the construction industry. The American Institute of Architects, the Associated General Contractors of America jointly with the American Society of Civil Engineers, and various branches of the federal, state, and municipal governments have all developed and published standardized sets of general conditions.

Although most of these documents bear a superficial similarity to one another, certain federally-produced documents depart widely from the normal industry standards. One such document, widely used by a number of federal agencies including the Economic Development Administration (EDA), the Environmental Protection Agency (EPA), and the Department of Housing and Urban Development (HUD) sparked such controversy, however, that a substitute document was produced and agreed upon for certain types of projects. The new document is the previously referred to ''Contract Documents for Construction of Federally-Assisted Water and Sewer Projects,'' which was developed in cooperation with numerous public and private agencies for use by borrowers and grantees in federally-assisted projects funded by the following federal agencies:

Economic Development Administration, Department of Commerce
Environmental Protection Agency

Farmers Home Administration, Department of Agriculture
Department of Housing and Urban Development

One redeeming feature of the new documents is the fact that the substitution or revision of some individual sections is allowed where they conflict with local state law. The original documents of these agencies (which are still used in some instances) contain one of the most difficult and conflict-producing provisions that has even been written into any set of General Conditions. It is always "Article 41," no matter which agency's documents are used, and it creates a contractual condition wherein the General Conditions must take precedence over any conflicting provisions in any other portion of the specifications! It is quoted below:

41. CONFLICTING CONDITIONS

Any provision of the Contract Documents which may be in conflict or inconsistent with any of the paragraphs in these General Conditions shall be null and void to the extent of such conflict or inconsistency.

Think of what that could do to a contract! The new General Conditions referred to are voluntary, but at the urging of the following organizations who jointly prepared and endorsed them in cooperation with the previously listed federal agencies, they are quite widely used by many engineering firms on water and sewer projects. The endorsing agencies who assisted in their preparation are the following:

American Consulting Engineers Council
American Public Works Association
American Society of Civil Engineers
Associated General Contractors of America
National Society of Professional Engineers
National Utility Contractors Association

Standard forms of General Conditions have many advantages. Not only are they generally the result of collaboration with industry leaders, and thereby represent a fair and equitable method of handling a construction contract, but they have normally had the advantage of being thoroughly critiqued by members of both the architect/engineering profession and the legal profession. Furthermore, many have been tested in court and can be relied upon to provide similar protection to all who use them. Another, and frequently overlooked advantage, is that such documents have evolved into a form that has withstood the test of time and experience and have become familiar to the contractors who use them. After repeated usage, a contractor will clearly understand all of its terms, meaning, and implications. This is often reflected in a stability of bid prices, as it has already been established as to the full effect of its provisions on the contractor.

It must be remembered, however, that the mere fact that a document *is* so "general" in nature, means that certain types of specific data cannot be included, otherwise it would not be applicable to all of the projects on which it is used. For example, a provision in the

General Conditions for "liquidated damages" or for "bonds" will normally only cover the limitations, procedures, or other unchanging elements—but *not* the actual monetary amount. The specific dollar amounts must be referred to in the Supplementary General Conditions, a document that will be discussed later.

Some of the well-known standardized "General Conditions" documents in current usage are those of the following organizations:

AGC/ASCE	Associated General Contractors/American Society of Civil Engineers
AIA	American Institute of Architects
CEC	Consulting Engineers Council
EDA	Economic Development Administration, Department of Commerce
EPA	Environmental Protection Agency
FHA	Farmers Home Administration, Department of Agriculture
HUD	Housing and Urban Development
JPL	Jet Propulsion Laboratories
NASA	National Aeronautics and Space Administration
NAVFAC	Department of the Navy, Naval Facilities Engineering Command
NSPE	National Society of Professional Engineers
SCS	Soil Conservation Service
USBR	U.S. Bureau of Reclamation
USCE	Corps of Engineers, U.S. Army
(joint)	Contract Documents for Federally-Assisted Water & Sewer Projects (EDA; EPA; FHA; HUD; ACEC; APWA; ASCE; AGC; NSPE; NUCA)

Obviously, there is no shortage of "standards" and the choice of which to use on any given project may be influenced by many things, including the specific owner requirements source of construction funds, type of work to be constructed, whether the project is being built by a public or a private agency, and, last but not least, whether a particular set of General Conditions contains provisions with which the owner and architect/engineer are willing to live.

From the multitude of standard General Conditions available, there would seem to be little valid reason to generate a new one, yet many architects and engineers and owners are doing just that when they type their own General Conditions to fit a particular job. Each time that a new set is written, there is always the danger that its provisions may contain subtle wording that may not afford the same contractual protection as those contained in the existing standard forms that have had their days in court—and survived.

General Conditions Portions of Standard Specifications

On some projects where the basic contract is written around a set of Standard Specifications, the General Conditions of the contract are usually contained in the early chapters of the Standard Specifications book. For example, a project for construction of a bridge under the Virginia Road and Bridge Specifications has its General Conditions specified in Division I, "General Provisions," which includes Sections 101 through 110 of that document.

Similarly, the American Public Works Association in cooperation with the Associated General Contractors published a book of Standard Specifications entitled "Standard Specifications for Public Works Construction," usually simply referred to as the "Green Book." Here, as in the standard state highway specifications, the General Conditions are actually Part 1, "General Provisions," Sections 1 through 9 of the standard specifications book. The principal difference between the two books lies in two areas: (1) the "Green Book" contract provisions are designed to accommodate a broader type of construction, while the state highway and bridge specifications are primarily designed for highways, bridges, and drainage facilities; and (2) the state highway standard specifications are designed for use only in one state and, therefore, contain all of the special legal requirements that must be a part of public contracts in that state, while the "Green Book" is written for use in several states, and the inclusion of such specific information would seriously limit its use in other states.

USING THE GENERAL CONDITIONS

Unforseen Underground Conditions

Several of the provisions of the General Conditions deserve special discussion because of their importance to the inspector and to the contractor as a result of the possible interpretations of their provisions. One of the most misunderstood of all contract provisions, and the one that is frequently the cause of large contractor claims for additional work and change orders, is the provision for *subsurface conditions*.

Subsurface and latent physical conditions at the site present a special problem. If they differ significantly from what is printed in the contract documents, the contractor may well be entitled to additional payment for any increased work involved. When this happens, it usually comes as a great surprise to the owner. The architect or engineer should explain the possibility of such claims to the owner before the construction contract is signed. He should also be particularly careful that he gives no assurance as to the accuracy of any subsurface exploration, even when a special soils consultant was employed. Failure to advise the contrator of any available data regarding subsurface conditions may not only entitle the contractor to additional payment, but may possibly be the cause of a significant delay in the project when underground conditions are discovered that are quite different than shown on the plans.

One can no longer say that the responsibility for all such conditions and the delays that accompany them will always be that of the contractor. There are recent court decisions relieving the contractor from such responsibility even where the wording of the contract documents states that the contractor must familiarize himself with all conditions at the site that might affect the performance of the work. In fairness to the contractor and to avoid risk of blame for causing delays on the job, the design firm or the owner should make all data used in design available to the contractor.

Materials and Equipment

One of the most common occurrences during construction is the constant search by the contractor to obtain products that cost less than those actually specified, and offer them to the architect/engineer as substitutes (sometimes without offering a share of the savings to the owner). The ever-present desire to use cheaper materials that frequently have not had the test of time to show that they will perform as well as a specified product frequently leads to claims against the architect or engineer for negligence if it is determined later that the product did not perform as required. Great care must be used in the approval of new, substitute products as well as in the application of some established ones. The architect or engineer has the duty to see that the products furnished in compliance with his drawings and specifications are actually suitable for the particular uses intended. Reliance on producer's sales literature is hazardous at best. There are several court decisions in which the architect or engineer has been held liable for failure to have a new material tested, or an established item tested for a new application prior to approving it. Thus, it is easy to understand his occasional reluctance to try new products.

It may even be desirable to require that the manufacturer of such new products furnish guarantees that extend beyond the usual time. The refusal of a producer to provide such guarantees may be sufficient reason for rejecting the product. In any case, the authority for acceptance of a product offered as an ''or equal'' item is reserved to the architect or engineer of record—not to the resident project representative or other inspector.

The Contractor and Subcontractors

Almost all of the construction contract General Conditions are based upon having the resident inspector dealing solely with the general contractor; not directly with subcontractors, materialmen, or fabricators. The General Conditions generally state that the general contractor is fully responsible for all the acts and omissions of his subcontractors, and nothing in the General Conditions is intended to create any contractual relationship between any subcontractor and the owner or design firm or any obligation to assure that the contractor has paid his subcontractors or material suppliers.

The fact that only the *general* contractor is recognized should end the frequent disputes of subcontractors that revolve around definitions of the scope of their portion of the work (usually the result of the failure of the general contractor to provide his subcontractors with a complete set of specifications and drawings). The general contractor may complain that it is the design architect's or engineer's fault because he failed to include certain items in a specification section that would be performed by a specialty subcontractor, and thus he believes that additional funds should be paid to cover the added charges to the general contractor by the specialty subcontractors. Obviously, the answer is simple from a contractual standpoint—only one contract was let; the total scope of the work was specified;

and it is not the responsibility of the architect or engineer to determine how the successful bidder plans to subcontract the work. Furthermore, the scope of any one class of work can often vary significantly even from one county to the next, due to differences in trade union contracts and the resultant jurisdictional agreements. One contract means one job; it is the general contractor's responsibility to properly contract with his subs to assure a clear understanding of the scope of each such subcontract.

Shop Drawings and Samples

Normally, the contractor is obligated to submit a preliminary schedule of the submittals of shop drawings and other submittals required under the contract. This schedule should be reviewed by the design firm or the owner's engineering staff and finalized prior to construction. Shop drawing submittal procedures are one of the topics for discussion at the *preconstruction conference* described in Chapter 9. Careful attention to these preliminary matters can avoid misunderstandings at a later date, and an agreed procedure should be set out on paper and copies circulated to all affected parties.

One of the most important and misunderstood facts about shop drawings is that a shop drawing approval does *not* authorize changes from the contract provisions [Appeal of *Whitney Brothers Plumbing & Heating, Inc.,* ASBCA No. 16876, 72–1 BCA 9448 (1972)]; these may only be accomplished by *change order.* Many field superintendents firmly believe that in a case in which a detail has been shown differently on a shop drawing than on the original contract drawings, the shop drawings will take precedence. This is a fallacy created by the belief that the architect's or engineer's so-called ''approval'' of shop drawings is a carte blanche acceptance of everything that is contained on those drawings. Actually, shop drawing approval is intended only to determine that they are in conformance with the design concepts of the project and compliance with the information provided in the contract documents. The contractor is still responsible for dimensions to be confirmed and correlated at the job site; for information that pertains solely to the fabrication processes or to techniques of construction; and for coordination of the work of all trades.

Therefore, a shop drawing cannot be considered as a change order, and any variation from the design drawings and specifications must be the result of a change order. Otherwise it is not authorized. [Appeal of Community Science Technology Corp., Inc., ASBCA No. 20244, 77–1 BCA 12,352 (1977).]

In a recent example, a reservoir was to have a precast, prestressed (pretensioned) concrete roof provided under a contract with a fabricator who specialized in furnishing such work as a complete package; that is, they provided the design (within the criteria set by the architect/engineer); the fabrication of all the prestressed, precast concrete structural members; and the erection at the site of all such members into a complete roof system. On shop drawings transmitted during the execution of this contract, a small but significant design detail was changed from that shown in the original design concept that was approved by the engineer and the local building and safety department. The contractor contended that approval of shop drawings with the design change on them meant that they should build according to the shop drawings instead of the contract drawings. However, the contract provided that any change from the contract drawings must be accompanied by an authorized change order, and therefore the contractor was required to conform to the original detail as shown on the contract drawings.

Again, only a *change order* can authorize a deviation from the contract provisions, and a change order must normally be signed by the owner, as it is he who is a party to the contract, not an outside design firm. It cannot be done legally by simply showing changes on a shop drawing unless the architect/engineer creates an informal change order out of the shop drawing by adding the proper authorization and signature of the owner to the drawing sheets. This, of course, would be somewhat irregular and certainly undesirable from the record keeping viewpoint.

Disapproving or Stopping the Work

Many general conditions allow the resident project representative, as a representative of an outside design firm, the right to stop the work. This is a very sensitive area and can lead to serious legal consequences if the contractor can show that it was unjustified and that he was subjected to added cost by this action. However, upon receipt of information from the architect or engineer that the work is defective, the *owner* may order the contractor to stop the work on these grounds. In any case, the more risky right to stop the work should be left to the owner, as a party to the construction contract, not to an outside design firm or their resident project representative.

In some cases where the owner is relatively ''unsophisticated,'' as the term relates to construction, there is a tendency to allow an architect/engineer or his field representative to exercise greater control over the project. It should be kept in mind at all times, however, that certain additional risks accompany such added responsibility.

One prime exception to the ''stop the work'' discussion above is the case where the work is being carried on in an unsafe manner. Under these conditions, moral standards or the law may impose a duty on both the resident project representative and the contractor for the benefit of employees and third parties to stop such work as a means of lessening the risk of death or serious injury that could result if such conditions were allowed to continue (see ''Imminent Hazards'' in Chapter 8).

Any disapproval or rejection of the work should be communicated to the contractor in writing, stating the reasons for the disapproval. This should be done as early as possible after rejecting the work. In addition, the resident project representative normally has the power to require special testing or inspection of all work that has been covered up without his consent, including work that has been fabricated, installed, or completed.

SUPPLEMENTARY GENERAL CONDITIONS

As the name implies, the Supplementary General Conditions are simply an extension of the General Conditions. It is in this document that the special legal requirements of the contract are expanded to include provisions that apply solely to the project at hand. In some cases the titles of Articles within the Supplementary General Conditions will duplicate titles already mentioned in the General Conditions. This is neither repetitious nor necessarily a superseding provision. In most cases both such paragraphs still apply. However, the provisions in the General Conditions may contain only procedural and responsibility clauses, while the same subject in the Supplementary General Conditions will add specific requirements that apply only to this job, such as amounts of liquidated damages or the amounts of bonds, or amounts of insurance required.

The Supplementary General Conditions portion of the contract documents may appear under several titles, without actually changing the nature of the document. Often under older formats this portion of the specifications is known as "Special Conditions" or on some of the newer formats Supplementary General *"Provisions"* instead of *"Conditions."*

In addition to items that are expansion of addition to items that are expansions of Articles already specified in the General Conditions, there are numerous other subjects that may, in all likelihood be encountered in the Supplementary General Conditions. A sample of the contents of one such document follows:

1. Scope (of the entire project
2. Supplementary Definitions (not covered in the General Conditions)
3. Legal Address of the Architect/Engineer and the Owner (needed for service of legal documents)
4. Amounts of Bonds (actual dollar or percentage values)
5. Amount of Liquidated Damages (actual dollar value)
6. Permits and Inspection Costs (who pays what)
7. Contract Drawings (complete list, by number and title of all drawings that are made a part of the contract)
8. Applicable Laws and Regulations (specific requirements for this job)
9. Insurance (amount of coverage; additional insurance not specified in the General Conditions and amount of its coverage)

TECHNICAL PROVISIONS OF THE SPECIFICATIONS

It should be noted that two of the three parts to which the specifications document is usually divided have "General" clauses in them. They are Part II Conditions of the Contract and Part III Technical Provisions. Some distinction should be noted between these two portions of the specifications to avoid confusion.

First, the "general" provisions of the *Conditions of the Contract* relate to the contractual relationships and legal obligations of the parties to the contract. On the other hand, the "general" provisions of the *technical* portion of the specifications should relate to those requirements of a technical nature that apply generally to the work of the entire project, rather than to work of one trade, for example. Thus, the General Conditions of the contract refer to legal and contractual relationships, while the General Requirements Section of Part III Technical Provisions relates to construction details, project features, procedural requirements for handling the work, and similar project-related functions.

Under the CSI Format, Division 1 of the 16-Division format was reserved for this purpose, and the subjects generally included (if applicable to the project) would usually be either those shown in the following list, or similar subjects that the architect/engineer deems necessary to perform properly the work of the project (see also Figures 5.2 and 5.3):

GENERAL REQUIREMENTS—DIVISION 1
1. Summary of Work
    Work by others
    Items provided by owner
    Work included in this contract
    Work to be performed later
2. Alternatives
3. Project Meetings
    Preconstruction conferences
    Progress meetings
    Job site administration
4. Submittals
    Construction schedules
    Network analyses
    Progress reports
    Survey data
    Shop drawings, product data, and samples
    Operation and maintenance Data
    Layout Data
    Schedule of values
    Construction photographs
5. Quality Control
    Testing laboratory services
    Inspection services
6. Temporary Facilities and Controls
    Temporary utilities (power, lighting, water, phones, sanitary)
    Construction elevators and hoists
    Guards and barricades
    Shoring, falsework, bracing, scaffolding, and staging
    Access roads
    Control of dust, noise, water, vapors, pollutants
    Traffic control; parking; storage of materials
    Temporary field offices
7. Products
    Quality transportation and handling
    Storage and protection

8. Project closeout
   Cleaning up
   Project record documents
   Touch up and repair
   Operational testing and validation
   Maintenance and guaranty
   Bonding requirements during guarantee period

These and similar provisions are generally representative of the types of subject matter that are expected to be contained in Division 1 of the Technical Provisions where the CSI Format is being used. A comparison of these subjects with the subject area covered under the General Conditions of the Contract, Part II of the specifications, should give some idea as to the accepted grouping of the various subject matter.

ADDENDA TO THE SPECIFICATIONS

Addenda to the specifications, or in singular form an ''addendum'' to a particular set of specifications, are documents setting forth the changes, modifications, corrections, or additions to the contract documents that have been issued after the project has been advertised for bids, but *before* the time of opening bids—sufficiently in advance of the bid opening date, one hopes, to allow the bidder time to make the necessary changes in his bid.

The addenda may be specified as ''Addendum to the Specifications'' or as an ''Addendum to the Notice Inviting Bids.'' Each has the same legal effect. Many public agencies prefer the latter. Normally, the addenda must be delivered to each party who has obtained a set of specifications in such manner as to provide the owner with written assurance of completed delivery before the opening of bids. This may be accomplished by sending a copy to each person who has obtained a set of plans and specifications, via certified mail with a return receipt requested. The return receipt is the confirmation of receipt by the bidder and it should be carefully filed. A further safeguard to assure that all parties who bid the job are using the same edition of the documents is to use one of the following listed methods of assurance:

1. Require that the bidder sign an acknowledgment for the receipt of each addendum issued. Then, at bid opening time, all such acknowledgments are checked before considering the bid as admissible.
2. Require that the bidder simply submit copies of all addenda along with his bidding documents at the time of opening bids. This is a fairly common procedure by many public agencies, who frequently require that the bid forms not be removed from the specification document, and that the entire book be submitted intact with the bid.

One of the first things to be done upon receipt of addenda is to carefully check the specifications and drawings, and carefully mark all corrections, changes, modifications, or additions to the original documents. The next step is to cross-check to see if any of the

THE METROPOLITAN WATER DISTRICT
OF SOUTHERN CALIFORNIA

Supplement No. 2 to Notice Inviting Bids
under Specifications No. 923

To all prospective bidders under Specifications No. 923 for constructing the Live Oak Reservoir, for which bids are to be received by the Metropolitan Water District of Southern California at its office at 1111 Sunset Boulevard, Los Angeles, California (Post Office Box 54153, Los Angeles, California 90054) until 10 a.m., September 7, 1973:

I.   The following changes are hereby made in the text of the above-described specifications:

(A)   In Division 2, on page 1, Section 2-3 (a), in the report entitled: "Site and Laboratory Investigation for Final Design for Live Oak Reservoir," April 1972, the logs of drill holes Nos. D-34 to D-43, inclusive, have been revised and are attached hereto.

(b)   In Division 21, on page 2, Section 21-3 (9) (f) shall be changed to read as follows: "Angle valves for exterior wet standpipes shall be Crane No. 117 with cap and chain, Powell Fig. 1040H with cap and chain, or an approved equal."

II.   The following drawings have been revised, as shown on the prints of the drawings attached hereto, and these drawings as revised shall be controlling for purposes of the required work in lieu of the drawings as originally issued:

(A)   Sheet No. 6C-2, Drawing No. B-58664, has been revised by adding the pipe class on Detail 3/6C-2.

(b)   Sheet No. 10C-8, Drawing No. B-58675, has been revised by changing the slope shown on "Typical Section, from Station 87+50 to Station 90+25".

III.   Specifications No. 923 as originally issued shall be used in submitting bids and a copy of Supplement Nos. 1 and 2 to Notice Inviting Bids and of Specifications No. 923 shall accompany the bid.

THE METROPOLITAN WATER DISTRICT
OF SOUTHERN CALIFORNIA

By   Frank M. Clinton
General Manager

August 24, 1973

Figure 6.1   *Specifications addendum.*

data that were changed involves interfacing with other sections of the specifications or any other drawings. In the issuance of addenda, the architect or engineer seldom if ever provides cross-references. The resident inspector must check his own copy for this and should mark all of his set of contract documents to reflect all such changes by addenda.

It should be remembered that addenda can only be issued *during the bidding period*; any changes that are made after the opening of bids should be issued as a change order during the construction phase. Thus the resident project representative will have access to all such changes by addenda long before reporting to the project site.

Of prime importance is the fact that an addendum to the specifications (or to the *Notice Inviting Bids,* as it is sometimes addressed) will always take precedence over any portion of the plans or specifications that is in conflict with it. The inspector should always check all addenda before requiring compliance with provisions of the original specifications or drawings.

STANDARD SPECIFICATIONS

By definition, a set of *standard specifications* is a preprinted set of specifications, usually comprising both a set of General Conditions and complete Technical Specifications for all types of construction and materials that the originating agency expects to normally cover in their kind of work. When adopted by a public agency or by a design firm working on a project for a public agency, then the total content of the Standard Specifications become a part of the contract documents, subject only to changes set forth in a separate project-related document called the "Special Provisions," which adapts the rather general treatment of the Standard Specifications to the specific needs of a particular project. In this manner, where alternatives are offered in the Standard Specifications, the Special Provisions serve to indicate which of the available choices apply to this specific project. Under this type of contract, contractually anything not modified by the terms of the Special Provisions is required to comply with *all* applicable provisions of the Standard Specifications.

In direct contrast to the above, if a project does not cite the Standard Specifications as the principal contract document, but merely references certain sections from it, then nothing in the Standard Specifications will apply to the subject project except those items specifically referenced in the specifications. The resident inspector must be very careful with regard to citations from Standard Specifications to assure proper application.

Particular attention should be paid to the exact numerical designation of a citation as well. For example, if a citation read:

"per Section 223.02(d) of the Virginia Road and Bridge Specifications"

such a specific reference would preclude the use of anything that is not in that particular subsection (d) ...in this case it would mean that concrete must be cured solely by the use of the "liquid membrane seal" method, which is specified in detail. On the other hand, if the citation read:

"per section 223 [or 223.02] of the Virginia Road and Bridge Specifications"

then the contractor would be free to select any of four specified acceptable methods of curing his conrete; it would be the contractor's option.

Under California Department of Transportation Specifications, the coverage of each Section is broader; Section 90 of that document includes not only portland cement, but also aggregates, curing materials, admixtures, and similar items. The effect of making a reference as general as the following:

"per Section 90 of the CalTrans Standard Specifications"

in a contract where the Standard Specifications was the principal document, would be to require the contractor's compliance with *all* provisions of that section, including a choice of each alternative provided. If the engineer wanted to limit the use of curing methods, for example, the Special Provisions would have to include a qualifying statement to that effect.

The use of a set of Standard Specifications without an accompanying set of Special Provisions is like asking to read a copy of a book, and being handed a dictionary instead with the comment "all the words are here; just read the ones that apply."

MASTER SPECIFICATIONS

A master *specification* is another matter entirely. It is equivalent to a Standard Specification only in that it is a preprinted set of specification provisions. It is never used on a job in the preprinted form, however. Each time it is to be used the master specification must be physically modified to meet the specific job requirements. This precludes any need to issue a set of Special Provisions or to issue sections of specifications that do not a apply to the project at hand. MasterSpecs are in-house tools to enable the architect/engineer or other agency to more effectively produce project specifications that reflect a fixed corporate or agency policy, and that may be readily updated to reflect current changes in construction methods, materials, and laws.

SPECIAL MATERIAL AND PRODUCT STANDARDS

If every time an item were specified for a project the specifications would have to contain all of the provisions that were necessary to assure that the product met all physical, chemical, geometrical, or performance standards required, every project specification would have to be from 10 to 100 times bulkier than it is now—some of them would look like a set of encyclopedias. Worse yet, every architect/engineer without the benefit of coordination would each have enough subtle difference in his description of a product as compared with another architect or engineer's description of the same product so that the manufacturers would be solely in the business of manufacturing "custom" materials for every different project. Even if this could be successfully accomplished, the construction costs would skyrocket to astronomical levels.

As a means of providing the uniformity necessary, various nonprofit associations as well as government agencies and manufacturers have established voluntary standards, which are actually Standard Specifications for separate individual products. Thus, by referring to the published data for each of these products, an architect or engineer can design his project subject to the specified product limitations, with full assurance that such products are not only marketed, but carefully regulated by each manufacturer to assure compliance with the previously established standards.

The agencies that issue such standards are sometimes governmental, sometimes industry trade associations, and sometimes independent standards associations whose only function is the preparation of such industry standards with the voluntary cooperation of industry, of course. In each case, the standards have been established as the coordinated effort between the manufacturer, the architect engineer, the academic community, and other influences as applicable.

Such standards become a part of a construction contract only if specifically called out in the specifications or drawings—and then only to the degree referred to. If a specification calls for a particular product by its ASTM Designation, but includes something that was not a part of that ASTM standard, the product must conform to the cited standard *subject to the modifying provision*. Thus, it would actually be a "special" product requiring the manufacturer to make as a "custom" item with appropriate increase in cost and delay in delivery schedule.

Such standards may be loosely divided into two basic classifications: (1) Government Standards, and (2) Nongovernment Standards. Of the first category the following are most commonly used:

Government Standards

Federal Specifications:

Federal specifications describe essential and technical requirements for items, materials, or services that are normally bought by the federal government. They are also extensively referred to in specifications for nonfederal projects when commercial standards are not available for a particular item. They are generally characterized by the unique letter-number type of designations used, such as: "SS-C-192(G)3" for portland cement concrete in the following illustration:

NUMERICAL LISTING OF FEDERAL AND INTERIM FEDERAL SPECIFICATIONS

DOCUMENT NUMBER	QPL	TITLE	FSC	PREP	DATE	PRICE
SS-A-674B(1)		Asphalt, Paving, Emulsion	5610	FSS	2 Sep 58	.05
SS-A-00674D		Asphalt, Petroleum, Paving Emulsion, Grade RS-1	5610	FSS	15 Sep 69	
SS-A-00694C		Asphalt, Petroleum (Coating, Brushing And Spraying Consistency)	5610	FSS	1 Aug 68	
SS-A-701		Asphalt-primer; (For) Roofing And Waterproofing	5610	YD	1 Aug 33	.05
SS-A-00701A		Asphalt, Petroleum (Primer, Roofing, And Waterproofing)	5610	YD	26 Jan 67	
SS-A-706C		Asphalt, Petroleum: Road And Pavement Construction	5610	ME	15 May 67	.05
SS-B-656B		Brick, Building, Common (Clay Or Shale)	5620	ME	18 Feb 66	.05
SS-B-663B		Brick, Building, Concrete	5620	ME	9 Jun 65	.05
SS-B-668A		Brick, Brick, Facing, Clay, Or Shale	5620	FSS	15 Feb 66	.05
SS-B-671C		Brick, Paving	5620	ME	2 Jun 65	.05
SS-B-675B		Brick, Rubbing	5345	SA	8 Feb 68	.10
SS-B-681B		Brick, Building, Sand-lime	5620	ME	22 Dec 65	.05
SS-B-691B		Brick, Sewer, (Clay Or Shale)	5620	FSS	9 Jun 65	.05
SS-B-750B		Building Board, Asbestos-cement, Corrugated	5640		23 Nov 60	.05
SS-B-755A(1)		Building Board, Asbestos-cement Flat And Corrugated	5640	ME	21 May 68	.05
SS-C-153		Cement; Bituminous, Plastic	5610	FSS	1 Aug 33	.05
SS-C-00153A(2)		Cement, Bituminous, Plastic	5610	FSS	12 Aug 70	
SS-C-160(2)		Cements, Insulation, Thermal	5640	ME	6 Feb 69	.05
SS-C-161		Keene's, Cement	5610	ME	7 Feb 33	.05
SS-C-181E(1)		Cement, Masonry	5610	MO	18 Oct 65	.05
SS-C-185A(1)		Cement, Natural, (For Use As A Blend With Portland Cement)	5610	MO	18 Oct 65	.05
		Cement, Plastic, Cutback Pitch Base	5610	YD	1 Feb 56	.10
SS-C-192G(1)		Cement, Portland	5610	ME	18 Oct 65	.05
SS-C-197C(1)		Cement, Portland Blast Furnace Slag	5610	MO	18 Oct 65	
SS-C-208C(1)		Cement, Portland-pozzolan	5610	MO	18 Oct 65	
SS-C-218D(1)		Cement, Slag	5610	ME	18 Oct 65	
SS-C-255		Chalk, Carpenters' And Railroad	7510	FSS	30 Aug 49	.05
SS-C-00255A		Chalk, Carpenters' And Railroad	7510	FSS	10 Jan 69	
SS-C-266D		Chalk, Marking, White And Colored	7510	FSS	15 Jan 63	.05
SS-C-00266E(3)		Chalk, Marking, White And Colored	7510	FSS	30 Sep 70	
SS-C-450A						

Figure 6.2   Federal Specifications Index.

Military Specifications (Department of Defense):

Military specifications, or "Mil-Specs" as they are often called, specify products that are usually unique to the needs of the military; however, in some rare cases such as certain electrical devices, they may be the only source of an appropriate material specification. Their use is generally discouraged in civil projects because of the difficulty in obtaining copies of the standards as well as the restricted availability of manufacturers who produce to these standards. Mil-Specs are characterized by designations such as: "MIL-R-0039016A" for an electrical relay.

ALPHABETICAL LISTING

TITLE		DOCUMENT NUMBER	FSC	PREP	DATE		CUSTODIAN		
Valves, Aircraft Hydraulic Shuttle	Q	MIL-V-5530B (4)	*1650	71	24 Mar 70	AV	AS	71
Valves, Aircraft Hydraulic Unloading	Q	MIL-V-5519C (1)	1650	71	05 Aug 64			71
Valves, Aircraft Power Brake		MIL-V-5525C	1630	AS	21 Oct 59	AV	AS	11
Valves, Aircraft, Hydraulic Pressure Relief, Type Ii Systems (Asg)	Q	MIL-V-8813	*1650	AS	20 Nov 57		AS	71
Valves, Aircraft, Hydraulic Thermal Expansion Relief (Supersedes AN-V-28)	Q	MIL-V-5527A	1650	AS	14 May 51		AS	71
Valves, Angle, Shut-off, Packed, Receiver, REFRIGERANT-12		MIL-V-22854A (1)	4130	GL	30 Sep 68	GL	YD	82
Valves, Astern (For Shipboard Use)	L	MIL-V-22682A (2)	4820	SH	15 Aug 63		SH	
Valves, Ball	L	MIL-V-23611	4820	YD	19 Mar 63		YD	
Valves, Ball, Naval Shipboard, For Air, Nitrogen, Helium Or Hydraulic Service (Sizes 2-1/2 Inches I.p.s. And Below)	Q	MIL-V-22687B (1)	4820	SH	16 May 66		SH	
Valves, Blocking	L	MIL-V-21517D (3)	1440	OS	17 Oct 63		OS	
Valves, Blow Off, Boiler	L	MIL-V-18406A	4820	YD	11 Jan 68		YD	
Valves, Boiler Blow, Shipboard Use	L	MIL-V-17737D	4820	SH	01 Feb 71		SH	
Valves, Check		MIL-V-18436C	4820	YD	30 Apr 70	ME	YD	82
Valves, Check Swing, Cast-iron And Steel		MIL-V-10386B (3)	4820	ME	17 Feb 67	ME	YD	82
Valves, Check, Controllable, Hydraulic, Aircraft, Type Ii Systems (Asg)	Q	MIL-V-19067A	1650	AS	30 Apr 57		AS	71
Valves, Check, Oxygen, High Pressure (Asg)	Q	MIL-V-5027D	1660	AS	12 Mar 68	AV	AS	71
Valves, Combined Vent-check For Submarine Mbt Blow Lines	QL	MIL-V-23953A (2)	4820	SH	12 Feb 70		SH	
Valves, Compressor Service, REFRIGERANT-12		MIL-V-22862B	4130	GL	30 Jul 68	GL	YD	82
Valves, Control, Air Diaphragm-operated	L	MIL-V-18030C (1)	4820	SH	26 Jan 70			
Valves, Cylinder, Gas, Carbon Dioxide Fire Extinguisher		QPL-17360-13	4210	SH	20 Nov 68			
Valves, Diaphragm, Stop	L	MIL-V-82026	4820	YD	13 Jul 64		YD	
Valves, Expansion, Thermostatic, REFRIGERANT-12		MIL-V-23450	4130	GL	10 Jun 71	GL	YD	82
Valves, Fuel Selector		MIL-V-5018A (2)	4530	AS	31 Oct 63	MO	AS	84
Valves, Fuel Shutoff Solenoid Operated, 28 Volt, D.c. (Asg)		MIL-V-8610A (1)	2990	82	05 Nov 71		AS	82
Valves, Fuel Shutoff, Electric Motor Operated		MIL-V-8608A (2)	2915	11	09 Nov 66	AV	AS	11
Valves, Gate, Bronze, 300 Psi	L	MIL-V-18827A	4820	YD	15 Dec 71		YD	
Valves, Gate, Cast Or Forged Steel And Alloy Steel, Outside Screw And Yoke (Basically Commercial Valves)	Q	MIL-V-1811GD	4820	SH	24 Jul 61	MO	SH	82
Valves, Gate, Globe And Angle, Steel		MIL-V-18434B	4820	YD	28 May 71		YD	
Valves, Gate, Rising Stem, Double Acting Aluminum		MIL-V-58039B	4820	ME	20 Jun 66	GL	MC	
Valves, Globe, Angle And Y, Flanged Bonnet, Manually Operated (Sizes 1-1/2 Inches And Below)		MIL-V-22094B (1)	4820	SH	3 Oct 61	MO	SH	82
Valves, Globe, Angle, And Y, Cast Or Forged, Steel, And Alloy Steel, Outside Screw And Yoke (Sizes 2-1/2 Inches And Above) (Basically Commercial Valves)	Q	MIL-V-22052C (3)	4820	SH	24 Aug 64		SH	
Valves, Globe, Angle, Quick Change Cartridge Trim, High Pressure (H.p.) Hydraulic And Pneumatic (Sizes 1/8 - 1 1/4 Inches)	QL	MIL-V-24109A	4820	SH	31 Aug 71		SH	
Valves, High-pressure, Oxygen cylinder Automatic Opening (Aeronautical Use) (Asg)		MIL-V-8522	1660	AS	21 Mar 50		AS	

Figure 6.3 Index of Mil-Spec Standards.

UBC Standards

Although technically not a governmental agency, the UBC Standards, wherever referred to are actually backed up by local ordinances, thus carrying the force of law. All cities and counties who have adopted the Uniform Building Code include the UBC Standards as a part of their requirements by virtue of the fact that they are covered by reference in the Uniform Building Code. The majority of UBC Standards are in fact other commercial standards that have been adopted as UBC standards and renumbered. The UBC designations are characterized by the following type designation: ''UBC Standard 26-1-73'' for portland cement. This standard is identical to ASTM Designation C 150.

Nongovernmental Standards

ASTM (American Society for Testing and Materials):
> By far the most recognized of all American standards. It covers not only materials specifications, but contains testing requirements and in rare cases some performance standards as well. Its listings are characterized by designations such as ''ASTM Designation C 150-74,'' where the ''74'' denotes the year of the particular edition or revision of that particular standard. All ASTM Standards are divided systematically

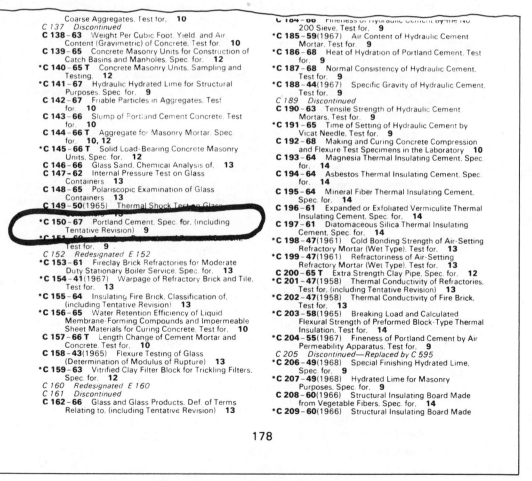

Coarse Aggregates. Test for. **10**
C 137 *Discontinued*
C 138 – 63 Weight Per Cubic Foot. Yield, and Air Content (Gravimetric) of Concrete. Test for. **10**
C 139 – 65 Concrete Masonry Units for Construction of Catch Basins and Manholes. Spec. for. **12**
*•**C 140 – 65 T** Concrete Masonry Units. Sampling and Testing. **12**
*•**C 141 – 67** Hydraulic Hydrated Lime for Structural Purposes. Spec. for. **9**
C 142 – 67 Friable Particles in Aggregates. Test for. **10**
C 143 – 66 Slump of Portland Cement Concrete. Test for. **10**
C 144 – 66 T Aggregate for Masonry Mortar. Spec. for. **10, 12**
*•**C 145 – 66 T** Solid Load-Bearing Concrete Masonry Units. Spec. for. **12**
C 146 – 66 Glass Sand. Chemical Analysis of. **13**
C 147 – 62 Internal Pressure Test on Glass Containers **13**
C 148 – 65 Polariscopic Examination of Glass Containers **13**
C 149 – 50(1965) Thermal Shock Test on Glass
*•**C 150 – 67** Portland Cement. Spec. for. (including Tentative Revision) **9**
*•**C 151**
Test for. **9** .
C 152 *Redesignated E 152*
*•**C 153 – 61** Fireclay Brick Refractories for Moderate Duty Stationary Boiler Service. Spec. for. **13**
*•**C 154 – 41**(1967) Warpage of Refractory Brick and Tile. Test for. **13**
*•**C 155 – 64** Insulating Fire Brick. Classification of. (including Tentative Revision) **13**
*•**C 156 – 65** Water Retention Efficiency of Liquid Membrane-Forming Compounds and Impermeable Sheet Materials for Curing Concrete. Test for. **10**
C 157 – 66 T Length Change of Cement Mortar and Concrete. Test for. **10**
C 158 – 43(1965) Flexure Testing of Glass (Determination of Modulus of Rupture) **13**
*•**C 159 – 63** Vitrified Clay Filter Block for Trickling Filters. Spec. for. **12**
C 160 *Redesignated E 160*
C 161 *Discontinued*
C 162 – 66 Glass and Glass Products. Def. of Terms Relating to. (including Tentative Revision) **13**

C 184 – 66 Fineness of Hydraulic Cement by the No. 200 Sieve. Test for. **9**
*•**C 185 – 59**(1967) Air Content of Hydraulic Cement Mortar. Test for. **9**
*•**C 186 – 68** Heat of Hydration of Portland Cement. Test for. **9**
*•**C 187 – 68** Normal Consistency of Hydraulic Cement. Test for. **9**
*•**C 188 – 44**(1967) Specific Gravity of Hydraulic Cement. Test for. **9**
C 189 *Discontinued*
C 190 – 63 Tensile Strength of Hydraulic Cement Mortars. Test for. **9**
*•**C 191 – 65** Time of Setting of Hydraulic Cement by Vicat Needle. Test for. **9**
C 192 – 68 Making and Curing Concrete Compression and Flexure Test Specimens in the Laboratory **10**
C 193 – 64 Magnesia Thermal Insulating Cement. Spec. for. **14**
C 194 – 64 Asbestos Thermal Insulating Cement. Spec. for. **14**
C 195 – 64 Mineral Fiber Thermal Insulating Cement. Spec. for. **14**
C 196 – 61 Expanded or Exfoliated Vermiculite Thermal Insulating Cement. Spec. for. **14**
C 197 – 61 Diatomaceous Silica Thermal Insulating Cement. Spec. for. **14**
*•**C 198 – 47**(1961) Cold Bonding Strength of Air-Setting Refractory Mortar (Wet Type). Test for. **13**
*•**C 199 – 47**(1961) Refractoriness of Air-Setting Refractory Mortar (Wet Type). Test for. **13**
C 200 – 65 T Extra Strength Clay Pipe. Spec. for. **12**
*•**C 201 – 47**(1958) Thermal Conductivity of Refractories. Test for. (including Tentative Revision) **13**
*•**C 202 – 47**(1958) Thermal Conductivity of Fire Brick. Test for. **13**
*•**C 203 – 58**(1965) Breaking Load and Calculated Flexural Strength of Preformed Block-Type Thermal Insulation. Test for. **14**
*•**C 204 – 55**(1967) Fineness of Portland Cement by Air Permeability Apparatus. Test for. **9**
C 205 *Discontinued—Replaced by C 595*
*•**C 206 – 49**(1968) Special Finishing Hydrated Lime. Spec. for. **9**
*•**C 207 – 49**(1968) Hydrated Lime for Masonry Purposes. Spec. for. **9**
C 208 – 60(1966) Structural Insulating Board Made from Vegetable Fibers. Spec. for. **14**
*•**C 209 – 60**(1966) Structural Insulating Board Made

178

Figure 6.4 *ASTM Index of Standards.*

into groupings with separate letter prefixes, which enable a user to identify the type of material referred to from the number designation alone. The following is a complete listing of all current letter prefixes and the material categories they refer to:

A Ferrous metal
B Nonferrous metals
C Cementitious, ceramic, conrete, and masonry materials
D Miscellaneous materials
E Miscellaneous subjects
F End-Use materials
G Corrosion, deterioration, and degradation of materials

ANSI (American National Standards Institute):
Perhaps the second most commonly known of commercial and industrial standards organizations. It is often mistaken for a governmental entity because of its name; however, it is a voluntary, nonprofit organization without any governmental connections whatever. Its listings are characterized by designations such as: ''ANSI A37.79-1970'' for sheet material for curing concrete (identical to ASTM C 171-69). In an effort toward unification, many ANSI standards are in fact the standards of other agencies that have been renumbered and given an ANSI designation in addition to that of the originating agency. The last number of an ANSI designation, as with ASTM, denotes the year of issue of that particular edition of the standard.

ANSI standards have been a source of confusion to some members of the construction industry, as they have twice changed their name since 1967. First known for years as the American Standards Association (ASA), many of their publications still bear this designation. The standards have not necessarily changed, however, and many valid standards still exist today with an ASA designation. The first change of name from ASA was the United States of America Standards Institute (USASI), but this was short-lived, and shortly thereafter the name was changed to ANSI, as we know it now.

As with the ASTM, the ANSI standards are grouped under letter prefix designations each of which identifies a particular group of standards.

The following is a complete list of all ANSI letter prefixes and the categories that each represents (also applies to ASA and USASI):

A   Construction
B   Mechanical
C   Electrical and electronics
D   Highway traffic safety
G   Ferrous metals and metallurgy
H   Nonferrous metals and metallurgy
J   Rubber
K   Chemical

L Textile
M Mining
MC Measurement and automatic control
MD Medical devices
MH Materials handling
N Nuclear
O Wood
P Pulp and paper
PH Photography and motion pictures
S Acoustics, vibration, mechanical shock, and sound recording
SE Security equipment
W Welding
X Information systems
Y Drawings, symbols, and abbreviations
Z Miscellaneous

American National Standards

A   civil engineering and construction

(Special price of series $625.00, including applicable abbreviation and symbol standards)

A1.1-1970 Portland Cement, Specification for (ASTM C150-69a)................................ 1.50

A1.2-1970 Sampling Hydraulic Cement, Methods of (ASTM C183-68a)................................ 1.50

A1.3-1970 Masonry Cement, Specification for (ASTM C91-69)..... 1.50

A1.4-1965 Compressive Strength of Hydraulic Cement Mortars (Using 2-In. Cube Specimens), Method of Test for (ASTM C109-64; AASHO T106-631) *(ISO R679)*........................... 1.50

A1.5-1970 Chemical Analysis of Hydraulic Cement, Methods for (ASTM C114-69) *(ISO R681, R682)*...................... 1.50

A1.7-1967 Fineness of Portland Cement by the Turbidimeter, Method of Test for (ASTM C115-67)........................ 1.50

A1.8-1969 Autoclave Expansion of Portland Cement, Method of Test for, (ASTM C151-68)........................ 1.50

A1.9-1961 (R1969) Air Content of Hydraulic Cement Mortar,

A1.31-1969 False Set of Portland Cement (Mortar Method), Method of Test for, (ASTM C359-67T (1969))................ 1.50

A1.32-1969 Potential Expansion of Portland Cement Mortars Exposed to Sulfate, Method of Test for, (ASTM C452-68).......... 1.50

A1.33-1970 Apparatus for Use in Measurement of Length Change of Hardened Cement Paste, Mortar, and Concrete, Specification for (ASTM C490-69)........................ 1.50

A1.34-1965 Bleeding of Cement Pastes and Mortars, Method of Test for (ASTM C243-65)........................ 1.50

A1.35-1969 Shrinkage and Coefficient of Thermal Expansion of Chemical-Resistant Mortars, Method of Test for, (ASTM C531-68)........................ 1.50

A1.36-1969 Compressive Strength of Chemical Resistant Mortars, Method of Test for (ASTM C579-68)................ 1.50

A1.37-1969 Flexural Strength and Modulus of Elasticity of Chemical-Resistant Mortars, Method of Test for (ASTM C580-68)........................ 1.50

A2.1-1970 Fire Tests of Building Construction and Materials,

Figure 6.5   ANSI Index of Standards.

AWWA (American Water Works Association):
Not as well known as the ASTM or ANSI, except in the public works sector where it has been the standard of the water industry. Its standards are broad, and many specify a single fabricated item, or an entire project feature, such as the designation "AWWA D100-73" for the construction of welded steel elevated water tanks, standpipes, and reservoirs. The AWWA publishes their data in several forms includ-

ing reference books, handbooks, manuals, standards, and periodicals and pamphlets. As with the other standards organizations, a system of letter prefixes has been established for the orderly grouping of subject matter for easier recovery of data:

A Source
B Treatment
C Distribution
D Storage
E Pumping

ACI (American Concrete Institute):

This possibly represents the most respected of concrete standards in the United States. Most of the ACI provisions have been adopted into all other codes and regulations, with minor changes. ACI is a nonprofit technical society. It is not industry-supported [its nearest industry-supported counterpart is Portland Cement Association (PCA)]. ACI publications are produced by standing committees, each of which is identified by a committee number. All publications are identified by a numbering system in which the ACI committee number forms the publication number, followed by the revision date. Thus committee 318 is the code committee, and each new revision of the ACI Building Code carries the same number 318, followed by the latest revision date.

There are numerous other standards that have not been mentioned, but the methods of identifying their publications are similar to the organizations already mentioned. The following is a partial listing of other organizations that publish standards:

AASHTO	American Association of State Highway and Transportation Officials
AISC	American Institute of Steel Construction
AISI	American Iron and Steel Institute
AITC	American Institute of Timber Construction
APA	American Plywood Association
ASHRAE	American Society of Heating, Refrigerating, and Air Conditioning Engineers
ASME	American Society of Mechanical Engineers
AWPA	American Wood Preservers Association
AWPI	American Wood Preservers Institute
AWS	American Welding Society
CRSI	Concrete Reinforcing Steel Institute
IES	Illuminating Engineering Society
NEMA	National Electrical Manufacturers Association
NFPA	National Fire Protection Association
SSPC	Steel Structures Painting Council
UL	Underwriters Laboratories, Inc.
WIC	Woodwork Institute of California
WRI	Wire Reinforcement Institute, Inc.

BUILDING CODES, REGULATIONS, ORDINANCES, AND PERMITS

Building codes have been adopted by most cities, counties, and states. They are adopted by each governmental entity by ordinance or other means at their disposal to impart the force of law behind them. The codes carefully regulate design, materials, and methods of construction and compliance with all applicable code provisions is mandatory. Most of these codes are based in whole or in part on the various national codes that are sponsored by different national groups. Changes, where made in the parent code, have generally been to accommodate local needs and conditions, and to make portions of the code more stringent than may have been provided for in the code as it was originally written.

There are, of course, many codes that are not based upon such national codes, but have been specifically written for some particular locality. Many large cities do this.

Although the Uniform Building Code is the basis for the majority of codes in use in the western states, there are several prominent codes in use throughout the United States that are equally important in the areas that they serve. Some of the more prominent codes are listed below:

1. *National Building Code:* Compiled by the American Insurance Association adopted in various localities across the country.
2. *Uniform Building Code:* Compiled by the International Conference of Building Officials (ICBO); widely used in the western states.
3. *Basic Building Code:* Compiled by the Building Officials and Code Administrators International (BOCA); used mainly in the eastern and north central states.
4. *Southern Standard Building Code:* Compiled by the Southern Building Code Congress (SBCC); used in most southern and southeastern states.
5. *National Electric Code:* Compiled by the American Insurance Association; widely adopted in all parts of the country.
6. *National Plumbing Code:* Compiled by the American Public Health Association and the American Society of Mechanical Engineers; used widely in all parts of the country.
7. *Uniform Plumbing Code:* Compiled by the International Association of Plumbing and Mechanical Officials (IAPMO); widely used in the west.

Of particular importance to the inspector as well as the constractor is the ''edition'' date on the code. Even though a new code edition has been published, there can be no assurance that a particular jurisdiction will adopt it at any certain time, if at all. A case in point is a city that for years used an old edition of the Uniform Building Code, which it kept updated by adopting a series of city ordinances annually to meet the requirements of the local building official. Thus, in fact it was a special code, and only by carefully studying the basic old code edition plus all ordinances adopted afterward could an inspector be aware of the conditions that affected his project in that jurisdiction. That particular city has since adopted a newer version of the Uniform Building Code, and the cycle must begin all over again.

In addition to the provisions of any applicable codes, the contractor is obligated to conform to the provisions of all permits issued by public agencies having jurisdiction. Many of these permits are several pages long, and resemble a small specification.

Projects Subject to Control by More than One Agency

Often a project will involve property or facilities that are under the jurisdiction of another public agency. If a pipeline project, for example, crossed an interstate freeway route, a flood control right-of-way, or the pipeline of another public agency or utility, the contractor could well be facing the prospect of having not only the regularly assigned resident inspector on the job, but a battery of other inspectors who represent each of the other affected agency properties. In each such case, a permit may be required from each affected agency, and the contractor would be not only bound by the terms of the contract documents for the project, but by the terms of each such permit as long as he was working in an area within the jurisdiction of the issuing agency. Whenever the pipeline referred to crosses any of these other improvements, the requirements of the agency owning such improvement will usually govern over the terms of the project specifications, unless their requirements are less stringent than those of the project specifications, in which case the affected agency may agree to the project specification requirements in lieu of their own.

TYPES OF DRAWINGS COMPRISING THE CONSTRUCTION CONTRACT

The drawings or plans that were prepared especially for the project are generally referred to as the ''contract drawings'' and they are for the express purpose of delineating the architect or engineer's intentions concerning the project that he has conceived and designed. The drawings normally show the arrangement, dimensions, geometry, construction details, materials, and other information necessary for estimating and building the project.

Occasionally, ''standard drawings'' of public agencies are defined as being a part of the contract documents. These drawings usually portray the repetitive details of certain types of construction that may be required by the local public agency for all similar work in their jurisdiction. A typical example is the design of drop inlet structures and other drainage structures that have been standardized in each community throughout the years. Instead of redrawing the same details over and over, the architect or engineer simply refers to a certain ''standard drawing'' of the jurisdictional agency involved.

''Shop drawings'' are those details and sketches prepared by the contractor or his material suppliers or fabricators that are necessary to assure the fabricator that his basic concept is acceptable before beginning costly fabrication. Shop drawings frequently contain information that is not related to the design concept, or information that is relative only to the fabrication process or construction techniques in the field, all of which are outside the scope of the duties and responsibilities of the architect or engineer. In approving shop drawings, the architect or engineer only indicates that the items conform to the design *concept* of the project and compliance with the plans and specifications prepared by him (see "Shop Drawings and Samples" in this Chapter). The contractor remains wholly responsible for dimensions to be confirmed in the field, for information that pertains solely to the fabrication process or to techniques of construction, and for coordination of the work of all the trades.

Change orders are issued to accompany a written agreement to modify, add to, or otherwise alter the work from that originally set forth in the contract drawings at the time of opening bids. A change order is normally the only legal means available to change the contract provisions after the award of the contract, and normally requires the signature of the owner.

Some confusion seems to accompany the use of the terms "record drawings" and of "as built" drawings. Generally speaking, the *record drawings* are a marked set of prints prepared by the contractor or the resident inspector in the field. Record drawings are contract drawing prints upon which the contractor or inspector records all variations between the work as it was actually constructed and the work as it was shown in the original contract drawings as they existed at the time the contract was awarded. All change orders should be reflected in appropriate marks on the record drawings. The term "as built" drawings is unpopular because of some of the legal difficulties that have resulted in attempting to have the architect or engineer certify that a set of drawings truly represented the project "as built." If, some years later, an underground pipeline is struck because it was not at the location or depth indicated in the certified "as built" drawings the architect or engineer could find himself the defendant in a civil action pressed by his one-time client.

ORDER OF PRECEDENCE OF CONTRACT DOCUMENTS

In order to assist in the resolution of field disputes in cases where a discrepancy exists between the various parts of the contract documents, it is desirable to establish some system of order to indicate the relative order of importance of each. Although through legal precedent some degree of order has already been established, many General Conditions cite the specific order anyway so that a dispute may be settled without the need for interpretation or arbitration.

Although a specific listing of order, if specified in the contract documents, will govern over any policy listed here, the following guide is based upon the NSPE General Conditions with some modifications:

The contract documents are complimentary; what is called for in one is as binding as if called for in all. If the contractor finds a conflict, error, or discrepancy in the contract documents he must call it to the attention of the engineer in writing before proceeding with the work affected thereby. In resolving such conflicts, errors, and discrepancies, the documents shall be given preference in the following order (see Chapter 5):

1. Agreement
2. Specifications
3. Drawings

Within the specifications the order of precedence is as follows:
1. Addenda
2. Supplementary General Conditions (Special Conditions)
3. Instructions to Bidders
4. General Conditions of the Contract
5. Technical Provisions
6. Standard Specifications

With reference to the drawings the order of precedence is as follows:
1. Figures govern over scaled dimensions
2. Detail drawings govern over general drawings
3. Change order drawings govern over contract drawings
4. Contract drawings govern over standard drawings
5. Contract drawings govern over shop drawings

The approval of shop drawings that deviate substantially from the requirements of the contract documents must be accompanied by a written change order.

Bibliography

Commentary on Contract Documents, by John R. Clarke, Esq., 1974 edition, by Professional Engineers in Private Practice, a practice division of the National Society of Professional Engineers, Washington, D.C.

CONSTRUCTION LAWS AND LABOR RELATIONS

COMPLIANCE WITH LAWS AND REGULATIONS

As with most endeavors, the performance of construction contracts is regulated by law. The difference seems to lie in the fact that there are more jurisdictional agencies involved than in most other businesses, and thus more laws to contend with.

Simply stated, it can be said in general that these laws fall into four major categories:

1. those laws and regulations that affect the making of contracts, both public and private;
2. those that relate to the conduct of the work being performed under the contract—and this includes the issuance and conformance to the conditions of the various permits, regulations, ordinances, and other requirements of the many jurisdictional agencies that are frequently involved;
3. the laws that relate to the settling of differences and disputes that may develop out of the performance of the contract;
4. the licensing laws that govern not only the business practices but also the personal qualifications standards of the various people involved in the construction process.

These last include the licensing of architects and professional engineers in every state in the United States, as well as the licensing of contractors in many states, the licensing of construction managers in a few states, and the licensing of inspectors in some states. In addition to these licenses, which all require the demonstration of proficiency standards by some type of examination, there are the local business licenses, permits to do business in certain areas, and sales tax permits that authorize the collection of sales tax by businesses. Of the more common laws that are encountered on most projects are the following:

Davis-Bacon Act requirements (for federal or federally-funded projects)
OSHA and state safety requirements for industrial applications
OSHA and state safety requirements for construction
State Labor Code requirements
U.S. Department of Labor requirements, as applicable
State housing laws
Local Building codes and ordinances
Sales and use tax regulations
Air pollution control laws
Noise abatement ordinances
Business licenses to conduct business in *each* locality
Mechanics lien laws of the state
Unemployment insurance code requirements
Workmen's compensation laws
Corps of Engineers & Coast Guard regulations for work in navigable waterways
Subletting and subcontracting laws
Licensing laws for architects, engineers, surveyors, contractors, and inspectors
Permits by special local agencies for construction, including:

> Building permits, grading permits, encroachment permits, street work permits, police permits for interrupting traffic, excavation permits, Environmental Protection Agency permits, special hauling permits, Department of Agriculture permits, and many others.

Civil Rights Act of 1964 (federally assisted programs)
All local city and county codes and ordinances

There are, of course, many others but the above list serves as a means of calling attention to the fact that a project cannot be built without regard for the regulations of the many jurisdictional agencies affected by the work. These include federal, state, county, city, special districts, including the many federal and state bureaus that have a legal interest in the effects of the proposed work on the area they have a legislative mandate to control, and all others who have a legitimate interest in the work that affects facilities or improvements over which they have legal jurisdiction and responsibility.

PUBLIC VERSUS PRIVATE CONTRACTS

As a means of protecting the public interest in projects involving the expenditure of public funds, or the public administration of projects built with private funds but intended for public use, the majority of all public contracts are required to conform to the general laws governing the execution of public contracts in that state.

Although every contractor has a legal obligation to observe the law in the conduct of his business, many state and federal regulations are required to be spelled out in the project documents, even though the failure to repeat their terms and conditions would not relieve the contractor of the responsibility to conform to their requirements.

Some of the significant differences between the requirements for public contracts and private projects can be noted by observing the following restrictions that apply to public contracts in most jurisdictions:

1. Project must be publicly advertised.
2. Bids must be accompanied by a bid bond, usually 5 or 10 percent.
3. Notice Inviting Bids must normally contain a list of prevailing wage rates for all crafts to be used in the work. If federal funds are involved, an additional listing of the federal wage rates must be published.
4. Insurance policies and bonds covering public liability and property damage are required.
5. In some jurisdictions a list of all subcontractors who will perform work on the project must be listed and filed with the general contractor's bid.
6. Wherever a "brand name" product is specified, the specifications must give the names of two brand name products, *plus* the words "or equal."
7. Performance Bond and a Payment Bond (for labor and materials) must be provided in the amounts specified by law.

TRAFFIC REQUIREMENTS DURING CONSTRUCTION

Often the work on a project involves a degree of restriction on the local traffic in the project area. The contractor is obligated to get a permit from the local agency empowered to enforce traffic regulations whenever he needs to close a street or intersection, or to restrict its traffic. The terms and conditions of this permit will become a part of the contract provisions, and must be enforced. The inspector should take careful note of the specific restrictions, which are sometimes spelled out in the project specifications as well. Frequently, as in cases involving streets that handle rush-hour traffic, the traffic requirements may vary depending upon the time of day. The inspector should watch in particular for requirements that a flagman be provided and used by the contractor to direct traffic through restricted traffic lanes, and to be certain that the conduct of the flagman is in full accordance with the traffic requirements of the jurisdiction having control. Whenever there is only one lane of traffic open on a street that must provide two-way travel, a flagman or a detour route will generally be required. In general, the minimum number of lanes allowed during construction affecting a city street is one 10-foot traffic lane *in each* direction. The inspector should watch for requirements that excavations be continually fenced or covered, as might be the case in the vicinity of schools; or that not less than a specified length of pipe trench be allowed open at any one time ahead an behind a pipelaying operation; or that the contractor be required to provide temporary "bridges" over excavations that might otherwise prevent safe access to businesses and residences in the vicinity of the work.

CODE ENFORCEMENT AGENCY REQUIREMENTS

Whenever privately owned buildings are to be constructed, and frequently in the case of most public buildings or public works projects, the building code enforcement agency will be involved. In some jurisdictions, a public project built by another agency within the same jurisdiction enjoys immunity from the regulations imposed by another agency of the same government. Thus, a project constructed by that agency might apply its own rules to govern design and construction. Generally, however, it will be found that even the structures of agencies not obligated to conform to a sister agency's requirements will design in accordance with its code requirements, and in some cases will even submit to its inspection requirements. If a permit fee is levied, however, it would simply be a paper transaction between departments.

Wherever the code enforcement agency has jurisdiction over a project under the Uniform Building Code, the provisions of Section 305(a) specify the conditions under which a project must be under the continuous inspection of a "special inspector" approved by the building official. In some jurisdictions, such approval is only granted after passing a written examination administered by the local department of building and safety. Where such programs are provided, even an architect or registered engineer may not be allowed to perform the inspections unless he has passed the building department's examination. In other jurisdictions, no formal program exists, and the process of "approval" of the inspector by the building official is an informal one, usually simply upon recommendation of the architect or registered engineer of record on the project.

A complete listing of all specialty areas that require the employment of a special inspector is found in Section 305 of the Uniform Building Code, and similarly in some other codes.

WORK WITHIN OR ADJACENT TO NAVIGABLE WATERWAYS

It may not be frequent that an inspector will encounter a project subject to these requirements, but every now and then the inspector may be called upon to provide inspection of a project at a waterfront, such as where barge-mounted pile drivers or similar equipment may be used. On such work, some items that might not otherwise be thought of can be encountered.

For one thing, the contract documents should provide that the contractor must furnish, at the request of the design firm, the owner, or any inspector assigned to the work, suitable transportation from all points on shore designated by the design firm or owner to and from all offshore construction. If these provisions are not in the specifications, they should be arranged for with the contractor at the preconstruction meeting.

As for the transportation of the contractor's personnel and equipment to offshore sites, it is the contractor's own responsibility to obtain boat launching facilities, or to make arrangements with local water carriers. He is similarly obligated to avoid the creation of navigation hazards or interference in any way with navigation routes except upon special permit from the agencies having jurisdiction.

If a contractor, during the course of his work, throws overboard, sinks, or misplaces anything overboard that could be interpreted as a hazard to navigation, the contractor must be required to recover such items as soon as possible. The contractor's first requirement after such an incident is to give immediate notice to the inspector, along with a description and location of such obstructions. If necessary, he may also be required to place a buoy or other mark at the location until recovery. It is an item that must be conducted at the contractor's sole cost and expense unless specifically provided otherwise in the contract. His liability for the removal of a *vessel* wrecked or sunk without fault or negligence is limited to that provided in Sections 15, 19, and 20 of the Rivers and Harbors Act of March 3, 1899, which is still very much alive and enforced.

All work being constructed in or involving the use of "navigable waterways" is subject to the orders and regulations of the Department of the Army, Corps of Engineers, and to the U.S. Coast Guard as they apply to the construction operations affecting property or improvements within the jurisdiction of these agencies. The principal jurisdiction on all construction matters lies with the Corps of Engineers, while the Coast Guard is primarily concerned with the movement of vessels. The term "navigable waters" is much broader now than in previous years, and is administratively defined in *Permits for Activities in Navigable Waters or Ocean Waters* on page 31324 of the Federal Register of 25 July 1975.

In addition, the Federal Water Pollution Control Act amendments of 1972 (Public Law 92-500) requires a Corps of Engineers permit, under Section 404 of the Act, for the discharge of any more than one cubic yard of dredged or fill material into any navigable waters.

FAIR SUBCONTRACTING LAWS

For work on public projects in some areas of the United States, laws have been enacted to protect subcontractors and the public against the practice of "bid shopping" or "bid peddling" by general contractors. Such laws were prompted by the realization that projects that had been subject to bid shopping practices often resulted in poor quality material and workmanship to the detriment of the public, and because it deprived the public of the full benefits of fair competition among prime contractors and subcontractors, and in addition it led to insolvencies, loss of wages to employees, and other evils.

Generally, such laws provide that any bidder on a public project must list all subcontractors he intends to use on the work, whose work, labor, or services exceed a specified percentage of the prime contractor's total bid.

Under the provisions of such "fair subcontracting" laws, if the general contractor fails to list a subcontractor for any portion of the work, he must perform all such work himself.

It is the resident project representative's responsibility when the job begins construction to check carefully the identity of all subcontractors on projects subject to such laws to ensure that their provisions have not been violated. This may have to be monitored at intermittent intervals to assure compliance at all times.

FEDERAL LABOR LAWS

Labor-Management Relations Laws

The history of federal labor laws goes back to 1890 when the Sherman Anti-trust Act was enacted. This provided the statutory beginnings for labor management legal policy. Although it is debatable whether the Act was ever intended to apply to labor unions, a Supreme Court decision in 1908 ruled that the labor unions were indeed covered by the act.

During the intervening years, Congress passed other labor-related laws that more clearly outline federal labor policy. Today's labor policy is the outcome of the combined provisions of the Norris-LaGuardia Act of 1932 (Anti-Injunction Act), the National Labor Relations Act of 1935 (Wagner Act), the Labor Management Relations Act of 1947 (Taft-Hartley Act), and the Labor Management Reporting and Disclosure Act of 1959 (Landrum-Griffin Act).

Equal Employment Opportunity Laws

In recent years, many of the federal labor laws have been aimed at eliminating discrimination in employment for any cause such as age, sex, race, religion, or nationality. The first of these was the *Civil Rights Act of 1964* in which Congress confirmed and established certain basic individual rights with regard to voting; access to public accommodations, public facilities, and public education; participation in federally-assisted programs; and opportunities for employment. Administration is handled through the Equal Employment Opportunity Commission (EEOC) that was created by the act. Under this act it is unlawful for any employer to refuse to hire or to discharge any individual or otherwise discriminate against him or her with regard to conditions of employment because of race, color, religion, sex, or national origin.

In 1965, the President issued *Executive Order 11246,* which applies to contracts and subcontracts exceeding $10,000.00 on federal and federally-funded construction projects. Under this Executive Order, the contractors not only are prohibited from discrimination but also must take positive action to see that applicants are employed and that employees are treated during their employment without discrimination. Originally limited to discrimination based upon race, creed, color, or national origin, it was supplemented in 1968 by *Executive Order 11375,* which prohibits discrimination in employment based upon sex in all federal and federally-funded contracts. If a contractor fails to conform he may be barred from future contracts involving federal funds, his present contract can be cancelled or suspended, and the OFCC has the additional power to withhold progress payments from contractors who appear to be in violation.

In 1967, the *Age Discrimination in Employment Act* was passed. This act prohibits arbitrary age discrimination in employment. The act protects persons of 40 to 65 years old from age discrimination by all employers of 25 or more persons in an industry affecting interstate commerce. Employment agencies and labor organizations are also covered. The prohibitions against age discrimination do not apply when age is a valid occupational qualification; when differentiation is based upon reasonable factors other than age; when differentiation is caused by the terms of a valid seniority system or employee benefit plan; or when the discharge or discipline of the individual is for good cause.

Wage and Hour Laws

The *Davis-Bacon Act* of 1931, as subsequently amended, is a federal law that determines the minimum wage rates and fringe benefits that must be paid to all workers on all federal and federally-assisted projects. The law applies to all projects over $2000 and it states that the wages of the workmen must not be less than the wage rates specified in the schedule of prevailing rates of wages as determined by the Secretary of Labor for similar work on similar projects in the vicinity in which the work is to be performed. Under its terms, the contractor is required to pay once a week to all workmen employed directly on the site of the work, at wages no lower than those prescribed. The federal minimum wage rates are currently published every Friday in the Federal Register, and all changes are reflected in the various trades and areas of the United States.

As passed in 1934, the *Copeland Act* (Anti-Kickback Law) forbids an employer to deprive any employee on a federal or federally-assisted construction job of any portion of the compensation to which he is entitled under federal law. Other than deductions provided by law, the employer may not require "kickbacks" from his employees. Violation may be punished by fine, imprisonment, or both. The Copeland Act applies to all projects on which the Davis-Bacon prevailing wage law applies.

The Fair Labor Standards Act, usually known as the *Wage and Hour Law,* was enacted by Congress in 1938, and has since been amended several times. The act contains provisions governing minimum wage, maximum hours, overtime pay, equal pay, and child labor standards. An employer who violates the wage and hour requirements is liable to his employees for double the unpaid minimum wages or overtime compensation, plus associated court costs and attornies' fees. Willful violation is a criminal act and may be prosecuted as such. Several classes of employees are exempted from coverage under the act, such as executive, administrative, and professional employees who meet certain tests established for exemption.

The Fair Labor Standards Act, as amended by the *Equal Pay Act of 1963,* provides that an employer may not discriminate on the basis of sex by paying employees of one sex at rates lower than he pays employees of the other sex for doing equal work on jobs requiring comparable skill, effort, and responsibility and performed under similar working conditions.

The basic minimum age for employment covered by the act is 16 years, except for occupations declared to be hazardous by the Secretary of Labor, to which an 18-year age minimum applies. Construction, as such, is not designated as hazardous, although some of its specific work assignments are designated as such by name.

The *Contract Work Hours and Safety Standards Act* passed by Congress in 1962 (Work Hours Act of 1962), which has since been amended, applies to federal construction projects and to federally-assisted projects. It does not apply if the federal assistance involved is in the form of a loan guarantee or insurance. Its main requirement is that workers be paid not less than 1½ times the basic rate for all hours worked in excess of 8 hours per day *or* 40 hours per week.

The National Apprenticeship Act

In 1937 Congress passed the National Apprenticeship Act. One of its prime objectives was to promote cooperation between management and organized labor in the development of apprenticeship programs. Traditionally, apprenticeship programs have been a joint effort between union-shop contractors and the AFL-CIO Building Trades unions. However, in 1971 the Bureau of Apprenticeship and Training approved national apprenticeship standards for the employees of open-shop contractors. This was the first time a unilateral apprenticeship program was approved on a national basis and placed under the direct supervision of employers only.

LABOR RELATIONS

The involvement of the resident project representative in the labor relations for his project is seldom extensive. In most cases he plays the part of an impartial observer, although he enjoys the advantage of being close to the work and can often feel the undercurrents at work there. Because of this closeness, he can be invaluable to the owner and the design firm as a barometer of on-site labor conditions. If he is employed on a construction management contract, this insight may be of even greater value, as his construction manager may be directly involved in the labor relations processes on his project.

One of the most important rules for the inspector to follow is to maintain himself in an observer category only. He should express no opinions at the site with anyone except his project manager, and then only while in confidence. Neither should the resident project representative or other inspector take sides on any labor issue, or even express any sympathy for either side of a potential controversy.

All direct relations of the resident inspector on the job are to be conducted through the foremen and superintendents only, with the one possible exception of the emergency handling of an ''Imminent Hazard'' as defined in Chapter 8, Construction Safety.

While the resident inspector is not expected to take part in labor negotiations, he may be called upon to confirm that the contractors and their labor forces are in conformance with both the contract provisions and the labor laws of the state and federal governments.

Construction Unions

The labor union movement is deeply involved in the construction industry. There is no denying that their contribution has been an important one. They have had a stabilizing influence on what is a potentially unstable industry, although this is viewed as having both its good and its bad points. The unions do provide direct access to a pool of skilled and experienced labor from which a contractor can draw, as his needs require, and through the medium of negotiated labor contracts, fixed wage levels have been established, thus serving the dual purpose of upholding the living standard for the labor force as well as providing added stability to the bids of the contractor by eliminating the labor rates as a competitive bid item. The unions also help by maintaining discipline among their membership as well as setting achievement standards for the different skill levels.

Contractor-Employee Relationships

Since the advent of the large labor union in the construction industry, the old personal relationships that formerly existed between an employer and his employees are all but gone. Loyalties of a building tradesman are now largely to his union, who handles all of the employee's business relationships on a scale well beyond the confines of a single employer's shop. Thus, the rates of pay, holidays, overtime, and other employment conditions are not negotiated with the employee himself, but with the union business agents. Thus, each employee is bound by the terms of the resultant labor contract just as the contractor is.

As a result of such relationships, the employees are not generally "company-minded" men, but feel that they owe their allegiance to their respective unions, instead. Even their social lives are intertwined with their unions. In a manner of speaking, it could be said that the tradesmen are employees of a single large employer—their union—who contracts with various contractors to provide their services. The paternalistic attitude of the unions to their members through the retirement benefits and similar allowances seems further to bear this out.

Collective Bargaining in Labor Relations

Under the provisions of the National Labor Relations Act, both management and labor are required to bargain in good faith. This does not necessarily mean that concessions must be made or that the two sides even agree, for that matter—just that they bargain in good faith.

Lack of good faith on the part of a contractor could be interpreted from his ignoring of a bargaining request, failure to appoint a bargaining representative with power to reach an agreement, attempts to deal directly with employees during negotiations, refusal to consider proposals, failure to respond with counterproposals, anti-union activities, or refusal to sign an agreement.

Although some contractors bargain with unions independently by dealing directly with the unions, the most prevalent form of labor negotiations in the construction industry is for contractor associations to bargain with the unions for all of the members of the association. In this manner the contractor has greater bargaining power than as an individual. Local associations of general contractors generally bargain with the locals of the basic trades: the carpenters, cement masons, laborers, operating engineers, and construction teamsters. In some areas, iron workers are also included. The basic trades may bargain either as individual locals or as a group of locals affiliated with the same international union, or even through groups of locals of different unions such as building trades councils. The resulting labor agreements are generally referred to as "Master Labor Agreements." The resulting agreements apply only within the jurisdiction of the union locals involved, and then only to the extent of the particular trades involved.

Administration of the Union Contract

The matter of union–contractor labor relations is not closed simply because a labor agreement has been reached, however. There is still the matter of administering the labor contract and assuring that all its provisions are being met. Any project is likely to have some disputes or disagreements between either the union and the contractor, or between two unions representing different crafts. The labor agreements typically contain procedures for the settlement of such disputes. When a dispute occurs that cannot be resolved by a conference of the steward, business agent, superintendent, and any other party directly involved, the grievance procedure set forth in the agreement is followed. This procedure generally forces the matter up to progressively higher echelons of the contractor and the union, during which time no work stoppage is supposed to occur. If the matter cannot be resolved, arbitration of the matter may or may not be provided for in the labor agreement. Generally, the unions have resisted the concept of binding arbitration; however, there is a greater tendency now to provide for arbitration as a means of resolving or settling contract disputes without resort to work stoppages.

Prejob Labor Agreements

On some project where special employment conditions exist, and where the project is large enough to justify the procedure, a prejob conference is held with the local labor officials to establish standard conditions for field operations for the life of a particular project. The intended purpose is to establish a meeting of the minds between the contractor and the unions involved regarding job conditions of employment, work rules, or jurisdictional responsibilities. In a project located in a remote area, for example, the contractor is interested in running the job in as economical a manner as possible, while the unions want fair labor standards to be maintained. The locals having jurisdiction must be checked to see that they have enough men available to do the job. If not, arrangements must be made to bring workers in from the outside, either by the union local or by the contractor. Although some contractors are tempted to resist prejob labor conferences on the grounds that the unions will be tempted to make exorbitant demands, most available evidence seems to indicate that the unions are more reasonable at this stage because they do not feel that the contractor is trying to hide something. On one project in which the author was involved, such cooperation with the local building trades council allowed an open shop condition to exist at a federal project, involving both union subcontractors and non-union subcontractors on the same project, thus preserving the jobs of the members of an otherwise economically depressed community. Through an agreement involving mutual understanding of the various problems involved, no union member of the community with the skills necessary for this particular project was deprived of his livelihood as a result of the agreement, and thus the purposes of the owner, the contractor, and the labor force were realized.

Open Shop Contracting

Open shop contracting, so called because it is unhampered by union agreements or representation, has suffered more than its share of troubles in its lifetime. In recent years, however, it appears to have made rapid and possibly lasting strides to where it is now established as a fact of life in the labor market. There is a strong movement by many smaller contractors and subcontractors to embrace the open shop concept, and it is estimated that close to 40 percent of the annual construction volume is now done by non-union contractors. In recent years, even some of the larger contractors have gone non-union.

Contrary to the first impression usually received, open shop contractors are not necessarily anti-union. Although they do usually pay somewhat less than the union scale, the average non-union worker is provided with full-time employment instead of working by the job. Thus, his income comes closer to being a guaranteed annual income, and as such often exceeds that of his union counterparts. The fringe benefits of most of the companies are similar to those paid by union contractors. This does not mean that none of an open shop's employees are union members. Many such shops have a mixture of union and non-union help. One of the basic rights an open shop contractor stands for is the right of the contractor to decide for himself the size of his work crews and to what job a man may be assigned. Similarly, they are free to use prefabricated materials and are not subject to jurisdictional disputes, featherbedding, forced overtime, and work slowdowns. Workers are paid according to their work and performance. If, however, an open shop contractor bids a federal job subject to the Davis-Bacon Act, then he, too, must pay his employees the same minimum wage rates published in the Federal Wage Rate Determination, and his bids will have to be computed accordingly. Thus, he may have a tough time competing in some markets for a project. If he does win a federal job, however, there is nothing in the federal law to prohibit an open shop contractor from being awarded a contract.

Bibliography

Richard H. Clough, *Construction Contracting,* 3rd ed., Wiley, New York, 1975.

California Contractor's License Law and Reference Book, Contractor's State Licensing Board, Sacramento, California.

Professional Index of Private Practice, the National Society of Professional Engineers, Washington, D.C.

California Public Contract Law Conference, published papers, Sacramento, California, 3–4 April 1970.

8
CONSTRUCTION SAFETY

AS MENTIONED in Chapter 4, the general contractor has the prime responsibility for construction safety; however, there are certain areas of concern for construction safety that the resident project representative should not ignore. The degree of the inspector's involvement is, to some extent, influenced by the specific terms of the construction contract, but some recent court decisions point out the need for concern by the inspector on the job.

In the Illinois case of *Miller vs. DeWitt* (37 Ill.2d 273, 226 N.E. 2d 630), where a steel roof had to be shored up while construction took place beneath it, the roof fell and injured a worker. In this case, the court stated: "As a general rule it has been said that the general duty to 'supervise the work' merely creates a duty to see that the building when constructed meets the plans and specifications contracted for." Thus, the court said, under ordinary circumstances the architect would not be regarded as a person in charge of the work. But in the DeWitt case, the courts added that despite the argument of the architects that the shoring was "a method or technique of construction over which they had no control, we believe that under the terms of the contracts the architects had the right to interfere and even stop the work if the contractor began to shore in an unsafe and hazardous manner."

In the New York State case of *Clinton vs. Boehm* (124 N.Y.S. 789), it was ruled that the architect owed no duty to the workers to supervise the contractor's methods to assure the workers' safety, and in 1960 the rule was again upheld [*Olsen vs. Chase Manhattan Bank* 175 N.E. 2d 350]; however, this rule was seriously challenged in Arkansas in 1960 when the court said that the "supervising" architect who saw that an excavation wall was badly shored had a duty to the workers to *stop the work* to make repairs and that his failure to do so made him [the architect] liable for the death of three workmen in a cave-in [*Erhart vs. Hummonds* 334 S.W. 2d 869].

In southern California an unsupported wall of a 14-foot deep trench caved in, resulting in the death of a laborer who was in the trench at the time. The project was a large residential development involving not only separate construction contracts for the various types of structures being built, but also for underground pipelines for water and sewer. An inspector was assigned to the entire project to monitor the progress of several of the different contracts then under construction. One of these projects involved a large underground sewer main, and it was on this project that the disaster occurred. It was reported that the inspector had observed an unshored trench prior to the accident and knew that workers were in the unshored trench. The widow of the deceased worker filed suit, and in the resulting decision, the court held that the excavation contractor had contributed to the accident through negligence, but also held that the engineer's office must share the responsibility. In the view of the court, the engineer had an inspector on the job during construction and although the inspector saw the contractor's employee "descend into the trench, he voiced no objection." [Widman vs. Rossmoor Sanitation, Inc. (1965–70, 97 Cal Reg. 52)].

Both the Arkansas and the California cases seem to support the proposition that an architect/engineer who has knowledge of a safety problem has a duty to the workers to prevent harm to them. Without the knowledge of a safety hazard, it appears that he has no such duty to them. Thus, if a design or construction management firm has a contract for construction management or continuous inspection, as might be the case where a resident project representative is employed, there would seem to be no way of pretending no knowledge of such conditions.

Thus, using the above as but a few examples of the inspector's involvement simply due to his presence on the project, it can be seen that the inspector has an important involvement in construction safety hazards that pose a threat to life or health. It is of particular note that the case just mentioned involved an inspector who was providing only *part-time* inspection on that particular project. It is from cases such as the one just mentioned that policies have been adopted by many agencies, both public and private, that spell out the obligations of an inspector with regard to his knowledge of safety hazards on the job.

EFFECT OF INCLUDING CONTRACTOR'S SAFETY OBLIGATIONS IN THE SPECIFICATION

The resident project representative is the person who is most directly involved in the administration of contract provisions and should have the responsibility of assuring that the contractor is in full compliance with all aspects of the contract, including applicable major safety requirements. The degree of control that the inspector may have over the contractor in requiring compliance with the OSHA construction safety requirements depends at least partly on the following conditions:

1. If no mention is made in the contract documents, whether on the drawings or in the specifications themselves, safety obligations of the contractor are primarily a legal obligation between himself and the state or federal agency administering the provisions of OSHA. Although an inspector would seem to be obligated to call attention to observed deficiencies that constitute a serious hazard, and to notify the contractor that they should be remedied, the contractor's failure to respond can only be handled by the inspector through the service of a written notice to the contractor, with copies to the organization administering the construction contract and by filing an official notice to the local OSHA enforcement agency, which is administered at state level in many areas. Otherwise, the contractor's failure to comply is difficult to control, as the inspector normally possesses no police powers over the work.

2. If, on the other hand, the contractor's compliance with the safety requirements of OSHA is specified in the contract specifications, the inspector's subsequent demand that a contractor comply with certain OSHA provisions takes on a different light. In this case, the safety requirements, in addition to being the *legal* obligation of the contractor, have become a *contractual* one as well. Thus, the contractor's failure to comply can be interpreted as a breach of contract, and the design firm may recommend that the owner withhold payments for that portion of the work until the contractor complies. This does not take the place of the official notice mentioned under the previous paragraph, but merely provides an additional recourse to the design firm and the owner beyond the steps previously mentioned. Furthermore, under these conditions, assurance that the contractor is living up to his obligations with regard to safety is now a part of the inspector's responsibility because it is written into the specifications and must therefore be considered as one of the inspector's field administrative responsibilities.

Wherever the construction safety provisions are written as a part of the terms of the construction contract, the inspector in the administration of his part of the contract is required to see that the contractor properly provides for the safety of the workmen. Under no circumstances should the contractor be instructed orally or in writing as to *how* to correct a deficiency. The unsafe condition should simply be *identified* and the specific regulation, if it is known, should be cited.

APPLICABILITY OF STATE AND FEDERAL OSHA PROVISIONS TO A PROJECT

As a way of setting the groundwork, it should first be mentioned that the federal OSHA provisions are in two volumes. The first book, officially called *"OSHA Safety and Health Standards* Code of Federal Regulations Title 29, Part 1910," deals with safety features that are intended to be included in the design of the project. This is the responsibility of the designer to include on his plans as a part of the project design. The second book is the one that relates to the construction phase of the work and generally concerns the temporary hazards and conditions that exist as a direct result of the construction activities. This volume is officially entitled *"Construction Safety and Health Regulations,* Code of Federal Regulations Title 29, Part 1926.'' In addition, under the federal safety program, each state has the right to enact a safety code that is at least equivalent to the federal OSHA provisions and by so doing, retains the right to be the sole safety enforcement agency within its jurisdictional borders. If a state does not choose to exercise this option, construction in that state will be subject to inspection by both federal and state safety inspection agencies. If a state elects to upgrade its safety code to meet the OSHA requirements, it has a three-year period to accomplish this. Under these conditions, local safety enforcement will be by state agency only, both during and after enactment.

SPECIAL APPLICATIONS

Although ordinarily it would be assumed that a state safety program would not have jurisdiction within the confines of a federal reservation, and that only the federal OSHA program would govern there, an interesting state government interpretation has been made on this subject, as described in the following paragraph.

A federal military reservation was the site of a construction project that was planning to base its safety requirements on federal OSHA requirements administered by federal safety inspectors. The state announced jurisdiction, based upon the fact that its safety provisions were a part of its Labor Code, which was enacted to protect workers in their various occupations. It was further stated that none of the construction workers on the military base were federal employees, and as such were all subject to the provisions of the State Labor Code. This appears valid, as all other provisions of the State Labor Code apply to the contractor's employees, and the fact that a particular construction project takes them into federal property does not strip them of the protection afforded by the Labor Code.

It appears then that a project on a federal reservation, if built by nonfederal employees from off the reservation, will be subject to local state safety regulations—possibly in addition to federal OSHA if the state involved has failed to meet, or has not participated in, the OSHA upgrading program.

PROCEDURAL GUIDELINES

In carrying out the owner's and the design firm's responsibilities of assuring safety compliance as a contract requirement, the following guidelines are suggested.

1. IMMINENT HAZARD—A condition that if not corrected would most likely result in an accident causing severe or permanently disabling injury or death.
   PROCEDURE: When an imminent hazard condition is known to exist, or when a contractor either delays in correcting or permits repeated occurrences of a hazardous condition, the resident project representative should immediately order the contractor to suspend the operations affected, and not permit work to resume on these operations until the condition has been corrected. The project manager of the design

firm and the owner and the state or federal agency having jurisdiction over construction safety should be notified of the hazardous condition and of the action taken. In addition, a letter giving all the details should be prepared, covering all the events leading up to the suspension, and this letter should be submitted to the project manager.

2. DANGEROUS CONDITION—a condition that does not present an immediate danger to workers, but if not corrected could result in a disabling injury and possibly death, or could develop into an imminent hazard as described above.

PROCEDURE: When a dangerous condition is known to exist, the resident inspector should notify the contractor in writing of the conditions and allow a reasonable period of time for correcting the condition. If the resident inspector is not certain of the remedial measures proposed or taken by the contractor, then the services of a construction safety engineer should be requested. If the contractor does not correct the dangerous condition, or if the condition is deteriorating into an "imminent

Figure 8.1 Example of an imminent hazard.

Figure 8.2   Example of a dangerous condition.

hazard,'' then the design firm should consider recommending that the owner suspend the affected operations.

3. MINOR OR NONSERIOUS CONDITION—Conditions that could result in minor or less serious injuries, or that are small in nature, but so that they may still be classified as a
threat to health.

PROCEDURE: When a minor or nonserious condition is known to exist, the resident
project representative should advise the contractor of the conditions and of the
necessity of eliminating them. If the contractor fails to correct the problem or
permits its repeated occurrence on subsequent operations, then the design firm or
owner should be notified.

The construction safety activities of both the contractor and all project personnel must
be documented in the inspector's diary. It is important for the inspector to realize that he is

only responsible for seeing that the contractor complies with the project safety requirements through the use of normal administrative procedures. The legal enforcing agency is the federal or state OSHA officers. The inspector should keep the name and telephone number of the local safety compliance officer handy—it is often one of his most effective compliance "tools."

It should be noted that the mention of "suspension" of portions of the work in the foregoing procedural guidelines *relate to the immediate area* of the hazardous condition only. Nothing described here is intended to suggest that the inspector, the design firm, or the owner would be justified in closing down an entire project for such local conditions.

References to the capability of payment retention by the owner upon the recommendation of the design firm on contracts where safety provisions have been made contractual requirements as well as legal obligations are presented solely as a matter of interest to the inspector. It must be kept in mind that only the project manager has the authority to approve or recommend that part or all of a contractor's monthly progress payment be withheld. However, recommendations of the resident project representative may bear a heavy influence on the decision of the project manager in such cases.

SHORING AND BRACING

The federal OSHA Part 1926 *Construction Safety and Health Regulations* require that all trenches and earth embankments over five feet deep be adequately protected against caving in by a system of sheeting, shoring, and bracing or by sloping the sides of the trench or other excavation to an acceptable angle.

Trench and excavation shoring is one of the critical safety hazards referred to in the OSHA Construction Safety and Health Regulations. Numerous fatalities have resulted from failure of the contractor to provide adequately for worker safety under these conditions. The inspector should take particular note of the fact that *all* trenches or other excavations on any project, public or private, require sheeting, shoring, or bracing if they are five feet deep or deeper. Details of safety codes vary somewhat from state to state, but there is a trend toward greater uniformity and the safety codes of each jurisdiction should be carefully checked prior to beginning work in another state to confirm the specific limitations and regulations that will control.

SAFETY REQUIREMENTS IN CONSTRUCTION CONTRACTS

Many public agencies include safety standards as a part of the construction contract documents, which then become a contractual obligation as well as a legal one, as previously explained. Many state highway departments include a safety code in their construction contracts. Several federal agencies, including the U.S. Army Corps of Engineers, the Naval Facilities Engineering Command, and the U.S. Bureau of Reclamation include health and safety standards in their construction contracts. OSHA provides that such federal agencies may continue to provide their own safety inspection and enforcement; however, this does not preclude the state from requiring compliance through its own safety enforcement officer. Thus it can be seen that the inclusion of safety requirements as a part of the contractual obligations of the contractor is a growing practice. Each inspector upon beginning a project should make a careful study of the plans and specifications to determine whether such safety provisions are included as a contractual requirement, thus placing an additional burden of responsibility upon the inspector to assure compliance, and to take appropriate administrative action in case of default by the contractor.

Bibliography

State of California, Department of Transportation, *Construction Manual*, Section 1–60 Safety; issued by the Division of Construction and Research, Office of Construction, Sacramento, California, 1975.

9
PRECONSTRUCTION OPERATIONS

DESCRIPTION OF APPROACH

On a project involving a field staff of two or more persons, the organizational structure of the resident project representative's field office is often determined by a design or construction management firm as the representative of the owner of the project. It should be clearly understood before the work on the project commences that all assignments and limits of authority and responsibility are as delegated to the resident project representative by his employer. On larger projects it might be desirable to draft an organizational diagram or chart that clearly defines all levels of responsibility and authority on the proposed project. Such a chart can be of immeasurable help in expediting the work when new tasks must be done and the normal procedures are not applicable.

Preconstruction operations can be generally grouped into five phases:

1. Advertise and award phase
2. Development of quality control program or construction surveillance and inspection plan on CQC projects
3. Field office organization phase (planning)
4. Preconstruction conference
5. Establishment of a field office at the construction site for the administration and quality control of the work for the owner.

Frequently, the resident project representative is not involved in the project during the advertise and award phase at all; however, this phase of the work will be covered in this chapter for the benefit of those whose obligations do include this phase of the work. In such cases, the resident project representative's tasks may be limited to the performance of items 3, 4, and 5 only of the foregoing list.

ADVERTISE AND AWARD PHASE

During the advertising phase, the resident project representative should review the contract documents carefully to make certain that all important field considerations have been provided for in the specifications. If during the award phase omissions are noted in the plans or specifications or if conditions are specified that may create conflicts in the field, there is still time to provide written notice to the design firm of any such omissions or conflicts so that it can issue an addendum to the specifications prior to bid opening time. Thus the problem can be corrected in time to eliminate the need of a change order during construction.

An example of such omission might be the failure of the design firm to specify that the contractor shall furnish a field office for the resident project representative's use throughout the life of the project, unless the design firm or owner intends to provide such facilities. The omission of a requirement for a field office in the specifications was once the cause of the author spending a long uncomfortable year at a project site in a prefabricated tool shed that he was able to talk the contractor into providing as a field office at no additional cost. Anyone who has ever had this experience will realize its shortcomings. In rainy weather the choice was to close the window flaps and keep dry—in the dark, or to leave the flaps open and get plenty of light—and get wet. It was hot in the summer and freezing in the winter, and the dirt was often so thick the floor was obscured.

Another thing to look for in the specifications is a requirement for a field telephone. If a free phone is not specified, the contractor will either provide no phone in the inspector's field office or if a phone is provided, he will invariably provide a pay phone—after all, if a phone was not in the specifications, there is no valid reason for the contractor to have included the cost of a free phone for the resident project representative in his bid. If a pay phone is installed, the resident project representative will have to keep a pocket full of change at all times to be capable of communicating with his home office. The ideal approach is to require that the contractor provide and maintain, at his own expense, and for the full term of the project, a field telephone in the resident project representative's field office as well as in his own field office. This is fair to the contractor as well as to the owner for it allows him to bid a fixed telephone cost as part of his proposal. This phone should also be specified to be connected to an established exchange for toll service and with all other phones that may be used by the contractor. This may sound like an unnecessary precaution, but consider the fix the author found himself in some time ago when the telephone in the field office was part of a private telephone system of the contractor and *could not be connected* to a regular public telephone service for local or toll calls! It is equally important to see that the telephones provided in the contractor's field office and in the resident project representative's field office be on separate trunk lines. A party-line or extension telephone, including key phones that allow selection of both the

Figure 9.1   *Typical tool shed adapted for use as a construction field office.*

contractor's and the inspector's trunk line, is undesirable, as it allows no security of communications for either party.

Naturally, the mention of toll service may scare the contractor unless some prearranged agreement has been reached concerning the use of the phone for long distance calls. It is recommended that the contractor permit the resident project representative, the design firm, the owner, or any of their authorized representatives to use the phone without cost for all calls that do not involve published toll charges. Calls that do involve toll charges should then be billed to the owner by the contractor *at the actual rate charged to him* by the telephone company.

There are many other points to watch for in the specifications as well; many of them involve technical matters. In all cases, if a description of the problem can be submitted to the design firm in time, and if they agree with the inspector's recommendations, this item can become a part of the contract requirements before bid opening time.

Prior to bid opening time, the resident project representative should meet with the project manager to develop an agenda and a list of key subjects to be discussed at the preconstruction conference. In addition, the project manager should contact the owner to see if he will want assistance during the preparations for, and during the bid opening.

During the bid holding period following the opening of all bids, but prior to determination of the award of the construction contract, the resident project representative should be available, if requested by the design firm or the owner to assist in the evaluation of bid data, costs, and other contractually significant items. In this manner the architect's or engineer's job of making recommendations to the owner for award of the contract can be made much simpler and easier.

DEVELOPMENT OF A QUALITY CONTROL OR ASSURANCE PROGRAM

On many federal projects, one of the construction phase requirements is that the architect/engineer or his field representative develop a *construction surveillance and inspection plan* for submittal to the contracting officer (Fig. 9.2).

A prerequisite to the development of a surveillance and inspection plan is the development of a *quality requirements control system*. The purpose of this system is to develop a method of control for all specification requirements that are required to be done in writing, plus some other items that the architect/engineer may add. The *quality requirements control system* should contain a record of all quality control requirements in tabular form or other equivalent method. Typical examples of the data that must be presented in the form of tables or lists as a checking method throughout the job are:

1. Proofs of compliance (from the various specification sections)
2. Qualifications for soil testing service
3. Tests for proposed soil materials
4. Reports required
5. Excavation methods (approval of)
6. Concrete testing and inspection service (approval of)

In addition, such federal contracts often include the requirement that the architect/engineer's resident project representative review the *construction contractor quality control plan* (CQC) plan. This involves a review of the contractor's QC plan for clarity and completeness and a recommendation to the owner's contracting officer for acceptance, rejection, or revision.

Initially, in order to develop a successful quality control program, a complete definition of each and every task must be determined. This is done in coordination with the drawings and specifications and other controlling documents. Following completion of the quality control program, personnel assignments must be made, along with a definition of the duties and responsibilities of each person on the quality control team.

Prior to the time when the need actually arises, arrangements should be made for the selection of the testing laboratory that will provide testing services under contract and, if required, supplementary inspection personnel for specialized tasks of short-term duration.

Though not universally done on private or local public agency projects, a requirement of many federal agency construction services contracts calls for the preparation of a *quality control plan,* as mentioned in earlier paragraphs. Actually, this is a good idea to use on any job, and it not only eases the work burden during the job but also provides for a

Figure 9.2   *Construction surveillance and inspection plan for a NASA project.*

more orderly administration of the entire construction phase of the job. It does call for a great deal of effort at the beginning of a project, however, as it not only requires that all the policy matters that apply to the quality control functions be set out in writing, but it also requires the preparation of technical check lists for all work on the project as a means for reminding the inspector of each item that must be checked, as well as setting forth the standards for each such inspection. Normally, a quality control plan also sets out, in tabular form, a complete listing of all testing that is required on all materials and equipment for which tests are specified, and it further specifies the frequency of such tests (Fig. 3.8). It can be said that a quality control plan is actually a separate "specification" for the testing and inspection phase of an entire project, and such a document can easily run over a hundred pages of typewritten text.

Work flow diagrams should be developed before the work on the project has begun. In this manner, preliminary planning efforts will not interfere with the orderly flow of the inspector's work after the contractor has mobilized at the site. The inspector's work flow diagrams are inteded solely for the use of the field office staff, and should include reminders to the resident project representative as to when certain important events are to happen, as well as the assignment and responsibility for them. Generally, all these things can be shown in a simple chart form with a few explanatory sentences.

A significant part of the input data needed to prepare the work flow diagrams can be obtained from the contractor's CPM or bar charts. These charts are the key to each significant construction event, as no other document can provide too much data in such a usable form. To be sure, adjustments will be required throughout the life of the job, but in general the CPM or bar chart will set the stage for all construction events to follow.

FIELD OFFICE ORGANIZATION OF THE OWNER OR HIS FIELD REPRESENTATIVE

Mission

The mission of the field engineer or inspector as the design firm's or the owner's resident project representative is to assure compliance with the plans and specifications and to cause the end product to meet the needs of the ultimate user. In certain cases, where public agencies are involved, the resident project representative is further charged with the responsibility of checking on the ocmpliance by the contractor with certain legislation such as that pertaining to labor and the use of domestic materials.

The Planning Stage

In the early stages of design, or in some cases prior to that time, the owner must decide who is going to operate his field office to monitor construction. There are many current practices, some of which are described in the following paragraphs.

As practiced in many cases, the owner may engage his own resident project representative to monitor the construction phase of the project (under the responsible charge of an architect or professional engineer) or the owner may hire an architect/engineer or construction management firm to perform this function. Another approach is to engage the services of an independent agency such as a testing laboratory or, on public projects, one governmental agency may solicit the help of another government agency for furnishing construction services. An example of this was the employment of the U.S. Corps of Engineers in the early post-war hospital construction program of the Veterans Administration, and later for Post Office construction.

Another practice is for the owner to enter into a professional construction management contract (PCM) wherein the construction manager oversees both design and construction and may actually contract with the construction contractor. Or, the owner may hire a single contractor to perform design, construction, and supervision of construction on either a lump sum or a cost-plus-fixed-fee (CPFF) basis. The latter is a combined engineering and construction contract often called a ''turnkey'' job. For special inspection, the services of a testing laboratory may be hired for testing soils, aggregates, lumber, masonry units, steel, and concrete. Likewise, there are expert free-lance technicians who inspect steel framework to assure soundness of connections (riveted, bolted, or welded) as well as the leveling and plumbing of beams and columns.

Having decided who is to perform the inspection, the extent and scope of the inspection services must be determined. Sometimes contracts provide that the builder will arrange for inspection by a testing laboratory and furnish test results to the owner or his architect/engineer. The degree of inspection required often depends upon the importance of the work or the function of the item in question. For instance, it is hardly worthwhile to take test cylinders on 2000-psi conrete used for sidewalks around a single-story residence, but it is absolutely essential that it be done on a prestressed concrete bridge girder. The inspector should be cautioned at this point, however, as the determination of the frequency and level of tests required is a decision that must be made by the engineering staff of the design firm or owner, not by field personnel unless specifically authorized to do so by the project manager of the owner or design firm, as applicable. The extent of the inspection is a major factor in the cost of operating the owner's field office. Another item to be considered by the owner in the construction planning stage is the provision of adequate funds to cover the field office costs of whatever agency he chooses to inspect the project.

Establishment of the Field Office

Arrangements will have to be made to set up the field office for the resident project representative and his field staff prior to the beginning of the work on the project. If it is the contractor's responsibility to do this under the project specifications, the inspector should monitor this provision closely, as there are often last-minute field problems that tend to delay implementation. Also, the contractor may make last-minute attempts to offer facilities that do not meet the provisions of the specifications, such as the setting up of one-half of his own field office trailer for the use of the inspector—even though the specifications may call for a separate structure.

The resident project representative should make certain that the field office telephone has been ordered in time, if it is the contractor's responsibility to provide such utilities to the inspector's field office. Without it, the resident project representative will be out of communication with the design firm's or the owner's office during the early portion of the job. In addition, if the contractor is obligated under the provisions of the specifications to provide an electronic pager (radio "beeper") or other communications equipment, be sure that such equipment is provided in time to cover the critical early part of the job.

Finally, a requisition should be made and sent to the office of the design firm or the owner by the resident project representative in sufficient time to enable them to make up a supply order on a routine basis, and to be able to obtain the office equipment that may be needed in the field office.

Field Office Responsibilities

In the establishment of a field office, the owner, or his design or construction management firm, is guided by many of the criteria that are considered by the contractor for setting up his own field office: the delegation of authority, the functions to be performed, the remoteness of the work site, and the extent and complexity of the job.

Figure 9.3   Modern trailer type field office.

The delegation of authority from the design firm or the owner to the resident project representative or from the contractor to his CQC representative can vary within wide limits. In some cases it is merely to inspect the work; in others, the greater task of construction project administration is assigned. Costs of field office operation will vary widely with the extent of the work delegated. Usually personalities, experience, remoteness of the job site, and functions performed are serious considerations governing the delegation of authority. With respect to the resident project representative's or CQC representative's *delegated* functions, the following factors must be considered:

1. What specific functions of the resident project representative or CQC representative are specified in the contract?
2. How much testing will be performed by the resident project representative or CQC representative and his staff and how much will be contracted out to commercial testing laboratories?
3. How much of the materials specified will require pre-inspection at the factory before being shipped to the job site?
4. How much use will be made of special inspectors such as for concrete, masonry, or structural steel and welding inspections?
5. Is the contract lump-sum, unit-price, or cost-plus-fixed-fee?
6. What is the authority of the architect/engineer to initiate, estimate, negotiate, and execute contract modifications?
7. What authority will be granted to the design or construction management firm by the owner to approve partial and final pay estimates?

8. How much of a check on the contractor's costs must be maintained by the resident project representative, particularly on unit-price and cost-plus-fixed-fee contracts?
9. What responsibilities will the resident project representative have, in the case of public agency contracts, for enforcement of such labor laws as the Davis-Bacon Act, the 8-hour law, and the Copeland Act or other similar laws?

Other questions more specifically related to the *direct* responsibilities of the resident project representative or CQC representative include the following:

1. To what degree must testing be conducted? In cases such as cement or steel, will mill certificates be accepted or will specific tests be required?
2. How much surveying must be supplied by the design firm or owner's field office?
3. Will record drawings be required to be prepared by the contractor or by the resident project representative of the owner or design firm?
4. What reporting and other documentation requirements will be imposed on the resident project representative or CQC representative and his field office staff?
5. What will be the responsibility of the resident project representative or CQC representative with regard to intermediate and final acceptance of test results?
6. Will the resident project representative or CQC representative be asked to participate in any portion of the review phase of shop drawings? If so, to what degree?
7. What if any safety responsibilities will be expected of the resident project representative or CQC representative?

In the establishment of the resident project representative's field office, the matter of staffing should be considered together with the assignment of individual responsibilities. The number of personnel needed to perform the administrative and quality control functions normally associated with the resident project representative's field office may vary from one part-time construction administrator/inspector to a staff of 15 or 20 people on an exceptionally large project. Most commonly, the small projects involve the use of one part-time construction coordinator who provides construction administration and general technical inspection, supplemented by special inspectors where necessary. On slightly larger projects a full-time resident project representative may be justified. Although he is the only full-time member of the field office staff, he may be supplemented by special inspectors where necessary. Beyond this level, the full-time resident project representative is usually provided with a full-time clerk-typist to assist in the numerous routine office tasks involved. In addition, one or more full-time field inspectors may also be assigned to the project, supplemented by part-time special inspectors as necessary.

Projects of a size and complexity that require a larger or more specialized staff are generally under the direction of a resident engineer who is a registered professional engineer or architect as the resident project representative.

Outline of Field Office Cost Items

Among the items contributing significantly to the cost of establishing and operating a construction field office for the owners or design firm are the following:

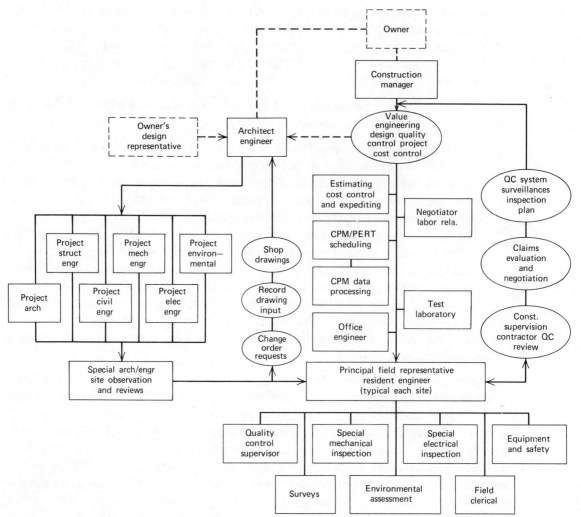

Figure 9.4 *Representative operational diagram for a large project.*

1. *Supervision:* Usually, on the larger projects a full-time resident project representative is assigned to each job site. He may work under the direct supervision of a project manager in an architect/engineer's office who often is in charge of several projects and many different contracts. The project manager *is* the architect/engineer so far as his project is concerned. A resident project representative may be assigned to supervise the inspection of more than one project on an intermittent basis——usually for the same project manager. In addition to supervising the inspection forces, the resident project representative maintains liaison with the contractor's project superintendent and sometimes with a representative of the owner. He is often asked to conduct on-the-job conferences.

2. *Operations:* This generally comprises the inspection group. It may be subdivided into functional areas such as the dam, the spillway, or the powerhouse; or on a contract basis such as the paving contract, the drainage facilities contract, the pump station contract, or similar tasks. Also to be considered are the various special inspectors such as the mechanical, electrical, control systems, welding and structural steel, masonry, concrete, soils, and paving inspectors. Laboratory operations may also be assigned to test soils, aggregates, concrete masonry units, sealants, asphalt, and other construction materials.

Keeping a daily diary (log) is the duty of each inspector (Chapter 4) and all activities must be documented thoroughly. The resident project representative is also responsible to check the contractor to assure that all insurance, bonding, and permits are in order. The operations tasks also include review of payment requests, measurements of work completed as a means of verifying payment requests (Chapter 14), the evaluation of requests by the contractor for change orders (Chapter 16), and the submittal of recommendations to the design firm or the owner regarding the recommendations of the resident project representative for action to be taken on such requests. Although the resident project representative does not perform any construction surveys, he should be involved to the extent of coordinating the survey tasks required for the project.

The field office operations include estimating of costs of construction for partial and final payments, change order requests, and value engineering proposals. All transmittals of samples, shop drawings, and other material intended for the design firm or the owner should be routed through the resident project representative; he should log all such submittals prior to forwarding to the design firm or the owner for action. The responsibility of the resident project representative does *not* include his approval of shop drawings, samples, approval of substitutions of materials, *nor* the interpretation of the intent of the plans and specifications—these should be reserved for the architect or engineer's project manager. On a very large project, a professional engineering staff may be assigned the job of field administration of the project, in which case exceptions to the above responsibilities may be established by the design firm.

3. *Administration:* In addition to the administrative tasks included in the foregoing paragraph, the resident project representative and his field office staff must perform general clerical services, communications services, limited personnel functions, mailing and shipping, ordering and maintaining of supplies and equipment, administration of transportation and travel of personnel, expense account submittals, minor purchasing, maintenance of company-owned vehicles, and similar functions. In addition, on some governmental projects, particularly federal work, the resident project representative field office may be required to check the contractor's payrolls for compliance with labor legislation, and assist in negotiations with craft unions and labor relations. Wherever owner-furnished equipment is to be installed by the contractor, the resident project representative also may be called upon to expedite delivery and control, and provide for the storage and issuance to the contractor of such owner-furnished equipment.

"In addition to the administrative tasks—the resident inspector must perform purchasing, checking of the contractor's payroll—and similar functions."

THE PRECONSTRUCTION CONFERENCE

In communicating with the contractor and his personnel it is important that the design firm or the owner and his resident project representative make their positions very clear right from the start of the job. It is far better to get started on a basis of administering the contract firmly in accordance with the plans and specifications than it is to correct a difficult situation later in the job that is the result of a lax relationship with the contractor.

As a means of establishing the "ground rules" and calling the contractor's attention to the critical areas of construction, the preconstruction conference is an invaluable tool. Initially, it allows the key personnel of both sides to be introduced, and the responsibilities and authorities of each can be defined at that time. It also allows the parties to get a clear understanding of the procedures involved in contractor submittals, sampling and testing, construction surveys, inspections by outside agencies, payment requests, procedures for claims and disputes, unforeseen job conditions, change order requests, and similar items. The contractor can take this opportunity to raise questions about any of these items and clear up any misunderstandings.

During the course of the preconstruction meeting, mention can be made of the contractor's responsibility to provide insurance documents, as specified, and all required bonds as well as to obtain (and usually pay for) all permits from building departments, street departments, police departments (for traffic control), flood control districts, environmental protection agencies, or other agencies having jurisdiction. He should be reminded at the preconstruction meeting that all such documentation is required to be submitted before work can begin, and that his contract has a specified length of time after

PRECONSTRUCTION CONFERENCE AGENDA

Introduce key personnel of owner; engineer/architect; and contractor
    Define authority and responsibilities of each

Outline procedures for the following:
    Contractor submittals
    Sampling & testing (who pays)
    Construction surveys (how to order; who pays)
    Inspections by outside agencies; procedures
    Payment request timetable
    Procedures for claims and disputes
    Handling of unforeseen conditions
    Change order request procedures

Contractor to provide the following permits at his own expense (before starting)
    Building department
    Street department excavation permit
    Police department (traffic control)
    Flood control districts
    Utilities
    State highway department special permits
    Environmental Protection Agency

Time and order of the work
    Time of contract; importance of timely completion
    Liquidated damages; penalties; bonus clauses
    Schedules required to be submitted and regularly updated
    Engineer has right to review schedules and require changes
    Jobsite management meetings; frequency; who attends; where held?
    Submittal of contractor's safety program

Special Technical Concerns
    Level of inspector control
    Intent of plans and specifications; order of precedence of documents
    Concrete criteria and level of control
    Waterstop welding procedures
    Protective coating quality control devices to be furnished by contractor
    Order of precedence of contract documents
    Procedures in case of discrepancies in documents

Time schedule for providing inspector's field office and facilities

Submit names and both home and business telephone numbers of all key personnel

Figure 9.5 Sample agenda for a preconstruction conference

the signing of the contract or the issuance of a Notice to Proceed within which he is to begin the work.

Another item that should be brought up at the preconstruction conference is the schedule of job site and management meetings, the location and frequency of such meetings, and who should be in attendance.

Before closing the conference, the subject of the construction schedule should be raised. It may be necessary to remind the contractor that the initial project schedule submitted at the beginning of the project will require periodic adjustment, and that all such adjustments must meet with the approval of the design firm and the owner. It should also be emphasized that the design firm or the owner, through his resident project representative, has the right to require the contractor to revise his work schedule, increase his work hours or personnel, or to make other adjustments that will assure completion of the project within the agreed upon time schedule. Before making any such demands upon the contractor, however, be certain that the provisions of the contract will allow the architect or engineer to exercise such authority. Also, check both the time allowed to complete the job and whether the exact wording of the contract makes specific reference to "time" as "the essence of the contract." Failure to specify time as the essence of the contract may place the owner in a weak position for requiring the contractor to accelerate the work in order to complete the work "on time." [c.f. *Kingery Construction Co. v. Scherbarth Welding, Inc*. 185 N.W. 2d 857 (1971)].

STUDY PLANS AND SPECIFICATIONS

Prior to the beginning of any actual work on the project, and preferably prior to mobilization by the contractor, the resident project representative or CQC representative *and all other inspectors* assigned to the project should obtain a complete set of project plans and specifications, *plus all addenda,* and all key reference books or standards that are cited in the specifications. The plans, specifications, addenda, and references should be carefully studied and the inspector's copy of the plans and specifications should be marked with a highlighter pen or other marker to identify all key inspection provisions. The placing of index tabs at the beginning of each section of the specifications is also a good idea, as it will facilitate rapid reference to each section when needed. If the construction documents review can be conducted in the office of the architect/engineer, it is even better, as the inspector will be in a better position to get factual answers to specific questions from the project manager and the design engineers and architects themselves. In addition, this one-to-one level of communication allows the supervisor of each design discipline to meet the project field representative and develop a working relationship. At the same time, contacts can be made with the mechanical and electrical department heads to determine their schedules for requesting special inspections of those portions of the work for which they are personally responsible.

KEY DATES

The resident project representative or CQC representative should note on his field calendar each and every date that has special significance on the project, whether it be for tests, special inspections, payment request due dates, delivery dates, or other important milestones. All such data should be obtained from either the specifications (if listed there) or from the contractor's CPM or bar chart schedule.

AGENCY PERMITS

At the beginning of the job, the resident project representative should see that all required permits have been obtained, and should prevent any construction work from proceeding

NOTICE OF AWARD

To: ______________________

____

____

____

____

PROJECT Description: ____

____

____

The OWNER has considered the BID submitted by you for the above described WORK in response to its Advertisement for Bids dated __________, 19 __________, and Information for Bidders.

You are hereby notified that your BID has been accepted for items in the amount of $______________.

You are required by the Information for Bidders to execute the Agreement and furnish the required CONTRACTOR'S Performance BOND, Payment BOND and certificates of insurance within ten (10) calendar days from the date of this Notice to you.

If you fail to execute said Agreement and to furnish said BONDS within ten (10) days from the date of this Notice, said OWNER will be entitled to consider all your rights arising out of the OWNER'S acceptance of your BID as abandoned and as a forfeiture of your BID BOND. The OWNER will be entitled to such other rights as may be granted by law.

You are required to return an acknowledged copy of this NOTICE OF AWARD to the OWNER.

Dated this __________ day of ______________, 19__________.

____
Owner

By ______________________________

Title ______________________________

ACCEPTANCE OF NOTICE

Receipt of the above NOTICE OF AWARD is hereby acknowledged

by ____,

this the ______________________day of ______________________, 19______

By ______________________________

Title ______________________________

CONTRACT DOCUMENTS FOR CONSTRUCTION OF
FEDERALLY ASSISTED WATER AND SEWER PROJECTS

Document No. 8
Notice of Award: Page 1 of 1

Figure 9.6 *Example of Notice of Award.*

NOTICE TO PROCEED

To: ______________________ Date: ______________________

______________________ Project: ______________________

______________________ ______________________

______________________ ______________________

______________________ ______________________

You are hereby notified to commence WORK in accordance with the Agreement dated __________, 19______, on or before __________, 19______, and you are to complete the WORK within __________ consecutive calendar days thereafter. The date of completion of all WORK is therefore __________, 19______.

____
Owner

By ______________________

Title ______________________

ACCEPTANCE OF NOTICE

Receipt of the above NOTICE TO PROCEED is hereby acknowledged by ______

______________________,

this the ______________________ day

of ______________________, 19______

____

By ______________________

Title ______________________

CONTRACT DOCUMENTS FOR CONSTRUCTION OF
FEDERALLY ASSISTED WATER AND SEWER PROJECTS

Document No. 9
Notice to Proceed: Page 1 of 1

Figure 9.7 Example of Notice to Proceed.

whenever a required permit controlling such work has not been obtained. It should be noted that sometimes the terms of a permit may be quite lengthy, and the permit conditions may read like a specification in itself. Such terms and conditions of a permit must be considered as binding upon the contractor, and will normally take precedence over the terms of the project specification in case of conflict.

STARTING A PROJECT

The beginning of a construction project normally starts with the award of the construction contract. This may be accomplished in the minutes of a City Council or County Board of Supervisors action, by letter, or by issuance of a preprinted *Notice of Award* form (Fig. 9.6). The giving of a Notice of Award is similar in its legal effect to the issuance of a letter of intent, since it obligates the owner to sign the construction contract if the contractor does what is required of him within the time specified. The Notice of Award *does not authorize the start of construction* since no work is supposed to start until after the owner/contractor agreement has been signed by both parties. Under the terms of the NSPE General Conditions, the contract time will commence running on the thirtieth day after the owner has signed and delivered a fully executed agreement, but it may start sooner if a formal Notice to Proceed is issued. Under the AIA General Conditions, if no Notice to Proceed is issued the contract time will commence as of the date of signing of the agreement.

The issuance of a *Notice to Proceed* formalizes the date that the project is to begin, and sets the stage for computation of the total project construction time. This will greatly facilitate the establishment of an accurate count of construction time for the computation of liquidated damages. It is considerably more reliable than relying solely upon the Notice of Award, as can be seen by the variation in terms within the contract provisions of the two major societies who offer standardized General Conditions to be used in the project specifications. Many public agencies allow a ten-day period after the issuance of a formal Notice to Proceed for the contractor to begin work at the site.

10
CONSTRUCTION PLANNING AND SCHEDULING

PLANNING FOR CONSTRUCTION

Construction planning and scheduling should not be considered as one of the deep mysteries of life, but rather as an application of common sense, a logical analysis of a construction project along with all of its parts, and a thorough knowledge of construction methods, materials, and practices.

The process of planning is simply an application of the thought process that must be entered into before the actual scheduling can begin. The planning process should include answers to the following *preliminary* questions:

1. *Long lead purchases:* Are there any items that will require purchase orders to be placed long in advance of the time that the item is needed on the job because of material shortages, fabrication time, or similar delay factors?
2. *Utility interruptions:* Is there any part of the project that will involve an outage of utility services such as water, power, gas or other essential services? If so, has the utility owner been contacted to determine the maximum length of the outage; the time of day that outages will be permitted; the calendar dates during which outages will be permitted, or similar restrictive controls?
3. *Temporary utilities:* Will temporary utility lines be required to be built to bypass the construction area, and will temporary roads be required to provide detour routes for street traffic?
4. *Temporary construction utility service:* Who provides temporary construction utility service, and from where must it be obtained?

5. *Labor:* Have representatives of labor been contacted in the area of construction to establish the jurisdictional responsibilities of the various trades to be used in the work, as well as to determine the union work rules in the affected area?

6. *Work and storage areas:* Have provisions been made for contractor's work and storage areas?

7. *Traffic requirements:* Have local traffic control regulations been investigated? Will construction equipment be allowed to operate on public streets; will street closures in the construction area be permitted; and will special traffic control and flagmen be required to direct traffic around construction?

8. *Temporary access:* Will temporary access, including temporary bridges, be required to provide continued access to residences and places of business during the construction period?

9. *Other contractors:* Will other contractors be working in the same area, thus requiring schedule coordination with them in order to complete the work of this contract?

10. *Interdependency of tasks:* Are some of the tasks in this project dependent upon the completion schedule of another contractor or utility owner before they can be started?

11. *Environmental controls:* Will special environmental controls be required; if so, what?

12. *Special regulations:* Are there special regulations, such as FAA requirements for work at airports, that may affect the construction scheduling or construction time?

13. *Special construction equipment:* Will special equipment be required for construction? If so, is it off-road equipment that will require special haul routes? What are the load limits and bridge clearances for roads in the area?

14. *Time for construction:* Is the time allowed to complete the project adequate for the location and the seasons, or will it require increased crew sizes or premium time?

Each of the above items is an important consideration in the planning stage of a project. After determination of the various limitations and constraints on the conduct of the work, the task of planning the actual construction effort can begin. Many large contracts can be divided into separate stages of construction. In some cases there may be a single general contractor responsible for the construction of all of the stages, which may have simply been planned to accommodate a fixed order or sequence of construction. In other cases, it may be possible that portions of a construction project may begin even before the entire work of design has been completed. This is generally accomplished by the owner entering into phased-construction contracts (''fast-track''), in which each stage of the work is let for construction as soon as the design effort on that particular phase of the work has been completed.

As previously mentioned, this approach has the added advantage that it can result in completion of a project at an earlier date than would be possible if it were necessary to wait until all design work had been completed. It also may offer a distinct financial advantage to the owner in many cases by allowing the early bidding of completed portions of the work so as to avoid the added costs that could result from the cost inflation spiral if

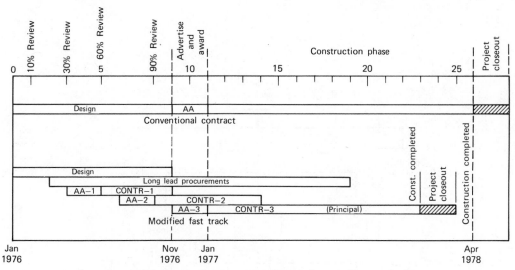

Figure 10.1 *Conventional versus phased (fast-track) construction.*

the work were to be delayed. The fast-track method of construction is often a money saver for the owner in spite of added field administration costs, as the earlier construction completion date is often money in the owner's pocket.

Phased construction (fast-track) has its disadvantages, too, as it creates considerably more work for the project manager and the resident project representative, and may require a larger field staff to administer. One of the difficulties that may have to be overcome is created by the fact that under a fast-track system of construction, numerous other *prime* contractors are on the job. Because of this, the added responsibility for coordination of each of these various prime contractors falls upon the shoulders of the resident project representative as there is no general contractor with this responsibility. Similarly, interfaces between the various scopes of the work of each of the separate prime contracts have been very carefully worked out in the contract documents. Furthermore, if the project in which these various separate contractors are involved concerns separate elements that must ultimately become a part of a single operational system, the question of responsibility for the proper functioning of the overall system may pose a serious problem for the owner.

Generally, under a system of fast-track contracts, it is most desirable to operate under a design/build (turnkey) or a construction management contract, wherein such responsibilities can be handled by the construction manager and his project team. In such cases the task of administration of the construction will be carried by an on-site project manager, and the resident inspector will normally be performing the functions of a quality control supervisor.

Another approach to the problem of responsibility over fast-track contract operations that has not yet come into common use is one in which all but one of the prime contracts awarded contains an assignment clause that allows one of the other prime contractors to

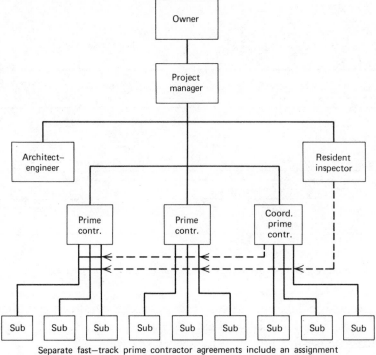

Separate fast—track prime contractor agreements include an assignment clause to allow principal (coordinating) contractor, when he is brought onto the project, to have authority for coordination and interface responsibility. This is NOT AN ASSIGNMENT OF CONTRACT.

Principal (coordinating) contractor's agreement will contain a clause requiring him to provide overall coordination between his own forces and those of all fast—track prime contractors as well as maintain interface control between the work of all tasks.

Figure 10.2 *Phased (fast-track) construction with assigned coordination.*

function as a lead contractor. In this capacity, the lead contractor will have responsibility for coordinating the work of all the contractors on the project and assuring that all work will interface properly without gaps or overlaps of responsibility.

The planning problem is further complicated by the fact that consideration must be given to the work of each of the trades to assure that there will be no interference by others whose work takes them into the same construction area; nor will the work of one trade be held up because of the failure of another to complete its work. Costs of mobilization must also be considered, as it would certainly be both uneconomical and time consuming to move heavy earthmoving equipment to a site for construction of the work of one phase and move off the site, only to be moved back again to execute the earthwork requirements of another phase of the work if all of the earthwork could have been completed at the same time.

Obviously, in order to get a clear picture of all the interrelated problems at a construction site, some kind of a graphic picture must be drawn to enable the contractor and the resident project representative to get a clear understanding not only of the sequence of events, but also of their times of beginning and anticipated completion as well.

SCHEDULING METHODS

There are relatively few basic scheduling systems in use today, although numerous variants of each are in use. Generally, scheduling methods can be classed in two major categories:

1. Bar Charts
2. Network Diagrams

Bar charts seem to have been with us since the beginning of time, and they are still in extensive use today. They are still an extremely useful tool, and may often be seen accompanying a network diagram. The bar chart as it is used today is somewhat similar to the charts discussed by one writer in the nineteenth century involving a work-versus-time graphical representation. It was Henry L. Gantt and Frederick W. Taylor, however, who popularized its use in the early 1900s. Their ''Gantt'' charts are the basis of today's bar graphs or bar charts. Although their work was originally aimed at production scheduling, it was readily accepted for planning construction and recording its progress. One of its principal advantages is that it is readily understood by all levels of management and supervision.

Network diagrams represent the development of systems that not only record the graphical work-versus-time relationships of each phase of the work, but also enable the user to see the interrelation and dependencies that control the project. Network planning did not come into being until the middle of the 1950s when the U.S. Navy Special Projects Office set out with their consultants to devise a new method of planning for special weapons systems. The result was called Program Evaluation Review Technique, now universally called ''PERT.'' It was an *event-oriented* system, and was designed primarily as a project monitoring system. The attempt to apply PERT to the construction industry was not too successful, primarily because of event orientation, the use of three time estimates instead of one, and the technique of starting at the end and working toward the beginning. Consequently, further research was done by others in the construction field, and the result was the Critical Path Method, known as CPM. This method was *activity oriented,* used single time estimates, and usually started at the beginning and worked to the end of the project.

In actual practice the CPM and PERT techniques are almost identical. Network planning is the basis for both systems, and although in contemporary usage a computer is generally used, they can be done by manual methods as well.

By comparing the bar chart methods with network diagramming methods, the user can see the advantages of one system over the other. With a network diagram, it can be shown to be obvious that work item ''E'' could not proceed until work item ''D'' had been completed, whereas a bar chart could only indicate the scheduled date that task ''E'' was to be performed, and if task ''D'' was late there was no way of determining from the bar chart that task ''E'' would be delayed also because of the interrelationship between the two tasks. In the preparation of a bar chart, the scheduler is almost necessarily influenced by the desired completion dates, often working backward from the completion dates. The resultant mixture of planning and scheduling is often no better than wishful thinking.

BAR CHARTS

If a bar graph is carefully prepared, the scheduler goes through the same preliminary thinking process that the network planner does. However, a bar graph cannot show or record the interrelations or dependencies that control the progress of the project. At a later date, even the originator of a bar graph may find it difficult to explain his plan using the bar graph. In the example, Figure 10.3, a simplified bar chart is shown of a small one-story office building. Suppose that, after this 10-month schedule has been prepared, the owner asks for a six-month schedule instead. By using the same time for each activity, the bar chart can be changed as shown in Figure 10.4. Although this may look correct at first, it is not based upon logical planning; it is merely the juggling of the original bar graph.

Note that in Figures 10.3 and 10.4 the general contractor's work is broken down in some detail, while the mechanical and electrical work are each shown as a continuous line, starting early and ending late. In conformance with the bar chart, the general contractor often pushes the subcontractors to staff the project as early as possible with as many mechanics as possible, while the subcontractors would like to come on the project as late as possible with as few mechanics as possible. The general contractor often

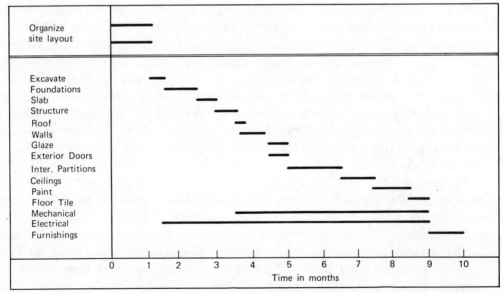

Figure 10.3 Bar chart of small one-story office building.

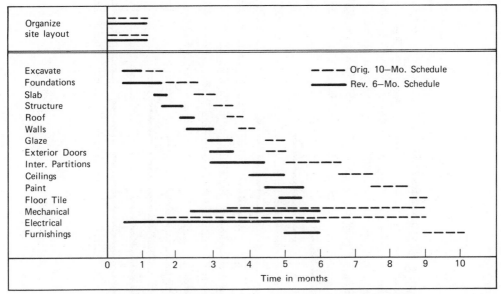

Figure 10.4 *Revised bar chart of small one-story office building.*

complains that the subcontractor is delaying the job through his lack of interest in the progress of the work. At the same time the subcontractor is complaining that the general contractor is not turning work areas over to him and that he, the subcontractor, will have to go into a crash effort to save the schedule. As in most matters, the truth is probably somewhere between both extremes. Network diagrams offer the means to resolve many of these differences with specific information rather than generalities.

The bar chart is often actively used early in the project, but seems to be nowhere to be found later in the project. One can assume the reasons for this may be that somewhere before the construction phase the design firm and owner are all trying to visualize the project schedule in order to set realistic completion dates, and once this is accomplished, lose interest in the specifics of the schedule. Most specifications require the submittal of a schedule in bar graph form by the contractor soon after the award of the contract. When the project begins to take shape in the field, the early bar charts become as useful as last year's calendar, because the bar graph does not lend itself to planning revisions.

In one form, the bar chart persists, and rightfully so. As a means of communicating job progress information to nontechnically trained people, or even to construction experts whose need to know is limited to progress data only, the bar chart excels as a means of showing such data in a clear and concise manner. Such charts record progress in each of the major elements of construction as a solid bar along a corresponding time scale, and are generally updated monthly. Another type of chart frequently used for showing a comparison of anticipated construction progress to actual progress is the ''S'' curve, illustrated in Figure 10.6. Another variation of this curve is frequently used for cost control.

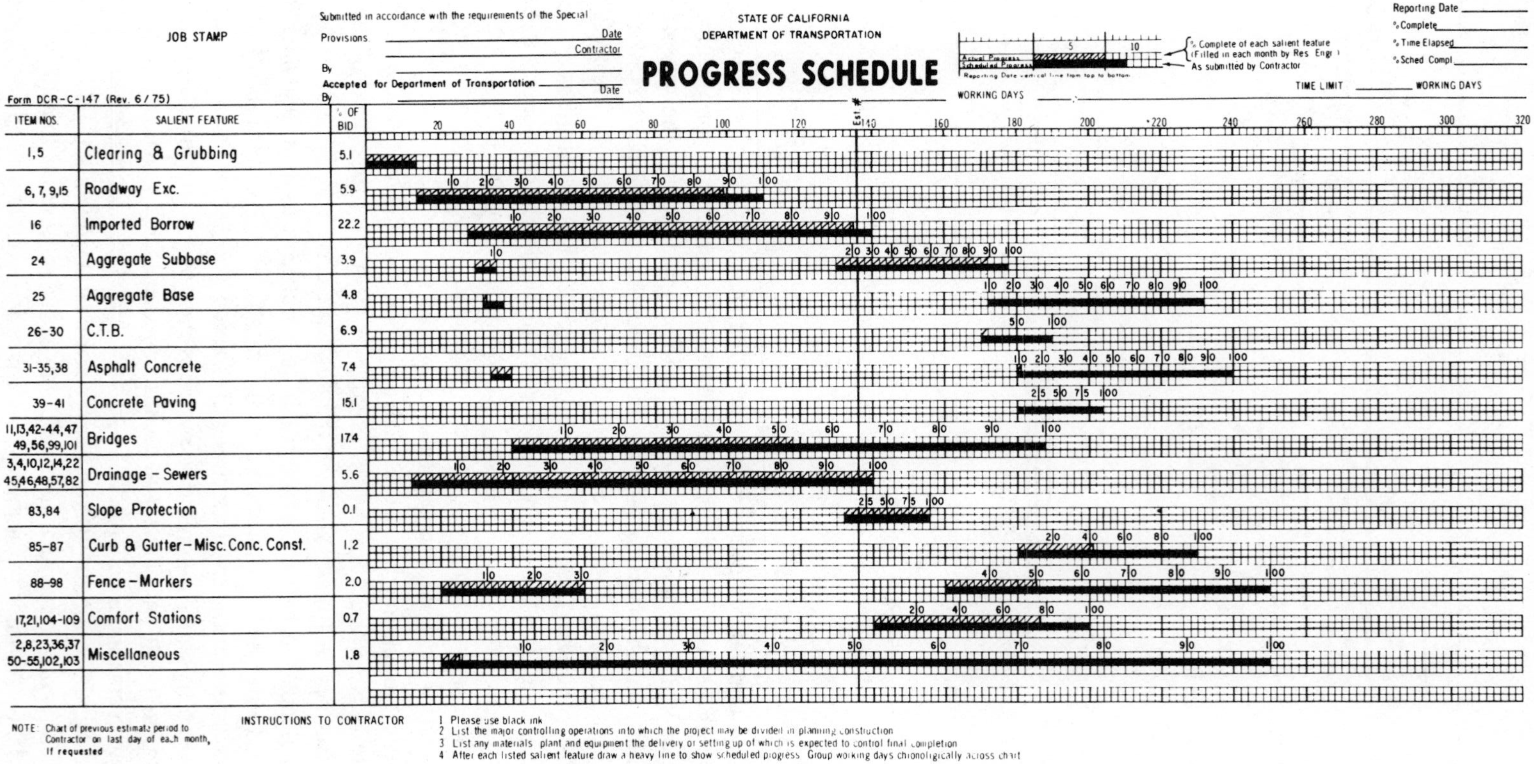

Figure 10.5 Bar chart progress schedule.

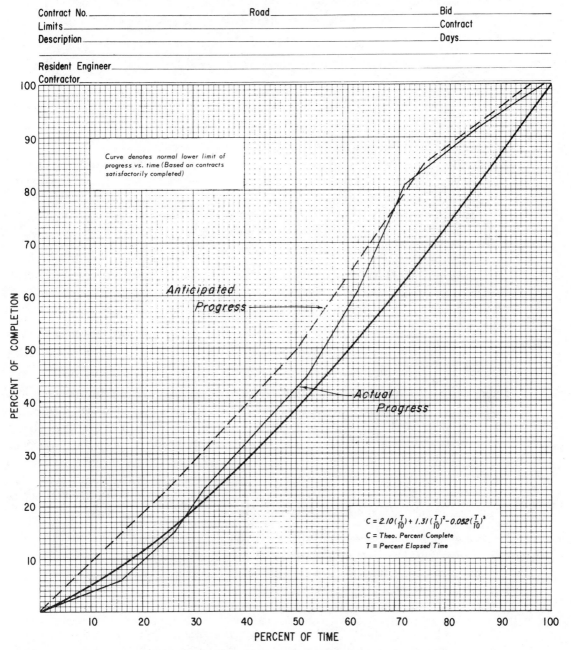

CONSTRUCTION PROGRESS

Contract No._____ Road_____ Bid_____
Limits_____ Contract
Description_____ Days_____

Resident Engineer_____
Contractor_____

Curve denotes normal lower limit of progress vs. time (Based on contracts satisfactorily completed)

Anticipated Progress

Actual Progress

$$C = 2.10\left(\frac{T}{10}\right) + 1.31\left(\frac{T}{10}\right)^2 - 0.052\left(\frac{T}{10}\right)^3$$

C = Theo. Percent Complete
T = Percent Elapsed Time

PERCENT OF COMPLETION

PERCENT OF TIME

Figure 10.6 *Construction progress curve.*

NETWORK DIAGRAMS

General Summary of Systems in Use

Network diagrams, so called because of the net effect of the interconnecting lines used to indicate dependencies and interrelationships, can be divided into three basic categories for use in construction:

1. *CPM* or *Critical Path Method,* which was originally developed specifically for the planning of construction.
2. *PERT* or *Program Evaluation Review Technique,* which was originated by the Special Projects Office of the Navy Bureau of Ordinance, and with few exceptions is used almost exclusively in military and aerospace work. Adaptations of the basic technique have been developed for use in construction.
3. *CMCS* or *Construction Management Control System,* of the General Services Administration, is a management program covering both design and construction phases of the work, using critical path method for overall project control. It is required on many GSA projects, and instructions for use as well as program tapes are available from the Associate Commissioner for Project Management, Public Buildings Service, General Services Administration, Washington, D.C. 20405.

Occasionally, modifications are used that utilize some of the separate features of the above systems. Contractors for construction of ground support and launching facilities for missiles in space may encounter PERT in construction; otherwise it appears that little will be seen of it in construction in an unmodified form.

Critical Path Method

The work horse of network scheduling methods used in construction is the popular critical path method, which is used almost universally wherever network scheduling methods are called for. The CPM system shows the order and interdependence of activities and the sequence in which the work is to be accomplished. The basic concept of the network analysis diagram is to show the start of each given activity and its dependence upon the completion of preceding activities, and how its completion also restricts other activities to follow. The CPM network provides for the construction phase only, using either manual or automated methods, involving the following activities:

1. Long lead purchases and deliveries of critical materials
2. Fabrication, installation, and testing of critical equipment
3. Submittal and approval of material samples and shop drawings
4. All activities that affect progress on the job
5. Required dates of completion for all activities

If a project is of such size that a single network cannot be easily shown on a single sheet, a summary network diagram will probably be provided. The summary sheet is usually a network of from 50 to 150 activities, and is based upon the detailed diagrams of all the remaining tasks. The mathematical analysis of the CPM network diagram includes the following information for each activity:

1. Preceding and following event numbers
2. Activity description
3. Estimated duration of activities
4. Earliest start dates (calendar dates)
5. Earliest finish dates (calendar dates)
6. Scheduled or actual start date
7. Scheduled or actual finish date
8. Lastest start date (calendar date)
9. Latest finish date (calendar date)
10. Monetary value of activity
11. Responsibility for activity (prime; subs; suppliers; etc.)
12. Manpower required
13. Percentage of activity completed as of each report
14. Contractor's earnings based upon portion of work completed
15. Bid item of which the activity is a part

In addition to the tabulation of activities, the CPM computer printout should also include an identification of activities that are planned for expediting by the use of overtime or double shifts to be worked, including possible Saturday, Sunday, or holiday work. It should also provide an on-site manpower loading schedule and a description of the major items of construction equipment planned for operations on the project. Where portions of the work are to be paid for under unit costs, the estimated number of units in an activity that was used in developing the total activity cost should be shown.

The computer printout generally sorts certain classes of frequently used data into groups or "sorts." Generally, the data on a CPM will be grouped into the following sorts:

1. By the preceding event number from the lowest to the highest, and then in order of the following event number
2. By the amount of slack, then in the order of earliest allowable start dates
3. In order of the latest allowable start dates, then in order of preceding event numbers, then in order of succeeding event numbers.

PBS Project Management Control System

The PBS–CMCS or Public Buildings Service—Construction Management Control System is a newer network system for management control now in use by the General Services Administration of the federal government, which they require to be used by private architect/engineers in the construction management of numerous GSA projects. The CMCS provides for the design and construction phases of the project using both manual and automated procedures as a support for the following functions:

1. Planning
2. Organizing
3. Scheduling
4. Budgeting
5. Reporting of design and construction progress
6. Reporting of design and construction expenditures
7. Accounting
8. Documentation
9. Identification of variances and problems
10. Decision-making
11. Decision implementation

The data provided must be timely, must be responsive to the needs of management at all levels, and must be fully capable of providing a sound basis for management decisions. The computer printouts, in which automated methods are used, will include the following:

1. Sorts by early and late start, criticality, responsibility, and building area
2. Allocation of material and labor costs to each work item
3. Generation of cash-flow projections and contractor payment request verifications
4. Master schedule; design schedule; preconstruction schedule; and occupancy schedule
5. Separate reports, including summary and bar charts, contractor payments, purchase orders, shop drawings, and samples

Learning to Use a Network Diagram

Network diagrams may seem unduly complicated to read at first, but if you happened to be called upon to try to develop one, they would indeed *be* complicated. Fortunately, the resident project representative's responsibility in network diagramming is limited to reading, understanding, and using the diagrams to good advantage on his project. The skill of learning to read and understand them is not that complicated, and can be acquired by anyone willing to apply himself to the task of learning a few of its basic principles. These will be explained in more depth in Chapter 11.

It is essential that the resident project representative should become reasonably familiar with the principles of network diagramming so as effectively to perform his duties and responsibilities on those projects that use them. The inspector must not only understand the network diagrams themselves, but also should be capable of reading and interpreting the computer printouts of all CPM data received by the field office. Admittedly, the system may only be encountered on the larger projects, but a basic knowledge of the general principles of network diagramming should be a part of every resident project representative's education.

Bibliography

F. Thomas Collins, *Network Planning and Critical Path Scheduling,* 1st ed., Know-How Publications, Berkeley, California, 1964.

R. L. Peurifoy, *Construction Planning, Equipment, and Methods,* 1st ed., McGraw-Hill, New York, 1956.

State of California, Department of Transportation, *Construction Manual,* Section 2–08 Prosecution and Progress; issued by the Dvision of Construction and Research, Office of Construction, Sacramento, California, 1975.

General Services Administration, Public Buildings Service, Project Management Division, Washington, D.C.

U.S. Army, Corps of Engineers, Guide Specifications.

11
FUNDAMENTALS OF CPM CONSTRUCTION SCHEDULING

CONSTRUCTION PROJECTS are complex, and a large job will literally involve thousands of separate operations. If a project is to be completed within the time called for in the contract, the work must be very carefully planned and scheduled in advance. If all the tasks would simply follow each other in consecutive order, the job of scheduling would be much easier. Unfortunately, the problem is not that simple. Each operation within the project has its own time requirement, and often it cannot start until certain other operations have been completed. On the other hand, there are many other tasks that can be carried on simultaneously because they are entirely independent of one another. Thus, a typical project involves many tasks that are dependent upon one another as well as many other tasks that are totally independent of each other, and when interrelated in a project, they create a tangled web of individual time and sequence relationships. When all these tasks are superimposed, it becomes obvious that project planning and scheduling is a very complicated and difficult management function.

It is not the intent of this book to go into the subject of CPM scheduling in sufficient depth to enable the resident inspector to be able to set up a project schedule by CPM, but certainly deep enough so that he should be capable of reading and understanding them. It is often one of the resident project representative's responsibilities to make regular evaluations of the contractor's construction schedules so as to determine whether he is meeting the schedule requirements and will complete the work within the agreed time. The inspector should know the subject well enough to know what to look for, and be fully capable of recognizing a logical and an illogical chart when he sees one.

The traditional basis in years past for scheduling construction work had always been the bar and "S" charts. There is no question but that these are still useful tools for showing the established schedule of operations and recording its progress. However, the bar chart falls somewhat short of being an adequate tool for project planning, and the resulting construction schedule is based more upon the contractor's experience and intuition than on any rational analysis of the work to be performed. Its major weakness lies in the fact that it does not show the interrelationships and interdependencies that exist among the various phases of the work. Also, there is no way to determine which operations actually control the overall time progress of the project.

THE DEVELOPMENT OF CPM

Since about 1957, a new concept in planning and scheduling has been developed and utilized. The new system allows the analysis of sequences and time characteristics by the use of network diagrams. Although the new system has not entirely replaced the bar chart system, it has become widely used among contractors as a part of their management systems. Very often, construction contracts will contain a requirement in the specifications that the contractor provide CPM control during the life of the project.

Frequently you will hear the terms "CPM" and "PERT" as though they mean the same thing. Although both have certain fundamental similarities, the two methods differ considerably in their applications and objectives. PERT (Program Evaluation Research Task) was originally started by the U.S. Navy as a tool to assist in the planning and control of the Polaris missile system. It is primarily used as a management system on military and aerospace projects. The PERT system is concerned with estimating the probability of completing a project within a specified time.

CPM (Critical Path Method) is primarily a tool of the construction industry. It lends itself well to projects on which times can be predicted with a higher degree of certainty. It is a method that allows the contractor to achieve improved time control over construction projects or similar work that has been done before, and therefore a reasonably accurate estimate of time can be made of each of the work elements involved. In many cases, there are systems in use that are essentially a combination of some of the features of both the PERT and the CPM methods. Generally, however, it has been found that the original CPM methods are best suited to construction projects.

CPM—WHAT IT IS AND WHAT IT DOES

The CPM is essentially a project management system that covers the construction phase of a project and allows the user to aid his decision-making process by guiding the contractor in selecting the best way to expedite the job, as well as the fact that it provides him with a prediction of future manpower requirements as well as equipment needs.

Project planning is the first step in a CPM procedure. This step consists of the following:

1. Identify the elementary work items needed to complete the job

2. Establish the logical order in whic these work items must be done

3. Prepare a graphic display in the form of a network diagram

The next step is the scheduling phase, and it requires an estimate of the time required to accomplish each of the work items previously identified. With the use of the network diagram, computations are made to provide information concerning the time schedule characteristics of each work item, and the total time necessary to complete the project.

Although these comments seem to suggest that CPM must follow a definite step-by-step order, this is not the case in actual usage. For example, the three planning steps often proceed simultaneously. For the purposes of this discussion, it will be assumed that they are treated separately in the order listed.

The computations previously mentioned are actually only simple additions and subtractions. Although the actual computation is simple and very easy, there are usually so many of them required on an actual project that the process becomes very tedious. For this reason, many contractors use computers to produce their CPM schedules. Furthermore, with the use of the computer, the schedule may be updated even on a weekly basis without undue hardship. Many computer management firms now exist that will provide all levels of service for network scheduling to contractors, architects, and engineers. With the addition of some programmed logic in a computerized network system, complex scheduling problems can be worked out rapidly and optimum solutions can be reached. A task that would be impossible within the allowable time if it had to be done by hand methods can be accomplished in minutes by computer after developing the input data required.

For a full understanding of the method, some understanding of the calculations that are necessary and an understanding of the terminology used is required. In addition, there are many applications of CPM in which manually developed data are adequate and quite usual. Therefore, the following explanations are based upon manual procedures, followed by some examples showing how the data developed are printed out when computer methods are used along with some elementary instructions as to the use of the computer printouts by the resident project representative.

BASIC PROCEDURE IN SETTING UP A CPM SCHEDULE

Normally, the network scheduling is started right after the award of the project. Because the prime purpose of the system is to produce a coordinated project plan, the principal subcontractors must also be entered into the planning stage. Normally, the general contractor sets the general timing for the project; the individual subcontractors then review their portions of the work, and the needed alterations are made.

The basic procedure used by the planning group is to "talk" the project through first. This way the project is subject to careful, detailed, advance planning. This planning alone justifies the time spent on CPM. Usually, the network diagram is then constructed in a rough form, and the job is broken up into basic elements; then the sequential order of construction operations is discussed. It is often helpful to list the major operations of the project and use them as a means of developing the preliminary diagram.

PROJECT PLANNING

The first phase of CPM is that of planning. The project must first be broken down into time-consuming "activities." An "activity" in CPM is defined as any single identifiable work step in the total project. The extent to which the project is subdivided into activities depends upon the number of practical considerations; however, the following factors must be taken into account:

1. Different areas of responsibility, such as subcontracted work, which are distinctly separate from that being done by the prime contractor directly.
2. Different categories of work as distinguished by craft or crew requirements.
3. Different categories of work as distinguished by equipment requirements.
4. Different categories of work as distinguished by materials such as concrete, timber, or steel.
5. Distinct and identifiable subdivisions of structural work such as walls, slabs, beams, and columns.
6. Location of the work within the project that necessitates different times or different crews to perform.
7. Owner's breakdown for bidding or payment purposes.
8. Contractor's breakdown for estimating or cost accounting purposes.
9. Outage schedules or limiting times that existing utility services may be interrupted to construct the project.

    The activities chosen may represent relatively large segments of the project or may be limited to only small steps. For example, a concrete slab may be a single activity or it may be broken into separate steps necessary to construct it, such as: erection of forms, placing of steel, placing of concrete, finishing, curing, and stripping of forms or headers.

    As the separate activities are identified and defined, the sequence relationships between them must be determined. These relationships are referred to as "job logic" and consist of the necessary time and order of construction operations. When the time sequence of activities is being considered, "restraints" must also be considered; these are the practical limitations that can influence the start of certain activities. For example, an activity that involves the placing of reinforcing steel obviously cannot start until the steel is on the site. Therefore, the start of the activity of placing reinforcing steel is "restrained" by the time required to prepare and approve the necessary shop drawings, fabricate the steel, and deliver it to the job. It is quite common to treat restraints much the same as activities and to represent them as such on the network diagram.

FUNDAMENTALS OF CPM

The first step in understanding the CPM is to learn the meaning of the terms used, the symbols involved, and the rules of network scheduling. The following paragraphs are presented to define the principal terms and summarize the most important of the rules for network planning and scheduling.

Activities

After the activities have been identified and their logic established, it is time to construct the job graphically in the form of a network diagram. The basic symbol for an activity is an arrow. It is general practice to think of th arrow as moving from left to right, and that "time" also passes from left to right on the diagram. A basic relationship is that of the event to an arrow or activity. An "event" as distinguished from an activity is the instant of time at which an activity is just starting or finishing. An activity is preceded by an event and followed by an event, in other words it has to have both a starting point and a stopping point. The arrows representing activities are *not* vectors, and their lengths are *not* significant. Also, the arrows can be straight, bent, curved, or whatever shape the user chooses. The real essence of the diagram is the manner in which the activities are joined together into a total operational pattern or network.

Each activity in a network diagram is shown as an arrow, along with a pair of activity numbers for identification. These are referred to as "i–j" designations. In diagram usage, the letter "i" is used as a general symbol to designate the tail or *start* of an activity and the letter "j" is used to designate the head or finish of the activity.

In the activity arrow in Figure 11.1, the activity is "place concrete" and its "i–j" designation is (9–10). As an illustration of some of the activities that might be involved in a "project" to drill a hole 24 inches in diameter by 15 feet deep and fill it with concrete, the activities involved might be as follows:

Approve and sign contract	Locate and lay out the hole
Obtain building permit	Drill hole
Order and deliver drill rig	Place conrete in hole
Order and deliver concrete	Clean up the site

Job Logic

The job logic or time sequence relationships among the various activities involved in the previously mentioned project are the next step to determine. The sequence of operations will be the following:

Activity	Sequence	Symbol	Activity Following
Get signed and approved contract	1.	SC	BP–OD–OC
Get building permit	2	BP	LH
Subcontract for drill rig	2	OD	DH
Subcontract for ready-mix concrete	2	OC	CH
Lay out and accurately locate hole	3	LH	DH
Drill hole	4	DH	PC
Place concrete in hole	5	PC	CS
Clean up the construction site	6	CS	none

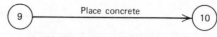

Figure 11.1 *Activity arrow.*

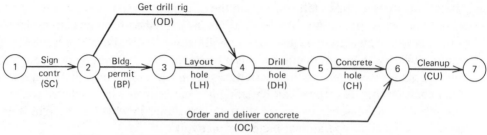

Figure 11.2 *Arrow diagram showing job logic of sample problem.*

In elementary form, this is the type of information that is generated while a project is being "talked through." For the purposes of CPM, job logic requires that each of the activities in the network have a definite *event* to mark its starting point. This event may be either the start of the project or the completion of preceding activities. It is not possible in CPM to have the finish of one activity overlap beyond the start of a succeeding activity. When such a condition appears to present itself, it is a sign that the work must be further subdivided. It is a fundamental rule that *a given activity cannot start until all those activities immediately preceding it have been completed.* Normally, the job logic is not written down. It is only for the purposes of presenting a clear example that a separate tabulation is made here. In practice, the arrow diagram is drawn along with the development of the job operational plan.

In the course of explaining the structure of a CPM diagram sufficiently to enable the resident project representative to read and understand the symbolism involved, a few special symbols and conventions will be covered in the following paragraphs.

Dummy Arrows

Frequently, a dotted or dashed line arrow will be found in a CPM arrow diagram. These are the generally accepted symbols for a "dummy arrow," which is a way of indicating that the completion of one activity restrains the start of two or more other activities. The dummy is nothing more than a slightly awkward way of representing such a dependency.

In Figure 11.3, the dashed arrow (15–16) is an example of a dummy arrow, because the start of (16–20) cannot begin until both (05–15) and(05–16) have been completed, whereas activity (15–20) can begin immediately after (05–15) has been completed, regardless of whether (05–16) has been completed or not. The direction of the arrow indicates the time flow of construction operations and the sequential order cannot back up against a dummy arrowhead.

Another common usage of dummy arrows is to give each activity its own numerical

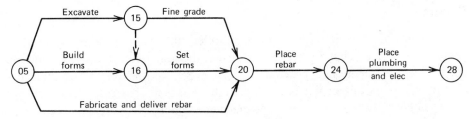

Figure 11.3 Dummy arrows.

"i–j" designation. In Figure 11.4 three activities are shown that are parallel to one another and share a common start and finish point. As indicated in the figure, however, each of the three activities would have to be identified by the same i–j number of (19–25). While this may be no particular hardship if the network was being prepared manually and the diagram was always in front of the user, if the CPM was being computer-generated, there would be no possible way of separating the three activities in the computer, as they would all appear as the same number, thus cancelling one another out.

When a situation is encountered such as that previously illustrated, and they are fairly frequent occurrences, dummy arrows can be utilized as shown in Figure 11.5 so as to allow separate i–j numbers to be assigned to each of the three activities and still show the dependent relationships.

Thus in the preceding figure, the three parallel activities as a result of the dummy arrows could now be identified as activity (20–25), (29–25), and (21–25), which will satisfy the computer requirement that all activities must have separate i–j number identities, while the dashed dummy arrows retain the original relationship of each activity to the others.

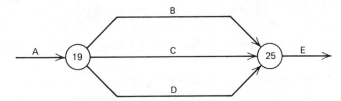

Figure 11.4 Three parallel activities.

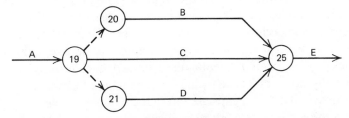

Figure 11.5 Use of dummy arrows to preserve activity identities.

Events

At the ends of each activity arrow are circles (the most common system) or another geometrical figure. These circles are placed at the junction of the arrows and they represent events. As mentioned previously, an "event" is the instant of time at which an activity is just starting or finishing. Although CPM is not basically event oriented, that is, it does not usually emphasize or name the events, but merely refers to them by numbers, if some events are particularly important they may be referred to as "milestone events" and may be specially identified and named on the diagram.

The basic rule applying to any event is that *all* activities leading into an event must be completed before *any* of the activities leading out of the event can be started. This is basic network logic.

Event Numbering

In all CPM diagrams, the events are identified by a number. The number assigned to the starting event is referred to as the *i;* the number assigned to the completion of the event is the *j.* The resulting i–j number can be used as a name for the activity as well as being used as a storage address in the computer storage register. Most CPM diagrams follow two basic rules in numbering of events:

1. Each activity must have its own i–j designation (see Fig. 11.5)
2. When event numbers are assigned, the number at the head of the arrow should be greater than the event number at the tail of the arrow.

Although it is possible for a CPM diagram to be prepared using random numbering, especially where an activity was inserted into an arrow network that was already numbered, if rule 2 were strictly applied, then all numbers in the entire network would have to be renumbered to allow the new activity to have consecutive i–j numbering. In many cases, a CPM network involves thousands of separate activities, and such renumbering would be very impractical. The preferable system of numbering involves the assignment of i–j numbers only after the entire network has been completed and is ready for its first computation.

There are two basic practices used in the assignment of i–j numbers, the horizontal and the vertical methods. In the horizontal method the event numbers are assigned along a line of activities until they meet at a point involving two or more other activities. This is then repeated until all horizontal lines into the junction point have been numbered; then they continue horizontally to the next junction point in the same fashion.

In the vertical numbering method, which is more commonly used, the numberer numbers all events in vertical fashion, moving from top to bottom and from left to right. He still observes the basic rule of keeping the *j* value of each activity greater than its *i* value. There is actually no significance to the event numbers themselves except as a means of identifying an activity. Often gaps are left in the numbering system so that spare numbers are available for subsequent work refinements or revisions. One advantage to the use of

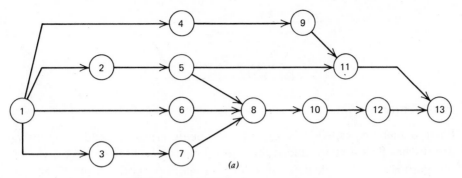

Figure 11.6a Vertical event numbering.

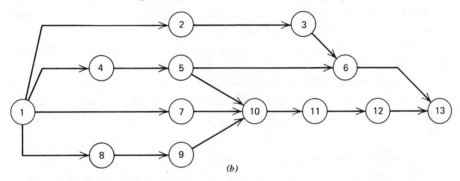

Figure 11.6b Horizontal event numbering.

sequential numbering over that of random numbering of activities is that it is easier to locate events and activities on the network diagram, and it also helps prevent the inclusion of "logical loops," which will be discussed next.

Logical Loops

The "logical loop" is a paradox in network planning. It indicates the requirement that an activity be followed by another activity *that has already been accomplished*. In Figure 11.7, a simple example of a logical loop is shown. The term "logical loop" is a misnomer, since if anything, a logical loop is extremely *illogical*. Although this is perfectly obvious in the simple example illustrated, logical loops can be inadvertently included in large or complex networks without the scheduler realizing that they are there. Because such loops are representative of impossible conditions, the network planner will take precautions to try to prevent their inclusion. The use of a random i–j numbering system allows a greater likelihood of error by allowing logical loops to remain undiscovered, as a computer printout cannot indicate any clues as to its presence under such conditions. It is wise to study the network diagram carefully at the beginning of the job to confirm the logic of its structure.

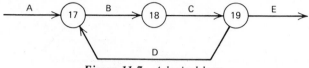

Figure 11.7   A logical loop.

Float Time

Float, sometimes called "slack," can best be described as scheduling leeway. When an activity has float time available, this extra time may be used to serve a variety of scheduling purposes. When float is available, the earliest starting time of an activity can be delayed, its duration extended, or a combination of both can occur. To do a proper job of monitoring of the schedules for noncritical items, the resident inspector should understand the working of float times on a project.

Arithmetically, float time is easy to compute, as it is simply the difference between the early and late dates for an activity. It represents the available time between the earliest time in which an activity can be accomplished (based upon the status of the project to date) and the latest time by which it must be completed for the project to finish by its deadline. There are three important timing facts that can be determined from a CPM network:

1. The earliest time an activity can start and finish.
2. The latest time an activity can start and finish without delaying the project completion.
3. The amount of leeway available in scheduling an item.

There are two types of float time: "free float" and "total float." *Free float* is defined as the amount of time that any activity can be delayed without adversely affecting the *early start of the following activity*. In other words, free float is the least difference between the early finish of an activity and the early start of all following activities. *Total float* is defined as the amount of time that an activity can be delayed without adversely affecting the *overall time for the project completion*. It should be clearly understood that just because an activity has a certain amount of *total float* does not necessarily mean that that activity can use it all without creating tighter scheduling restraints on all of the other activities. It must be remembered that *total float* is shared with all other activities. Free float, on the other hand, is not shared with other activities; thus, it provides a true measure of how much an activity can be delayed or extended without adversely affecting any other activity. In the accompanying illustration in Figure 11.8, an arrow diagram is used to

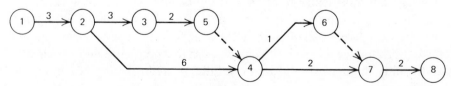

Figure 11.8   Arrow diagram for CPM network.

show a CPM network involving seven different activities. The i–j numbers are shown in the circles and the numbers on the arrows represent the time required to complete each activity in days.

In order to illustrate float time, the arrow diagram in Figure 11.8 is time-scaled and shown in bar schedule form in Figure 11.9. Each activity is shown on the chart twice; once plotted for early start and finish (the white bar), and once plotted for late start and finish (the shaded bar). Free float for activities (3–5) and (4–6) is indicated by the times (3–5)F and (4–6)F in the time-scaled chart. Activity (2–3), on the other hand, has no free float because the early start of (3–5) is actually the same as the early finish of (2–3).

Total float is shown on the chart as (2–3)T, (3–5)T, and (4–6)T. In the example shown, if (2–3) is delayed up to the amount of (2–3)T, it will delay the start of (3–5) but will not change the completion time for the project. Similarly, if (3–5) starts on time but is not completed on time, its completion may be delayed as much as (3–5)T without holding up the completion of the project.

It is important to note that the total float shown on the time-scaled chart is equal for both (2–3) and (3–5). However, if (2–3) falls behind schedule, it actually uses up some of the total float time that is shared by all activities in the line 1–2–4.

If a series of activities are on the "critical path" of the project, then no float exists; the early and late dates are the same. Sometimes, when a project is behind schedule, the earliest time at which an activity can begin is after the latest time it can be done to remain on schedule. Then, not only does no float exist, but the difference between the early and

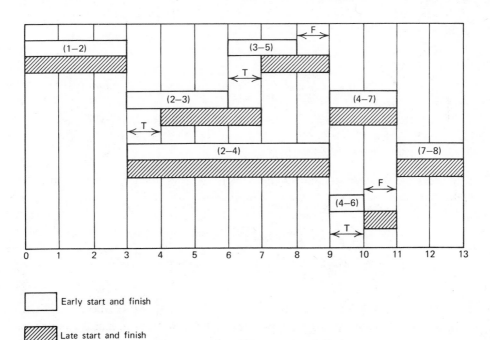

Early start and finish

Late start and finish

Figure 11.9 Time-scaled chart showing comparison of early versus late start and finish.

late dates is less than zero (therefore negative), and is now a measure of how far behind schedule the project is.

PRECEDENCE OR NODE DIAGRAMMING

Another method of network diagramming is called "node" notation, or precedence diagramming. In this method, the nodes (boxes) represent the activities instead of arrows, and the arrows between the nodes simply indicate the logic dependencies among the activities. However, other than the difference in the way in which the diagram is drawn, the workings of an arrow diagram and a node diagram are essentially identical. Nodes may be represented either as circles or boxes. However, rectangles are better suited for the entry of activity identification and time information than circles; hence they become more frequently used.

When precedence diagramming is used, the length and direction of the arrows have no significance because they only indicate dependency of one activity upon another. Furthermore, node diagramming eliminates the need for dummy activities, although in one sense all of the arrows in a node diagram could be considered as dummies because they are all of zero time duration. When using node notation the arrowheads are not really necessary and frequently are not even used on such diagrams. For the purposes of clarity, however, the arrows shown in this text will have arrowheads.

Although it has been said that the job logic is precisely the same, the two methods of drawing networks produce diagrams that are quite different in appearance. In a precedence diagram, the arrow shown in Figure 11.10(a) would be represented by the rectangular block shown in Figure 11.10(b):

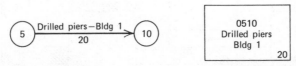

Figure 11.10 (a) Arrow activity ←6 → (b) Precendence network activity.

When two activities are shown in series in the traditional arrow diagram method, they appear as shown below:

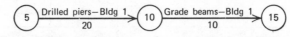

Figure 11.11 Arrow notation of two activities in series.

The "j" node of the first activity becomes the "i" node of the second activity. The computer relies on this basic principle, and it is for this reason that the node identification must be numeric. Sometimes a dummy must be used, as when the completion of an activity restrains the start of two more activities:

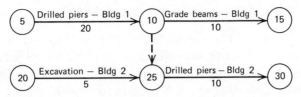

Figure 11.12 *Arrow diagram of four activities with dummy arrow to show dependency.*

In precedence diagramming, however, the two activities shown in series in Figure 11.11 would be shown as follows:

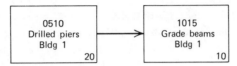

Figure 11.13 *Node notation of two activities in series.*

The line between the two rectangles indicates the relationship between them; in a way it is a sort of "dummy" arrow. However, explicit dummy activities are not required. In the example of the four activities shown in Figure 11.12, a precedence diagram version of the same activities and dependencies would appear as shown in Figure 11.14, following:

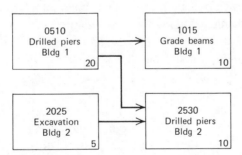

Figure 11.14 *Node notation of four activities with a restraint.*

The analogy is apparent. If processed on a computer, the output would be identical, except that the i–j printout would contain one dummy, the precedence diagram would contain no dummy. However, the printout of the precedence diagram would have to contain a supplementary list of relationships in order for the user to determine and maintain the logic in the computer memory. With some computer programs, this supplementary list can be quite awkward to use.

COMPARISON OF NODE AND ARROW DIAGRAMMING

It is generally felt that node diagramming, otherwise known as "precedence diagramming," is easier to learn and understand by field personnel than arrow diagramming. Learning the significance and proper usage of dummies requires time and experience, and false dependencies are a real hazard. It is also easier to modify and correct a node diagram than an arrow diagram.

Arrow notations have some advantages, however. Most of the computer programs in current usage have been written for arrow diagrams and will not accept node notation. There are no events in node diagrams, which makes it impossible to use "milestones" and to interface events between networks. Those who are familiar with bar charts will find arrow diagrams to be more meaningful and easier to associate with the time flow of job activities.

The adoption of one diagramming method over another is simply a matter of choice. Node diagramming has found considerable favor in many quarters and its usage seems to be increasing.

READING A MANUAL CPM NETWORK SCHEDULE

As the use of arrow diagramming is probably more frequently utilized, the emphasis in this book will be placed upon the reading of CPM arrow diagrams and the associated tabular data. The term "critical path," of course, refers to that portion or portions of the work that are the bottlenecks in the construction process. Obviously, the total project cannot be completed earlier than those portions of the work that require the most time to complete. On complex schedules it is impossible to determine by examination of the network diagram which paths represent the critical path—thus computers have come into the picture. In this manner, all possible combinations of tasks and activity times, early and late starts and finish dates, and float times can be analyzed by the computer until all of the key times can be determined from the computer printout. In addition, the computer determines the critical path or paths, as the case may be, and any overruns in time along the critical path will result in a schedule overrun.

If performed manually, CPM does not have the benefit of tabular printouts, which give key time data; thus, the user must rely upon observation of the diagram itself. Although on a very simple arrow diagram it may be possible to determine the critical path, it is normally necessary to construct a time-scaled network from the arrow diagram before any true scheduling can be determined. The arrow diagram of Figure 11.16 simply shows the logical relationships between the various project activities:

Before time-scaling the arrow diagram in Figure 11.16, observe the effect of adding activity times from 1–3–6–8–13–16–17–18. Activity "B" (1–3) has a time of 7 days; activity "F" (3–6) has an activity time of 4 days; activity "L" (6–8) has an activity time of 8 days; activity "M" (8–13) has a time of 10 days; activity "U" (13–16) has a time of 10 days; activity "X" (16–17) has a time of 4 days; and activity "Y" (17–18) has a time of 4 days. Added together they total 47 days. Compare this with the path through

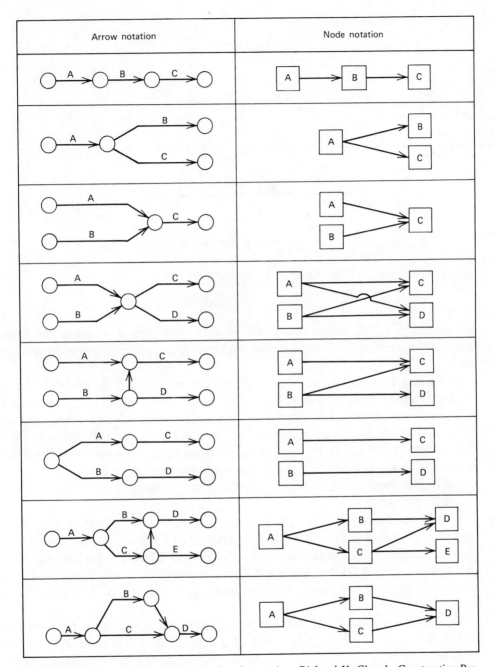

Figure 11.15 *Comparison of arrow and node notation. Richard H. Clough,* Construction Project Management, *John Wiley & Sons, Inc. New York, N.Y., 1972.*

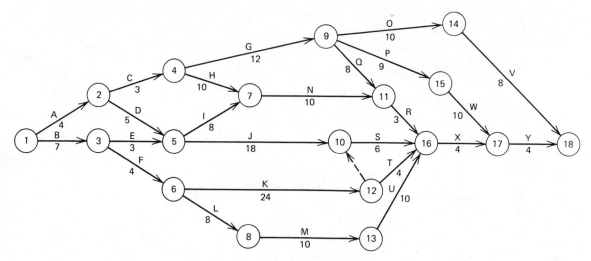

Figure 11.16   *Arrow diagram problem.*

1–3–6–12–16–17–18, which also totals 47 days. From this it might at first appear that both paths are critical, and that the minimum time to complete the project was 47 working days.

By plotting each activity on a time-scale chart (Figure 11.17) and adjusting the start and finish times to be compatible with the logic expressed in the arrow diagram, it can be seen that some motable limitations come into view. The chart is based upon early start and finish dates with float time indicated by the wavy lines. The numbers in the circles represent the i–j numbers for the activities, based upon early start and late finish. The number in brackets is the "j" value for early finish of each activity if there is slack present. The numbers over the bars represent the amount of time required in days to complete the activity.

First of all, the path of 1–2–5 would appear from the arrow diagram to be simply the sum of activity times of "A" and "D," which totals 9 days. Yet, it should be noted that path 1–3–5 adds up to 7 days plus 3 days, or a total of 10 days to get from the same event No. 1 to event No. 5. Thus, the controlling time to reach event No. 5 is of course 10 days, not 7 as it might at first appear, and obviously path 1–3–5 then includes 1 day of float time.

By careful inspection of the time-scale network it can now be seen that path 1–3–6–8–13–16–17–18 contains a total of 2 days of total float time. By continuing the inspection of the arrow diagram and the time-scaled chart it can be further noted that the path through activities "B," "E," and "J" (1–3–5–10) cannot proceed past event No. 10 until the completion of activity "K" (6–12), as indicated by the dummy arrow. Therefore, event No. 10 must be delayed until the completion of event No. 12. (On the time-scaled chart they are equivalent to being completed on the same day.)

It should be noted that the path from event Nos. 10 to 16 is a total of 6 days in contrast

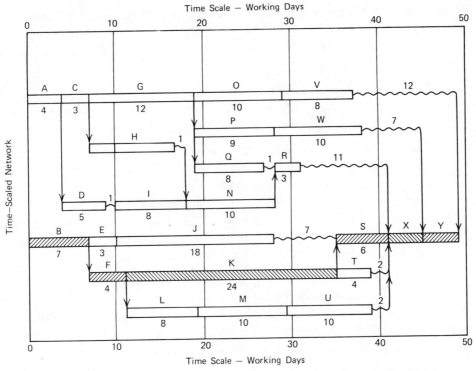

Figure 11.17 *Time-scaled chart of arrow diagram problem shown in Fig. 11.16.*

to the 4 days required from event Nos. 12 to 16. Also, since both events are held up until the completion of activity "K" (event No. 12), the new path becomes:

$$(1–3–6–12–10–16–17–18)$$

The new path then follows through activities B–F–K–dummy–S–X–Y, which totals:

$$7 + 4 + 24 + 6 + 4 + 4 = 49 \text{ days}$$

not the 47 days at first supposed!

It now appears that in comparison with the other paths analyzed, the above is the critical path for this sample project, as all of the other paths contain float time.

Many of the questions that arise in construction involve the establishment of early and late start and finish dates for each activity. These dates represent the earliest or latest that any event can be started or finished without changing the critical path of the project. Any change in the starting time of any event on the critical path must result in a change in the completion date of the project. Thus, if activity "F" (3–6) started 3 days late, the time required to complete the project would be 52 days because activity "F" is on the critical path. On the other hand, if event No. 11 started 10 days late, the completion date of the project would probably not be affected, as it has 11 days of free float time following it on the time-scale chart. Note, however, that the early start date for activity "R" cannot change because it is contingent upon the completion of activities "I" and "N," which allow no time variations.

Other questions may be asked, such as: Before Activity "R" can begin, what other activities must be completed?

Working back from event No. 11 on the arrow diagram of Figure 11.16, it can be seen that both activities "N" and "Q" must be completed first, plus all the activities that must necessarily precede activities "N" and "Q," as outlined below:

1. Working back from event No. 11, note that "N" and "Q" must be done.
2. Then, back from event No. 9, only activity "G" must be done.
3. Back from event No. 7, both activities "H" and "I" must be completed.
4. From event No. 4, only activity "C" must be done.
5. Back from event No. 5, both activities "D" and "E" must be completed.
6. Back from event No. 3, only activity "B" must be done.
7. Finally, back from event No. 2, only activity "A" must be done.

Do not overlook the significance of the dummy arrow, however. It should be noted that before any work can proceed beyond event No. 10, it is required that activity "K" must be completed. In order to proceed beyond event No. 10, not only must activities "E" and "J" be completed, but because of the dependency upon completing activity "K," all three activities "B," "F," and "K" must be completed before activity "S" can start.

Float Time in the Sample Problem

As stated before, the float of an activity represents the potential scheduling leeway. When an activity has float time available, this extra time may be utilized to serve a variety of scheduling purposes. When total float is available, the earliest start of an activity can be delayed, its duration extended, or a combination of both can occur as long as the late finish time is not exceeded. To do a proper job of scheduling of noncritical activities, it is important that the user understand the workings of float or "slack" time.

As mentioned previously, the total float of an activity is the maximum time that its actual completion can go beyond its earliest finish time and not delay the entire project. It is the time leeway that is available for that activity if the activities preceding it are started as early as possible and the ones following it are started as late as possible. If all of the available total float is used on one activity, a new critical path is created. The free float of an activity is the maximum time by which its actual completion date can exceed its earliest finish time without affecting either the overall project completion or the times of any subsequent activities. If an operation is delayed to the extent of an activity's free float, the activities following it are not affected, and they can still start at their earliest start times.

Thus, in the illustration in Figures 11.16 and 11.17, the total float of the activity "T" (12–16) would be as follows:

Critical path from event No. 12 to event No. 16 is:

12(10) to 16 = 6 days time

Completion time for activity "T" is 4 days

Total float time is $(6 - 4)$ days $= 2$days

Early start time for activity "T" (from event Nos. 12 to 16):

Path 1–3–6–12, which totals 35 days

Late start for activity "T" would be:

Path 1–3–6–12 plus float time for activity
"T" $= (35 + 2) = 37$ days

Thus, as long as the time required to complete activity "T" does not exceed $(4 + 2) = 6$ days, the critical path time will not change. As soon as activity "T" goes to 7 or more days, the time to complete the work will change. Similarly, if such would occur on a noncritical path and cause that total path to exceed the original critical path, then a new critical path is created.

The danger is that if one activity uses all of the total float, it is gone for good. From then on the contractor is on critical path.

A good example can be seen by considering two sequential activities, such as placing conduit for a concrete pour and actually making the pour. Assume that these activities are not on the critical path, and that the difference between the early and the late dates is a total of 10 days. Assuming that no other activities will have any effect on the two mentioned, how much total float does the "conduit" activity have? The answer, of course, is 10 days—the difference between the early and late start or the early and late finish. Now, how much total float does the "pour" activity have? The answer to that, too, is 10 days, computed in the same manner. Then, how much total float does the entire sequence of activities have—20 days? NO, because total float cannot be added; the sequence or chain of activities still has only 10 days.

What if the electrician is 3 days late in starting? As of the time he starts, he only has 7 days of total float. The general contractor has also been reduced to 7 days of total float. What if the electrician finishes 7 days late? Now the general contractor has *no* float—he is on critical path.

The point is that individual activities do not really have total float individually. Chains of activities have total float, and all of the activities in the chain share the same total float time. If one activity uses it up, it is gone for good and is no longer available for the other activities.

READING A COMPUTERIZED CPM NETWORK SCHEDULE

By far the majority of the cases of CPM scheduling that will be encountered by the resident project representative will involve the use of computer-generated scheduling data. Two type of documents will normally be made available to the resident project representative: the arrow diagram and the computer printout of the various types of scheduling data required by the contractor.

Although the majority of the printouts will include contractor cost data as well as time scheduling data, the inspector will probably be interested in the time scheduling data alone. Each of the jobs is run through the computer and the data recomputed on a regular basis so that all information is up to date. Of particular concern might be the redistribution of slack times if portions of total slack have been used by certian individual activities. The usual groups of data are sorted and arranged into separate lists, and all such separate lists or "sorts" are printed out separately.

As an example, a CPM schedule prepared for the NASA Orbiter Mating Device built at the Dryden Flight Research Center in California for the John F. Kennedy Space Center in Florida provided printouts of the following types of data grouped into separate printouts:

1. Bar chart by early starts (dummies and finished activities omitted)
2. Sort by total slack/late start dates
3. Sort by activity numbers
4. Cost by activity numbers
5. Schedule of anticipated earnings

In the example of the bar chart in Figure 11.18, it can be seen how the computer can even be used to produce a bar chart from the network analysis data, thus providing the user with several types of statistical data for use in his scheduling operation. In the "sort by activity numbers" shown in Figure 11.19, the user is provided with all of the activities arranged in numerical order, based upon the i–j numbers assigned to each activity. If random numbering of activities were used, this would be a cumbersome and almost meaningless document to use—thus one more example of the importance of providing sequential numbering of all activities. Especially valuable would be the use of interrupted numbering so as to allow for late inclusions without destroying the effectiveness of the sequential system. It should be kept in mind, however, that under such a system, the printout would be in numerical order, but not necessarily consecutive numbering as the allowances for future number additions will not show up in the printout.

In the "sort-by-slack" type printouts, the activities are all arranged in the numerical order of the amount of total slack available for each activity. The order is based upon listing the activities with the most slack first, then in decreasing order. In addition to the total slack, the amount of free slack is also listed along with early and late start and finish dates for each activity. The first two columns at the left show the i–j node numbers for the activities listed, followed by a verbal description of each activity.

The sort-by-slack printout shown in Figure 11.20 is significant in that some of the activities show negative slack, a sign that the activity is behind schedule. The amount of float indicated is then negative (see right-hand column) and shows how far behind schedule the various activities of the project actually are. Note, too, the effect on the printed out schedule dates for the activities that are shown negative—the computer subtracts the calendar dates because of the negative sign and the early start dates appear later than the late start dates.

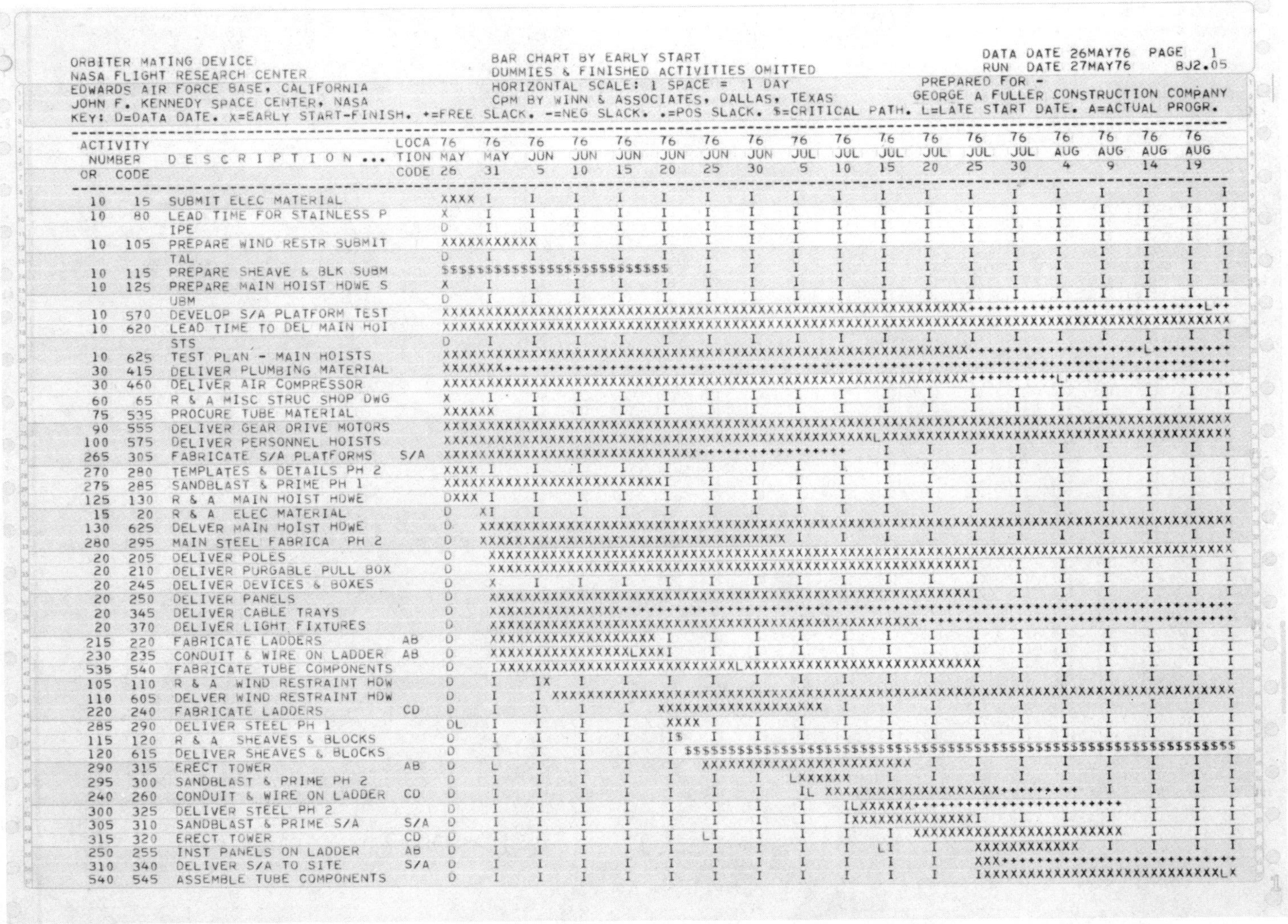

Figure 11.18 Computer printout of bar chart by early starts. CPM by Winn & Associates, Dallas. Contractor: George A. Fuller Construction Company, Dallas. Owner: John F. Kennedy Space Center, Florida.

I NODE	J NODE	DESCRIPTION	LOCATION CODE	RESP CODE	BID ITEM	DURATION	EST REM	PCT COMP	ACTUAL START	ACTUAL FINISH	EARLY START	EARLY FINISH	LATE START	LATE FINISH	FREE SLA	TOT SLA
20	210	DELIVER PURGABLE PULL BOX		ELEC		55	55	0			31MAY76	25JUL76	20MAY76	14JUL76	0	-11
20	250	DELIVER PANELS		ELEC		55	55	0			31MAY76	25JUL76	20MAY76	14JUL76	0	-11
210	250	DUMMY									25JUL76	25JUL76	14JUL76	14JUL76	0	-11
250	255	INST PANELS ON LADDER	AB	ELEC		12	12	0			25JUL76	6AUG76	14JUL76	26JUL76	0	-11
255	260	DUMMY						0			6AUG76	6AUG76	26JUL76	26JUL76	0	-11
260	375	INST PANELS ON LADDER	CO	ELEC		12	12	0			6AUG76	18AUG76	26JUL76	7AUG76	13	-11
260	205	DELIVER POLES		ELEC		106	106	0			31MAY76	14SEP76	21MAY76	4SEP76	0	-10
205	995	INSTALL POLES & LIGHTS	SITE	ELEC		60	60	0			14SEP76	13NOV76	4SEP76	3NOV76	42	-10
365	370	DUMMY						0			12OCT76	12OCT76	4OCT76	4OCT76	0	-8
370	405	INSTALL LIGHT FIXTURES	ABCD	ELEC		20	20	0			12OCT76	1NOV76	4OCT76	24OCT76	12	-8
10	105	PREPARE WIND RESTR SUBMITTAL				73	11	85	11DEC75			6JUN76		30MAY76	0	-7
105	110	R & A WIND RESTRAINT HDW		NASA		7	11	80	26APR76			7JUN76		31MAY76	0	-7
110	605	DELVER WIND RESTRAINT HDW		GENR		150	135	10	13MAY76			20OCT76		13OCT76	13	-7
385	480	DUMMY				0	0	0			12OCT76	12OCT76	6OCT76	6OCT76	0	-6
365	475	DUMMY				0	0	0			12OCT76	12OCT76	6OCT76	6OCT76	0	-6
475	485	PURGE AIR SYSTEM	AB	MECH		14	14	0			12OCT76	26OCT76	6OCT76	20OCT76	0	-6
480	485	PURGE AIR SYSTEM	CD	MECH		14	14	0			12OCT76	26OCT76	6OCT76	20OCT76	0	-6
485	490	PURGE AIR SYSTEM	CL	MECH		7	7	0			26OCT76	2NOV76	20OCT76	27OCT76	0	-6
490	995	TEST PURGE AIR SYSTEM		MECH		7	7	0			2NOV76	9NOV76	27OCT76	3NOV76	46	-6
215	220	FABRICATE LADDERS	AB	ELEC		20	19	5	3MAY76			19JUN76		17JUN76	0	-2
220	240	FABRICATE LADDERS	CD	ELEC		20	19	5	3MAY76			8JUL76		6JUL76	0	-2
240	260	CONDUIT & WIRE ON LADDER	CD	ELEC		20	20	0			8JUL76	28JUL76	6JUL76	26JUL76	9	-2
270	280	TEMPLATES & DETAILS PH 2		FABR		10	4	65	5APR76			30MAY76		30MAY76	0	0
280	295	MAIN STEEL FABRICA PH 2		FABR		35	35	1	24MAY76			4JUL76		4JUL76	0	0
295	300	SANDBLAST & PRIME PH 2		FABR		7	7	0			4JUL76	11JUL76	4JUL76	11JUL76	24	0
300	325	DELIVER STEEL PH 2		FABR		7	7	0			11JUL76	18JUL76	11JUL76	18JUL76	25	0
255	355					7	7	0			6AUG76		7AUG76				1
60	65	R & A MISC STRUC SHOP DWG		NASA		7	1	98	26JAN76			27MAY76		30MAY76	0	3
385	465	DUMMY				3	3	0			12OCT76	17OCT76	17OCT76	20OCT76	0	5
465	470	TEST AIR COMPRESSOR		MECH		3	3	0			12OCT76	15OCT76	17OCT76	20OCT76	0	5
520	995	TEST SHOP AIR SYSTEM		MECH		14	14	0			15OCT76	29OCT76	20OCT76	3NOV76	57	5
335	615	DUMMY				0	0	0			31AUG76	31AUG76	8SEP76	8SEP76	60	8
365	530	DUMMY				0	0	0			12OCT76	12OCT76	24OCT76	24OCT76	0	12
385	530	DUMMY				0	0	0			12OCT76	12OCT76	24OCT76	24OCT76	0	12
530	995	TEST ELECTRICAL SYSTEMS		ELEC		10	10	0			12OCT76	22OCT76	24OCT76	3NOV76	64	12
470	490	DUMMY									15OCT76	15OCT76	27OCT76	27OCT76	18	12
285	295	DUMMY									20JUN76	20JUN76	4JUL76	4JUL76	14	14
225	230	DUMMY									31MAY76	31MAY76	16JUN76	16JUN76	16	16
230	235	CONDUIT & WIRE ON LADDER	AB	ELEC		20	20	0			31MAY76	20JUN76	16JUN76	6JUL76	0	16
235	240	DUMMY						0			20JUN76	20JUN76	6JUL76	6JUL76	18	16
335	465	PAINT AND CAULK STRUCTURE		PAIN		30	30	0			31AUG76	30SEP76	17SEP76	17OCT76	12	17
10	620P	LEAD TIME TO DEL MAIN HOISTS		NASA		274	107	39	11DEC75			10SEP76		29SEP76	71	19
335	415	DUMMY				0	0	0			31AUG76	31AUG76	19SEP76	19SEP76	0	19
415	425	DRAINS	AB	MECH		21	21	0			31AUG76	21SEP76	19SEP76	10OCT76	0	19
415	445	POTABLE WATER PIPING	CD	MECH		21	21	0			31AUG76	21SEP76	19SEP76	10OCT76	0	19
415	440	DRAINS	CD	MECH		21	21	0			31AUG76	21SEP76	19SEP76	10OCT76	0	19
415	435	FIRE WATER PIPING	CD	MECH		21	21	0			31AUG76	21SEP76	19SEP76	10OCT76	0	19
415	420	FIRE WATER PIPING	AB	MECH		21	21	0			31AUG76	21SEP76	19SEP76	10OCT76	0	19
415	430	POTABLE WATER PIPING	AB	MECH		21	21	0			31AUG76	21SEP76	19SEP76	10OCT76	0	19
420	445	DUMMY				0	0				21SEP76	21SEP76	10OCT76	10OCT76	0	19
420	430	DUMMY				0	0				21SEP76	21SEP76	10OCT76	10OCT76	0	19
435	445	DUMMY				0	0				21SEP76	21SEP76	10OCT76	10OCT76	0	19
425	430	DUMMY				0	0				21SEP76	21SEP76	10OCT76	10OCT76	0	19

Figure 11.19 CPM sort by activity numbers. CPM by Winn & Associates, Dallas. Contractor: George A. Fuller Construction Company, Dallas. Owner: John F. Kennedy Space Center, Florida.

ORBITER MATING DEVICE
NASA FLIGHT RESEARCH CENTER
EDWARDS AIR FORCE BASE, CALIFORNIA
JOHN F. KENNEDY SPACE CENTER, NASA

SORT BY ACTIVITY NUMBERS
ALL ACTIVITIES INCLUDED
CONTRACT NUMBER NAS10-8921
CPM BY WINN & ASSOCIATES, DALLAS, TEXAS

DATA DATE 26MAY76   PAGE 1
RUN DATE 27MAY76   BF L1.53
PREPARED FOR -
GEORGE A. FULLER CONSTRUCTION COMPAN

RECEIVED JUN 1 1976 FLIGHT RESEARCH CENTER KSC-GRO

I NODE	J NODE	DESCRIPTION	LOCATION CODE	RESP CODE	BID ITEM	DUR EST	REM	PCT COMP	ACTUAL START	ACTUAL FINISH	EARLY START	LATE START	EARLY FINISH	LATE FINISH	FREE SLA	TOT SLA
5	10	NOTICE TO PROCEED FULL184				0	0	100	11DEC75	11DEC75						
5	902	DUMMY				0	0	100	26APR76	26APR76						
5	903	DUMMY				0	0	100	26APR76	26APR76						
5	904	DUMMY				0	0	100	26APR76	26APR76						
5	905	DUMMY				0	0	100	26APR76	26APR76						
5	906	DUMMY				0	0	100	26MAY76	26MAY76						
10	15	SUBMIT ELEC MATERIAL		ELEC		73	4	95	11DEC75				30MAY76	19MAY76	0	-11
10	25	SUBMIT PLUMBING MATERIAL		MECH		73	0	100	23FEB76	14APR76						
10	35	SUBMIT FRAMING PLANS		FABR		46	0	100	26JAN76	23MAR76						
10	40	SUMIT MAIN STEEL SHOP DWG		FABR		73	0	100	26JAN76	24MAR76						
10	50	SUBMIT S/A PLATFORM S D		FABR		46	0	100	26JAN76	23FEB76						
10	70	SUBMIT TELESCOPING TUBES		TUBE		73	0	100	23FEB76	23FEB76						
10	80P	LEAD TIME FOR STAINLESS PIPE		NASA		110	1	1	11DEC75				27MAY76	60CT76	0	132
10	85	PREPARE GEAR DRIVE SUBMITTAL				73	0	100	11DEC75	1APR76						
10	95	SUBMIT PERSONNEL HOISTS				73	0	100	27FEB76	27FEB76						
10	105	PREPARE WIND RESTR SUBMITTAL				73	11	85	11DEC75				6JUN76	30MAY76	0	-7
10	115	PREPARE SHEAVE & BLK SUBM				73	26	65	11DEC75				21JUN76	30APR76	0	-52
10	125P	PREPARE MAIN HOIST HDWE SUBM				73	1	1	11DEC75				27MAY76	13MAY76	0	-14
10	265	PICK-UP GFE STEEL		FABR		20	0	100	15DEC75	22DEC75						
10	290	MOBILIZE				30	0	100	7APR76	3MAY76						
10	570	DEVELOP S/A PLATFORM TEST		FABR		50	60	0			26MAY76	21AUG76	25JUL76	200CT76	111	87
10	620P	LEAD TIME TO DEL MAIN HOISTS		NASA		274	107	39	11DEC75				10SEP76	29SEP76	71	19
10	625	TEST PLAN - MAIN HOISTS				60	60	0			26MAY76	14AUG76	25JUL76	130CT76	132	80
15	20	R & A ELEC MATERIAL		ELEC		106	1	90	24MAR76				31MAY76	20MAY76	0	-11
20	205	DELIVER POLES		ELEC		106	106	0			31MAY76	21MAY76	14SEP76	4SEP76	0	-10
20	210	DELIVER PURGABLE PULL BOX		ELEC		55	55	0			31MAY76	20MAY76	25JUL76	14JUL76	0	-11
20	215	DELIVER UNISTRUT		ELEC		7	0	100	3MAY76	10MAY76						
20	225	DELIVER CONDUIT		ELEC		7	0	100	3MAY76	10MAY76						
20	230	DELIVER WIRE		ELEC		7	0	100	3MAY76	10MAY76						
20	235	DELIVER DEVICES & BOXES		ELEC		7	1	90					1JUN76	14JUL76	0	43
20	250	DELIVER PANELS		ELEC		55	55	0				20MAY76	25JUL76	14JUL76	77	101
20	345	DELIVER CABLE TRAYS		ELEC		15	15	0				9SEP76	24SEP76		85	77
20	370	DELIVER LIGHT FIXTURES		ELEC		76	49	35			31MAY76	19JUL76		40CT76		
25	30	R & A PLUMBING MATERIAL		NASA		7	7	0				2JUN76	19SEP76		90	109
30	415	DELIVER PLUMBING MATERIAL		MECH		7	7	5	3MAY76	10MAY76						
30	460	DELIVER AIR COMPRESSOR		MECH		60	60	0			26MAY76	4AUG76	25JUL76	30CT76	37	70
35	45	R & A FRAMING PLANS		NASA		7	0	100	26JAN76	25MAY76						
40	45	R & A MAIN STEEL SHOP DWG		NASA		7	0	100	26JAN76	25MAY76						
45	270	TEMPLATES & DETAILS PH 1		FABR		15	0	100	9FEB76	24MAR76						
50	55	R & A S/A PLATFORM S D		NASA		7	0	100	26JAN76	9FEB76						
50	60	MISC STRUCTURAL SHOP DWGS		FABR		27	0	100	9FEB76	15MAR76						
55	265	TEMPLATES & DETAILS S1A	S/A	FABR		14	0	100	9FEB76	24MAR76						
55	270	DELIVER MISC STEEL		FABR		5	1	98			27MAY76		30MAY76		0	3
60	65	R & A MISC STRUC SHOP DWG		NASA		7	0	100	26JAN76	24MAY76						
65	280	DELIVER MISC STEEL		FABR		30	1	98	15JAN76	24MAY76						
70	75	R & A TELESCOPING TUBES		NASA		7	0	100	23FEB76	24MAR76						
75	535	PROCURE TUBE MATERIAL		TUBE		60	6	90	23MAR76				1JUN76	28JUN76	0	27
80	475	DUMMY		NASA		0	0	100			27MAY76	60CT76	27MAY76	60CT76	138	132
85	90	R & A GEAR DRIVE MOTORS		NASA		0	0	100			27MAY76	60CT76	27MAY76	60CT76	138	132
90	555	DELIVER GEAR DRIVE MOTORS		GENR		150	150	100	23FEB76	13MAR76	26MAY76	230CT76	6MAY76	230CT76	0	-20

Figure 11.20 CPM sort by total slack/late start dates. CPM by Winn & Associates, Dallas. Contractor: George A. Fuller Construction Company, Dallas. Owner: John F. Kennedy Space Center, Florida.

Texas A&M University Project

The CPM network consisted of one 30 × 42-inch size summary network and three 30 × 42-inch sheets of detailed net for the Animal Industries and Poultry Science Center Amphitheater Building, supplemented by 84 pages of computer printouts covering a single reporting period.

On the detailed network plan shown in Figure 11.21, the critical path is indicated by a heavy broken line. Of particular note on this sheet is the fact that there is more than one critical path during this phase of the work. Thus, if any change occurs to delay the work along *any* of the critical paths, then that one path will become the only critical path unless similar delays would occur along another path that would exceed those of the one just affected.

By observation, note that the node numbering is based upon the horizontal method (see Fig. 11.6), and that the system of diagramming is an arrow diagram with activity-on-arrow notation. The Schedule Reports (computer printouts) are provided for the following data:

(Work Item: Sort by i–j numbers)
(Sort by total float)
(Sort by early start dates)

By observation of each of the computer printouts, it can be seen that the column headings are all identical. The only difference between them is the arrangement of the activities on the sheets. On one, all activities are arranged in numerical order by i–j node numbers; in another they are all arranged in the order of dates of early start of each activity; in another they are all arranged in the order of the amount of float time per activity.

As an example of this, activity 0246–0248, which is included in each of the three sample Schedule Reports shown in Figures 11.22, 11.23, and 11.24, is shown identically on each of the three sheets. In each case, its early start date is 25 Dec 1975 and early finish date is 30 Dec 1975; its late start date is 26 Jan and late finish is 31 Jan 1976; and its total float time is 32 and its free float time is 2. Thus the only difference is the way that the data are arranged on the sheet. The reason for this is to make it easier to use the data. If you wanted all items with a particular start date of the early start dates and all that was available was a list of all activity data arranged in numerical order of their node numbers, it would take a great amount of time to go through all of the data to look for a particular date needed.

Note activity 0254–0256 in Figure 11.22. The total float indicated for this activity is 28 days, yet the amount of free float is zero. This indicates that there is no leeway in the individual schedule for that activity, but any float is the result of slack time somewhere else in the network. By comparison, see activity 0226–0228 in Figure 11.22, which shows that there is no float time of any kind available for this activity. This is an indication that the activity is on the critical path. By locating this activity on the CPM network in Figure 11.21, it can be seen that this is truly the case.

On the schedule report shown in Figure 11.22, an example of the effect of using total

BID ITEM	I	J	DURATION SCD	R/A	AMOUNT SCHED.	EARNED	PER CNT	DESCRIPTION	T/C	SCHED START	ACT FINISH	START EARLY	START LATE	FINISH EARLY	FINISH LATE	FLOAT T/F	F/F
0224	0224	0234	0	0				DUMMY				20NOV75	04DEC75	20NOV75	04DEC75	14	0
0224	0224	0236	7	7				COMP. SECT 2 FORM / LOWER LEVEL				20NOV75	04DEC75	27NOV75	11DEC75	14	0
0226	0226	0228	14	14				SECT 3 START FORM / LOWER LEVEL				27NOV75	27NOV75	11DEC75	11DEC75	0	0
0228	0228	0230	0	0				DUMMY				11DEC75	10JAN76	11DEC75	10JAN76	30	0
0228	0228	0238	7	7				COMP. SECT 3 FORM / LOWER LEVEL				11DEC75	11DEC75	18DEC75	18DEC75	0	0
0230	0230	0232	7	7				START SECT 4 FORM / LOWER LEVEL				11DEC75	10JAN76	18DEC75	17JAN76	30	0
0232	0232	0244	7	7				COMP.SECT 4 FORM / LOWER LEVEL				18DEC75	17JAN76	25DEC75	24JAN76	30	0
0234	0234	0236	7	7				SET PAN #1 / LOWER LEVEL				20NOV75	04DEC75	27NOV75	11DEC75	14	0
0236	0236	0238	7	7				SET PAN #2 / LOWER LEVEL				27NOV75	04DEC75	04DEC75	18DEC75	14	14
0236	0236	0240	5	5				EMBEDS & POUR #1 / LOWER LEVEL				27NOV75	13DEC75	02DEC75	18DEC75	16	16
0238	0238	0240	0	0				DUMMY				18DEC75	18DEC75	18DEC75	18DEC75	0	0
0240	0240	0242	0	0				DUMMY				18DEC75	17JAN76	18DEC75	17JAN76	30	0
0240	0240	0244	5	5				EMBEDS & POUR #2 / LOWER LEVEL				18DEC75	19JAN76	23DEC75	24JAN76	32	2
0240	0240	0252	0	0				DUMMY				18DEC75	15JAN76	18DEC75	15JAN76	28	0
0240	0240	0268	0	0				DUMMY				18DEC75	18DEC75	18DEC75	18DEC75	0	0
0242	0242	0244	7	7				SET PAN #3 / LOWER LEVEL				18DEC75	17JAN76	25DEC75	24JAN76	30	0
0244	0244	0246	0	0				DUMMY				25DEC75	26JAN76	25DEC75	26JAN76	32	0
0244	0244	0248	7	7				SET PAN #4 / LOWER LEVEL				25DEC75	24JAN76	01JAN76	31JAN76	30	0
0246	0246	0248	5	5				EMBEDS & POUR #3 / LOWER LEVEL				25DEC75	26JAN76	30DEC75	31JAN76	32	2
0248	0248	0250	5	5				EMBEDS & POUR #4 / LOWER LEVEL				01JAN76	31JAN76	06JAN76	05FEB76	30	0
0250	0250	0258	0	0				DUMMY				06JAN76	05FEB76	06JAN76	05FEB76	30	2
0252	0252	0254	7	7				SECT #1 FORM & POUR / LOWER LEVEL				18DEC75	15JAN76	25DEC75	22JAN76	28	0
0254	0254	0256	7	7				SECT #2 FORM & POUR / LOWER LEVEL				25DEC75	22JAN76	01JAN76	29JAN76	28	0

Figure 11.22. CPM sort by i-j numbers. CPM by Forward Engineering, Inc., Jacksonville, Florida. Contractor: George A. Fuller Construction Company, Dallas. Owner: Texas A & M University.

BID ITEM I	J	DURATION SCD	R/A	AMOUNT SCHED.	EARNED	PER CNT	T SCD	C ACT	SCHED/ACT START	FINISH	DESCRIPTION	START EARLY	LATE	FINISH EARLY	LATE	FLOAT T/F	F/F
0240	0244	5	5								EMBEDS & POUR #2 LOWER LEVEL	18DEC75	19JAN76	23JAN76	24JAN76	32	2
0244	0242	0	0								DUMMY	25DEC75	26JAN76	25DEC75	26JAN76	32	0
0246	0248	5	5								EMBEDS & POUR #3 LOWER LEVEL	25DEC75	26JAN76	30DEC75	31JAN76	32	2
0764	0768	0	0								DUMMY	10NOV76	12DEC76	10NOV76	12DEC76	32	0
0768	0772	14	14								DRYWALL CEILINGS THIRD FLOOR	10NOV76	12DEC76	24NOV76	26DEC76	32	16
0770	0772	0	0								DUMMY	24NOV76	26DEC76	24NOV76	26DEC76	32	16
0254	0260	0	0								DUMMY	25DEC75	29JAN76	25DEC75	29JAN76	35	0
0256	0262	0	0								DUMMY	01JAN76	05FEB76	01JAN76	05FEB76	35	0
0260	0262	7	7								SECT #1 FORM & POUR LOWER LEVEL	25DEC75	29JAN76	01JAN76	05FEB76	35	0
0262	0264	7	7								FORM & POUR WALLS LOWER LEVEL	01JAN76	05FEB76	08JAN76	12FEB76	35	7
0732	0746	21	21								MISC. FINISHES SECOND FLOOR	1MAR77	24APR77	08APR77	15MAY77	37	0
0742	0744	0	0								DUMMY	01APR77	08MAY77	01APR77	08MAY77	37	0
0742	0746	7	7								ELECT TRIM SECOND FLOOR	01APR77	08MAY77	08APR77	15MAY77	37	0
0744	0746	7	7								GRILLS & REGISTERS SECOND FLOOR	01APR77	08MAY77	08APR77	15MAY77	37	0
0746	0748	7	7								PUNCH OUT SECOND FLOOR	08APR77	15MAY77	15APR77	22MAY77	37	0
0748	0826	0	0								DUMMY	15APR77	22MAY77	15APR77	22MAY77	37	21
0684	0686	0	0								DUMMY	13OCT76	19NOV76	13OCT76	19NOV76	37	0
0686	0692	30	30								FINISH DRYWALL SECOND FLOOR	13OCT76	19NOV76	12NOV76	19DEC76	37	0
0692	0694	0	0								DUMMY	12NOV76	19DEC76	12NOV76	19DEC76	37	0
0694	0696	21	21								ACOUSTICAL FRAMING SECOND FLOOR	12NOV76	19DEC76	03DEC76	09JAN77	37	0
0696	0698	0	0								DUMMY	03DEC76	09JAN77	03DEC76	09JAN77	37	0
0698	0702	21	21								FL.TO CLG.METAL STUD SECOND FLOOR	03DEC76	09JAN77	24DEC76	30JAN77	37	0
0702	0704	14	14								FL.TO CLG.DRYWALL SECOND FLOOR	24DEC76	30JAN77	07JAN77	13FEB77	37	0

Figure 11.23 CPM sort by total float. CPM by Forward Engineering, Inc., Jacksonville, Florida. Contractor: George A. Fuller Construction Company, Dallas. Owner: Texas A & M University.

BID ITEM I	J	DURATION SCD	R/A	AMOUNT SCHED.	EARNED	PFR CNT	DESCRIPTION	T	C	SCHED/ACT START	FINISH	START EARLY	LATE	FINISH EARLY	LATE	FLOAT T/F	F/F
0246	0248	5	5				EMBEDS & POUR #3 / LOWER LEVEL					25DEC75	26DEC75	30DEC75	31JAN76	32	2
0254	0254	7	7				SECT #2 FORM & POUR / LOWER LEVEL					25DEC75	22JAN76	01JAN76	29JAN76	28	0
0254	0260	0	0				DUMMY					25DEC75	29JAN76	25DEC75	29JAN76	35	0
0260	0262	7	7				SECT #1 FORM & POUR / LOWER LEVEL					25DEC75	29JAN76	01JAN76	05FEB76	35	0
0248	0250	5	5				EMBEDS & POUR #4 / LOWER LEVEL					01JAN76	31JAN76	06JAN76	05FEB76	30	0
0256	0258	7	7				SECT #3 FORM & POUR / LOWER LEVEL					01JAN76	29JAN76	08JAN76	05FEB76	28	0
0256	0262	0	0				DUMMY					01JAN76	05FEB76	01JAN76	05FEB76	35	0
0262	0264	7	7				FORM & POUR WALLS / LOWER LEVEL					01JAN76	05FEB76	08JAN76	12FEB76	35	7
0250	0258	0	0				DUMMY					06JAN76	05FEB76	06JAN76	05FEB76	30	2
0258	0264	7	7				SECT #4 FORM & POUR / LOWER LEVEL					08JAN76	05FEB76	15JAN76	12FEB76	28	0
0270	0272	30	30				COMP.FORM EMBEDS / FIRST FLOOR					08JAN76	20JAN76	07FEB76	19FEB76	12	0
0270	0274	0	0				DUMMY					08JAN76	08JAN76	08JAN76	08JAN76	0	0
0270	0284	0	0				DUMMY					08JAN76	08JAN77	08JAN77	08JAN77	366	0
0270	0286	0	0				DUMMY					08JAN76	08APR77	08APR77	08APR77	456	0
0270	0444	0	0				DUMMY					08JAN76	01APR77	08JAN76	01APR77	449	30
0274	0276	21	21				START WALLS & COLS / FIRST FLOOR					08JAN76	08JAN76	29JAN76	29JAN76	0	0
0284	0288	120	120				R/I VACUME ACID WAST / CRAWL SPACE					08JAN76	08JAN77	07MAY76	08MAY77	366	0
0286	0288	30	30				ELECTRICAL R/I / CRAWL SPACE					08APR77	08APR77	07FEB76	08MAY77	456	90
0264	0266	7	7				FORM & POUR WALLS / LOWER LEVEL					15JAN76	12FEB76	22JAN76	19FEB76	28	0
0266	0272	0	0				DUMMY					22JAN76	19FEB76	22JAN76	19FEB76	28	16
0276	0278	0	0				DUMMY					29JAN76	29JAN76	29JAN76	29JAN76	0	0
0276	0280	21	21				COMP.WALLS & COLS / FIRST FLOOR					29JAN76	29JAN76	19FEB76	19FEB76	0	0
0276	0492	0	0				DUMMY					29JAN76	03NOV76	29JAN76	03NOV76	279	0

Figure 11.24 CPM sort by early start dates. CPM by Forward Engineering, Inc., Jacksonville, Florida. Contractor: George A. Fuller Construction Company, Dallas. Owner: Texas A & M University.

Figure 11.25 Page from report by i-j numbers of Kajakai Project. CPM by Winn & Associates, Dallas. Contractor: Fischbach & Moore International.

KAJAKAI HYDROELECTRIC PROJECT   REPORT BY IJ NUMBERS   DATA DATE 30JUN76   PAGE 1
110KV & 44KV TRANSMISSION LINES & SUBS   ALL ACTIVITIES INCLUDED   RUN DATE 22JUL76   8F L1,53
FISCHBACH & MOORE INTERNATIONAL,GC   PREPARED FOR -

CPM BY WINN & ASSOCIATES, DALLAS, TEXAS

I NODE	J NODE	DESCRIPTION	LOCA TION CODE	RESP CODE	BID ITEM	DURATION EST	REM	PCT COMP	ACTUAL START	ACTUAL FINISH	EARLY START	LATE START	EARLY FINISH	LATE FINISH	FREE SLA	TOT SLA
5	10	COMMENCE JOB SITE OPNS				30	0	100	25NOV74	25DEC74						
5	15	LETTER OF CREDIT				30	0	100	25NOV74	25DEC74						
5	20	PREL ORDER PP & FORMS				30	0	100	90DEC74	11DEC74						
5	25	ORDER TOWERS				30	0	100	17DEC74	17DEC74						
5	30	APPLY FOR RADIO FREQUENCY				30	0	100	18FEB75	10MAR75						
5	40	ORDER CONDUCTOR				60	0	100	14JAN75	23APR75						
5	45	ORDER INSULATORS & HDWE				60	0	100	15JAN75	14MAR75						
5	55	ORDER TOWER GRNDNG MATL				75	0	100	15JAN75	17FEB75						
5	65	ARRANGE FOR KANDAHAV FACILITIES				120	0	100	25NOV74	6APR75						
5	70	ORDER POWER TRANSFORMERS				180	0	100	7MAR75	21MAY75						
5	75	ORDER COMM EQUIPMENT				180	0	100	7MAR75	21MAY75						
5	80	ORDER SWITCHYARD EQUIPMENT				180	0	100	7MAR75	21MAY75						
5	81	ORDER SWITCHYARD STRUCT				180	0	100	7MAR75	21MAY75						
5	105	ORDER & DELIVER EXCAV EQUIP				185	0	100	7JAN75	6AUG75						
5	130	AR FOR REHAB & SU LASHKAR GAH FA				180	0	100	15FEB75	30SEP75						
5	135	ORDER & DELIVER CEMENT FOR && FN				180	0	100	15MAR75	20AUG75						
5	175	ORDER & DELIVER TYPE II CEMENT				250	0	100	10DEC74	16JUN75						
5	180	ORDER & DEL POLE & CROSS ARM REB				240	0	100	8JAN75	13AUG75						
5	185	ORD & DEL CROSS ARM FORM & HDWE				270	0	100	6JAN75	30DEC75						
5	220	ORDER & DELIVER MATL FOR SS BLDG				270	0	100	2JUN75	24JAN76						
5	260	ORDER & DELIVER FENCING				240	0	100	11FEB75	5AUG75						
5	295	SET UP KAJAKAI FACILITIES				60	0	100	25NOV74	24JAN75						
5	335	ORDER & DELIVER RIGGING EQUIP				60	0	100	7JAN75	6AUG75						
5	385	ORD & DEL STRNGNG TOOLS & EQUIP				210	0	100	7FEB75	6AUG75						
10	90	APPROVE AGG				150	0	100	25NOV74	30SEP75						
10	135	PREPARE POLE PLANT SITE				180	0	100	6APR75	1MAY75						
10	140	PREP ACCESS & GHDE TWR SITES				180	0	100	15APR75	15OCT75						
15	20	DUMMY				0	0	100	30SEP75	30SEP75						
15	585	REVOLVING FUND				1	1				30JUN76	24MAY77	1JUL76	25MAY77	328	328
20	35	FINALIZE ORDER PP & FORMS				30	0	100	3JAN75	20JAN75						
20	135	DEL ANC BOLTS & IMBEDS PP FDN				150	0	100	26MAY75	26AUG75						
25	50	DESIGN TOWERS				30	0	100	180CT74	10JAN75						
35	335	ORDER PROJ COMM SYST LICENSE				210	0	100	18FEB75	18MAR75						
35	235	DELIVER POLE PLANT				240	0	100	20JAN75	18NOV75						
40	95	APPROVE CONDUCTOR				120	0	100	6MAY75	12NOV75						
45	60	APPROVE INSULATORS & HDWE				40	0	100	31JAN75	9APR75						
50	145	APPROVE TOWER DESIGN				155	0	100	11JAN75	22APR75						
60	295	DELIVER TOWER GROUNDING				225	0	100	19APR75	20OCT75						
65	535	DEL INSULATORS & HDWE				368	0	100	9APR75	10MAY76						
65	85	REHAB & SETUP KANDAHAR FACIL				60	0	100	1JAN75	30SEP75						
70	210	SUBMIT & APPROVE POWER TRANSF				290	0	100	21MAY75	8MAR76						
75	150	SUBMIT COMM EQUIP				177	0	100	9SEP75	14NOV75						
80	155	SUBMIT SWITCHYARD EQUIP				270	27	99	11AUG75		27JUL76	23AUG76			0	27
81	82	SUBMIT + APPR ELEC ARRANGEMENT				182	0	100	21MAY75	19NOV75						
81	170	SUBMIT + APPR SS FOUND PLAN				182	0	100	21MAY75	19NOV75						
82	83	DESIGN SWITCHYARD STRUCT				69	0	100	19NOV75	27FEB76						
83	84	APPROVE STRUCT				30	0	100	16FEB76	29MAR76						
84	365	DEL JUNCTION STRUCTURES				93	19	80	2MAR76		19JUL76	27OCT76			0	100
84	386	DEL KANDAHAR STRUCTURES				140	42	70	18MAR76		11AUG76	22OCT76			0	72
84	405	DEL LASHKAR GAH STRUCTURES				175	70	60	31MAR76		8SEP76	12OCT76			0	34
85	100	GRADE KANDAHAR SUBSTATION				10	0	100	7AUG75	15AUG75						

KAJAKAI HYDROELECTRIC PROJECT
110KV & 44KV TRANSMISSION LINES & SUBS
FISCHBACH & MOORE INTERNATIONAL,GC

REPORT BY TOTAL SLACK
FINISHED ACTIVITIES OMITTED

DATA DATE 30JUN76
RUN DATE 22JUL76
8F L1.53

PREPARED FOR -

CPM BY WINN & ASSOCIATES, DALLAS, TEXAS

I NODE	J NODE	DESCRIPTION	DURATION EST	REM	PCT COMP	ACTUAL START	EARLY START	LATE START	EARLY FINISH	LATE FINISH	FREE SLA	TOT SLA
210	340	MFG & DEL PWR TRANS-KANDAHAR	270	149	45	9MAR76			26NOV76	26NOV76	0	0
340	395	INST. TRANS. - KANDAHAR	60	30	0		26NOV76	26NOV76	26DEC76	26DEC76	0	0
395	400	CONN EQUIP KANDAHAR	60	60	0		26DEC76	26DEC76	24FEB77	24FEB77	0	0
400	580	TEST KANDAHAR	30	30	0		24FEB77	24FEB77	26MAR77	26MAR77	0	0
580	585	SYSTEMS TEST	30	60	0		26MAR77	25MAY77	25MAY77	25MAY77	0	0
585	590	CLEAN UP & MOVE OUT	30	30	0		25MAY77	24JUN77	24JUN77	24JUN77P	0	0
590	9999	DUMMY					24JUN77	24JUN77	24JUN77P	24JUN77P	0	0
80	155	SUBMIT SWITCHYARD EQUIP	270	27	90	11AUG75			23JUL76	30AUG76	0	27
155	165	APPROVE SWITCHYARD EQUIP	30	3	90	13AUG75			30JUL76	26AUG76	0	27
165	395	DEL SWITCHYARD EQUIP	184	92	50	14JAN76			30OCT76	26NOV76	0	27
355	410	DUMMY	0				30OCT76	26NOV76	30OCT76	26NOV76	0	27
355	390	DUMMY	0				30OCT76	26NOV76	30OCT76	26NOV76	0	27
410	415	SET EQUIP. - LASHKAR GAH	30	30	0		30OCT76	26NOV76	29NOV76	28DEC76	27	27
390	395	SET EQUIP. - KANDAHAR	30	30	0		30OCT76	26NOV76	29NOV76	26NOV76	0	27
415	420	CONN EQUIP. - LASHKAR GAH	60	60	0		29NOV76	26DEC76	28JAN77	24FEB77	27	27
420	580	TEST LASHKAR GAH	30	30	0		28JAN77	24FEB77	27FEB77	26MAR77	27	27
210	345	MFG & DEL PWR TRANS-LASHKAR GAH	214	118	45	12JAN76			26OCT76	26DEC76	4	31
345	415	INST. TRANS. - LASHKAR GAH	30	30	0	31MAR76			25NOV76	120CT76	7	34
84	405	DEL LASHKAR GAH STRUCTURES	45	45	0		8SEP76	120CT76	230CT76	26NOV76	0	34
405	410	ERECT LASHKAR GAH STRUCTURES	152	15	90		15JUL76		15JUL76	26NOV76	0	40
95	385	DELIVER CONDUCTOR	14	14		12NOV75			26OCT76	24AUG76	0	40
385	555	TRAIN STRINGING CREWS	62	62	0		29JUL76	24AUG76	7SEP76	7SEP76	0	40
555	570	STRING WIRE ON TOWERS	108	108	0		29JUL76	7SEP76	29SEP76	8NOV76	0	40
570	575	STRING WIRE ON CONC STRUCT 80%	30	30	0		29SEP76	8NOV76	8NOV76	24FEB77	0	40
575	580	STRING WIRE ON CONC STRUCT 100%	168	101	40		15JAN77	24FEB77	15JUL76	26MAR77	40	42
425	515	CONC POLE STRUCTURE TESTS	65	65	0	19MAR76	9OCT76	20NOV76	90CT76	20NOV76	0	42
515	520	ERECT POLES & C.A.'S - 92%	21	21	0		13DEC76	20NOV76	130CT76	24JAN77	0	42
520	556	ERECT POLES & C.A.'S - 100%	10	10	0		3JAN77	24JAN77	24JAN77	14FEB77	2	42
556	575	INST INS & HDWE ON CONC STR 100%	95	57	40	16JUN76		14FEB77	14FEB77	14FEB77	0	42
430	450	DELIVER TYPE I CEMENT - 100%					26AUG76	270CT76	26AUG76	270CT76	0	62
450	455	DUMMY	0				26AUG76	270CT76	25SEP76	26NOV76	0	62
455	460	ERECT JUNCTION STRUCTURES	30	30	0		25SEP76	26NOV76	250CT76	26DEC76	0	62
460	465	SET JUNCTION EQUIPMENT	30	30	0		250CT76	26DEC76	24DEC76	24FEB77	0	62
465	470	CONNECT JUNCTION EQUIPMENT	60	60	0		24DEC76	24FEB77	24FEB77	26MAR77	0	62
470	580	TEST JUNCTION	30	30	0		24FEB77	26MAR77	23JAN77	26MAR77	62	62
84	386	DEL KANDAHAR STRUCTURES	140	42	70	18MAR76			11AUG76	220CT76	45	72
386	390	ERECT KANDAHAR STRUCTURES	35	35	0		11AUG76	220CT76	15SEP76	26NOV76	0	73
370	375	STRUCT. FDN'S KANDAHAR	30	18	40	10NOV75			23JUL76	5SEP76	0	73
375	380	STRUCT. FDN'S JUNCTION	30	8	75	10DEC75			40CT76	120CT76	39	73
380	405	STRUCT. FDN'S LASHKAR GAH	70	67	5	25NOV75			120CT76	24JAN77	42	84
450	520	MFG POLES 100%	93	19	80	29JUN76			24JAN77	270CT76		100
84	365	DEL JUNCTION STRUCTURES	43	43	0	2MAR76			19JUL76	270CT76	58	100
510	515	ERECT POLES & C.A.'S - 67%					30JUN76	8OCT76	12AUG76	2NOV76	38	107
365	455	DUMMY					19JUL76	270CT76	19JUL76	270CT76		107
160	330	DELIVER COMM EQUIP	208	42	80	5DEC75			11AUG76	26NOV76	45	107
350	460	DUMMY	0				11AUG76	26NOV76	11AUG76	26NOV76	80	107
350	355	DUMMY	0				11AUG76	26NOV76	11AUG76	26NOV76	80	107
375	386	DUMMY	0				5JUL76	220CT76	5JUL76	220CT76	37	109
490	495	MFG CROSS ARMS 100%	30	16	47	11JUN76			16JUL76	20NOV76	0	127
495	515	DUMMY	0				16JUL76	20NOV76	16JUL76	20NOV76	85	127
132	515	100% POLE EXCAVATION	90	2	98	26NOV75			2OCT76	20NOV76	99	141

Figure 11.26 Page from report by total slack of Kajakai Project. CPM by Winn & Associates, Dallas. Contractor: Fischbach & Moore International.

float for a given activity can be shown. Activities 0252–0254 and 0254–0256 are consecutive operations, a fact that can be noted both on the printouts as well as on the Detailed Network plan. Each shows zero free float and each shows 28 days of total float. The fact that there are 28 days of total float indicates that each of these activities is not on a critical time schedule, and that by altering the schedules of other activities in the chain, up to 28 days slack can be realized for *either one or the other,* but not both. By description of the activity involved it is evident that one cannot proceed until the other has been completed. The early completion date of 0252–0254 is shown on the schedule as 25 Dec 1975 and the early start date of 0254–0256, which cannot start until the former activity has been completed, is also 25 Dec 1975. Note that 0260–0262 is shown on the network diagram as also being dependent upon the completion of 0252–0254. Thus, any overrun in the completion of this activity would have an immediate effect upon two other activities —thus, the reason for indicating zero free float.

Kajakai Hydroelectric Project

Another example of CPM network scheduling and computer reports is that of the Kajakai Hydroelectric Project, which, unlike the previous example, only shows major activities such as: "Structural Foundations, Kandahar" in which a single activity includes all of the subsidiary tasks that are sometimes scheduled as separate activities on other projects, such as: excavation; build forms; fabricate rebar; erect forms; place rebar; place concrete; etc.

As with all printouts based upon a sorting by i–j node numbers, the order in which the activities appear on the list bears no relationship to either the order of construction or any other real life condition. It is simply an aid to finding an activity by knowing its i–j number. This is quite an aid when, working from the network diagram, you have found the activity on the diagram and you want the computer data on that activity.

Of particular note on the Kajakai project are the number of paths shown on the network sheet as being critical; however, many of them involve the ordering and delivery of large fabricated-to-order turbines and generating and transmission equipment as well as heavy earthmoving equipment. Delays in any such items could easily affect adversely the entire project schedule.

Bibliography

James J. O'Brien, *CPM in Construction Management,* 2nd ed., McGraw-Hill, New York, 1971.

Richard H. Clough, *Construction Project Management,* 1st ed., Wiley, New York, 1972.

Richard H. Clough, *Construction Contracting,* 3rd ed., Wiley, New York, 1975.

F. Thomas Collins, *Network Planning and Critical Path Scheduling,* 1st ed., Know How Publications, Berkeley, California, 1964.

Robert C. McLean, "Construction Planning and Scheduling" from Havers and Stubbs, *Handbook of Heavy Construction,* 2nd ed., McGraw-Hill, New York, 1971.

Network Float—What Is It and Who Owns It?, and *Some Comments on the Precedence Diagramming Technique of Network Analysis Systems,* by Winn & Associates, Dallas, Texas, 1976.

12
CONSTRUCTION
OPERATIONS

ALTHOUGH MOST of the material in this book could be classed as a part of the resident project representative's normal construction operations, separate chapters have been presented to cover material that relates to the more complex functions that are necessary, as well as the more lengthy subjects that require special clarification. Thus, the subject of this chapter is of more general nature. The day-to-day considerations experienced by the resident project representative, along with an understanding of who is responsible for what, are the principal items covered. That is not to imply that the material is unimportant or noncontroversial, as some of the day-to-day activities that must be endured by the resident project representative would challenge the patience of a stone statue.

Following are the paraphrased words of Gene Sheley, editor of *Western Construction* magazine*, who admittedly was not thinking about inspectors when he wrote:

> The resident inspector must be an expert in engineering, architecture, construction methods, labor relations, barroom brawls, public relations, and should have an extensive vocabulary in graphic and colorful construction terms. He must be able to work closely with contractors, subcontractors, engineers, architects, owners, and agree with frequent directives that make no sense from people who know less than he does; he must be able to understand then ignore environmental impact reports and regulations without the Sierra Club finding out, and he must cooperate with construction superintendents and contractor quality control representatives, and avoid backing his automobile into the privy while they are inside.

*Used with permission of Gene Sheley, Editor, *Western Construction*.

The resident inspector must have skin like an alligator, the stomach of a billie goat, the temperament of a Presbyterian minister, nerves of chrome-molybdenum steel, the fortitude of Job, and the physical strength to take care of a situation when all else fails. He should enjoy his job, and will probably love the working conditions, except for the dust, numbing cold, searing heat, knee-deep mud, mosquitos, rattlesnakes, scorpions, muck-covered office trailers, questionable toilet facilities, and physical assault by frustrated foremen.

If you still want to be a resident construction inspector, the job is yours.

AUTHORITY AND RESPONSIBILITY OF ALL PARTIES

The owner as a contracting party has several rights especially reserved for him. Depending upon the type of contract and its specific wording, he may be authorized to award other contracts in connection with the same work; to require contract bonds from the contractor; to approve the surety proposed; to retain a specific portion of the contractor's monthly progress payments; to make changes in the work; to carry out portions of the work himself in case of contractor default or neglect; to withhold payments from the contractor for adequate cause; and to terminate the contract for cause. The right of the owner to inspect the work as it progresses, to direct the contractor to expedite the work, to use completed portions of the work before contract completion, and to make payment deductions for incomplete or faulty work are also common contract provisions.

The contract between the owner and the contractor also imposes some responsibilities on the owner. For example, most construction contracts make the owner responsible for furnishing property surveys that describe or locate the project on the site, for making periodic payments to the contractor, and for making land surveys that establish the boundaries of the property upon which the project is to be located. The owner is also obligated to make extra payment in case of eventualities that were not anticipated in the contract, as well as to allow extensions of time to complete the work for such unanticipated conditions.

It is important to note, however, that the owner cannot intrude into the direction and control of the work. By the terms of the usual construction contract, the contractor is classed as an "independent contractor" and even though the owner has certain rights with respect to the conduct of the work, he cannot issue direct instructions as to methods or procedures unless specifically provided for under the terms of the contract. The owner does not have the authority to interfere unreasonably with construction operations, or otherwise unduly assume the functions of directing and controlling the work. If the owner were to assume such authority, it would relieve the contractor from the responsibility for the completed work as well as for the negligent acts committed by the contractor in the course of the construction operations—in short, the owner would be acting as a "general" contractor, and would thus have to expect to inherit all of the responsibilities of that position.

The Architect/Engineer as a Separate Design Organization

Except for cases in which both design and construction are performed by the same contracting party (turnkey construction), or in which the owner has his own in-house design capability, the architect/engineer, as a separate design firm, is not a party to the construction contract, and no contractual relationship exists between him and the contractor. He is a third party who derives his authority and responsibility from his contract with the owner. When private design professionals are utilized by the owner, the construction contract substitutes the architect/engineer for the owner in many important respects under the contract. However, the jurisdiction of the architect/engineer to make determinations and render decisions binding under the construction contract is limited to the specific terms of the construction contract. The architect/engineer often represents the owner in the administration of the contract and acts for him in the day-to-day administration of construction operations. In such contracts, the architect/engineer advises and consults with the owner, and communications between the owner and the contractor are usually made through the architect/engineer. Paragraph 2.2 of the AIA General Conditions of the Contract for Construction contains typical provisions regarding the architect/engineer's role in construction contract administration.

Construction contracts of this type impose many duties and bestow considerable authority on the architect/engineer. All construction operations are to be constructed under his surveillance, and he is generally responsible to oversee the progress of the work. It is his direct responsibility to see that the workmanship and materials are in conformance with the requirements of the drawings and specifications. To assure fulfillment of these conditions, he or his resident project representative (resident inspector) exercises the right of job inspection and approval of materials. In addition, he may exercise the privilege of inspecting the contractor's general program of field procedure and even the equipment that he plans to use, as well as the schedule and sequence of operations to complete the work. Should the work be lagging behind schedule, he may reasonably instruct the contractor to speed up the work.

The fact that the architect/engineer retains the privilege of approval of the contractor's methods does not mean that he is assuming responsibility for them. The rights of the architect/engineer are essentially those of assuring that the contractor is proceeding in accordance with the provisions of the contract documents, and that the contractor's methods or equipment are capable of accomplishing this objective.

The contract documents often authorize the architect/engineer to interpret the requirements of the contract. The usual wording is that the "decision of the architect/engineer shall be binding and final, and shall bind both parties." Actually, the jurisdiction of the architect/engineer is limited to the settlement of questions of *fact* only, such as what materials, quantities, or quality are required, or whether the work meets the contract requirements. The answers of questions of fact require the professional knowledge and skill of the architect/engineer, and it is proper that he should make such decisions. In the absence of fraud, bad faith, or gross mistake, the decision of the architect/engineer may, in fact, be considered as final unless the terms of the contract contain provisions for appeals or arbitration.

With respect to disputed questions of law, however, the architect/engineer has no jurisdiction. He cannot deny the right of a citizen to due process of law, and the contractor has the right to submit a dispute containing a legal aspect of the contract to arbitration or to the courts. Whether a particular matter is one of fact or one of legal construction can depend upon the language of the contract. Matters concerning time of completion, liquidated damages, and claims for extra work are usually points of law, not fact.

The General Contractor

As you might assume from a document prepared by and especially for the owner, the contractor appears to have fewer rights and more obligations under the contract. His major responsibility, of course, is to construct the project in accordance with the drawings, specifications, and other contract documents. Despite all the troubles, delays, adversities, accidents, and other misoccurrences that may happen, the contractor is generally expected to deliver a completed project in the allotted time—just as if nothing had happened to slow him down. Although some casualties are considered justifiable for him to receive more construction time, only severe contingencies such as impossibility of performance can serve to relieve him from his obligations under the contract.

The contractor is expected to give his personal attention to the work, and either he or his authorized representative must be on the site at all times during working hours. The contractor is further required to conform to all laws and ordinances concerning job safety, licensing, employment of labor, sanitation, insurance, zoning, building codes, and other aspects of the work. In many cases, failure of the design firm to research properly restrictions on his project result in designs that in themselves are not in conformance with all applicable regulations. Thus, the contractor really inherits a bucket of worms when the contract calls for his conformance to some technical requirement, and at the same time requires him to conform to all codes and laws that clearly show the original design to be a violation—sometimes, you just can't win. Many contracts now include tough new rules designed to decrease air pollution, noise pollution, dust, and similar restrictions as well as rules concerning trash disposal, sanitary wastes, pile driving, blasting, riveting, demolition, fencing, open excavations, traffic control, and housekeeping.

The general contractor is further held responsible for and must guarantee all work and materials on the project, whether constructed by his own forces or whether constructed by his subcontractors, because the subcontractors have no contractual relationship with the owner—only with the general contractor. Every restriction in the construction contract that refers to the "contractor" is binding solely upon the general contractor, as far as the owner is concerned. The general contractor may subcontract portions of the work, but the terms of such subcontracts are not subject to review by the owner, and are solely an agreement between himself and the subcontractor with whom he is entering into agreement. Even though the contractor has no direct responsibility for the adequacy of the plans and specifications, he can incur contingent liability for proceeding with faulty work whose defects should be evident to one in his business. Should an instance occur in which the contractor is directed to do something that he feels is not proper, and is not within the realm of good construction practice, he should protect himself by filing a letter of protest to the design firm or the owner through the resident inspector, stating his position and the facts as he sees them before proceeding with the matter in dispute. The contractor, if ordered to proceed by the design firm or the owner, must continue with the work even if he disagrees with it, or even in case of dispute for other causes. Settlement of disputes then follows concurrently with the prosecution of the work.

Insurance coverage is an important contractual responsibility of the contractor, both as to type of insurance and the policy limits. The contractor is generally required to provide insurance not only for his own direct and contingent liability, but also frequently for the owner's protection. He is expected to exercise every reasonable safeguard for the protection of persons and property in, on, and adjacent to the construction site.

Some of the contractor's most important rights concern progress payments, and the contractor's recourse in case the owner should fail to make such payments, as well as the right to terminate the contract for cause, the right to extra payment and extensions of time as provided in his contract, appeals from decisions of the owner or the design firm. Subject to contractual requirements and limitations in his contract, the contractor is free to subcontract portions of his work, purchase materials where he chooses (but not necessarily the right to select such materials), and to proceed with the work in any way or order that he pleases, if permitted under the terms of the contract documents.

The Resident Project Representative

The resident project representative normally works as the agent of the owner, the design firm, or a construction management firm, and as such may under the terms of such agency exercise such authority as is normally reserved to the owner, design firm, or construction firm, so long as he acts within the scope of his delegated authority and subject to the restrictions of law that prohibit such persons from performing certain functions reserved by law to the practice of professional engineering or architecture.

The purpose of inspection is to detect, recognize, and report deficiencies in material or workmanship, or noncompliance with applicable plans, specifications, or other contract documents, procedures, standards, codes, or regulations. The inspector's job is to inspect the workmanship, materials, and manner of construction of all buildings and appurtenant structures, or portions of such structures, to determine whether the requirements described by the plans, specifications, contract documents, codes, ordinances, or other statutory provisions are met by the observed work. This responsibility is basic. Any authority or responsibilities beyond these stated above are limited to that delegated by his employer and should be clearly established before reporting to the job.

The CQC Representative

A contractor quality control (CQC) representative is a position unique to federal contracts. Under a contractor quality control (CQC) provision, a construction contractor has the responsibility to inspect his own work on some federal contracts, and to present for federal acceptance only such work that complies with the contract plans and specifications. Under a contract requiring a contractor quality control program (usually construction projects with a budget estimate of over $1,000,000), the contractor is required to assign a responsible and competent individual to the position of CQC representative, and to delegate certain responsibilities and authority to him. The primary function of a CQC representative at the site is to assure that all inspections and tests are made and to give all approvals unless specifically reserved to the federal agency. This includes the checking of all material and equipment delivered to the site. One of his objectives is to achieve quality construction acceptable to the agency and to contribute to the contractor's profits by preventing defective work rather than discovering deficiencies that may result in costly removal and replacement. In those cases in which unacceptable work is started or completed, the CQC representative must have the authority to take any action necessary to correct the deficiency event though it means stopping the work of his employer on a particular portion of the job. The CQC representative must also coordinate and assure the performance of all tests required by the specifications. He is an agent of the contractor, and as such will be held responsible by the federal agency for any fraudulent acts or certifications made by him. In his day-to-day contact with the federal agency involved, he works through a federal construction representative assigned to the project.

TIME OF INSPECTION AND TESTS

The provisions of the various general conditions of the construction contract generally treat the subject of when and under what conditions the inspections and tests will be performed. Although each standard document now in use seems to treat the subject in different words, they all say essentially the same thing. Generally, the provisions cover the following:

1. Contractor must give the architect/engineer timely notice.
2. Tests and inspections required by public agencies must usually be paid for by the contractor.
3. Tests and inspections, other than the above, that are required by the contract documents will be paid for by the owner.
4. Work covered prior to required inspections must be uncovered for inspection and then recovered, all at the contractor's expense.
5. Failure of an inspector to observe a deficiency does not relieve the contractor of his obligation for performance.
6. Extra inspections required as the result of a deficiency noted by the inspector must be paid for by the contractor.
7. The contractor must provide all materials for testing at his own cost and expense.

The resident project representative is urged to refer to Articles 13.2, 13.3, and 13.4 of the NSPE Standard General Conditions of the Contract, and to Articles 7.8.1, 7.8.3, and 7.8.5 of the AIA General Conditions of the Contract for Construction, for examples of specific terms covering such inspections. Similarly, the General Conditions of the Contract for Engineering Construction of the Associated General Contractors in collaboration with the American Society of Civil Engineers places similar restrictions upon the contractor in Section 15 of that document.

CONTRACTOR SUBMITTALS

All submittals from the contractor should be handled in a systematic, consistent, and orderly manner. Changes in systems or procedures during a job lead to confusion, errors, and abuses. There should be no "special cases" or exceptions in the routine established for submittals—these lead to breaks in communication, and occasionally result in gross error. Whenever a resident project representative is provided on a project, the most desirable method is to require that *all* submittals required under the contract be transmitted directly to him, who in turn should forward such items to the project manager of the design firm or owner. This serves a two-fold purpose. First, the resident project representative will be fully aware of the status of all phases of his project; secondly, it will serve to emphasize to the contractor that the resident project representative speaks for the owner and the design firm, and that any efforts to bypass him will be rejected. Furthermore, it eliminates any arguments that certain submittals were "mailed on time" or that the subcontractors submitted their submittals directly to the design firm or owner.

Often, a contractor making a request that has already been denied by the resident project representative may try to approach the design firm or owner directly *without the knowledge* of the resident project representative. If this procedure is followed, the embarassing condition of a contractor's proposal being accepted by the project manager after it has already been rejected by the resident project representative will be eliminated. There are subsidiary dangers to the above situation, also. Once the contractor is successful, the effectiveness of the resident project representative is diminished measurably, and the project manager will find himself conducting most of the field business personally. It would seem that if a job warrants the presence of a resident project representative, he should be provided with the authority necessary to conduct his job efficiently and effectively—otherwise, the design firm or owner should save its money and eliminate the position.

OPENING A PROJECT

Opening a project involves many details to be completed before the contractor even moves a single piece of equipment onto the project site. Immediately after award of the contract, the contractor is expected to make arrangements for the required policies of insurance, obtain permits, order long-lead purchase items, check the site to determine the availability of storage and work staging areas, make arrangements for offsite disposal of surplus or waste materials, and numerous other tasks.

In addition, the owner and the design firm will usually want to schedule a preconstruction meeting (see Chapter 9). At this time they will be able to meet with the contractor and his key personnel, identify areas of responsibility, establish job philosophy (set the ground rules), set up requirements for on- or off-site job meetings and set the frequency of such meetings, determine who should be in attendance, point out particular problem areas anticipated in construction and discuss any special methods of treatment of such problems, and if necessary discuss special sequence of operations or scheduling limitations.

Although not universally followed, it is desirable for the owner, either directly or through the design firm or construction manager, to issue a written *Notice to Proceed* to the contractor, which will designate the actual beginning of the contract—very important later when attempting to establish the amount of liquidated damages where the contractor has exceeded his contract time. The *Notice to Proceed* sets a precise date that the job began, and eliminates any later argument over the time of the contract.

The representative of the design firm or owner should visit the site early after the Notice to Proceed has been issued to assure that all the requirements of the contract documents relating to temporary facilities and utilities are being properly implemented. This includes, particularly for the resident project representative, that the proper field office facilities are being provided, that they are on time, that they are separate from those of the contractor (if specified as such), and that telephone service, temporary power, and sanitary facilities have been arranged for so that they will be installed in time. Where initial temporary fencing is required around construction areas, the resident project representative should closely monitor this requirement.

Each of the construction milestones, such as contractor submittals of key items, materials testing, operational tests, reviews and updates required in schedules, delivery dates of major key pieces of equipment, the beginning of new elements of the work, and similar requirements of the contract should be outlined on paper and a calendar established for the systematic control and monitoring of these functions (see Fig. 3.3). The procedures for the handling of all communications should be explained at that time, if not previously covered at the preconstruction meeting, and printed directions issued as a guide to the handling of all construction related matters in conformance with the owner agency requirements. A simplified diagram showing the routing of all field communications and submittals is shown in Figure 3.7.

It is quite important that once the communications procedures have been agreed upon, neither the resident project representative nor members of his staff should allow informal changes to occur. Such departures from the formally accepted policy can otherwise be justifiably used by the contractor to allege a lack of communication as a defense in case of a dispute.

JOB PHILOSOPHY

A firm but fair policy should be adopted by the resident project representative to control the work and to require proper workmanship and materials as well as compliance with drawings, specifications, and other contract documents. The resident project representative should provide as much assistance to the contractor as possible to alert him to special job requirements or portions of the work requiring more critical control, and to provide him with any known information that may benefit the contractor in the completion of his work within the terms of the contract. Valid claims for extra work beyond the scope of the contract, as well as unforeseen underground conditions, should be fairly reviewed by the design firm and, if valid, presented to the owner with a recommendation for approval. Invalid claims should be rejected.

The requirement that the inspector be fair in his dealings with the contractor does not mean that he should be overly lenient or patronizing, as there is no point in having a resident project representative on the job if he is not effective. The basic philosophy is to get a good start on the job. The inspector's attitude at the beginning of each job should be one of *firmness*. This will minimize arguments later in the job. A job once started in a loose fashion is almost impossible to regain proper control of later in the work, even by replacing the resident project representative. An incorrect method is easier corrected the first time it is practiced than after it has been in use for a while.

Another important philosophy is that the inspector should not become a creature of habit. Do not get into the swing of a regular routine. No one should be capable of anticipating the inspector's moves from one day to the next. All inspection should be at irregular intervals—and, above all, the inspector should be one of the first ones at the job and one of the last to leave. Many substandard details have been accomplished during the brief time between an inspector's early departure and the contractor releasing his crew for the day. Don't get the idea that the resident project representative should become a policeman, nor that everyone in the contractor's camp is out to defraud him. The result will be more tension before the job is half over than either the resident project representative or the contractor can handle. By far, the majority of the contractors and their employees want to do a good job. Remember, that they must usually base their judgments upon previous work that they have personally been involved in, and may not recognize the significance of some of the architect or engineer's design requirements. In addition, the contractor's project manager, in most cases, is an individual with a practical outlook and he may not be easily convinced that the architect or engineer's design theory has approached such a degree of exactness so as to justify stringent inspection practices and low tolerance inspection procedures.

ADMINISTRATIVE ACTIVITIES

The job of the resident project representative involves the handling of numerous administrative responsibilities. Although most of the major tasks have been described in detail, the following list will serve as a summary of the principal administrative activities expected of the resident project representative:

1. Coordinate and provide general direction of work and progress
2. Review contractor's CPM schedules regularly
3. Assist in resolution of construction problems
4. Evaluate contractor claims for the design firm
5. Maintain log of change orders
6. Maintain log of contractor submittals

7. Develop and administer a quality control program
   Proofs of compliance
   Qualifications of testing services
   Define required tests
   Maintain QC reporting system
   Maintain QC records of all tests and test results
   Establish frequency of testing
8. Physically inspect all construction *every day*
9. Observe *all* contractor tests
10. Maintain daily log and construction records
11. Maintain record drawing data
12. Review contractor progress payment requests
13. Review contractor's change order requests for design firm
14. Assure that construction area is safe
15. Participate in field management meetings
16. Provide negotiation assistance on contractor claims
17. Review and recommend on contractor value engineering proposals
18. Supervise inspection forces and field office staff
19. Report field conditions that prevent original construction
20. On unit price projects, obtain accurate field measurements
21. On all jobs, verify contractor's monthly work quantities
22. Assist scheduling and ordering required field services

While not exhaustive, the foregoing list summarizes the more commonplace activities expected of the resident project representative on a construction project.

SUSPENSION OF THE WORK

Much has been said about not "stopping the work," but little about the related act of "suspending" it. First, the word "suspension" as used in this context should be very carefully qualified. Work may be suspended in whole or in part, and the nature of a suspension is to cease all or part of the work without actual contract termination.

Temporary suspension is subject to the specific terms of the General Conditions of the contract for each particular project. In general, however, suspensions can be said to fall into two major categories:

1. The first category relates to the failure of the contractor to carry out orders or to perform any provision of the contract. Any letter ordering such suspension must include reference to applicable sections of the specifications and, if possible, state the conditions under which the work may be resumed. Such action must be taken only after careful consideration of all aspects of the problem, and then only under the direct authority of the design firm, construction manager firm, or owner. This is a legally risky area, however, and the NSPE feels that the right to reject defective work was a sufficient weapon for the architect/engineer, and the severe and more

risky right to stop the work should be left to the owner. However, as often stated before, in certain circumstances, moral standards or the law may impose a duty on the architect or engineer for the benefit of employees and third parties to stop work that is being carried on in an unsafe manner, or advise the owner to do so. This is so even when the General Conditions state that safety precautions are the sole responsibility of the contractor. The inspector as the authorized on-site representative of the design firm or owner, is then the only party who will normally observe such hazards and can serve such notices at the site.

2. The second category under which a suspension may be ordered relates to unsuitable weather *or* conditions unfavorable for the suitable prosecution of the work. Normally, such suspensions are not necessary for periods of 30 days or less, since these are best handled on a day-to-day basis when determining nonworking days.

   a. *Suspension of an Item or an Operation:* A suspension may be ordered that affects an item or several items only if desired. This is usually done when either the work or the public will be adversely affected by continuous operation. Such action is recommended for situations where the probable end result is based upon the architect's or engineer's experience and judgment as opposed to factors that are directly specified. Although this type of suspension is an option generally available only to the design firm or owner, the contractor's opinion on such suspension should also be considered.

   b. *Suspension of the Entire Project:* In areas subject to severe weather it is considered permissible to suspend an entire project if this is considered as being in the best interests of the owner. However, the authority of the architect or engineer to suspend is limited to the specific terms of the contract documents. In some cases it might even be necessary to have the contractor's concurrence to suspend an entire project.

The contractor must be advised of the conditions under which maintenance will be performed during any suspension, and who will be responsible for the condition of the unfinished work during any such suspension. It may be possible under many contracts that the contractor may be entitled to receive extra payments to maintain the project during this time.

When the reason for a suspension no longer exists, or when it can be expected that favorable conditions for resumption of the work will soon prevail, the contractor should be notified in writing. The letter should state the date when the count of working days will be expected to be resumed, and the notice should allow a reasonable amount of time for the contractor to regroup his labor forces and equipment. Generally, 10 working days is considered as a reasonable length of time for this.

13

VALUE ENGINEERING

VALUE ENGINEERING —what is it and what part does the resident project representative plan in its application? The latter question will be answered in this chapter. The first question, however, deserves special consideration. It has been said that value engineering is not the proper role for a project administrator, but rather for the decision maker, such as the project manager. As far as the concept of initiating or granting final approval to a value engineering proposal is concerned, this appears to be true. Nevertheless, it may involve construction methods regarding which the inspector may have valuable knowledge to contribute to the decision maker, and under many federal contracts it is also a part of the contract requirements of the general contractor to propose value engineering ideas *during the construction phase*. There is no way that a resident project representative can avoid the issue as long as the contractor is involved; thus, it is highly desirable for the inspector to know what value engineering is and how to work with value engineering proposals. In this chapter the inspector will be introduced to the subject in sufficient detail to understand what it is all about and where it fits into his responsibility area.

A great deal of lip service has been paid to the concept of "value engineering" in recent years, and the suggestion is that it is a new, previously undeveloped branch of the construction industry. There are entire engineering organizations devoted solely to the promotion of value engineering and at least one federal agency that lets contracts for large construction projects now requires its use during the design phase of every project. Value engineering concepts are desirable on any project; however, it must be said that *all* engineering has always involved *value engineering* concepts, though not under that title.

In fact, an architect or engineer who did not consider maximum economy and value in the selection and use of construction materials and methods, within the limits dictated by his design, was simply not doing his job. During the *design phase* of a project there should be no need for a separate value engineering effort if the architect or engineer is providing competent professional services to his client.

The concept of providing value engineering incentives to the construction contractor during the *construction phase* of a project, however, is a more deserving one. Often the selection of materials and methods by the architect/engineer is dictated by an evaluation of the average market conditions or contractor methods. Upon awarding a contract for construction to a specific contractor, his particular skills, equipment, materials sources, and knowledge of his local trade area and labor market can often be used to reduce beneficially the cost of a portion of a proposed project without necessarily compromising the design concepts involved. The final judgment of the acceptability of such suggestions would be up to the architect or engineer and the owner, of course.

DEFINITION

The first question to arise is usually, "What is value engineering, anyway?" Value engineering is a systematic evaluation of a project design to obtain the most value for every dollar of cost. By carefully investigating costs, availability of materials, construction methods, shipping costs or physical limitations, planning and organizing, cost/benefit values, and similar cost influencing items, an improvement in the overall cost of a project can be realized.

The entire value engineering effort is aimed at a careful analysis of each function, and the elimination or modification of anything that adds to the project cost without adding to its functional capabilities. Not only are first costs to be considered, but even the later in-place costs of operation, maintenance, life, replacement, and similar characteristics must be considered. Thus, although the name is new, value engineering is simply a *systematic* application of engineering economy as taught in every engineering course long before anyone ever thought up a catchy name for it.

The principal difficulty of applying value engineering principles to construction is the problem of having a third party, who may not possess the same degree of expertise in the subject area that the architect or engineer does, cause changes in design that simply substitute the value engineer's judgment for that of the designer—a risky process at best. Theoretically, the value engineer does not actually "cause" a design change, but by placing the architect or engineer in the position of having to defend his original design, he threatens the entire production schedule.

In the construction phase, however, it is a completely new ball game. Now the value engineer is the contractor, whose experience is in construction methods, techniques, and costs. His input can often offer the benefit of construction experience and a knowledge of the marketplace and labor force that the designer did not possess. It is here that the greatest cost benefit can result with a minimum of conflict with the designer. Often on

CONTRACT SCHEDULE
SECTION VII—COST & PRICE/PAYMENT

ARTICLE 8

VALUE ENGINEERING INCENTIVE (MARCH 1975)

(a)   Application. This clause applies to a Contractor developed and documented Value Engineering Change Proposal (VECP) which:

   (1) requires a change to this contract to implement the VECP; and

   (2) reduces the contract price without impairing essential function or characteristics, provided that it is not based solely on a change in deliverable end item quantities.

(b)   Documentation. As a minimum, the following information shall be submitted by the Contractor with each VECP:

   (1) a description of the difference between the existing contract requirement and the proposed change, and the comparative advantages and disadvantages of each; justification where function or characteristics of a work item is being altered; and the effect of the change on the performance of the end item;

   (2) an analysis and itemization of the requirements of the contract which must be changed if the VECP is accepted and a recommendation as to how to make each such change (e.g., a suggested specification revision);

   (3) a separate detailed cost estimate for both the existing contract requirement and the proposed change to provide an estimate of the reduction in costs, if any, that will result from acceptance of the VECP, taking into account the costs of development and implementation by the Contractor (including any amount attributable to subcontracts in accordance with paragraph (f) below);

   (4) a prediction of any effects the proposed change would have on related costs to the Government such as Government furnished property costs, and costs of maintenance and operation;

   (5) a statement of the time by which a change order adopting the VECP must be issued so as to obtain the maximum cost reduction during the remainder of this contract, noting any effect on the contract completion time or delivery schedule; and

   (6) identification of any previous submission of the VECP, including the dates submitted, the agencies involved, the numbers of the Government contracts involved, and the previous actions by the Government if known.

(c)   Submission. 6 copies of each VECP shall be submitted to the Contracting Officer with a copy to the Resident Engineer at the worksite. Proposals shall be processed expeditiously; however, the Government shall not be liable for any delay in acting upon any proposal submitted pursuant to this clause. The Contractor has the right to withdraw, in whole or in part, and VECP at any time prior to acceptance by the Government.

(d)   Acceptance. The Contracting Officer may accept, in whole or in part, by contract modification any VECP submitted pursuant to this clause. The Contracting Officer may accept the VECP even though an agreement on price reduction has not been reached, by issuing the Contractor a notice to proceed with the change. Until a notice to proceed is issued or a contract modification applies a VECP to this contract, the Contractor shall remain obligated to perform in accordance with this contract. Contract modifications made pursuant to this clause will so state. The decision of the Contracting Officer as to the acceptance of any VECP under this contract shall be final and shall not be subject to the "Disputes" clause of this contract.

   (1) Definition.

      (i)   Instant contract savings to the Contractor (ICS) are the estimated reduction in the Contractor's cost of performance resulting from the acceptance of the VECP. The proposed cost reduction includes estimated allowable Contractor development and implementation costs (CC). The Contractor's development and implementation costs include any subcontractor development and implementation costs (see (f) below). For purposes of this clause, Contractor development costs are those costs incurred after the Contractor has identified a specific VE project and prior to acceptance and implementation by the Government.

Figure 13.1   Example of value engineering incentive in federal construction contract.

10-0038-5

CONTRACT SCHEDULE
SECTION VII - COST & PRICE/PAYMENT
ARTICLE 8 Cont'd

    (ii) Government Costs (GC) are those NASA costs which directly result from development and implementation of the VECP, such as test and evaluation of the VECP.

  (2) Calculations and Actions.
    Multiply ICS by 45% and GC by 55%. Add these two results, e.g., (.45 ICS + .55 GC) and subtract from the contract price.

(f)   Subcontracts. The Contractor shall include appropriate VE arrangements in any subcontract of $50,000 or greater, and may include such arrangements in contracts of lesser value. To compute any adjustment in the contract price under paragraph (e) above, the Contractor's cost of development and implementation of a VECP which is accepted under this contract shall include any development and implementation costs of a subcontractor, and any VE incentive payments to a subcontractor, which clearly pertain to such VECP. However, no such payment or accrual to a subcontractor will be permitted, either as a part of the Contractor's development or implementation costs or otherwise, to reduce the Government's share.

(g)   Data. The Contractor may restrict the Government's right to use any sheet of a VECP or of the supporting data, submitted pursuant to this clause, in accordance with the terms of the following legend if it is marked on such sheet:

    "This data furnished pursuant to the Value Engineering Incentive clause of contract _____ shall not be disclosed outside the Government, or duplicated, used, or disclosed, in whole or in part, for any purpose other than to evaluate a VECP submitted under said clause. This restriction does not limit the Government's right to use information contained in this data if it is or has been obtained, or is otherwise available, from the Contractor or from another source, without limitations. If such a VECP is accepted by the Government under said contract after the use of this data in such an evaluation, disclose any data reasonably necessary to the full utilization of such VECP as accepted, in any manner and for any purpose whatsoever, and have others so do."

In the event of acceptance of a VECP, the Contractor hereby grants to the Government all rights to use, duplicate or disclose, in whole or in part, in any manner and for any purpose whatsoever, and to have or permit others to do so, any data reasonably necessary to fully utilize such VECP.

Figure 13.1 (continued)

federally-funded construction contracts, a value engineering incentive clause may be provided, in which the government will allow the contractor to retain up to 50 percent of the cost savings realized in any value engineering proposal made by him that is accepted and implemented.

THE ROLE OF THE RESIDENT PROJECT REPRESENTATIVE

Although the resident project representative will generally have no part in the actual submittal of value engineering proposals, he may frequently be called upon by the architect or engineer to evaluate a value engineering (VE) proposal that has been submitted by the contractor. It is not being suggested here that the inspector should render judgment in the matter of whether a cost savings proposal is valid, as this would be no better than leaving the matter up to a single individual who either did not take part in the actual design, and quite probably did not possess sufficient technical and professional background in the subject area to justify the acceptance of his judgment over that of the design engineer. In addition, it should always be remembered that the design engineer is the *engineer of record,* and it is his license and professional reputation at stake, not that of a value engineer consultant. The inspector's part in this process is to relate to the real world surrounding the project he is assigned to, and evaluate the probable effect of the proposal on his project if it is accepted. All such observations should be written into a memorandum form and submitted to the architect or engineer so that when the final evaluation is made it can be based upon a full knowledge of both the design conditions as well as the field conditions as communicated by the resident project representative.

FUNDAMENTALS OF VALUE ENGINEERING (VE)

Function

In value engineering the *function* is defined as the specific purpose or use intended for something. It describes what must be achieved. For value engineering studies, this "function" is usually described in the simplest form possible, usually in only two words; a verb and a noun. "Support weight," "prevent corrosion," and "conduct current" are typical expressions of function.

Worth

Worth refers to the least cost required to provide the *functions* that are required by the user of the finished project. Worth is established by comparison, such as comparing it with the cost of its functional equivalent. The worth of an item is not affected by the possibility of failure under the value engineering concept embraced by the federal government. Thus, if a bolt supporting a key joint in a large roof truss fails, the entire roof of the structure may be caused to fail. Nevertheless, the worth of the bolt is the lowest cost necessary to provide a reliable fastening.

Cost

Cost is the total amount of money required to obtain and use the functions that have been specified. For the seller, this is the total of his costs in connection with his product. For the owner the total cost of ownership includes not only the purchase price of the product, but also the cost of the paperwork of including it in the inventory, operating it, and providing support in the form of maintenance and utility services for its total usable life. The cost of ownership may also include a proportional share of expenditures for development, engineering, testing, spare parts, and various items of overhead expense.

Value

Value is the relationship of *worth* to *cost* as realized by the owner, based upon his needs and resources in any given situation. The ratio of *worth* to *cost* is the principal measure of *value*. Thus, a "value equation" may be used to arrive at a *Value Index* as follows:

$$\text{Value Index} = \frac{\text{Worth}}{\text{Cost}} = \frac{\text{Utility}}{\text{Cost}}$$

The value may be increased by doing any of the following:

1. Improve the utility of something with no change in cost,
2. retain the same utility for the less cost, or
3. combine improved utility with less cost.

Optimum value is obtained when all utility criteria are met at the lowest overall cost. Although *worth* and *cost* can be expressed in dollars, *value* is a dimensionless expression showing the relationship of the other two.

The Philosophy of Value

If something does not do what it is intended to do, no amount of cost reduction will improve its value. Any "cost reduction" action that sacrifices the needed utility of something actually reduces its value to the owner. On the other hand, costs incurred to increase the functional capacity of something beyond that which is needed amounts to "gilding the lily" and provides little actual value to the owner. Therefore, anything less than the necessary functional capacity is unacceptable; anything more is unnecessary and wasteful.

Types of Value Engineering Recommendations

Within the Defense Department and some other federal agencies, there are two types of recommendations that are the result of a value engineering effort:

Value Engineering Proposal (VEP): A value engineering recommendation that originates from within the government agency itself, or one that was originated by the contractor and may be implemented by unilateral action. A VEP can only relate to changes that are within the terms of the contract and specifications, and thus would not require a change order to implement.

Value Engineering Change Proposal (VECP): A value engineering recommendation by a contractor that requires the owner's approval, and that, if accepted, requires the execution of a change order. This would apply to any proposed change that would require a change in the contract, the specifications, the scope of the work, or similar limits previously established by contract.

AREAS OF OPPORTUNITY FOR VALUE ENGINEERING

Value Engineering by the Architect or Engineer

Value engineering is a basic approach that takes nothing for granted, and challenges everything on a project, including the necessity for the existence of a product or project, for that matter. The cost of a project is influenced by the requirements of the design and the specifications.* Prior to completing the final design the architect or engineer should carefully consider the methods and equipment that may be used to construct the project. Requirements that increase the cost without producing equivalent benefits should be eliminated. The final decisions of the architect or engineer should be based upon a reasonable knowledge of construction methods and costs.

The cost of a project may be divided into five or more items:

1. Materials
2. Labor
3. Equipment
4. Overhead and supervision
5. Profit

While the last item is beyond the control of the architect or engineer, he does have some control over the cost of the first four items.

If the architect or engineer specifies materials that must be transported great distances, the costs may be unnecessarily high. Requirements for tests and inspections of materials may be too rigid for the purpose for which the materials will be used. Frequently, substitute materials are available nearby that are essentially as satisfactory as other materials whose costs are considerably higher. The suggestions of the contractor can be of value here.

---

*From *Construction, Planning, Equipment, and Methods* by R. L. Peurifoy. Copyright 1956, McGraw-Hill Book Company, New York. Used with permission of McGraw-Hill Book Company.

The specified quality of workmanship and methods of construction have considerable influence on the amount and class of labor required and upon the cost of labor. Complicated concrete structures are relatively easy to design and draw but may be exceedingly difficult to build. A high-grade concrete finish may be justified for exposed surfaces in a fine building, but the same quality of workmanship is not justified for a warehouse. The quality of workmanship should be in keeping with the type of project involved.

Architects and engineers should keep informed on the developments of new construction equipment, as such information will enable them to modify the design or construction methods to permit the use of economical equipment. The inspector is a vital link in the chain of information that supplies the architect and engineer with the latest up-to-date data on construction methods and equipment. The normal *daily construction report* (Fig. 4.3) contains sufficient information to keep the architect and engineer adequately informed, and upon noting new methods or equipment in the inspector's report he can follow these leads to determine the specific capabilities and advantages of each case. For example, the use of a dual-drum concrete paving mixer instead of a single-drum mixer can increase the production of concrete materially, and for most projects will reduce the cost of pavement construction. The use of a high capacity earth loader and large trucks may necessitate a change in the location, size, and shape of the borrow pit, but the resulting economies may easily justify the change.

The utilization of higher capacity delivery equipment does not always result in a cost saving, however. On some recent projects in a hot, dry climate as an example, the use of seven-cubic-yard transit mixers for delivering concrete to a project proved far more costly than making twice as many trips using three-yard mixers. The placing requirements involved the construction of thin concrete columns and wall sections with a high concentration of reinforcing steel, with the resultant reduction in the rate of placement. Before a seven-yard truck load of concrete could be completely discharged under the existing conditions, the concrete mix started to set in the delivery vehicles because of the high temperature, low humidity, and three-hour time span from the addition of water to the mix to the final placement in the forms. Long delivery routes are often the cause of this, combined with slow pour conditions. The resultant frequency of rejection of portions of the seven-yard load (retempering was prohibited by specifications) was more costly than the increase in the number of deliveries and the smaller batch size that allowed the use of a fresh load after every three yards placed.

The following are some of the methods that the architect or engineer may use to reduce the cost of construction:

1. Design concrete structures with as many duplicate members as practical in order to allow the reuse of forms without rebuilding.
2. Confine design elements to modular material sizes where possible.
3. Simplify the design of the structure wherever possible.
4. Design for the use of cost-saving equipment and methods.
5. Eliminate unnecessary special construction requirements.

6. Design to reduce the required labor to a minimum.
7. Specify a quality of workmanship that is consistent with the quality of the project.
8. Furnish adequate foundation information wherever possible.
9. Refrain from requiring the contractor to assume the responsibility for information that should have been furnished by the architect or engineer, or for the adequacy of the design.
10. Use local materials when they are satisfactory.
11. Write simple, straightforward specifications that state clearly what is expected of the contractor. Define the results expected, but within reason permit the contractor to select the methods of accomplishing the results.
12. Use standardized specifications that are familiar to most contractors whenever possible.
13. Hold prebid conferences with contractors in order to eliminate any uncertainties and to reduce change orders resulting from misunderstandings to a minimum.
14. Use inspectors who have sufficient judgment and experience to understand the project and have authority to make decisions.

Value Engineering by the Contractor

One desirable characteristic of a successful contractor from the standpoint of value engineering is a degree of dissatisfaction over the plans and methods under consideration for constructing a project (a characteristic not always appreciated by the architect or engineer). However, complacency by members of the construction industry will not develop new equipment, new methods, or new construction planning, all of which are desirable for providing continuing improvements in the construction industry at lower costs. A contractor who does not keep informed on new equipment and methods will soon discover that his competitors are underbidding him.

Suggestions for possible reductions in construction costs by the contractor include, but are by no means limited to the following items:

1. Study the project before bidding, and determine the effect of:
    a. Topography
    b. Geology
    c. Climate
    d. Sources of materials
    e. Access to the project
    f. Housing facilities, if required
    g. Storage facilities for materials and equipment
    h. Labor supply
    i. Local services
2. The use of substitute construction equipment, having greater capactiies, higher efficiencies, higher speeds, more maneuverability, and lower operating costs.

3. Payment of a bonus to key personnel for production in excess of a specified rate.
4. The use of radios as a means of communications between headquarters office and key personnel on projects covering large areas.
5. The practice of holding periodic conferences with key personnel to discuss plans, procedures, and results. Such conferences should produce better morale among the staff members and should result in better coordination among the various operations.
6. The adoption of realistic safety practices on a project as a means of reducing accidents and lost time.
7. Consider the desirability of subcontracting specialized operations to other contractors who can do the work more economically than the general contractor.
8. Consider the desirability of improving shop and servicing facilities for better maintenance of construction equipment.

Improvements in the *methods* of construction, long the sole domain of the contractor, can result in significant savings in the cost of the project. This type of cost saving, if implemented after award of a contract, is seldom if ever shared with the owner. However, such cost-reducing considerations are an integral part of the competitive bidding system. Thus, the owner benefits in lower bid costs. As an example, an estimator for a contracting firm prepared a bid for a project. When the bids were opened, it was discovered that his firm's bid was so low that the other members of the firm feared that a serious error had been made in preparing the bid. The estimator was called in and asked if he thought that he could actually construct the project for the estimated cost. He replied that he could if he were permitted to adopt the construction methods that he used in estimating the cost. The firm agreed; he was placed in charge of the construction of the project and he completed the work with a satisfactory profit to the contractor. At the same time the owner benefitted by receiving his project at a low cost.

METHODOLOGY IN GENERATING VE PROPOSALS

A task that is accomplished in a planned and systematic manner is much more likely to be successful than one that is unplanned and relies upon undisciplined ingenuity. Most successful value engineering organizations follow a "scientific method" to assure a planned, purposeful approach. This procedure is called a VE *Job Plan*. It is set up as a group action because it is unlikely that a successful value engineering proposal will be the product of a single individual. The group plan produces benefits that the efforts of one or two individuals can seldom match. Among the principal benefits are:

1. More talent is directly applied to the problem.
2. The scope and depth of the effort is increased.
3. More efficient use is made of the available time because problem areas are more readily resolved through direct communications.

4. Team participation provides productive training for those not previously exposed to formal VE training.

Several versions of a VE Job Plan can be found in current publications. Some texts list five phases, some six, and some refer to even more. However, the number of phases is less important than the systematic approach involved. As an example, Figure 13.2 shows a five-phase Job Plan. Although the illustration may suggest otherwise, there are actually no sharp lines of distinction between the phases. They tend to overlap in varying degrees.

An effective value engineering effort must include all phases of the Job Plan. However, the proper share of attention given to each phase may differ from one effort to another.

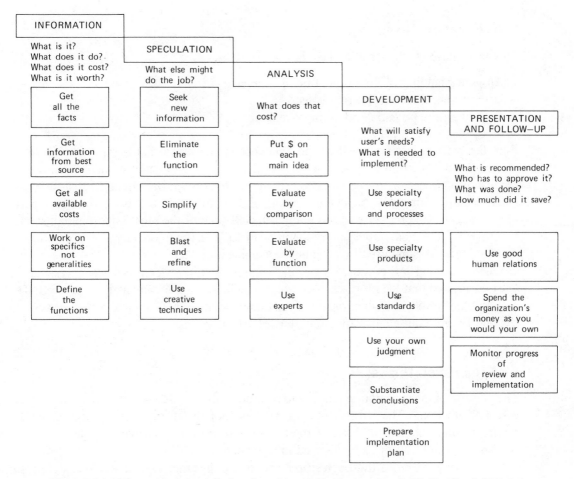

Figure 13.2 *Value engineering job plan chart from Value Engineering–DOD Handbook 5010.8-H.*

The Job Plan represents a concerted effort to furnish the best answers to the following key questions:

What is it?
What *does* it do?
What *must* it do?
What does it cost?
What is it worth?
What else might do the job?
What does the alternative cost?
What will satisfy all of the owner's needs?
What is needed to put the VE change into effect?

I—Information Phase

This first phase of the Job Plan has three objectives:

An understanding of the product being studied,
Determining the essential functions,
Estimating the potential value improvement.

Both the product itself as well as the general technical area that it represents must be studied to understand the subject of the VE effort. Data accumulated should include the predicted total cost of ownership; the present configuration; the quality, reliability, and maintainability attributes; the quantity involved; and the background information regarding the reason the product was originally selected (one of the most important considerations of all). It is most important to obtain qualified sources to obtain *facts,* not opinions. All data must be supported by adequate documentation.

When receiving VE proposals from the contractor, the resident project representative must be assured that the proposal is complete, including all documentation required. The proposal must include a functional analysis, an economic analysis, and a cost analysis to respond to the requirements for submittals of VE proposals.

II—Speculation Phase

The purpose of the speculation phase is to formulate alternative ways of accomplishing the essential functions. The effort begins as soon as enough information has been gathered, reviewed, and understood. Four of the methods used to help answer the basic question "What else might do the job?" raised in this phase are:

Simple comparison: A thorough search for other things that have at least one significant characteristic similar to the item being studied.

III—Analysis Phase

The purpose of the analysis phase is to select for further refinement the most promising of the alternatives that were developed during the speculation phase. During speculation there was a conscious effort to delay judgment so that the creative process would not be inhibited. During this phase those ideas are subjected to a preliminary screening to identify those that satisfy the following criteria:

Functional comparison: A creative session in which new and unusual contributions of known things or processes are combined and rearranged to provide different ways of achieving the function.

Scientific factors: A search for other scientific disciplines capable of performing the same basic function. This involves contributions from specialists in disciplines not normally considered in the original design.

Create and refine: Push to get off the beaten path and create by reaching for an unusual idea or another approach. Refine by strengthening and expanding ideas that suggest a different way to perform the function.

Will the idea work?
Is it less costly than the present design?
Is it feasible to put into effect?
Will it satisfy the owner's needs?
If the answer to any of the above is "no," can it be modified or combined with another to give a "yes" answer?

The ideas that survive the initial screening are then rated according to their relative ability to meet the above requirements. The advantages and disadvantages of each are also noted. Preliminary cost estimates are then developed for those ideas which appear technically and economically most promising. Following these preliminary estimates, one or more of the ideas with significant savings potential are selected for further detailed analysis. If relative cost differences among several alternatives are not conclusive at this point, they may all be subject to further analysis.

IV—Development Phase

In the development phase the alternatives that have survived the previous selection process are developed into firm recommendations (VE Proposals). This portion of the effort includes the development of detailed technical and economic data for the proposal. The proposal should include everything, including total ownership costs. This phase is also devoted to assuring that the proposal satisfies all of the owner's needs. For evaluation of mechanical equipment on a project, a checklist such as the following is often helpful:

Performance requirements
Quality requirements
Reliability requirements
System compatibility
Safety requirements
Maintenance considerations
Logistics support problems

At this stage the value engineering proposal should also include a written discussion designed to satisfy any objections likely to be raised concerning any aspect of the proposal. Conferences with specialists are often helpful in overcoming anticipated objections in advance. If a technical characteristic is either unacceptable or marginal, the alternative should be modified to correct the deficiency wherever possible. If it is not possible to overcome the deficiency, the alternative should be rejected. Of the technically feasible alternatives remaining, only the one that represents the lowest cost is selected for the detailed development of the technical and economic data necessary to support its selection.

If more than one alternative offers the possibility of valid savings, it is common for all of them to be recommended. One becomes the primary recommendation and the others are considered as alternative recommendations, and are usually presented in the order of their decreasing savings potential.

V—Presentation and Followup Phase

The final phase of the *Job Plan* includes the preparation and presentation of the value engineering proposal to those having approval authority. This phase also includes:

Preparing a plan for implementation,
Obtaining a decision regarding disposition of the proposal,
Assisting as needed in the implementation action,
Preparing a final report if appropriate.

When finally presented for approval, the VE proposal should be self-explanatory and leave no doubt concerning its justification. Only factual and relevant information should be included. All expected technical and cost variations from the existing design must be described. The following checklist represents the minimum information usually included in a value engineering proposal:

Identity of the project
"Before" and "After" descriptions
Cost of the original design
Cost of the proposed design change
Quantity basis for costs

Cost to put VE proposal into effect
Expected savings to the owner
Actions that are necessary to put the change into effect
Suggested schedule for putting the change into effect

The management personnel who are responsible for review and approval must base their judgment entirely upon the documentation submitted with a VE proposal, and this documentation must contain all of the data that the reviewer will need to reach a decision. VE proposals should contain sufficient information to assure the reviewer that:

The performance of the overall project is not adversely affected
Supporting technical information is complete and accurate
Potential savings are based upon valid cost analyses
Feasibility of the proposed change is adequately demonstrated

Failure to provide adequate VE proposal documentation is a major cause of proposal rejection. An analysis made of 90 rejected contractor-initiated Value Engineering Change Proposals revealed that approximately 40 percent of the rejections were due to incomplete or inaccurate technical or cost information.

INSPECTOR RESPONSIBILITY IN VALUE ENGINEERING

As previously mentioned, the inspector's part in the value engineering process is an indirect one. However, his participation may be requested in either of two areas: first to assist the architect or engineer in providing valuable, up-to-date construction information on materials, methods, availability, the capabilities of a particular contractor or contractor, and other similar field data. In addition, his judgment may be solicited during both the *Information* and *Speculation* phases to assist the architect or engineer in his own VE proposals. Secondly, his comments may be requested to evaluate the contractor's VE proposals and submit commentary to the architect or engineer. In this manner, the resident project representative may perform the function of one of the ''specialists'' that the architect or engineer may wish to consult during the analysis and evaluation of the contractors VE proposals.

Bibliography

Principles and Applications of Value Engineering, Department of Defense Joint Course Book, Volume I, U.S. Army Management Engineering Training Agency, Rock Island, Illinois.

Value Engineering, Department of Defense Handbook 5010.8–H dated 12 Sept 1968, Superintendent of Documents, U.S. Government Printing Office, Washington, D.C.

14

MEASUREMENT AND PAYMENT

CONSTRUCTION PROGRESS PAYMENTS

Among the most important items to the contractor are those provisions of the construction contract governing the making of monthly progress payments to the contractor throughout the job. He will be expected to submit a request for payment, stating amounts of work completed and the estimated value of such work to the resident project representative approximately 10 days before the payment due date. At this point, whether the project is a lump sum or a unit price contract, the work of the resident project representative is very similar. Before transmitting the payment request to the owner's or designer's project manager, the resident project representative is generally delegated the task of verifying and evaluating the contractor's payment request. The resident project representative, because of his nearness to the work, is often the only representative of the owner or the design firm who can truly verify the actual quantities of the various items of work completed, and determine the probable value of such work.

Although a unit price contract requires extreme care in the verification of the contractor's payment claim, a lump sum job can usually be handled a little more informally, as the overage claims will be compensated for ultimately by the fixed price nature of the contract. Nevertheless, it is undesirable to be so careless as to allow payments in excess of the amounts of work actually done, as first of all it cancels out the effect of the retention, if any, and secondly, if the contractor were to default on his contract, the inspector might be in the position of having approved for payment more work than was actually built, thus allowing the defaulting contractor a tidy, unearned profit.

APPROVAL OF PAYMENT REQUESTS

The responsibilities of the resident project representative in the approval stage of contractor partial payment requests are limited to checking of quantities and costs prior to submittal to the owner's or designer's project manager with a recommendation for payment if warranted.

The following is a list of possible tasks that might be delegated to the resident project representative during the validation phase of the contractor's payment request.

1. Quantity takeoff of work actually completed as of date of request
2. Inventory of equipment and materials delivered but not yet used in the work
3. Field measurements of quantities of work completed or claimed
4. Construction cost estimate of all completed work, using unit prices in bid or in cost breakdown submitted at beginning of job
5. Audit of invoices and costs (cost-plus jobs only)
6. Review of claims for extra work and completed change orders
7. Check of retention amount
8. On extra work and change orders, check the method used to determine profit and overhead, material costs, and proper application of each in accordance with the conditions of the contract
9. Prepare recommendation to the project manager and submit along with the contractor's payment request (Figs. 14.1 and 14.2).

BASIS FOR PAYMENT AMOUNTS

The basis of all progress payments is a determination, in the field, of the actual quantities of work that have been accomplished as of the date that the payment request is submitted. The accuracy required of these field measurements is determined by the type of contract involved. There are principally three types of construction contracts in current use:

1. Lump sum contract (fixed price)
2. Unit price contract
3. Cost plus fixed fee (CPFF)

Although each type of contract may be let on the basis of competitive bids, with the lowest bidder getting the job, several significant differences exist. On a lump sum contract, the contractor must complete the work for the fixed price shown as long as the scope of the contract has not been altered by change orders. Any cost overruns must come out of the contractor's pocket; similarly, any money that the contractor saves on the job, as long as he conforms to the plans and specifications, belongs to him.

On a unit price contract, the design firm provides a list of all individual bid items, along with an ''engineer's estimate'' of the quantities involved. Blanks are provided in the proposal document for the bidder to insert a price per unit for which he agrees to build the work, which when multiplied by the quantity shown in the engineer's estimate indicates the total amount of his bid for each item. In the example shown in the accompanying

(SUGGESTED FORM)

APPLICATION FOR PAYMENT

No._____

Owner's Project No. _____   Engineer's Project No. _____ _____

Project _____

Contractor _____   Contract Date _____

Contract for _____

Application Date _____   Application Amount _____

For Period Ending _____

ITEM	SCHEDULE LABOR MATERIAL	PERCENT COMPLETE LABOR MATERIAL	AMOUNT EARNED TO DATE LABOR MATERIAL TOTAL

(Note that appropriate breakdown be included here)

TOTAL SCHEDULE LABOR........$ _____ $ _____

TOTAL SCHEDULE MATERIAL ....$ _____ $ _____

TOTAL CONTRACT AMOUNT ....$ _____ $ _____

MATERIAL SUITABLY STORED NOT INCORPORATED INTO WORK $ _____

CONTRACT CHANGE ORDER NO. _____PERCENT COMPLETE _____$ _____

CONTRACT CHANGE ORDER NO. _____PERCENT COMPLETE _____$ _____

CONTRACT CHANGE ORDER NO. _____PERCENT COMPLETE _____$ _____

GROSS AMOUNT DUE ....$ _____

LESS _____% RETAINAGE ....$ _____

AMOUNT DUE TO DATE ....$ _____

LESS PREVIOUS PAYMENTS ....$ _____

AMOUNT DUE THIS APPLICATION ....$ _____

The undersigned Contractor hereby swears under penalty of perjury that (1) all previous progress payments received from the owner on account of Work performed under the contract referred to above have been applied by the undersigned to discharge in full all obligations of the undersigned incurred in connection with Work covered by prior Applications for Payment under said contract, being Applications for Payment numbered 1 through _____ inclusive; and (2) all materials and equipment incorporated in said Project or otherwise listed in or covered by this Application for Payment are free and clear of all liens, claims, security interests and encumbrances.

Dated _____ 197_____   _____

(Contractor)

By _____

(Name and title)

COUNTY OF

STATE OF   } ss

Before me on this _____ day of _____ 197_____ personally appeared _____ _____ known to me, who being duly sworn, did depose and say that he is the _____ of the Contractor above mentioned; that he executed the

(office)

above Application for Payment and statement on behalf of said Contractor; and that all of the statements contained therein are true, correct and complete.

_____

Notary Public

My commission expires:

NSPE 1910-8-E (1970 Edition) © 1970, National Society of Professional Engineers

Figure 14.1 Application for payment.

APPROVAL OF PAYMENT

No. ....

Owner's Project No. ....   Engineer's Project No. ....

Project ....

Contractor ....

Contract For ....

Contract Date ....   Application Date ....

Application Amount ....   For Period Ending ....

To ....
(Owner)

     Attached hereto is the Contractor's Application for Payment for Work accomplished under the above contract through the date indicated above. Accompanying the Application is the Contractor's Affidavit stating that all previous payments to him under this contract have been applied by him to discharge in full all of his obligations in connection with the work covered by all prior Applications for Payments.

     In accordance with above contract the undersigned approves payment to the Contractor of the Amount Due as shown below.

....
Engineer

Date ....   By ....
(Name)   (Title)

STATEMENT OF WORK

Original Contract Price	$	Work to Date	$ . . . .
Net Change Orders	$	Amount Retained	$ . . . .
Current Contract Price	$	Sub. Total	$ . . . .
Work to be Done	$	Previous Payments Approved	$ . . . .
		Amount Due This Payment	$ . . . .

NSPE 1910–8–C (1970 Edition)

Figure 14.2 Approval of payment.

illustration, the bid sheets that the contractor must fill out to submit his bid already contain a typed-in quantity. The contractor then fills in the price he will charge for each bid item:

The amount that the contractor shows in the "unit price" column is actually his firm bid. The amount under the "total" column is merely the product of his unit price bid multiplied by the *engineer's quantity estimate*. The actual amount of money that the contractor will finally receive to do the work will be based upon the actual *field-measured* quantities, *not* the quantities shown in the engineer's estimate. However, for the purposes of determining the lowest bid, the quantities shown in the engineer's estimate are used during the bidding so that all bids can be compared on the same basis.

On a cost-plus-fixed-fee project, the contractor agrees to a fixed profit level, and he is reimbursed for all costs of labor and material at their actual cost to himself, plus the addition of a fixed fee rate for his profit. Under this arrangement, the contractor's books must be open to the owner or his representative, and all of the contractor's costs must be regularly audited to establish the amount of progress payments.

EVALUATION OF CONTRACTOR'S PAYMENT REQUESTS

Submittal Requirements

At a prearranged date each month, the contractor is expected to submit a request for payment for the work he has performed during the preceding month (Fig. 14.1). Prior to forwarding these payment requests to the owner through the design firm or construction management firm for payment, the resident project representative must check to assure that all items for which the contractor has claimed payment have actually been accomplished. If a project was contracted for on a lump sum basis, a reasonable estimate of the fair value of the work that was accomplished might be very difficult, so under the terms of the General Conditions of the Contract for both the NSPE and the AIA, the contractor is required to submit a schedule of values of the various portions of the work, including quantities where required, so that these values can be used as the basis for determining the amount of progress payments to be made to the contractor each month. The contractor is normally required to show evidence at the time of submittal of his price breakdown that his pricing is correct, and that the total aggregate amount will equal the sum of the total contract amount. Each item should contain its own share of profit at overhead.

If a project is based upon a unit price bid, as many engineering contracts are, the actual unit prices stated in the original bid will be held as the basis for computation of all progress payment amounts. It is essential to note, however, that, because a unit price contract does not have a fixed price ceiling, but the actual final cost to the owner will be determined by the actual quantities actually completed, the determination of field quantities must be very precise. This is in direct contrast to the administration of a lump sum contract where even if a small error was made one month, it would be compensated for in later payments. The contractor cannot receive more money than the stated fixed price, even if some of the final quantities varied somewhat from the anticipated amounts. Under

BID SHEET

Schedule of Prices for the Construction of

PORTER STREET IMPROVEMENTS

Item No.	Description	Quantity and Unit	Unit Price	Amount
1.	Excavation and removal of existing asphalt concrete and aggregate base	1050 cu yd	$ 0.25	$ 262.50
2.	Asphalt concrete paving	560 tons	$ 30.00	$ 16,800.00
3.	Aggregate base	1500 cu yd	$ 5.50	$ 8,250.00
4.	Catch basin; double grate	1 each	$ 400.00	$ 400.00
5.	Reinforced concrete pipe 24-inch diameter	120 lin ft	$ 24.60	$ 2,952.00
6.	Reinforced concrete headwall	For the lump sum of		$ 5,000.00

TOTAL $ $ 33,664.50

NOTE:

All amounts and totals in the Bid Sheet will be subject to verification by the Owner. In case of variation between the unit price and the totals shown by the bidder, the unit price will be considered as the bid.

The quantities listed in the Bid Sheet are supplied to give an indication of the general scope of the work, but the accuracy of these figures is not guaranteed and the bidder shall make his own estimates from the drawings.

* * * * *

Figure 14.3 A unit price bid.

the concept of a lump sum contract, the contractor agrees to build a complete project that will perform the intended function indicated in the plans and specifications. Anything that is necessary to accomplish this must be considered as part of his contract, even if not specifically stated. On a unit price contract, however, the contractor may still be required to construct a complete functional project, but if any variation occurs in the quantities of any of the separate bid items listed, he is entitled to an amount of money equal to the unit price of the bid item multiplied by the actual quantity of that item that was constructed or furnished. In this manner, if the quantity of a bid item exceeds what the original quantity estimate indicated, the contractor will receive more money than shown in his bid; and if it is less than in the original bid, he will receive less than the amount of his bid. All such quantity differences must be based upon the unit price stated by the contractor in his bid, as that alone is the controlling amount, not the extension obtained by multiplying the bid price by the anticipated quantity. The one notable exception to this rule is if the quantity overrun or underrun is in excess of 25 percent of the bid item. Then the contractor is entitled to renegotiate his unit price for the item. Although this 25 percent figure is frequently mentioned in contract documents, in situations where it was omitted, the principle of allowing a price renegotiation in cases in which the actual quantities differed from the anticipated quantities by over 25 percent has been upheld by some state courts.

Equipment and Materials Delivered but not Yet Used in the Work

The inspector should check the specifications carefully on this point before he starts to total the amount of payment due to the contractor. Often, certain fabricated items of equipment or certain products are delivered to the site a considerable amount of time before they are actually needed or installed in the work. In some contracts no payment will be made for any such material until it is actually used in the work (such as large pipe mains, which may not be paid for until they have been laid, jointed, backfilled, tested, and paved over; or large pieces of equipment such as motors, generators, valves, or steel plate fabrications that had to be made up especially for the project as opposed to an off-the-shelf item). A second approach to this problem is to allow partial payment for materials or equipment as soon as they have been delivered to the site. In any case, the decision is not for the resident project representative to make, but must be determined by the provisions of the specifications.

Unit prices are often quoted for items as "installed-in-place." Wherever this is the case, it is not reasonable to allow full payment for any material solely on the basis of its having been delivered to the site. If the contract allows any payment at all, and the material is priced as "in-place" then the contractor should provide a copy of his invoice for the material to support his claim for payment of the delivery and storage of the material at the site. There is considerable justification for allowing some payment for certain types of materials, products, or equipment because the contractor is expected to pay his supplier within 30 days after delivery in most cases. Thus, if a fabricated item like mortar-lined-and-coated steel pipe, or precast prestressed roof members, or special pumps or large valves are ordered, there is often a long lead time required in placing the order to be certain of delivery in time. Often, when the item is actually delivered, the work may not yet be far enough along to allow its immediate installation; yet the contractor has already obligated himself to payment. Nevertheless, there is nothing that the inspector can personally do to alleviate the problem except to carefully read the provisions of the specifications to make certain whether such payments can be made under the terms of the contract. It can save a lot of arguments if the inspector can show the contractor the provisions of the specifications that control such payments.

A word of caution at this point. As long as a contract is based upon a lump sum price, or as long as a unit price contract shows separate line items for a material and its installation, no particular problem exists other than a need to exercise care in evaluating the amount of work and materials claimed for payment. However, on a unit price contract where a single line item covers both the cost of the material as well as its installation a serious risk of overpayment exists.

Take the example of an underground pipeline under a roadway. Often a single price may be quoted to cover the cost of the pipe and its installation, including all earthwork and even the pavement over the trench, as would be the case for Item No. 5 in the Bid Sheet shown in Figure 14.3. In such cases, the price per linear foot of completed pipeline already includes the price of the pipe material. If early payment was allowed for pipe that was delivered to the site, but not yet installed, the cost of the pipe would have to be subtracted from the price claimed later for construction of the pipeline in place, otherwise the contractor would be receiving payment twice for the same pipe.

Payment for Extra Work and Change Orders

Although in a unit price contract a prearranged value has been established for each item of work to facilitate the determination of the amount owed to the contractor, and on a lump sum job, a bid breakdown is often requested to establish a fair price for any work completed, as a means of arriving at the amount to be paid for each monthly progress payment, the cost of extra work that was not included in the original contract must be negotiated separately or a fair method agreed upon for determining its value.

Obviously, if no ground work were laid to establish a procedure for evaluating and determining the cost of such extra work, then the contractor would have the owner "over a barrel," so to speak. Thus, it is common in all standard forms of the General Conditions of a construction contract to specify the means of determining such costs. It should be kept in mind, however, that not all General Conditions treat this subject area the same. Many such documents, because they must be universally acceptable, have been so watered down in their provisions that extensive Supplementary General Conditions must be prepared to adapt these provisions to a particular job.

General Conditions documents such as the AIA General Conditions advocate the principle of completing such extra work on a cost-plus basis with "a reasonable allowance for overhead and profit." Unfortunately, what is reasonable to the contractor may not be considered as reasonable by the owner. Most of the General Conditions used by public agencies for their own use have established fixed policies, and their General Conditions reflect this. An example can be seen in the provisions of the *Contract Documents for Construction of Federally Assisted Water and Sewer Projects* shown in Figure 14.4, where a maximum of 15 percent of the actual cost of the work is allowed to cover the cost of general overhead and profit.

Similar to the above, but considerably more comprehensive, are the provisions for "Change Orders and Extra Work" in the contract provisions of several public agencies, as illustrated in Figure 14.5, following:

As it can be determined from the provisions shown in the accompanying examples, some questions may still be unanswered and are thus subject to negotiation at the time of the owner's incurring the cost of extra work. If all the possible contingencies and conditions could be anticipated, then and only then could a document be produced that would provide a definite answer to any question relating to the cost of such extra work. Obviously, this is an impossible task. However, the document illustrated in Figure 14.6 seems to come close to accomplishing this objective. In that example the contract terms have been clearly defined so as to minimize misunderstandings and eliminate ambiguities. It also reflects an understanding of the current pricing structure in construction within its jurisdictional area by establishing a scale of allowances based upon an understanding of the differences between the costs of administering labor, materials, and equipment.

As a part of the contractor's payment request, if extra work authorized by the issuance of a valid change order was completed during the payment period, the resident inspector must also evaluate, not only the regular bid items and quantities, but also under the terms of the specific contract documents controlling the project, he must determine the validity of the claims of the contractor for the amount of money claimed for completing such extra

---

14. *CHANGES IN CONTRACT PRICE*

14.1 The CONTRACT PRICE may be changed only by a CHANGE ORDER. The value of any WORK covered by a CHANGE ORDER or of any claim for increase or decrease in the CONTRACT PRICE shall be determined by one or more of the following methods in the order of precedence listed below:

    (a) Unit prices previously approved.

    (b) An agreed lump sum.

    (c) The actual cost for labor, direct overhead, materials, supplies, equipment, and other services necessary to complete the work. In addition there shall be added an amount to be agreed upon but not to exceed fifteen (15) percent of the actual cost of the WORK to cover the cost of general overhead and profit.

Figure 14.4 Provisions for "Change in Contract Price" from contract documents for construction of federally assisted water and sewer projects.

10. **CHANGE ORDERS AND EXTRA WORK** — (a) When construction conditions are such that it becomes necessary or desirable to modify the Contract Documents to cover unforseeen circumstances encountered during the progress of the work, the Engineer may by written order make reasonable changes in, additions to, or subtractions from the work on the project. No such change order by the Engineer shall be effective until approved in writing by the Owner.

(b)   The Contractor shall perform each item of extra work so ordered, furnishing all labor, materials, tools, equipment, supplies, transportation, utilities, and other facilities necessary for the proper execution and completion of such extra work, in the same manner as if such extra work were originally set forth in the contract documents.

(c)   Unless a lump sum or a unit price shall be mutually agreed upon before the change order pertaining thereto has been approved, the compensation for such extra work shall be in an amount equal to the actual necessary field cost incurred by the Contractor plus 15 percent of such field cost; provided, that such 15 percent shall apply only to straight-time field costs and shall not be allowed for any costs of overtime or holiday work may have been ordered by the Engineer in accordance with the provisions of Article 45.3 of these General Conditions; said percentage shall be understood to cover all related overhead expense and profit on the item of work involved. The field cost shall include all expenditures for labor directly engaged on such extra work, including compensation insurance, taxes on such labor, all materials and supplies furnished therefor by the Contractor, and a reasonable allowance for the use of his plant and equipment where required; but, such field cost shall in no case include any charge for or distribution of office and clerical expenses, general and field superintendence, bonds, insurance other than compensation insurance, and other expenses not directly occasioned by such extra work.

Figure 14.5 Provisions for "Change Orders and Extra Work" from a typical set of public agency documents.

work. In each case, the inspector should consult the project manager of the design firm or the owner to determine the exact terms of the agreement that cover the construction of such extra work, and apply these terms to his evaluation. In any case, the terms of the contract General Conditions should be carefully followed, as they form the basis for any specific agreement with the owner for establishing the costs of extra work.

STANDARD CONTRACT PROVISIONS FOR MEASUREMENT AND PAYMENT

Although each set of contract documents treats this subject slightly differently, the provisions of the project documents must be the final determining factor in establishing the method and procedure of handling contractor payment requests. The following references are provided as an aid to comparing the provisions of several General Conditions documents in current use:

1. NSPE—Article 14 of the General Conditions
2. AIA—Article 9 of the General Conditions.
3. JPL—Article GP-7 of the General Provisions (Jet Propulsion Labs)
4. GSA—Article 7 of the General Provisions (Federal Contracts)
5. Contract Documents for Construction of Federally Assisted Water and Sewer Projects—Article 19 of the General Conditions

Although the foregoing is typical of most stock forms of General Conditions, or General Provisions as they are sometimes called, the AGC/ASCE documents vary some-

reasonable time, the Engineer and the Contractor fail to agree upon the cost of the eliminated work, the Engineer will unilaterally fix the cost of the eliminated work based upon his estimates of decreased labor and material costs to be incurred by the Contractor. Whether established by agreement of the parties or unilaterally by the Engineer, to the cost of the eliminated work will be added the allowances for overhead and profit, in accordance with Section 11 (c). The sum of the cost of the eliminated work plus the allowance for overhead and profit will be the amount to be deductible from the contract price as a credit to the District for the eliminated work.

(d) The Contractor shall proceed to immediately revise his schedule to accommodate the changed work upon receipt of a written order to make the changes, notwithstanding the fact that an agreement has not been reached regarding the cost of the changes. The Contractor shall start and complete the changed work in accordance with the revised schedule. If, in the opinion of the Engineer, the Contractor is not performing the changed work in accordance with the revised schedule, the Engineer may withhold certification of estimates for payment until such time that the Contractor does perform in accordance with the revised schedule. Within 20 working days after receipt of a written order to perform changes, the Contractor shall submit to the Engineer his claim for an extension of time and for the increased compensation which he considers necessary as a result of performing the changes; such claim shall contain an itemized cost breakdown of claimed increased compensation. If the Contractor fails to submit in writing his claims for increased compensation or extension of time within 20 working days after receipt of a written order to perform changes, the Engineer may make an equitable adjustment of the contract completion time and compensation based on his judgment of increases or decreases in costs or in time required to complete the contract due to the changes.

(e) When required to perform and complete the changed work in accordance with the revised schedule, the Contractor shall provide additional labor, materials, equipment, or other factors of production in excess of those in use before the changed work was ordered. When the changed work is not the current controlling operation or does not comprise a part of such controlling operation, the additional factors of production provided by the Contractor for the purpose of performing changed work shall not be obtained by removing factors of production from any part of the current controlling operation of the contract as a whole when such removal would delay the time of completing such current controlling operation.

11. **Extra work.** — (a) If during the performance of the contract it shall, in the opinion of the Engineer, become necessary or desirable for the proper completion of the contract to order work done or materials or equipment furnished which, in the opinion of the Engineer, are not susceptible of classification under the unit-price items named in the Bidding Sheet, and are not included in any item for which a lump sum is bid, the Contractor shall do and perform such work and furnish such materials and equipment. Such labor, material, and equipment will be classed as extra work and shall be ordered in writing before such work is started. No extra work shall be paid for unless ordered in writing. All claims for extra work shall be submitted to the District on standard forms provided by the District, and shall be supplemented by such other data as the Engineer may require.

(b) Extra work and work involving a combination of increases and decreases in the work will ordinarily be paid for at a lump sum or unit price agreed upon in writing by the Engineer and the Contractor before the extra work order is issued. In the negotiation of lump sum or unit prices, the agreed estimated cost of the work plus an allowance for overhead and profit, not to exceed the allowances in Section 11 (c) shall be used. In the event the Contractor fails to submit his proposal within the prescribed time, or the Engineer and the Contractor fail to agree upon a price or time extension, or both, within a reasonable time, or if in the judgment of the Engineer, it is impracticable because of the nature of the work or for any other reason to fix the price or to adjust the time for completion before the work order shall be issued, equitable payment for the extra work and an equitable adjustment in the time for completion of the Contract will be made by the Engineer on the basis of his estimate of increases or decreases in the quantities of work required. To the Contractor's costs of the work due to changes will be added an allowance for overhead and profit in accordance with the schedule set forth in Section 11 (c), or at the option of the Engineer, on the basis of cost-plus pursuant to Section 11 (c).

(c) Extra work and work involving a combination of increases and decreases in the work ordered on the basis of cost-plus will be paid for at the actual necessary cost as determined by the Engineer, plus allowances for overhead and profit. For work involving a combination of increases and decreases in the work the actual necessary cost will be the arithmetic sum of the additive and deductive costs. The allowance for overhead and profit shall include full compensation for superintendence, bond and insurance premiums, taxes, office expense, and all other items of expense or cost not included in the cost of labor, materials, or equipment provided for under Subsections (d), (e), and (f), hereof. The allowance for overhead and profit will be made in accordance with the following schedule:

ACTUAL NECESSARY COST	ALLOWANCE
Labor	20 percent
Materials	15 percent
Equipment	15 percent

GENERAL CONDITIONS
PAGE C-10

Figure 14.6 *Provisions for payments for "Extra Work" from the General Conditions of the construction contract of a large metropolitan water agency.*

The actual necessary cost for labor, materials, or equipment will be computed in accordance with Subsections (d), (e), and (f), respectively, hereof. Superintendence, bond and insurance premiums, taxes, and other general expense will not be included in the computation of actual necessary cost. It is understood that labor, materials, and equipment may be furnished by the Contractor or by the subcontractor on behalf of the Contractor. When all or any part of the extra work is performed by a subcontractor, the allowance specified hereinbefore shall be applied to the labor, materials, and equipment costs of the subcontractor, to which the Contractor may add 5 percent of the Subcontractor's total cost for the extra work. Regardless of the number of tiers or layers of subcontractors, the 5 percent increase above the subcontractor's total cost which includes the allowances for overhead and profit specified hereinbefore may be applied 1 time only for each separate extra work transaction. The Contractor shall furnish the Engineer daily report sheets covering the direct costs of labor and materials and charges for equipment, whether furnished by the Contractor, subcontractor, or other forces, and the report sheets shall be signed by the Contractor or his authorized agent. The daily report sheets shall provide names or identifications and classifications or workmen, and hours worked; size, type, and identification number of equipment, and hours operated. Material charges shall be substantiated by valid copies of vendor's invoices. The Engineer will make any necessary adjustments and compile the costs of cost-plus work. When these reports are agreed upon and signed by both parties, they shall become the basis of payment for the work performed, but shall not preclude subsequent adjustment based on a later audit.

(d) *Labor.* — The cost of labor used in performing the work by the Contractor, a subcontractor, or other forces will be the sum of the following:

(1) The actual wages paid plus any employer payments to, or on behalf of workers for fringe benefits including health and welfare, pension, vacation, and similar purposes. The cost of labor may include the wages paid to foremen when determined by the Engineer that the services of foremen do not constitute a part of the allowance for superintendence included as part of the overhead allowance.

(2) All payment imposed by State and Federal laws including, but not limited to, compensation insurance, and social security payments.

(3) The amount paid for subsistence and travel required by collective bargaining agreements, or in accordance with the regular practice of the employer.

At the beginning of the contract and as later requested by the Engineer, the Contractor shall furnish the Engineer proof of labor compensation rates being paid or paid.

(e) *Materials.* — The cost of materials used in performing the work will be the cost to the purchaser, whether Contractor, subcontractor or other forces, from the supplier thereof, except as the following are applicable:

(1) Cash or trade discounts available to the purchaser shall be credited to the District notwithstanding the fact that such discounts may not have been taken.

(2) In materials secured by other than a direct purchase and direct billing to the purchaser, the cost shall be deemed to be the price paid to the actual supplier as determined by the Engineer. Markup except for actual costs incurred in the handling of such materials will not be allowed.

(3) Payment for materials from sources owned wholly or in part by the purchaser shall not exceed the price paid by the purchaser for similar materials from said sources on contract items or the current wholesale price for such materials delivered to the jobsite, whichever price is lower.

(4) If in the opinion of the Engineer the cost of materials is excessive, or the Contractor does not furnish satisfactory evidence of the cost of such materials, then the cost shall be deemed to be the lowest current wholesale price for the quantity concerned delivered to the jobsite less cash or trade discount. The District reserves the right to furnish materials for the work and no claim shall be made by the Contractor for costs and profit on such materials.

(f) *Equipment.* — The Contractor will be paid for the use of equipment at the rental rate listed for such equipment in the State of California Department of Transportation publication entitled, "Equipment Rental Rates and General Prevailing Wage Rates," which is in effect on the date upon which the work is accomplished. Such rental rate will be used to compute payments for equipment whether the equipment is under the Contractor's control through direct ownership, leasing, renting, or another method of acquisition. The rental rate to be applied for use of each item of equipment shall be the rate resulting in the least total cost to the District for the total period of use. If it is deemed necessary by the Contractor to use equipment not listed in the foregoing publication, an equitable rental rate for the equipment will be established by the Engineer. The Contractor may furnish cost data which might assist the Engineer in the establishment of the rental rate.

(1) The rental rates paid, as above provided, shall include the cost of fuel, oil, lubrication supplies, small tools, necessary attachments, repairs and maintenance of all kinds, depreciation, storage, insurance, and all incidentals. Operators of equipment will be separately paid for as provided in Section 11 (d).

GENERAL CONDITIONS
PAGE C-11

Figure 14.6 (continued)

(2) All equipment shall, in the opinion of the Engineer, be in good working condition and suitable for the purpose for which the equipment is to be used.

(3) Before construction equipment is used on the work, the Contractor shall plainly stencil or stamp an identifying number thereon at a conspicuous location, and shall furnish to the Engineer, in duplicate, a description of the equipment and its identifying number.

(4) Unless otherwise specified, manufacturer's ratings and manufacturer approved modifications shall be used to classify equipment for the determination of applicable rental rates. Equipment which has no direct power unit shall be powered by a unit of at least the minimum rating recommended by the manufacturer.

(5) Individual pieces of equipment or tools having a replacement value of $100 or less, whether or not consumed by use, shall be considered to be small tools and no payment will be made therefor.

(6) Rental time will not be allowed while equipment is inoperative due to breakdowns.

(g) *Equipment on the work.* — The rental time to be paid for equipment on the work shall be the time the equipment is in productive operation on the extra work being performed and, in addition, shall include the time required to move the equipment to the location of the extra work and return it to the original location or to another location requiring no more time than that required to return it to its original location, except that moving time will not be paid for if the equipment is used at the site of the extra work on other than the extra work. Loading and transporting costs will be allowed, in lieu of moving time, when the equipment is moved by means other than its own power, except that no payment will be made for loading and transporting costs when the equipment is used at the site of the extra work on other than the extra work. The following shall be used in computing the rental time of equipment on the work:

(1) When hourly rates are listed, any part of an hour less than 30 minutes of operation shall be considered to be 1/2-hour of operation, and any part of an hour in excess of 30 minutes will be considered 1 hour of operation.

(2) When daily rates are listed, any part of a day less than 4 hours of operation shall be considered to be 1/2-day of operation, and any part of a day in excess of 4 hours will be considered 1 day of operation. When owner-operated equipment is used to perform extra work to be paid for on a cost-plus basis, the Contractor will be paid for the equipment and operator, as follows:

(i) Payment for the equipment will be made in accordance with the provisions in Section 11(f).

(ii) Payment for the cost of labor and subsistence or travel allowance will be made at the rates paid by the Contractor to other workers operating similar equipment already on the project, or in the absence of such other workers, at the rates for such labor established by collective bargaining agreements for the type of workmen and location of the work, whether or not the operator is actually covered by such an agreement. A labor surcharge will be added to the cost of labor described herein in accordance with the provisions of Section 11(d), which surcharge shall constitute full compensation for payments imposed by State and Federal laws and all other payments made to or on behalf of workers other than actual wages.

(iii) To the direct cost of equipment rental and labor, computed as provided herein, will be added the allowances for equipment rental and labor as provided in Section 11(c).

(h) *Special services.* — Special extra work or services are defined as that extra work characterized by extraordinary complexity, sophistication, or innovation, or a combination of the foregoing attributes which are unique to the construction industry. The following may be considered by the Engineer in making estimates for payment for special services:

(1) When the Engineer and the Contractor, by agreement, determine that a special service or extra work is required which cannot be performed by the forces of the Contractor or those of any of his subcontractors, the special service or extra work may be performed by an entity especially skilled in the work to be performed. After validation of invoices and determination of market values by the Engineer, invoices for special services or extra work based upon the current fair market value thereof may be accepted without complete itemization of labor, material, and equipment rental costs.

(2) When the itemization of labor, material, and equipment rental costs is impractical, or not in accordance with established billing practices of the special service industry involved, the Engineer may accept other evidence of the cost of special services in lieu of itemized invoices.

(3) When the Contractor is required to perform extra work necessitating special fabrication or machining process in a fabrication or a machine shop facility away from the jobsite, the charges for that portion of the extra work performed at the off-site facility may, by agreement, be accepted as a

Figure 14.6 (continued)

special service and accordingly, the invoices for the work may be accepted without detailed itemization.

(4) All invoices for special services will be adjusted by deducting all cash or trade discounts offered or available, whether the discounts were taken or not. In lieu of the allowances for overhead and profit specified in Section 11(c), an allowance of 5 percent will be added to invoices for special services.

(i) *Right to audit.* — If the Contractor submits a claim to the Engineer for additional compensation for extra work, the Engineer shall have the right, as a condition to considering the claim, and as a basis for evaluation of the claim, and until the claim has been settled, to audit the Contractor's books to the extent they are relevant, as determined by the Engineer. This right shall include the right to examine books, records, documents, and other evidence and accounting procedures and practices, sufficient to discover and verify all direct and indirect costs of whatever nature claimed to have been incurred or anticipated to be incurred and for which the claim has been submitted. The right to audit shall include the right to inspect the Contractor's plants, or such parts thereof, as may be or have been engaged in the performance of this Contract. The Contractor further agrees that the right to audit encompasses all subcontracts and is binding upon all subcontractors. The rights to examine and inspect herein provided for shall be exercisable through such representatives as the Engineer deems desirable during the Contractor's normal business hours at the office of the Contractor. The Contractor shall make available to the Engineer for auditing all relevant accounting records and documents, and other financial data, and upon request, shall submit true copies of requested records to the Engineer.

(j) When extra work ordered by the Engineer is performed by forces other than the Contractor's organization, the Contractor shall reach agreement with such other forces as to the distribution of the payment made by the District for such work.

(k) All extra work performed hereunder shall be subject to all of the provisions of the contract and the Contractor's sureties shall be bound with reference thereto as under the original contract.

12. Temporary suspension of work — time of completion. — (a) By written order to the Contractor, the Engineer may suspend the work wholly or in part, for an indefinite period or for such period as he may deem necessary, for any of the following reasons:

(1) Weather conditions or other conditions which are unfavorable for the proper prosecution of the work,

(2) Failure of the Contractor to carry out orders given or to perform any provisions of the contract, and

(3) The convenience and benefit of the District.

Such suspension shall be effective upon receipt by the Contractor of the written order suspending the work and shall be terminated upon receipt by the Contractor of the written order terminating the suspension.

(i) If, under authority of (1) or (3), above, the Engineer orders a suspension of all or a portion of the work which is the current controlling operation, the days on which the suspension is in effect shall not be considered working days, as defined in subsection (b), hereof. If a portion of work so suspended is not the current controlling operation at the time of such suspension, but subsequently does become the current controlling operation, the days on which the suspension is in effect, after the date on which such portion of the work does become the current controlling operation, shall not be considered working days, as defined by subsection (b), hereof.

(ii) If a suspension of work is ordered by the Engineer under authority of (2), above, the days on which the suspension order is in effect shall be considered working days if such days are working days within the meaning of the definition set forth in subsection (b), hereof.

(iii) If the Contractor is delayed in completion of the work beyond the time named in the Detail Specifications for the completion of the work, by acts of God or of the public enemy, fire, floods, epidemics, quarantine restrictions, strikes, labor disputes, or by freight embargoes, the Contractor shall be entitled to an adjustment in the time of completion in like manner as if the work had been suspended for the convenience and benefit of the District. No such adjustment will be made unless the Contractor shall notify the Engineer in writing of the causes of delay within 15 days from the beginning of any such delay. The Engineer shall ascertain the facts and the extent of the delay, and his findings thereon shall be final and conclusive. No adjustment in time shall be made for delays resulting from noncompliance with the contract nor for ordinary delays and accidents and the occurrence of such shall not relieve the Contractor from the necessity of maintaining the required progress.

(iv) In the event the contract completion is delayed beyond the time named in the Detail Specifications by reason of shortages of materials, the Contractor shall be entitled to an adjustment in the time of completion in like manner as if the work had been suspended for the convenience and benefit of the District; provided, however, that the Contractor shall furnish documentation acceptable to the Engineer that he placed or attempted to place firm orders with suppliers a reasonable time in advance of the required date of delivery of the materials in question, that such shortages shall have developed following the date such orders were placed or attempts made to place same, that said shortages are general throughout the affected industry, and that the Contractor shall, to the degree possible, have made revisions in the

Figure 14.6 (continued)

what in that their provisions for progress payments to the contractor are covered as a part of the *Form of Agreement,* and only the provisions for "Acceptance and Final Payment" are covered in The General Conditions of Contract for Engineering Construction.

Similar provisions are made in the various Standard Specifications, as these documents generally include all general provisions as well as technical ones. The principal difference is that the majority of the Standard Specifications also contain provisions for measurement methods to be used in determining the payment quantities—an excellent way of minimizing field disputes resulting from disagreements over the method of measurement, which can result in significant differences. The following references are provided as an aid in comparing the measurement and payment provisions of some typical Standard Specifications:

1. American Public Works Association/Associated General Contractors Standard Specifications for Public Works Construction
   Measurement of Quantities for Unit Price Work: Section 9–1
   Measurement of Quantities for Lump Contracts: Section 9–2
   Payment: Section 9–3
2. California Department of Transportation Standard Specifications
   Measurement of Quantities: Section 9–1.01
   Payment: Sections 9–1.02 through 9–1.09
3. FAA Standard Specifications for Construction of Airports
   Measurement of Quantities: Section 80–01
   Payment: Sections 80–02 through 80–07
4. Florida Department of Transportation Standard Specifications for Road and Bridge Construction
   Measurement of Quantities: Section 9–1
   Payment: Sections 9–2 through 9–10
5. Virginia Road and Bridge Specifications
   Measurement of Quantities: Sections 109.01 through 109.02
   Payment: Sections 109.03 through 109.09

INTERPRETING THE CONTRACTOR'S BID

Interpretation of Bidding Errors

If the final field-measured amount of earth excavation shown in Figure 14.8 was determined to be 53,000 cubic yards instead of the 52,000 estimated by the engineer, then the actual payment to the contractor for completing that item would be 53,000 × $2.75 and he would be paid $145,750 instead of the $143,000 shown in the totals column of his bid sheet. If the contractor knew in advance that the engineer's estimate was incorrect on this item, it might be to his advantage to place a higher unit price on this item, thus assuring himself of higher profits without placing himself in a noncompetitive position against the other bidders (see "Unbalanced Bids").

Often, errors are made in bids submitted and a determination must be made as to what is the true value of a bid. One common error involves a multiplication of the unit price and the estimated quantity. In the example in Figure 14.7, it can be seen that the proper product of the unit price times the quantity should be $575,056 instead of the $175,056 shown:

Item No.	Description	Quantity and Unit	Unit Price	Amount
8.	Concrete Conduit	5,080 cu. yd.	$ 113.20	$ 175,056.00

Figure 14.7 Example of error in bid computation.

The owner at the time of opening and comparing bids is within his rights to recalculate the total amount, using the unit price and the engineer's estimate as the controlling figures. This could result in this bidder losing the job, as the true bid price would be the true product, not the total the bidder had listed. In some cases, contractors have been allowed to withdraw a bid after opening where a clerical error existed; however, in an apparent equal number of such cases, such withdrawal has been successfully refused.

Similarly, where a bid sheet asks for the amount in "words and figures," the *words* will govern over the figures, as there is less chance of error this way. This type of error is likely in either a lump sum or a unit price bid amount. If the amount of the bid read as follows:

"Four thousand two hundred and forty-seven dollars ($40,247.00)"

The amount of the bid would be held as $4,247 not $40,247.

Unbalanced Bids

For unit price contracts, a balanced bid is one in which each bid item is priced to carry its share of the cost of the work and also its share of the contractor's profit. Occasionally, contractors will raise prices on certain items and make corresponding reductions of the prices on other items, without changing the total amount of the bid for the project. The result is an unbalanced bid. In general, extremely unbalanced bids are considered as undesirable and should not be permitted when detected, although the practice sometimes seems justified from the contractor's viewpoint. Some of the purposes of unbalancing bidding are as follows:

1. To discourage certain types of construction and to encourage others that may be more favorable to the contractor.

BALANCED BID BASED UPON COMPETITIVE UNIT PRICES

Item No.	Description	Quantity and Unit	Unit Price	Amount
1.	Site preparation	For the lump sum of		$ 17,500.00
2.	Temporary sheeting	12,200 sq ft	$ 0.01	$ 122.00
3.	Permanent sheeting	71,700 sq ft	$ 1.81	$ 129,915.00
4.	Earth excavation	52,000 cu yd	$ 2.75	$ 143,000.00
5.	Rock excavation	9,000 cu yd	$ 16.25	$ 146,250.00
6.	Reinforcing steel	433 tons	$ 450.00	$ 194,850.00
7.	Conduit bedding	1,320 cu yd	$ 13.50	$ 17,820.00
8.	Concrete conduit	5,080 cu yd	$ 130.00	$ 660,400.00

TOTAL $ 1,309,857.00

Figure 14.8 Balanced bid based on competitive unit prices.

2. When the contractor believes that the engineer's estimate for certain items is low, by unbalancing his bid in favor of such items, he can obtain an increased (unearned) profit in the actual payment of the work without increasing the apparent total amount of his bid.

3. Unreliable contractors may increase their bid prices for the first items of work to be completed, with corresponding reductions elsewhere in the bid, with the intention of receiving excessive early payments, then defaulting on the contract. This could leave the surety to complete the contract with insufficient funds remaining in the contract.

4. By unbalancing his bid in favor of items that will be completed early in the progress of the work, a contractor can build up his working capital (front money) for the remainder of the work. This can also serve to eliminate the financial squeeze caused by the usual 10 percent retention money. This is a fairly common practice.

Of all of the mentioned reasons for unbalancing a bid, only the last item seems to have some justification when dealing with reliable contractors. The expenses of mobilizing the construction plant, bringing the equipment and materials to the site, and the general costs of getting the work started are significant. These items often do not appear on the bid as separate bid items, and therefore are paid for only by adding their cost to the items actually listed. This usually means, however, that they would get paid for only as the work progresses, even though the actual cost to the contractor was all incurred at the beginning of the job. This can cause a hardship on the contractor in that his working capital would be tied up in the work to the sole advantage of the owner.

The prevention of unbalanced bids requires a knowledge of construction costs in the project area in order that unreasonable bids on individual items may be detected. An obvious case of unbalanced bidding should be considered as grounds for rejecting the entire bid.*

Example of an Unbalanced Bid

Initially, a contractor must figure his bid normally without unbalancing it in order to produce a competitive price. The price thus determined will become the ''bottom line'' price for the future unbalanced bid. The following example is based upon a partial list of bid items from the low bid for a reinforced box culvert bid in Connecticut in 1976. All original bid items and the quantities are all furnished in the bidding documents by the engineer, and the unit prices and extensions are all filled in by the bidder:

As an example, let's assume that a bidder, upon carefully studying the plans, discovers that the engineer has made an error in the quantities he has shown for temporary and permanent trench sheeting. Instead of 12,200 sq. ft. of temporary sheeting and 71,700 sq. ft. of permanent sheeting as the engineer's estimate indicates, totalling 83,900 sq. ft. of trench sheeting all together, let us assume that the bidder has discovered that although the total of 83,900 sq. ft. of sheeting is correct, the engineer has the amounts wrong. According to the bidder's estimate, there are actually 73,900 sq. ft. of temporary sheeting and only 10,000 sq. ft. of permanent sheeting. Now, although the price of the temporary sheeting is low because of the contractor's ability to reuse the material, the opportunities presented by the knowledge that the quantities are in error might suggest to the bidder that if his price on this item is high enough, the added quantity over that indicated in the engineer's estimate could be a financial windfall. The bidder, of course, also knows that if he raises that bid item alone, the total bid price will be too high and he may not get the job. Therefore, he must reduce the prices of certain other items to compensate for the raise in the unit price for temporary sheeting. When completed, his new bid must have the same ''bottom line'' total as the balanced bid:

In the unbalanced bid in Figure 14.9 the bidder has raised the unit prices of Bid Items 2 and 3, and compensated by lowering the unit prices for Bid Items 6 and 8. At the same time he has increased the amount of money bid for site preparation because it will be the first item completed. In this way it could provide the bidder with additional working capital (front money). Note that the total bid price (bottom line) has remained the same as in the original balanced bid.

By holding the original competitive bid price, the bidder assures himself of a fair

*Robert W. Abbett, *Engineering Contracts and Specifications,* John Wiley & Sons, Inc., New York, 1951.

UNBALANCED BID BASED UPON KNOWN QUANTITY ERRORS IN ENGINEER'S ESTIMATE

Item No.	Description	Quantity and Unit	Unit Price	Amount
1.	Site preparation	For the lump sum of		$ 23,943.18 *
2.	Temporary sheeting	12,200 sq ft	$ 4.19	$ 51,118.00 *
3.	Permanent sheeting	71,700 sq ft	$ 2.53	$ 181,401.00 *
4.	Earth excavation	52,000 cu yd	$ 2.75	$ 143,000.00
5.	Rock excavation	9,000 cu yd	$ 16.25	$ 146,250.00
6.	Reinforcing steel	433 tons	$ 395.54	$ 171,268.82 *
7.	Conduit bedding	1,320 cu yd	$ 13.50	$ 17,820.00
8.	Concrete conduit	5,080 cu yd	$ 113.20	$ 575,056.00 *

TOTAL $ 1,309,857.00

(* Denotes unbalanced bid items)

Figure 14.9 *Unbalanced bid based on known quantity errors in the engineer's estimate.*

chance of being awarded the job. Then, if this bidder gets the job, the payments to him as the contractor will be based upon the *actual* quantities of each item of the bid sheet actually completed. Thus, the high bid price on the quantity that the engineer showed as low will yield high unearned profits, which are not reduced significantly by the redistribution of the other bid prices in the unbalanced bid:

A quick comparison of the amount of the contract price that the contractor would have received if the quantities estimated by the engineer were correct, with the amount that would actually be claimed by the contractor is shown in the following:

$1,309,857.00	Original bid price for the project (based upon engineer's quantities)
$1,412,279.00	Amount claimed by the contractor for actual quantities
$102,422.00	Additional unearned profit due to false unit prices

Note that the amount of increase in the price bid for site preparation did not alter the final payment amount; it only provided early money for the contractor to use in his operations.

ACTUAL PAYMENTS TO THE CONTRACTOR

Item No.	Description	Quantity and Unit	Unit Price	Amount
1.	Site Preparation	For the lump sum of		23,943.18
2.	Temporary sheeting	73,900 sq ft	4.19	309,641.00
3.	Permanent sheeting	10,000 sq ft	2.53	25,300.00
4.	Earth excavation	52,000 cu yd	2.75	143,000.00
5.	Rock excavation	9,000 cu yd	16.25	146,250.00
6.	Reinforcing steel	433 tons	395.54	171,268.82
7.	Conduit bedding	1,320 cu yd	13.50	17,820.00
8.	Concrete conduit	5,080 cu yd	113.20	575,056.00
			TOTAL $	$1,412,279.00

Figure 14.10 Actual payments to the contractor.

MEASUREMENT FOR PAYMENT

At first a person may be tempted to think, "What's so difficult about field measurements?" The actual problem is neither with the techniques nor with the accuracy of the measurements as taken, but rather the fact that certain types of measurements may not be representative of the true pay quantities. An example might be the determination of the amount of pipe to be paid for under the construction contract. Often, the contract documents may specify that payment will be made based upon the lengths *indicated on the drawings*. It should be noted that the lengths on the drawing are generally shown in *stations* (100-foot increments), which are always horizontal dimensions. Thus, they are not representative of the actual lengths of pipe furnished by the contractor! If the pipe is laid in trenches that have a steep profile grade, then the contractor must furnish a longer pipe than will show in the plan view, and his bid price must reflect this difference. An inspector who determines the amount of pipe to be paid for on this type of contract by

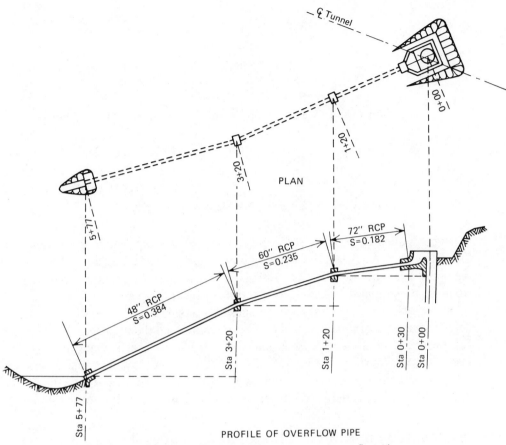

Figure 14.11 *Plan and profile of surge chamber overflow pipe.*

measuring the actual lengths of pipe laid in trenches may be approving an overpayment (Fig. 14.11).

Determination of Pay Quantities for Pipelines

The example shown in Figure 14.11 is an actual case involving an overflow pipeline from the surge chamber of a hydroelectric powerhouse project. In plan it can be seen that the pipeline is comprised of three reaches of pipe, each at a different slope in a trench on a hillside. The length of the pipe in plan, as determined from the indicated stations, is 577.00 feet, less the length of the upper structure. However, all lengths in stations are horizontal measurements only; thus, the true length is a calculated one. In the example shown, the lower reach of 48-inch diameter pipe has a slope of S = 0.384 (same as the tangent of the angle measured off the horizontal). The true length of this pipe *in place* is computed as follows:

$$\text{End station} \qquad = 5 + 77$$
$$\text{Upper station} \qquad = 3 + 20$$

$$2 + 57 \text{ stations} = 257.00 \text{ feet horizontal length}$$

For S = 0.384: vertical slope angle = 21.00678943 degrees

$$\text{True length} = \frac{257.00}{\cos 21.00678943°} = 275.30 \text{ feet (18.3 feet longer than indicated in plan view)}$$

By computing each reach of the entire length of the pipeline in the same manner, it is found that the actual length of the pipeline *in place* is 602.72 feet minus the length of the upper structure, or 572.22 feet. This is a total of 25.22 feet more pipe than indicated from the horizontal dimensions as determined from the plan.

The emphasis on the "in place" length of a pipe is based upon the fact that the actual delivered lengths of pipe will add up to even more than the indicated 572.22 feet to allow for the fitting of the spigot ends into the bell ends of each length of pipe. Thus, the inspector who measures delivered lengths of pipe for payment runs a serious risk of overpayment unless the specifications specifically call for payment to be made on the basis of lengths of pipe as delivered instead of laying length (in place dimension).

Determination of Earth and Rock Pay Quantities

It is appropriate to warn of the pitfalls involved in the determination of the quantities of earth or rock excavation or backfill. This is one of the most likely areas for miscalculation. In determining the amounts of excavation and embankment material in construction, an allowance must be made for the difference in space (volume) occupied by the material before excavation and the same material after it has been compacted in embankment. The various earth materials will be more compact in embankment (will occupy less space than they did in their original state) and rock will be less compact (will occupy more space than it did in its original state). This difference in volume between the same material as excavated and as replaced in fill is called *shrinkage* in the case of earth materials, and *increase* or *swell* in the case of rock materials.

The amount of shrinkage depends upon the kind of material and the method of placing it in the fill. Thus, a borrow area needed to provide 25,000 cubic yards of fill material may have to be capable of yielding 27,000 cubic yards of borrow material. As it can be seen, the resident project representative who is on a unit price job must be very careful to measure the material in strict accordance with the measurement for payment instructions of the job specifications. Obviously, a contractor who is excavating borrow material to be used as fill on his project would much rather be paid for the volume of earth embankment material hauled.

The actual percentages can only be determined by a qualified soils engineer; however, the following percentages are from the average of general experience. They express shrinkage in volume of several classes of materials:

Fine sand   6%
Sand and Gravel 8%
Ordinary Clay   10%
Loam   12%
Surface Soil   15%

If an understanding is reached in the contract to begin with, it does not matter which type of measurements are agreed upon. Thus the contractor would be able to structure his bid accordingly. But watch for the contractor who wants to change methods of measurement later. And, above all, the resident inspector should not yield to any pressure to count scraper or truck loads based upon loose volume!

Another method occasionally suggested by the contractor is that of paying for truck-loads of loose haul material by weight. This sounds acceptable at first, but with earth materials this is an extremely unreliable method. The principal problem lies in the variations of moisture content of the material being weighed. If the contractor uses his water truck extensively during excavation and loading into truck from the borrow area, which might be necessary in order to loosen some materials, the added weight of the damp or wet materials will be paid for as earth material, when in fact the added weight was actually due to the moisture content of the material. Although the contractor must water the material in order to achieve proper compaction when he is constructing earth embankments, this is usually done at the point of deposit. If, instead, the water is added before hauling, on a job where haul materials are paid for by weight, then the contractor can realize a tidy profit on the deal. The other way around he might even lose money if unit weight was based upon optimum moisture content, and the material was removed and weighed at a lower moisture content.

One common way of combatting the problem is to pay for materials in place *as calculated from the dimensions shown on the plans*. In this manner, the drawings represent "pay lines" and any material in excess of that shown on the plans would not be paid for. This has a disadvantage to the owner; on a heavy earthworks project it would be possible to unbalance the bid to provide a high unit price on backfill material, then if the contractor overexcavated by a few inches of depth where unit price payment is also made for excavation, the owner may end up paying twice for the same material.

Determination of Paving Quantities

On asphalt concrete pavement jobs where the asphalt concrete material was to be paid for by the ton, the inspector should watch closely for overexcavation as little as ½-inch depth. On a large roadway project the cost difference could be great. Similarly, *if* the price of asphalt concrete is priced by the square yard of material placed to a specific depth, any reduction in pavement thickness would simply assure the contractor the price for a full depth pavement while allowing him to pocket the difference between the estimated amount of material specified and the amount actually placed.

Many materials are subject to special conditions for the determination of pay quantities. Asphaltic prime coat, for example, is usually measured in gallons. However, the inspector should be certain that the volumes being paid for are based upon the volume that the material occupied at 60° F. If the material is placed hot, and the volumetric measurements are made at that time, an overpayment could result.

MEASUREMENT GUIDELINES FOR DETERMINATION OF UNIT PRICE PAY QUANTITIES

Bid Items Based Upon Linear Measure

Pipelines: Often paid for in terms of length in stations (horizontal measure) which is determined from the plans. Could possibly involve field measurements by a survey crew (also horizontal measurements).

Also paid for by measurement along the top of the pipe in place. This method will yield actual laying length. Do not allow measurement along the side of the pipe on the outside of curves. Do not accept lengths of pipe for measurement prior to laying.

Sometimes paid for by measurement in the field, *horizontally* along the centerline alignment of the pipe in place. This should result in the same quantity that would result from the stations indicated on the plans.

Curbs: Generally measured in the field by measurement along the top edge facing the street.

Watch for measurements made at the flow line, as the slope of the curb face may yield a slightly greater quantity this way under certain conditions.

Watch for measurements made at the sidewalk side of the top edge of the curbing. In some cases this can cause erroneous lengths also. The important thing is not so much *where* the measurements have been taken, but that all measurements are taken at the *same place* throughout the life of the job.

Channels: Where flood control channels or similar structures are to be lined, be sure to measure at the same location each time. If the point of reference is the toe of a slope, do not permit the measurements to be made on opposite sides, as this will alter the indicated length.

Sewer lines: Measurement of VCP sewer lines is generally made by measuement of the pipe in place. However, do not allow measurements to be made through sewer manholes, as the separate price paid for manhole construction already covers this cost.

Fencing: Measurement of chain link fencing can be accomplished by horizontal measurements or by measuring along the top rail of the fence in place, depending upon the method specified. As in the case of pipelines, the length indicated will be less when measured horizontally.

Bid Items Based Upon Area Measurements

Pavements: As mentioned before, the measurement of areas for payment usually presents no problem, but particular care must be exercised to assure that the proper pavement thicknesses have been attained. Watch, too, for underruns where the contractor is being paid both for excavation of the roadbed on a volume basis and pavement surfacing on an area basis.

A particular risk is involved where there are separate payments for pavements over small areas, such as trench resurfacing, and for larger paved areas that can be done with a paving machine. On one actual pipeline job in a city street, the unit price for repavement over trenches was quoted somewhat higher than roadway pavement because it would have to be done using hand methods. The contractor for this project, being an enterprising person, carefully studied his specifications and noted that the earthwork provisions permitted him to slope that portion of his trench walls that were above a plane lying one foot above the pipe; provided, that any excess excavation resulting from such methods was to be at the contractor's own expense. The contractor sloped all of the trench walls in the city street area, which allowed him to open up the entire width of one half of the city street, which he then repaved using a regular paving machine. The specifications for repavement of the area over the pipe trench were based upon the number of square feet of area to be actually paved, rather than upon the number of *linear* feet of pavement to be constructed over trenches. The result was that the contractor not only eliminated the added cost of trench shoring in deep trenches, but also "bought" a street repaving job to repave an entire half of the city street using a paving machine, but performing the work *at unit prices intended for hand work!* The only excess cost to him was the extra labor of the added excavation involved in the sloping of the sides of the pipe trench and the removal of the additional existing paving. The cost to the city was an additional $15,000, as there was nothing in the contract that would provide legal relief. Thus, the method of measurement for payment purposes can mean significant differences in a project cost. In this case it was the specifier's fault for not coordinating the paving specification with the earthworks specification. An alert resident project representative noticed this early, but unfortunately under the terms of the contract specifications, the contractor was fully within his legal rights to do this.

Retaining Walls: If a retaining wall is to be constructed around the periphery of a property, the inspector should be exceptionally careful of the method of making wall area measurements. If all measurements are around the outside of the wall, the cost to the owner will be excessive. On the other hand, if all measurements were on the inside face, the cost to the contractor would be unfair. Each wall surface should be taken as a prism, and any space occupied by

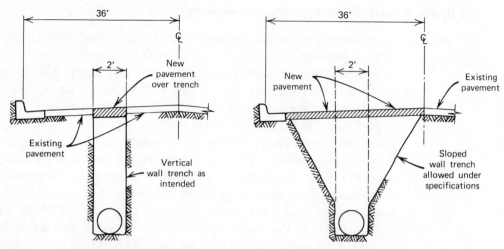

Figure 14.12 Effect of sloping trench walls on pavement width requirements.

the previously measured prism should not be included in any other measurement of adjoining surfaces.

Volume Measurements: Be certain of the method of measurement, particularly in the case of earth and rock materials, and of materials that must be placed at high temperatures. In many cases, volume measurements will have to be made using a survey crew to take cross sections of the affected area.

If a volume of material is to be placed in accordance with the lines shown on the drawings, be sure to get a survey crew on the site before the work commences, to establish the exact profile of the ground as it existed before the work began; otherwise, disputes may arise concerning the quantities because of a difference of opinion as to the condition that existed prior to the beginning of the work.

Weight: Establish at the beginning of the job what the basis of weight measurement is to be. Under the English system, which is slowly converting to metric, a "ton" can be either the *short ton* of 2000 pounds, or the *long ton* of 2240 pounds. Similarly, smaller units of weight must be clearly defined under the English system as well. Depending upon the material being weighed, the system may be avoirdupois, troy, or apothecary.

The foregoing is not intended to be an exhaustive listing of all the special areas of concern, but rather a sampling of some of the more common measurement problems encountered under a unit price contract project.

FINAL PAYMENT TO THE CONTRACTOR

After the Certificate of Substantial Completion has been filed (Chapter 18), the contractor will submit his application for final payment. Although the form he uses is the same as that previously used for monthly progress payments, there are several additional require-

NEER will make an inspection of that part of the Project to determine its status of completion. If the ENGINEER does not consider that it is substantially complete, he will notify the OWNER and CONTRACTOR in writing giving his reasons therefor. If the ENGINEER considers that part of the Project to be substantially complete, he will execute and deliver to the OWNER and CONTRACTOR a certificate to that effect, fixing the date of Substantial Completion as to that part of the Project, attaching thereto a tentative list of items to be completed or corrected before final payment and fixing the responsibility between the OWNER and CONTRACTOR for maintenance, heat and utilities as to that part of the Project. The OWNER shall have the right to exclude the CONTRACTOR from any part of the Project which the ENGINEER has so certified to be substantially complete, but the OWNER will allow the CONTRACTOR reasonable access to complete or correct items on the tentative list.

Final Inspection:

14.11. Upon written notice from the CONTRACTOR that the Project is complete, the ENGINEER will make a final inspection with the OWNER and the CONTRACTOR and will notify the CONTRACTOR in writing of any particulars in which this inspection reveals that the Work is defective. The CONTRACTOR shall immediately make such corrections as are necessary to remedy such defects.

Final Application for Payment:

14.12. After the CONTRACTOR has completed any such corrections to the satisfaction of the ENGINEER and delivered all maintenance and operating instructions, schedules, guarantees, Bonds, certificates of inspection and other documents—all as required by the Contract Documents, he may make application for final payment following the procedure for progress payments. The final Application for Payment shall be accompanied by such supporting data as the ENGINEER may require, together with complete and legally effective releases or waivers (satisfactory to the OWNER) of all Liens arising out of the Contract Documents and the labor and services performed and the material and equipment furnished thereunder. In lieu thereof and as approved by the OWNER, the CONTRACTOR may furnish receipts or releases in full; an affidavit of the CONTRACTOR that the releases and receipts include all labor, services, material and equipment for which a Lien could be filed, and that all payrolls, material and equipment bills, and other indebtedness connected with the Work for which the OWNER or his property might in any way be responsible, have been paid or otherwise satisfied; and consent of the Surety, if any, to final payment. If any Subcontractor or supplier fails to furnish a release or receipt in full, the CONTRACTOR may furnish a Bond satisfactory to the OWNER to indemnify him against any Lien.

Approval of Final Payment:

14.13. If, on the basis of his observation and review of the Work during construction, his final inspection and his review of the final Application for Payment—all as required by the Contract Documents, the ENGINEER is satisfied that the Work has been completed and the CONTRACTOR has fulfilled all of his obligations under the Contract Documents, he will, within ten days after receipt of the final Application for Payment, indicate in writing his approval of payment and present the Application to the OWNER for payment. Otherwise, he will return the Application to the CONTRACTOR, indicating in writing his reasons for refusing to approve final payment, in which case the CONTRACTOR will make the necessary corrections and resubmit the Application. The OWNER will, within ten days of presentation to him of an approved final Application for Payment, pay the CONTRACTOR the amount approved by the ENGINEER.

14.14. If after Substantial Completion of the Work final completion thereof is materially delayed through no fault of the CONTRACTOR, and the ENGINEER so confirms, the OWNER shall, upon certification by the ENGINEER, and without terminating the Agreement, make payment of the balance due for that portion of the Work fully completed and accepted. If the remaining balance for Work not fully completed or corrected is less than the retainage stipulated in the Agreement, and if Bonds have been furnished as required in paragraph 5.1, the written consent of the Surety to the payment of the balance due for that portion of the Work fully completed and accepted shall be submitted by the CONTRACTOR to the ENGINEER prior to certification of such payment. Such payment shall be made under the terms and conditions governing final payment, except that it shall not constitute a waiver of claims.

Contractor's Continuing Obligation:

14.15. The CONTRACTOR's obligation to perform the Work and complete the Project in accordance with the Contract Documents shall be absolute. Neither approval of any progress or final payment by the ENGINEER, nor the issuance of a certificate of Substantial Completion, nor any payment by the OWNER to the CONTRACTOR under the Contract Documents, nor any use or occupancy of the Project or any part thereof by the OWNER, nor any act of acceptance by the OWNER nor any failure to do so, nor any correction of defective work by the OWNER shall constitute an acceptance of Work not in accordance with the Contract Documents.

Waiver of Claims:

14.16. The making and acceptance of final payment shall constitute:

14.16.1. a waiver of all claims by the OWNER against the CONTRACTOR other than those arising from unsettled Liens, from defective work appearing after final payment or from failure to comply with the requirements of the Contract Documents or the terms of any special guarantees specified therein, and

14.16.2. a waiver of all claims by the CONTRACTOR against the OWNER other than those previously made in writing and still unsettled.

21

Figure 14.13 NSPE General provisions for final payment to the contractor. Copyright National Society of Professional Engineers.

ments that he must comply with before the architect/engineer should issue a final certificate for payment:

1. The contractor must pay all bills or other indebtedness
2. Under certain contracts he must submit receipts, releases, waivers of liens
3. Consent of surety where a surety is involved

Under the provisions of the AIA and the NSPE General Conditions, the final payment is withheld only until the contractor has provided evidence that each of the items in the above list has been complied with. Under the AIA and NSPE provisions, the making and acceptance of the final payment constitutes a waiver of all claims by the owner against the contractor other than those arising from unsettled liens, from defective work appearing after final payment, or from failure to comply with the requirements of the contract documents or the terms of any special guarantees that are a part of the contract. It is also a waiver of all claims by the contractor against the owner other than those previously made in writing that are still unsettled.

While the holding time for the release of the contractor's final payment under the AIA and the NSPE contract provisions is not specific, but is subject to the time it takes the contractor to submit his documentation, most public agency contracts note a specific period of time before release of the final payment to allow time for any lien holders to file before the owner releases the final payment to the contractor. In this manner, if liens have been filed, or valid claims are presented to the owner for unpaid bills, the owner can pay such indebtedness and deduct all the sums from the money due to the contractor.

Under the provisions for final payment of the Contract Documents for Construction of Federally Assisted Water and Sewer Projects (Figure 14.14), the owner retains all such sums for a period of 30 days before release. Under the terms of this document, the owner retains the right to withhold funds to satisfy liens or outstanding bills. In some states, however, this creates a potential problem; the period for the filing of liens against a construction project in many states where a Certificate of Substantial Completion has been executed and recorded has been established by statute. Because of this fact, many agencies set a holding period for all retention money equal to the statutory period plus 5 or 10

> 19.5 Upon completion and acceptance of the WORK, the ENGINEER shall issue a certificate attached to the final payment request that the WORK has been accepted by him under the conditions of the CONTRACT DOCUMENTS. The entire balance found to be due the CONTRACTOR, including the retained percentages, but except such sums as may be lawfully retained by the OWNER, shall be paid to the CONTRACTOR within thirty (30) days of completion and acceptance of the WORK.

Figure 14.14 *Provisions for final payment from contract documents for construction of federally assisted water and sewer projects.*

32.2 *Final Estimate and Payment.* — (a) Whenever the Contractor shall deem all work under this contract to have been completed in accordance therewith, he shall so notify the Engineer in writing and the Engineer will ascertain whether such be the fact and, if not, will advise the Contractor in detail and in writing of any additional work required.

(b)   Whenever in the opinion of the Engineer the Contractor shall have completely performed the contract on his part, the Engineer will so certify in writing to the Owner, and in his certificate he will state, from actual measurements, the whole amount of work done by the Contractor, and also the value of such work under and according to the terms of the contract. On the expiration of 35 days after the filing, in the office of the county recorder of the county or counties in which the work is located, of a Notice of Completion of the work herein agreed to be done by the Contractor, the Owner will pay to the Contractor the amount remaining after deducting from the amount or value stated in the first-mentioned certificate all such sums of money which by the terms hereof the Owner is or may be authorized or required to reserve or retain. All prior certificates upon which partial payment may have been made, being merely estimates, shall be subject to correction in the final certificate, which final certificate may be made without notice thereof of the Contractor.

Figure 14.15 Provisions for final estimate and payment from public agency contract documents.

days so as to allow the lien filing period to close before releasing the contractor's money. In this way, the owner can be assured that all potential lien holders have been satisfied before making final payment to the contractor. Another alternative would be a waiver of claims (see Chapter 19 on ''Project Closeout'').

As recommended in Chapter 19, it is desirable that a formal Certificate of Substantial Completion be executed *and recorded* in the County Recorder's Office. If this is not done, no reasonable retention period of the contractor's final payment may sometimes suffice. It would normally appear to be in the owner's best interest to see that a Certificate of Substantial Completion is filed and recorded within the statutory time allowed after substantial completion of the work, or to be sure of receiving a release or waiver of claims from the general contractor, all subcontractors, and material suppliers prior to releasing retention money.

Bibliography

W. H. Searles, H. C. Ives, and P. Kissam, *Field Engineering,* 22nd ed., Wiley, New York 1949.

Richard H. Clough, *Construction Contracting,* 3rd ed., Wiley, New York 1975.

Robert W. Abbett, *Engineering Contracts and Specifications,* 2nd ed., Wiley, New York 1948.

15

CONSTRUCTION
MATERIALS
CONTROL

ONSTRUCTION MATERIALS control is fully one half of what construction inspection is all about. The other half is control over workmanship. Many inspectors understand quality construction when they see it, or proper materials when they see them, but fail to understand fully what their authority and responsibility requires them to do. The implication often too firmly implanted in some inspectors' minds is that they are on the job to assure that the project will be constructed with only the "best" quality materials and the "highest" quality of workmanship. On numerous occasions, inspectors have been heard to remark, or even interrupt their instructions to say, supposedly reassuringly, "Don't worry about the specs; I'll see that you get a first-class job!"

Reassuring as it may sound at first, it is NOT the proper approach for an inspector to take. His real authority is *limited* to requiring the contractor to provide all that has been agreed to in writing in the contract documents. If an owner, through lack of funds or otherwise, chooses to purchase less than top quality goods or to accept adequate but somewhat less than first-class workmanship, it is his prerogative to do so. It would be an overstep of the authority of the inspector to attempt to require the contractor to provide anything in excess of the terms of the approved contract—and certainly would be unfair to the contractor. Remember, one of the basic principles of the law of contracts is that it must involve a meeting of the minds. Thus, anything that is not part of the written terms of the contract is not within the authority of the inspector to attempt to require without a supplemental agreement, such as a change order. If, on the other hand, an inspector observed a condition that, if performed in strict accordance with the plans and specifications, would result in an unsafe condition, or that might be considered as being of questionable judgment, the obligation of the inspector is to bring the matter to the direct attention of the architect or engineer or the owner. Then, if in the judgment of the architect or engineer or the owner a change should be made, it will be executed as a formal change order, with a possible appropriate adjustment in the contract price.

It all comes down to a simple axiom. If a man agrees to buy a Ford, the dealer should not be forced to deliver a Continental for the same price, just because it might represent a higher quality product in the eyes of the buyer's agent. Likewise, if it is found that the Ford will not do the job, but the Continental is required, then the buyer must make a new agreement to purchase and pay for the higher priced product.

In short, the inspector is not on the job to enforce what *he* believes to be proper construction, but rather to obtain the type and quality of construction that has been called for in the plan and specifications. This cannot be emphasized too strongly, as the wise contractor will generally provide exactly what the inspector demands, then file claims for extras for the cost differences between what was provided at the inspector's direction and what was called for in the plans and specifications—and, he will be entitled to get it.

REQUESTS FOR SUBSTITUTIONS OF MATERIALS

By far one of the most frequent requests received on the job will be requests by the contractor to use substitute materials for those actually specified by the architect or engineer. The conditions controlling the use of such alternate choices of materials differ somewhat between public and private construction contracts, and must be considered separately.

Whenever a substitute is offered, the contractor is obligated to give adequate notice of his intention to offer a substitute—not wait until it is already too late to get delivery in time for the product actually called for. Then, after submittal, sufficient time must be allowed for the architect or engineer to review the technical data submitted by the contractor in support of his claim that the product is the equal of the specified one.

On a private project, the design firm may specify a single proprietary item for every item on the project if he chooses to do so, and there is no obligation to anyone except the owner to consider substitutes unless the architect or engineer wishes to do so. Such instructions must be communicated to the inspector so that he can properly respond to the contractor in case of attempted submittals for consideration as substitutions. Furthermore, if in the judgment of the architect or engineer no substitutes may be considered, then only the specific brand or model of the specified product may be used in the work. All products delivered to the site for use on the work must be rejected if they fail to conform to the specific terms of the plans and specifications.

On public works projects, certain limitations exist all over the United States and in many foreign countries that limit the power of an architect or engineer to specify a single name brand of a product *if equivalent products are on the market*. All specifications for proprietary products in many states, as well as those for use either on federal contracts or contracts by other agencies in which part of the funding is from a federal agency, are required by law to name at least two brand names and the words "or equal" if a product is called for by brand name. Also, a prescriptive specification that upon analysis can be seen as applying only to a single brand name is considered the same as calling out only one brand name, and is thus considered illegal. The majority of the states have similar laws governing public projects within their jurisdiction, so even without federal funds these conditions usually prevail on public projects. In certain cases, the law controlling the specifying of brand names allows an exception to the rule: (1) if the product specified is required in order to be compatible with existing facilities; and (2) if the product specified is unique, and no other brand is made.

Furthermore, it is the opinion of many competent legal authorities that the specification of several brand names, where one brand is called for by manufacturer and that manufacturer's catalog number, and the remaining brands are called for only by manufacturer's name, is in violation of the intent of the law and will be judged as if no alternatives had been offered. Each product named must include the description in comparable terms. It sounds unreasonable at first, but consider the frequent case of a product called for by catalog number such as:

> "Well pump for the emergency water system shall be Jacuzzi 75S6A15, Byron-Jackson, or approved equal..."

In the first place only one *product* has actually been specified. There is no catalog number for the Byron-Jackson unit; thus it is not a product but only the name of a potential *manufacturer* of an "equal" product. Often, a little research turns up the fact that some of the manufacturers named in specifications in this manner do not even manufacture a similar product at all. The other possibility is that the alternative "product" opens up the specifications so broadly that hardly no offered substitute can be excluded. One of the inherent dangers of the "or equal" concept is that the products named may not be equal at all. Often the designer selected exactly what he wanted in one catalog, then hastily selected what appeared to be an equal from another manufacturer. In doing this, he may have unintentionally broadened the specifications to allow any other brand whose characteristics were anywhere within the extremes possessed by either brand. A product that contained all the worst features of both would still have to be considered as acceptable, as the simple naming of a second product that omitted a feature that was in the designer's primary choice of products automatically eliminated that particular feature as a minimum prerequisite for acceptance of a contractor-offered substitute

In some cases, there are also provisions for a public agency to specify a single proprietary product as part of a research or experimentation program in which the single product specified is the article being researched.

Basically, the architect or engineer is considered the final judge of the quality of a product, and the courts have upheld this concept. If in his determination the product offered is not equal, he has the power to summarily reject it. Furthermore, the contractor may be required to carry the burden of the cost that may be necessary to prove equivalency where a laboratory analysis or similar certification is required. A product may be judged as not being equal on the basis of physical or chemical properties, performance, selection of materials, or even due to dimensional incompatibility with the design of the finished structure where the use of the alternative product may require the redesign of portions of the previously designed structure to accommodate the substitute product. One case in Los Angeles, however, failed to uphold the owner's engineering staff in its refusal of a substitute product when its rejection was on wholly esthetic grounds, because the specifications in this case had not cited esthetics as being a proper criterion for the determination of product equivalency [*Argo Construction Co., Inc., vs. County of Los Angeles,* Court of Appeals, 2d Civil No. 32568 (1969)].

In any case, the product offered as a substitute to a specified article must be submitted to the architect or engineer or to the owner, through the resident project representative, for consideration and approval before such a substitute product may be used in the work. The inspector *must* reject any article that fails to satisfy one of the following two requirements:

1. It is the specific product called for in the plans and specifications.
2. It is a substitute product that the architect or engineer or the owner has approved in writing to the contractor.

In the absence of either of these conditions, the substitute product must be rejected by the inspector and required to be removed from the construction site. Failure to observe this requirement may be grounds for withholding partial payment to the contractor, and the inspector should make a careful survey at the time of payment requests to assure that all materials that have been installed or delivered to the site are in fact the same materials that have been specified or allowed by the design firm or the owner in writing as an approved substitute. If the contractor fails to meet these requirements, the inspector should submit a recommendation to the design firm or the owner along with the contractor's payment request that payment be disallowed for the nonconforming portion of the work.

INSPECTION OF MATERIALS DELIVERED TO THE SITE

It is the responsibility of the inspector to inspect promptly all materials delivered to the site *prior* to their being used in the work. The practice of withholding inspection until the job is done, then announcing to the contractor that the work fails to conform to the specifications, is totally unacceptable conduct for a resident project representative. Certain types of intermittent inspection as performed by government agencies, such as building departments, permit this type of inspection, but it is only because the responsibility for on-site quality control is that of the contractor and the owner's representative. The building department's responsibility is limited to assurance that all requirements of the code and the approved plans and specifications have been followed.

In certain cases it may be desirable to perform inspections of materials or fabricated products prior to their delivery at the site. A case in point would be an inspection of the precasting operation at a concrete precasting plant. Usually the product remains in the casting yard for an extended period before delivery to the site, and failure to make early discovery of patent defects may hold up a project for several months while the precasting yard clears the casting beds to work in a new casting schedule and set up the new forms on the beds between other scheduled operations just to recast defective work. Also, the placement of stirrups and similar conventional reinforcement in pretensioned, precast, prestressed concrete structural members must be carefully checked at the precasting yard before placing concrete, just as it must for cast-in-place conventional concrete. All too often the work of placing such reinforcing steel is not accurately done, and can result in major structural failures.

The author was personally involved in one project in which over 80 percent of all roof members on a 200 × 200 foot roof developed progressive failures that were traced to improper placement of stirrups at the precasting yard. In addition to checking of stirrups, the plant inspection will provide an opportunity to measure the net length of all prestressed beams and girders stored at the plant in time to compare their dimensions with the design spacing of supports to see that adequate bearing will be provided at the ends of all beams and girders. Failure to do this has also resulted in failures at several sites in the past.

REJECTION OF FAULTY MATERIAL

As described before, the inspector not only has a right to reject faulty materials, but is obligated to do so. Upon the rejection of nonconforming items, they should be clearly and indelibly marked in such manner that the article cannot be used in the work without the mark being clearly visible to the inspector. Such marks can be made with an indelible

Figure 15.1 Precast prestressed concrete members at casting yard.

felt-tip pen, paint, or impression-type markers. The inspector should require that all rejected articles be immediately removed from the construction area and placed in a separate pile to be transported off the site the same day. The inspector should assure himself that the rejection marks cannot be easily erased and the non-conforming article returned to the site as "new material."

Acceptability of any material, article, or equipment should be based upon accepted standards of the industry, such as ASTM Standards or trade association standards for the products involved (see "Special Material and Product Standards" in Chapter 6). If additional restrictions are imposed as acceptance criteria, they should be clearly spelled out in the specifications unless the requirements are so common in the industry that they are considered as unquestioned standards of the trade.

OWNERSHIP OF MATERIALS

Generally, it may be said that the ownership of all materials used in the work or stored at the site is vested in the contractor until final acceptance of the work by the owner at the end of the job. Thus, any risk associated with the protection of the work and the repair of damaged work, or the delivery of damaged materials is usually the responsibility of the contractor, not the owner. Similarly, the contractor's insurance carrier will normally be called upon to pay the costs of any such claims.

DELIVERY AND STORAGE OF MATERIALS

There is no firm formula for the determination of which facilities will be accorded the contractor as a working or staging area or for his storage of construction materials. Generally, it is the contractor's responsibility to make his own arrangements for such facilities if provisions have not been made by the owner. Although it is true that most owners do provide space, in some areas no such space is under the owner's direct control;

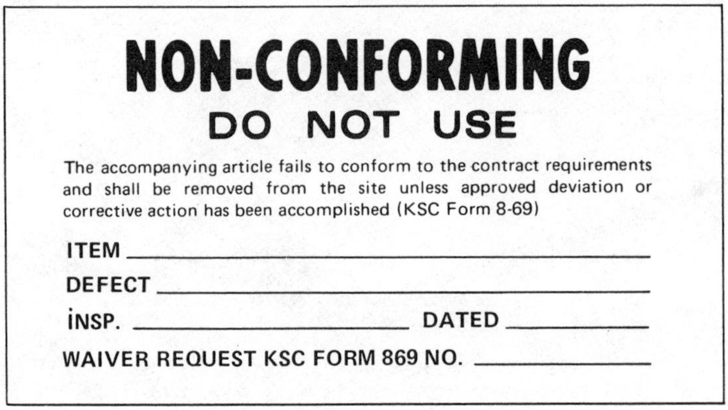

NON-CONFORMING
DO NOT USE

The accompanying article fails to conform to the contract requirements and shall be removed from the site unless approved deviation or corrective action has been accomplished (KSC Form 8-69)

ITEM _____

DEFECT _____

INSP. _____ DATED _____

WAIVER REQUEST KSC FORM 869 NO. _____

Figure 15.2 An inspector's rejection tag.

in such cases the contractor must make his own arrangements for space. Occasionally, this is done by the contractor actually entering into a rental agreement for space, which must accordingly be taken into consideration at the time of figuring his bid.

In no case should any contractor assume that he has the right to block public thoroughfares or to use public property of any kind, including parking lots, for his construction purposes, even when the work is being performed for the owner of the property under consideration, unless specific written authority has been granted. As a means of protecting the owner from such claims, the inspector should be assured that the space being used by the contractor for his work area has been properly granted by the owner of the affected property.

HANDLING OF MATERIALS

The inspector must be concerned not only with the quality of the materials as delivered and their methods of installation, but he should require that all such materials be properly handled during delivery, unloading, transporting, storage, and installation so that undue stresses will not result in latent defects that will not be detected until after the project has been signed off. When in doubt, the inspector should have the design firm or the owner contact the manufacturer of the affected material, who is generally just as interested in its proper handling in the field as the owner. This is because the manufacturer is often the victim of unjust claims for defective materials, when in fact the problem may have been due to improper handling during construction instead.

16

CONSTRUCTION QUALITY CONTROL AND CHANGE ORDERS

MATERIALS AND METHODS OF CONSTRUCTION

Most specifications, in their General Conditions, provide that unless specified otherwise, all workmanship, equipment, materials, and articles incorporated in the work are to be of the best available grade in the local trade area. Materials called for on the drawings that are not called for in the specifications, but that are known to be required for a complete project are similarly required to be of comparable quality. These phrases are usually found in specifications prepared by someone who doesn't really know what it takes to make a "complete" project, or how to properly specify quality in a product. The result is one of the all encompassing generalities such as noted above. It may get the job done, but not without many arguments in the field. It also saves the specifier the embarassment of having to tell someone how to build something that he may not know the first thing about. Apparently, the concept is legally sound, but it puts a considerable added burden upon the resident project representative who must be the one to interpret the terms "best" and "quality." Generally, an inspector can plan on some arguments over either of these terms, because that which one person considers high quality another may consider substandard and because the construction contract was supposed to represent a "meeting of the minds," unless both parties agree as to what the terms mean, there may be some doubt concerning that portion of the contract.

Often the specifications provide that all materials furnished must be free of defects or imperfections, and must normally be all new materials. Workmanship, similarly, is often stated in unenforceable terms. Phrases to the effect that "workmanship shall be of highest

263

quality'' or that something should be built using the ''best workmanship'' are almost useless, as the terms cannot be precisely defined, and therefore are largely unenforceable conditions. About all that can be rejected by the inspector under such provisions is craftmanship that is so obviously defective that even a layman can recognize it.

With the proper specification terms, the inspector has a useful tool that he can use to great advantage. Under the specific terms of a specification that clearly defines the quality of workmanship, an inspector has every right to reject all that does not meet the specified standards—in fact, he is obligated to do so. Specifications such as these are the products of professionals. A good specifications writer is one who has a good understanding of field construction as well as contract law, design principles, and a writing ability—a rare breed.

Interpretation of the Specifications

It should be kept in mind that the designer is the person who is most familiar with the intent of the contract documents and their provisions. To him none of its terms seem vague or ambiguous because he understood what it was he was trying to say when he wrote it in his specifications. The contractor, on the other hand, must attempt to interpret the strict wording of the specification in order to prepare his bid, and thus must rely on the ability of the specification writer to communicate accurately the designer's intent through the wording of the specifications. As a contractor once stated, after being told what was intended by the terms of a specification: ''I don't care what was intended—*this is what it says*!'' The contractor was right, of course. His contract was to provide what it *said,* not what it should have said. If the designer or owner chooses to interpret the terms differently, he must expect to pay for the privilege.

The courts also respect this concept. They have generally held that, all other things being equal, in case of a dispute over the meaning of the wordking of the specifications provisions, the binding interpretation will be in favor of the party who did not write the contract. This means that the judgment stands a good chance of being in the contractor's favor, as he is generally not the party who wrote the contract provisions. In this manner it is possible that in an imperfectly written set of documents, the contractor may actually be entitled to an extra to build the work according to the meaning that the designer intended in the first place when he wrote the specifications.

Access to the Work by Quality Control Personnel

The contractor is obligated to provide access to the work at all times tc the architect/engineer and the owner or their authorized representatives, and the contractor is responsible for their safety while they are at the site. Of course, the contractor may require that all such persons coming onto the site wear appropriate safety devices and conduct their operations in a safe manner. Similarly, the inspector is entitled, normally, to have access to the place of manufacture of materials or equipment that are to be used in the work. Work on offshore facilities may present a problem, however, if the designer or specification writer neglected to require the contractor to furnish transportation to such

Figure 16.1 Offshore construction.

facilities. In that case, the design firm's or owner's representatives may just have to provide their own boats to get to the project site. The contractor's obligation to *allow* inspector access to the site does not obligate him to provide transportation for the inspector as well, although few contractors will want to risk the adversary relationship that would be the inevitable result in case of refusal. Nevertheless, this is an added cost to the contractor, and where it is a significant amount the contractor will be justified in claiming extra payment for the service.

Construction Equipment and Methods

Generally, the selection of the type of equipment required to do a job is the responsibility of the contractor. However, if it can be clearly established that the use of a certain piece of equipment to do a specified job will in all probability result in inferior construction quality, it is within the authority of the architect/engineer or owner to require that appropriate changes be made. These instructions would normally be issued through the resident project representative. Also, if the inspector notes that certain equipment, such as a crane, is overloaded and can possibly lead to a serious accident, he is under some obligation to interrupt the use of the particular piece of equipment until the hazard has been eliminated.

One example of the right of a design firm or owner to limit the type of equipment to be used on a project concerns a concrete-lined reservoir where a 5-inch thick concrete lining was being placed in 24-foot square panels joined with PVC waterstops sealed with polysulfide joint sealant. The side walls were sloped to 1½ to 1, and the basin was 16 feet deep. The concrete lining was to be placed over a layer of polyethylene sheet, and the design requirements prohibited any penetration through the plastic sheet into the earth below. Thus, when the contractor planned to use 12-foot span mechanical vibratory screeds to span each panel, it was obvious that he would have to screed each panel using two passes. This would require the use of steel stakes to support a wood screed upon which one end of the vibratory screed was expected to ride. The result would have required a penetration through the polyethylene sheet, as well as some risk of substandard slab thickness in the area of the screed pins due to incomplete filling and consolidation of the screed pin holes. The contractor was informed that the equipment he planned to use was unsatisfactory and that an alternative method would have to be provided. It should be noted here that the resident project representative did not tell the contractor which method to use—only which method was unsatisfactory. It was still up to the contractor to select his own equipment and methods as long as they were capable of doing a satisfactory job within the terms of the specifications.

Similarly, any resident project representative can influence the methods of construction to be used by the contractor if it can be shown that the proposed method of the contractor will not provide a satisfactory product. As mentioned above, however, the inspector must be extremely careful as to how he words his statements to the contractor. He may indicate that a particular method of construction or piece of equipment is unsatisfactory, but must not go on to the next step and tell the contractor how the work should be done, or which particular piece of equipment should be used.

QUALITY LEVEL AND QUALITY CONTROL

Quality Level

Quality level is the specific degree of excellence, basic nature, character, and kind of performance possessed by a particular item or group of items required by the designer. The minimum quality levels are those called for in the specifications for the project. The items that control quality include the following:

1. Location of the project
2. Magnitude of each phase of construction
3. Availability of local materials
4. Contemplated life of the construction
5. Climatic and operating conditions
6. Cost limitations
7. The desires of the architect or engineer

Figure 16.2 Trussed screed for 24-foot wide panels.

Quality Control

Each quality level requires a quality control to assure that the established quality levels are met. The quality control may be by visual inspection, tests, certifications, reports, shop drawings, and similar procedures. Like the quality level, the quality control will vary from project to project. The quality controls that are the means to assure that construction is in conformance with the contract specifications and drawings are the responsibility of the resident project representative. Other quality controls are provided by the results of test, samples, shop drawings, and similar procedures.

QUALITY CONTROL PROVISIONS

The following quality control provisions are considered separately from the visual inspection requirements of the resident project representative. They are included in the specifications to assure that the quality of the items specified is actually provided by the contractor. When quality cannot be verified by routine field inspection, the quality control for material or equipment must be established by other means to assure satisfactory performance.

Testing

Testing is limited to those laboratory or field tests actually called for in the specifications, or allowed by them. Such tests may be performed by the contractor, the architect/engineer, the owner, or commercial testing laboratories. The commercial laboratories may be hired by the contractor, the owner, or the design firm, but in each case the project manager and the resident project representative should receive a copy of the test results.

Figure 16.3 Ultrasonic testing of structural field welds.

Testing is required for items of work that are critical and are particularly susceptible to unsatisfactory levels of quality, and that cannot generally be detected by observation. Examples are concrete; soil compaction; and similar materials. The specification determines which items are to be tested, which tests and procedures apply, and the required levels of performance. The specification also determines who should perform the test. Testing is necessary for any work that has a history of poor performance and involves an assembly of products furnished by more than one contractor and where the end of an item is critical.

Installation in Accordance with the Product Manufacturer's Instructions

In many cases, the specification requires that the product manufacturer provide instructions for the method of installation of products that are installed by subcontractors who are not directly affiliated with the product manufacturer. This provision is supposed to be used only where rigid adherence to the manufacturer's instructions is critical, where product composition and construction create limitations not likely to be understood by the installer, and where installation procedures are complex or subject to significant variations between different manufacturers. Unfortunately, it is also used by lazy specifications writers who either do not know enough about a product to specify it, or who won't take the time to research it.

Experience Qualification

An experience qualification is a requirement that a firm performing a certain type of work have an established reputation for the successful completion of similar work elsewhere for some specified amount of time. The use of an experience requirement is limited to those fields of work in which the ability to do a certain amount of work in the time normally allowed, as well as competence in performing installations and services requires a considerable amount of previous experience. Examples of such fields of work include:

1. Metal curtain walls
2. Foundation piles
3. Dewatering
4. Precast architectural concrete
5. Calking and sealing
6. Spray-on fire protection
7. Laboratory equipment
8. Mechanical & electrical equipment

This type of provision is devised to prevent "fly-by-night" firms from performing work for which they are not qualified or may not be able to complete. The disadvantage is that there is still no assurance that the selected firm will remain in business or will stand behind the work it performs. The provision is generally used for work that requires special qualifications for which there are a number of firms of long standing who are generally recognized in the industry as having this special capability, and where there is a history of "fly-by-night" operators.

Factory Inspection

Occasionally, a construction contract calls for inspection of production and fabrication facilities at a manufacturer's plant as a part of the quality control requirements of the project. The specification must tell the specific type of inspection to perform. This provision is used for assuring the quality control of custom products of such nature that on-site inspection or testing is either impossible or impractical. This provision is used mostly for large prefabricated products that are fabricated especially for each project, where it is impractical to perform tests and inspection at the jobsite or at a testing laboratory. Examples of such products are:

1. Precast concrete piles
2. Architectural precast concrete
3. Precast pretensioned concrete members
4. Fabricated steel plate specials
5. Pump station manifolds
6. Concrete or asphalt concrete batch plant facilities

Figure 16.4 *Precast prestressed concrete members at casting yard.*

Matching Samples on Display During Bidding

Sometimes a contractor is asked to base the quality of a product upon a sample that is placed on display during bidding. This provision is used only where important esthetic considerations cannot be adequately specified in words, and for which no known or local appearance standard can be furnished for prospective bidders to examine. To maintain effective quality control during construction, each such sample must later be stored at the construction site for ready reference as a basis of acceptance. Examples of such materials or items are:

1. Natural stone
2. Precast concrete panels with exposed aggregate
3. Concrete finishes
4. Special wood finishes and cabinetry standards

This method allows an effective means to assure that the desired visual characteristics of highly textured or grained materials, which are often difficult to describe verbally, can be provided. Additional advantages when used in public works construction are that trade names can be avoided and that disputes between the resident project representative and the contractor over the appearance of a material surface that may otherwise meet specification requirements can be avoided. The disadvantage is that facilities must be provided in one central location for displays of all samples during bidding, and again at the site during construction. Care must be taken to assure that sample panels represent the full range of colors and textures permitted, and that matching material is obtainable from more than one source in the case of public agency contracts.

Mockup

Another method of quality control is the requirement for the contractor to construct a mockup or a prototype constuction assembly that, after approval, will serve as the standard for the same type of construction throughout the project. This method is best used where it is impossible or impractical to specify critical esthetic characteristics that may be desired, or where an assembly is too large or complex to be fabricated prior to award of the contract. Examples are:

1. Certain masonry or natural stone assemblies
2. Architectural precast concrete

Mockups by the contractor prior to construction can be advantageous to control the quality of a complex construction system where the esthetic and other requirements cannot be accurately described in words or in drawings. The disadvantages are that:

1. The standard of production is established *after award* of the contract
2. Numerous arguments over fine points of esthetics may arise
3. The finally approved mockup may not conform to other specification requirements
4. Delays may result while awaiting approvals
5. Additional costs are normally reflected in the bids

The use of this system is usually confined to complex exterior wall assemblies on monumental buildings where esthetics are a major consideration, and where there is no other adequate way to describe the desired appearance.

Proven Successful Use

Under this provision the contractor is asked to provide proof that the same type of product or similar products or equipment have been successfully used in similar construction for a specific period of time. The use of this provision is generally limited to mechanical and electrical equipment that requires proof of safe, dependable, continuous operation for a number of years. This provision is not used for those items that would benefit by innovation. The primary advantage of this type of provision is that the risks usually associated with the experimental use of new products are avoided. It has the disadvantage of discouraging innovation, however, and it offers no insurance against faulty installation. It is generally used to specify items such as elevators, electrical equipment, large pumps, water and sewage treatment plant equipment, and similar items that must be in continuous and reliable service for many years. It is not generally used for architectural items or for products for which it is not possible to determine "successful use" clearly.

Qualified Products Lists

A "qualified products list" is a provision of the specifications that requires that the procurement of certain contract items be restricted to those items that have been previously tested and approved, and have been included in a list of approved items in the specifications. A qualified products list is not necessarily limited only to products that are named in the specifications, but may also be lists of products compiled by independednt authorities such as the Underwriters Laboratories, who assume the responsibility for testing and updating their lists. The advantage of using a qualified products list is that the sometimes long, complex, or expensive tests that may otherwise be required have already been performed and do not need to be done for each project. The disadvantages of a qualified products list are:

1. Possibility of less competition
2. Possibility of disclaimer by the contractor for defects in materials furnished under this system
3. Administrative difficulties in maintaining up-to-date lists

Certified Laboratory Test Reports

This is a requirement by which the contractor is asked to provide a certificate that indicates that a product meets specified quality requirements for performance or physical or chemical standards when the submitted sample is tested in accordance with certain specified laboratory standard tests. Submittal of test reports is required for those standard items for which there is a need for quality control testing, but for which the testing of the actual item to be installed cannot be justified. Requirements for this provision normally include a statement calling for exact test methods, minimum level of performance, and identification of the product to be tested to be sure that it is the same as the one to be used in construction. In addition, the tests are required to be performed by a recognized independent testing laboratory acceptable to the design firm or the owner. Examples of materials that may require such certified reports are:

1. Concrete reinforcing steel
2. Structural steel
3. Sound control ratings of materials
4. Fire spread ratings of materials
5. Polyvinyl chloride materials for waterstops
6. Masonry units

Where the contractor is responsible for obtaining the test reports, the disadvantage is the possible danger of apparent conflict of interest due to the contractor furnishing both the material and the testing. Additionally, the reliability of the testing laboratory could be open to question.

The manner in which this provision appears in specifications varies widely. Some of the more common requirements for certified laboratory test reports that are included in specifications are:

1. Test reports shall be based upon results of tests that have been made within a certain time on materials representative of those proposed for use; or
2. Test reports shall be based upon results of tests made on samples taken from materials proposed for delivery to the job site; or
3. Test reports shall be based upon results of tests made on installed items at the job.

Test reports included in the manufacturer's literature are often worthless, since the tests from which the data were derived are often nonstandard or are designed to dramatize certain properties and to conceal undesirable properties.

Certificate of Compliance or Conformance

Under these provisions the contractor is required to provide a certificate that says that the product complies with some specified reference standard. It is necessarily limited to products of standard manufacture for which quality can be clearly assured by the manufacturer, installation is not critical, and job testing is neither necessary nor justified. Examples of such products would include:

1. Glass
2. Paint
3. Aluminum windows
4. Wood

The primary advantage is that certificates can usually be obtained with very little if any increase in the price of the product. The disadvantage is that their validity and reliability depend entirely upon the integrity and knowledge of the certifier.

The requirements of the specifications that call for certificates of compliance are normally included only for those items for which the extra costs of certified laboratory costs cannot be justified. Usually, such certificates are reliable when they come from a member of an industry or trade that has a strong association that exerts some policing effort to maintain quality. When they do not come from such a source, their reliability may be subject to question. Generally, the inspector is protected by clauses in the specifications that reserve the right for him to inspect and test any article over and above the test requirements specified, and that the results of such inspections and tests are also binding upon the contractor. In such cases, the extra testing is usually at the expense of the owner unless it turns up a defect; then, often the contract provisions require payment by the contractor of both the corrective measures and the tests that disclosed the defect in the first place.

Warranties

The terms "warranty" and "guarantee" are often used interchangeably in construction contracts and are used to refer to the maintenance and repair obligations of the contractor for a specific period of time after the completion of construction. The General Conditions of the contract on most projects include specific requirements governing contractor warranties or guarantees. For the purposes of this definition, the term "warranty" will be used to describe this provision.

There are two types of warranties recognized under the law:

1. Implied warranties
2. Express warranties

The term "Implied warranties" means that the goods must be capable of passing in trade under the contract description and are fit for the purpose intended. Express warranties are those that are specifically set forth in the contract itself; they are in common use for many construction contracts. Warranties are generally for packaged items such as water heaters and compressors. Where the industry practice is to furnish a warranty for an item, the requirement for such a warranty may be included in the specifications. An express warranty is a means of achieving good procurement results by making the contractor responsible for his work and for failures of his work during some part of its useful life. The primary disadvantage of warranties is that they are often unenforceable. Moreover, a warranty clause costs money in the form of higher bid prices and it cannot be demonstrated that the owner recovers the cost of the warranty.

There are several obstacles to the strict enforcement of warranties; some of these obstacles are:

1. Even in what appears to be a clear-cut contractor responsibility under a warranty, certain action on the part of the owner or design firm may cloud the issue and result in litigation.
2. After acceptance of an item by the owner, the operation and maintenance of the item is performed by other than the contractor's or manufacturer's personnel. Thus, many defects that occur during the warranty period can be argued to result from faulty operation and maintenance by others rather than from a defect in the item itself.
3. Industry is becoming reluctant to accept several of the warranty clauses now in use. In particular, it will not accept the provision relating to third-party damages and the responsibility for an entire building and its contents, including damages to personnel, resulting from the failure of a single item.
4. Warranties of sole source items are generally unenforceable.
5. In practical application, warranties are generally enforceable only as to defects existing at the time of delivery and acceptance.

While the warranty clauses usually require the contractor to obtain and enforce warranties normally furnished by manufacturers and suppliers, the exact nature of the warranty is usually not stipulated in the specifications. Therefore, their effectiveness is subject to the wording used by the guarantor and can be expected to be something less than specific. Such a warranty depends almost entirely upon the integrity of the guarantor (the manufacturer or supplier). There are substantial differences in the warranty requirements of the many public and private agencies in their construction contracts. They range from requiring the contractor to warrant all work as to materials, workmanship, and contractor's design, to requiring the contractor to warrant only mechanical and electrical work. One agency may require the contractor to remedy all damage to equipment, site, building, and their contents resulting from a defect, while another agency may require the contractor to act as the owner's agent and obtain and enforce the subcontractors' and suppliers' warranties.

CHANGE ORDERS AND EXTRA WORK

A change order is a written agreement to modify, add to, or otherwise alter the work from that originally set forth in the contract documents at the time of opening bids, provided that such alteration can be considered to be within the scope of the original project; otherwise a contract modification may be required instead. It is the only legal means available to change the contract provisions after the award of the contract. Functionally, a change order accomplishes after award what the specifications *addenda* does prior to bid opening, except that an accompanying price change may be involved in a change order. A price change is not necessarily always in the contractor's favor, however, as it could also be in the form of a cash credit to the owner, or it may involve no price change at all.

It is standard practice in construction contracts to allow the owner the right to make changes in the work after the contract has been signed, and during the construction period. Depending upon the contract and its specific terms, such changes might involve additions to or deletions from the work, changes in the methods of construction or manner of work performance, changes in owner-furnished materials or facilities, or even changes in the contract time or order of the work. Changes may also be executed to correct errors in the plans or specifications, or they may be the direct result of contractor suggestions that are approved by the owner and the architect/engineer.

A contract change order is always used to effect a change within a contract. Such changes should always be in writing. Standard forms such as shown in Figure 16.5 are readily available for this purpose; however, they are not necessary, as a change order can be in the form of a letter if desired.

The following are some of the purposes served by change orders:

1. To change contract plans, specify the method and amount of payment, and changes in contract time therefrom.
2. To change contract specifications, including changes in payment and contract time that may result from such changes.
3. To effect agreements concerning the order of the work, including any payment or changes in contract that may result.
4. For administrative purposes, to establish the method of extra work payment and funds for work already stipulated in the contract.
5. For administrative purposes, to authorize an increase in extra work funds necessary to complete a previously authorized change.
6. To cover adjustments to contract unit prices for overrruns and underruns, when required by the specifications.
7. To effect cost reduction incentive proposals (value engineering proposals).
8. To effect payment after settlement of claims.

A contract change order is used in most instances when a written agreement by both parties to the contract is either necessary or desirable. Such use further serves the purpose of notifying a contractor of his right to file a protest if he fails to execute a change order.

When approved by the owner, the provisions of a contract change order become a part of the contract. If an approved change order is executed by the contractor, all of its provisions and terms are as equally binding upon the parties as those of the original contract.

Initiation of Change Orders

Change orders are usually initiated by construction personnel at the project site. However, changes are also requested from various other sources such as the contractor, the design firm, outside public agencies, private individuals, or other sources. In any case, they must be authorized by the owner before any change order authorizing extra work is valid.

A proposed contract change order is written only after the designers have given consideration as to the necessity, propriety, other methods of accomplishing the work, method of compensation, effect on contract time, estimate of cost, the contractor's reaction to the proposed change, and the probability of final approval.

Any change in the work which involves a change in the original contract price must be approved in writing by the owner before a change order can be executed. If it is not the owner who signs, then the party who does sign for him must have written authorization from the owner to sign on his behalf. The architect or engineer of record, by virtue of his position alone, has no authority to order changes to the contract. If he does act in this manner, he must be authorized in some way to act in the owner's behalf.

Change Order Preparation

A change order must be clear, concise, and explicit. It must tell the contractor what is to be done; where or within what limits; when the work is to be performed, if the order of the work is affected; how the contractor will be paid; and what consideration will be given to contract time (extensions, etc.).

Some clarification is in order at this time for users of AIA documents. The American Institute of Architects (AIA) uses two different forms to issue field change orders to the contractor during construction:

Change Order	AIA Document G701
Architect's Field Order	AIA Document G708

Although the use of the Change Order form is quite clear and it satisfies all the requirements for documenting and executing a change in the contract provisions, the same cannot necessarily be said of the Architect's Field Order. The field order is supposed to be an order from the architect to the contractor that either interprets the contract documents *or* orders minor changes in the work without changing either the contract sum or the contract time. As a document to interpret the contract provisions it serves its purpose admirably well. However, any document that changes any of the provisions of the plans, specifications or other contract documents *is* a change order no matter what you may choose to name it. As such, in the absence of a written authorization from the owner that allows the architect unilaterally to make such changes, only the owner can execute this document.

On a recent project where this document was used, it was desired to make a minor change in the work, for which there would be no additional charge by the contractor. The contractor, when confronted with this document, asked that a formal Change Order be issued instead, even though he had previously agreed to the terms and no charge was being made for the changes.

The contractor was not only within his rights in requesting a formal Change Order, but wise to do so. A formal Change Order provides the written authorization of the owner to

CHANGE ORDER

Order No. ____________________

Date: ____________________

Agreement Date: ____________________

NAME OF PROJECT: ____________________

____

OWNER: ____________________

CONTRACTOR: ____________________

The following changes are hereby made to the CONTRACT DOCUMENTS:

Justification:

Change to CONTRACT PRICE:

Original CONTRACT PRICE $____________

Current CONTRACT PRICE adjusted by previous CHANGE ORDER $____________

The CONTRACT PRICE due to this CHANGE ORDER will be (increased) (decreased) by: $____________

The new CONTRACT PRICE including this CHANGE ORDER will be $____________

Change to CONTRACT TIME:

The CONTRACT TIME will be (increased) (decreased) by__________calendar days.

The date for completion of all work will be ____________(Date).

Approvals Required:
To be effective this Order must be approved by the Federal agency if it changes the scope or objective of the PROJECT, or as may otherwise be required by the SUPPLEMENTAL GENERAL CONDITIONS.

Requested by: ____________________

Recommended by: ____________________

Ordered by: ____________________

Accepted by: ____________________

Federal Agency Approval (where applicable) ____________________

CONTRACT DOCUMENTS FOR CONSTRUCTION OF
FEDERALLY ASSISTED WATER AND SEWER PROJECTS

Document No. 10
Change Order: Page 1 of 1

Figure 16.5 Form of a change order.

make a change in the contract provisions; it states the effect on the contract sum, if any; it specifies the effect on contract time, if any; and could serve to release the contractor from liability that might result from making the change.

Any document that alters the terms of the original contract *in any way* must be considered as a change order. As such the document must either be signed by the owner or by someone with the power of attorney to act for him. The Architect's Field Order only provides for the signature of the architect and thus does not satisfy this requirement unless the architect also possesses written authority of the owner to execute such changes on his behalf. Even then, if a change in the work is intended, as opposed to an interpretation of the contract documents, it is still far more desirable to utilize the Change Order form for this purpose as a protection to all parties to the contract, even though there will be no change in contract price or time.

Cost of Delays Caused by Change Orders

Often, the execution of a change order involves slowdowns or delays of the contractor's operations. It should be kept in mind that all such delays involve extra cost to the contractor, and as such the costs are recoverable by the contractor. In a recent case involving construction delays resulting from defective specifications for a FAA Air Force Traffic Control Center, the U.S. Court of Claims ruled that a contractor working on a government contract is entitled to the extra costs incurred as a result of the government's defective specifications, even if only part of the job is delayed [*Chaney and James Construction Co., Inc., vs. United States,* U. S. Court of Claims No. 150–67 (Feb. 20, 1970].

This lends even more importance to the inspector's obligation to record all equipment and manpower at the site, and to note as to whether such equipment is being used on that day or not (Chapter 4). Such information can be the basis for defending claims of excessive charges for delays caused by extra work.

Bibliography

"Quality Level and Quality Control" NAVFAC P-455 *Construction Engineering Handbook,* July, 1974 ed., Book 1 — General Requirements. Department of the Navy, Naval Facilities Engineering Command, Alexandria, Virginia.

17
CLAIMS
AND
DISPUTES

CONSTRUCTION PROBLEMS

Every construction project seems to include its share of problems. To one way of thinking, perhaps if it weren't for these problems the job of resident project representative might never have been conceived. A good resident project representative is not simply a man who has the unique ability to solve problems, for generally the contractor can do this. It is the inspector's ability to apply his personal experience and knowledge to his project in such a way that he can look ahead, anticipate the occurrence of various events resulting from the various approaches that the contractor might take, evaluate these conditions, and offer constructive assistance in seeing that the potential problems either never occur or are minimized. An inspector who lacks this quality contributes nothing to the project—he simply adds to its cost.

In order to understand fully their application to the terms of the construction contract, several terms frequently used in this book will be defined. This chapter is divided into two major classifications. The first deals with the definition and the administrative procedures involved in the handling of protests, claims, and disputes under the terms of the construction contract; the second addresses itself to the methods available for the settlement of such differences as well as an explanation of the principles of arbitration under the rules of the American Arbitration Association, which is receiving growing respect as a fast, economical, and fair method for the resolution of construction contract disputes.

PROTESTS

The term ''protests'' as used here refers to disputes arising out of the issuance of a contract change order by the architect or engineer against the objections of the contractor. The terms of the contract documents for the orderly filing of written protests by the contractor as a means of establishing his claims for additional compensation or time to complete the work or claims of unfair treatment under the terms of the contract, short of turning the problem over to arbitration, is normally covered in the General Conditions (''boilerplate''). In the AIA General Conditions of the Contract for Construction, Articles 2.2.7 through 2.2.11 (1970 edition) and in the NSPE Standard General Conditions of the Construction Contract, Articles 9.9 through 9.10 (1974 edition) the procedures for the handling of protests and disagreements are specified in detail, up to the point of referring the matter to arbitration.

The normal procedure is for the resident project representative to discuss with the contractor any objections to a particular change order or other directions of the architect/engineer. If the contractor's objections can be satisfied by minor changes in the provisions of a proposed change order or direction given him, and such changes do not violate the contract provisions (this includes plans, specifications, addenda, previous change orders, codes, permit provisions, or similar constraints), then the change should normally be discussed with the architect/engineer's or owner's project manager and with his concurrence the change should normally be made. This will often avoid a formal protest, which is often costly even if you win.

In the event that the resident project representative cannot satisfy the contractor's objections, he should consult with the project manager to explore other possible means of settlement. When neither the resident project representative nor the project manager can resolve the problem through normal procedures, the pending change order or other direction of the architect/engineer or the owner should be issued in its original form and the contractor reminded of the provisions of the contract documents that require his conformance with any such order of the architect/engineer or owner even if he disagrees with it, under penalty of being considered in default on his contract. It should also be carefully noted in the inspector's diary (field log) that such reminder was given to the contractor. This does not take away the contractor's right to file a letter of protest that could be used as a later basis of claims against the owner, provided that such letter is submitted within the time schedules that are specified in the General Conditions of the construction contract.

When a protest letter is received from the contractor, it should be carefully examined prior to acknowledgment of its receipt to assure that the basic requirements of the specifications are included in the contractor's letter. The architect/engineer or owner should then review the merits of the contractor's protest. If the architect/engineer or owner decides that the protest is without merit, then he should issue a letter to the contractor advising him of his rights under the contract to file legal claims. Normally, if the contractor fails to file claims in accordance with the provisions of the contract, especially as to the time of filing, he may waive his rights under the contract.

furnished strictly pursuant to, and in conformity with the General Conditions of the Specifications, the Detail Specifications, and the lines and grades and other directions of the Engineer as given from time to time during the progress of the work under the terms of the contract, and also in accordance with the contract drawings and with working drawings to be furnished from time to time as provided herein. The Contractor shall complete the entire work to the satisfaction of the Engineer, and in accordance with the specifications and drawings herein mentioned, at the prices fixed in the contract.

16. Personal attention. — The Contractor shall give his personal attention constantly to the faithful prosecution of the work, and shall be present, either in person or by a duly authorized and competent representative, on the site of the work, continually during its progress, to receive directions or instructions from the Engineer. Whenever the Contractor is not present on any part of the work where it may be desired to give directions, orders may be given by the Engineer, and shall be received and obeyed by the superintendent or foreman who may have charge of the particular part of the work in reference to which orders are given.

17. Protests. — (a) If the Contractor considers any work demanded of him to be outside the requirements of the contract, or if he considers any record or ruling of the Engineer or of any inspector to be unfair, he shall immediately upon such work being demanded or such record or ruling being made, ask for written instructions or decision, whereupon he shall proceed without delay to perform the work or conform to the record or ruling, but unless the Contractor finds such instructions or decisions satisfactory, he shall, within 10 working days after receipt of same, file a written protest with the Engineer, stating clearly and in detail his objections and the reasons therefor. Except for such grounds of protest or objections as are made of record in the manner specified and within the time stated herein, the Contractor hereby waives all grounds for protest or objections to the records, rulings, instructions, or decisions of the Engineer, and hereby agrees that as to all matters not included in such protests the records, instructions, and decisions of the Engineer shall be final and conclusive.

(b) No later than 30 working days following the submission of a protest in accordance with subsection (a), the Contractor shall submit to the Engineer a statement of his factual and legal contentions concerning the matter so noticed. The statement shall set forth clearly and in detail, for each item of additional compensation or time adjustment claimed, the reasons for the protest, references to applicable provisions of the specifications, the nature and amount of cost or time involved, or both, the computations used in determining such cost or time, or both, and all other pertinent factual data. The Contractor shall furnish such clarification and further available information and data as may be requested in writing by the Engineer within the time specified in such request. In addition, he shall maintain complete and accurate daily records of the costs of any portion of the work for which additional compensation is claimed, and shall give the Engineer access thereto or certified copies thereof as requested.

(c) Any decision, order, instructions, notice or act or omission of the Engineer as to which the Contractor has submitted a protest shall be final and conclusive on the Contractor if he fails to submit or document a statement of his factual and legal contentions with respect thereto in the manner and within the times above specified, and such failure shall constitute a waiver of all claims in connection therewith, whether direct or consequential in nature. Provided, that the Engineer may, if the Contractor shows good cause and if the interests of the District will not be prejudiced, consider and decide a properly documented protest on its merits notwithstanding the Contractor's failure to submit it within the time above stated. The foregoing provision shall create no right in the Contractor, and failure or refusal of the Engineer to exercise his authority thereunder shall not be subject to claim by the Contractor.

(d) All protests will be disposed of by agreement between the Engineer and the Contractor; except that when agreement cannot be reached, the protest will be disposed of by the Engineer's decision. The Contractor will be informed of the Engineer's decision within 30 working days after the Contractor last submits data pertinent to the protest as provided for in Section 17(b). The Engineer's decision shall be final and conclusive.

(e) In all matters concerning the validity, interpretation, performance, effect, or otherwise of the Contract, the laws of the State of California shall govern and be applicable. Pending final disposition of a protest, the Contractor shall proceed diligently with the performance of the Contract and in accordance with the Engineer's decision.

(f) No action to enforce this Contract, or to interpret any provision thereof, or to assert any claim arising or alleged to arise in the course or out of its performance shall be brought by either party thereto in any court other than a State court of the State of California.

(g) Nothing herein contained shall relieve or be construed as relieving the Contractor of the obligation to file a claim in compliance with the requirements of Part 3 of Division 3.6 of Title 1 (beginning with Section 900) of the Government Code of the State of California in the event he intends to seek judicial relief from any decision of the Engineer on a protest and such protest involved a prior denial of claimed added compensation or relief from assessment of liquidated damages. For purposes of filing such claim, the cause for action shall be deemed to accrue no later than the date the voucher for final payment under the Contract is presented to the Contractor.

Figure 17.1 Provisions for handling protests under a public works contract.

CLAIMS

Potential Claims

The term "potential claim" applies to any differences arising out of the performance of the work that *might* reasonably lead to the later filing of a claim by the contractor if the difference cannot be resolved in the field.

It should be the policy of the architect/engineer or owner to consider the merits of a potential claim at the earliest possible time. As soon as the resident project representative has knowledge of the existence of a dispute that may lead to the filing of a potential claim, he should discuss the situation with the contractor. If the resident project representative determines that the contractor's preliminary arguments are valid, he should take such corrective neasures as are within the scope of his authority under the contract, including the possibility of making recommendation to the architect/engineer or owner to submit change orders to alleviate the problem.

In the event that the resident project representative cannot resolve the differences in the field, he should discuss the problem with the architect/engineer or owner. If the differences still cannot be resolved within the terms of the contract, the contractor should be reminded of the provisions of the contract documents relating to the time and methods for him to file claims, and such reminder should be recorded in the resident project representative's diary (field log).

Upon receipt of a potential claim in writing from the contractor, and prior to submitting it to the architect/engineer or owner for review, it should be reviewed by the resident project representative to see that it contains the basic information necessary, such as the reasons that the contractor believes additional consideration is due. It should also be reviewed to determine that the timeliness of the submittal is in accordance with the terms of the contract documents. If the contractor's letter is not sufficiently complete with respect to the nature of the claim, the architect/engineer or owner should request in writing that the contractor submit additional data before further processing of the contractor's claim.

Each poential claim should be reviewed by the architect/engineer or owner. If after this review the potential claim is considered as being without merit, then an answering letter should be sent to the contractor. The letter should include the statements referred to under "protests" in the previous paragraphs. If the contractor's notice of potential claim does not meet the requirements for timeliness as set forth in the specifications, then the architect/engineer or owner should advise the contractor in writing of this deficiency.

Claims and Disputes

The term "claim" applies to differences that *are* developed during the life of the contract under protests and potential claims, and that are not yet resolved at the time the contractor returns his proposed final estimate of the amount of additional money or time asked for. In other words, a protest or potential claim does not become a claim until the contractor repeats his objections by notifying the architect/engineer or owner at the time he returns the proposed final estimate for such claim.

There are normally two situations that become claims:

1. Protests and potential claims that have not been resolved during the progress of the work and that have been restated with the return of the final estimate.
2. Situations wherein the first notification of any problem is a claim submitted with the return of the proposed final estimate.

Procedures for resolving disputes over contractor claims are subject to the specific provisions of the contract documents; in some cases such disputes are directed to be resolved through binding arbitration under the rules of the American Arbitration Association. Arbitration of owner/contractor claims and disputes under the provisions of the AIA General Conditions of the Contract for Construction are specified in Articles 2.2.10 through 2.2.11 and 7.10 and under the provisions of the NSPE Standard General Conditions of the Construction Contract are specified in Articles 9.10 and 16. Similarly, the ASCE/AGC General Conditions of Contract for Engineering Construction cover resolution of such disputes by binding arbitration in Article 39 of that document.

RESOLVING DIFFERENCES

Even if a perfect set of contract documents were to be devised, there would still be disagreements between parties. Disagreements may arise between the contractor and the architect/engineer or owner concerning the interpretation of the contract; what constitutes extra work on the contract; payment for changes; extensions of time; damages for owner-directed acceleration or slowdown; costs occasioned by owner-caused delay; defective drawings or specifications; changed conditions (sometimes referred to as unforeseen conditions, based upon the logic that the conditions have not actually "changed" but were that way all the time. Discovery of the difference between the actual conditions and the way they were represented in the sepcifications or drawings is referred to under this concept as "unforeseen" differences). Other similar matters may affect contract cost or time required to complete the work. Contract documents routinely include procedures to be followed in the settlement of such claims and disputes. The greatest difficulty arises from the fact that there is no uniform method of handling such unforeseen conditions, and numerous books and technical articles have been written about it; many cases are brought to suit over such differences; and the matter isn't much closer to the development of a fair and equitable contract provision that will apply to all such cases than it was at the beginning.

Although their provisions may vary, construction contracts typically require the contractor to notify the architect/engineer immediately upon recognizing a situation that can lead to a claim or dispute. In cases of conflicts between the drawings and the specifications (a frequent cause of difficulty), it is the obligation of the contractor to notify the architect/engineer immediately without going further with what he knows to be improper work.

A word of caution at this point. An inspector should always be aware of the possibility that a contractor who is alert for extras may recognize a defect in the plans or specifications, yet hastily construct the work exactly as shown on the defective documents, knowing all the time that he will be directed to remove such work and reconstruct it later as soon as the architect/engineer or owner discovers the same defect. A situation such as this could be a race between the contractor and the inspector to see if the contractor can get the incorrectly specified or detailed work constructed before the inspector notices it and reports it to the architect/engineer or owner. The logic of the plan is simple. If a contractor can feign ignorance of the problem and simply claim that he was just following the plans and specifications (which, undoubtedly, he would be) then, when the architect/engineer or owner discovers the defect in the plans and specifications and orders the newly constructed work to be removed and reconstructed, the contractor will willingly rebuild the work in any manner subsequently ordered by the architect/engineer or owner—followed later by bills for extra work, which, of course, the owner then becomes obligated to pay.

If a dispute cannot be settled with the architect/engineer or owner, and he orders the contractor to continue with the work as directed by the architect/engineer or owner, the contractor cannot usually refuse without becoming potentially liable for breach of contract. Although the contractor may perform such work under written protest, he must continue to do the work and keep the operation on schedule, relying upon the contractual remedies in the contract documents to settle the question of compensation or additional time.

OBLIGATIONS OF THE CONTRACTOR

As might be expected from a document prepared by the owner, the contractor's rights under the terms of the construction contract documents are often few and his obligations many. However, certain standard forms of General Conditions of the Construction Contract such as those of the AIA, the NSPE, the ASCE/AGC, and many public agencies provide fairly equitable conditions for all parties to the contract, which is one reason that builders generally favor such standard forms over those typewritten, do-it-yourself varieties produced by the usually well meaning but often poorly informed specifier or even attorney who is unfamiliar with construction contract requirements.

The contractor is expected to give his personal attention to the work, and either he or his authorized representative must be on the construction site at all times that work is being performed there. Some contractors will leave the job site without adequate supervision in an attempt to entice the inspector into directing some of the construction work (actual direct supervision). Such action by the inspector would then shift a portion of the job responsibility to the owner or the architect/engineer. In cases of defects in construction in which the inspector has exercised such supervision, the contractor has grounds for being legally relieved of the financial responsibility of correcting such defects.

In addition to the requirements for providing continuous, adequate supervision, the contractor is also required to conform to all laws and ordinances concerning job safety, licensing, employment of labor, sanitation, insurance, zoning, building codes, environmental conditions, and similar constraints.

The general contractor, as the only party with a direct contractual relationship with the owner for construction, is responsible for and must guarantee all materials and workmanship, whether constructed by his own forces or by his subcontractors. The inspector should check the specifications thoroughly, as they may contain a provision that the contractor must arrange for an extension of his performance bond through the entire guarantee period, usually one year from the date of completion of the work and its acceptance by the owner. The requirement may call for the bond in full amount of the original contract price or may allow a reduced amount such as 5 or 10 percent for the term of the guarantee period.

Even though the contractor normally has no direct responsibility for the plans and specifications, he can incur a contingent liability for proceeding with faulty work whose defects should be obvious to one in his business. Thus, if the contractor is asked to do something that he feels is improper or not in accordance with good construction practice, he is entirely within his rights to submit a letter of protest to the architect/engineer or owner stating his position before proceeding with the matter in dispute. If, after the contractor has submitted his written protest, the architect/engineer or owner prefers to require that the contractor proceed anyway, the contractor has protected himself in case of later flaws that may develop. It may even be possible that the insuring firm could get out of paying a claim if it later turned out that a flaw developed as a direct result of not heeding the contractor's advice—a matter for the courts to decide.

Insurance coverage is an important contractual responsibility of the contractor, both as to type of insurance and policy limits. The contractor is required to provide insurance not only for his own direct and contingent liability, but also frequently for the owner's protection. He is expected to exercise every reasonable safeguard for the protection of persons and property in, on, and adjacent to the construction site.

Some of the most important of the contractor's rights include progress payments, recourse by the contractor if the owner fails to make payments, termination of the contract for cause, rights to extensions of time and extra payment as provided, and appeals from the decisions of the owner and the architect/engineer. Subject to contractual requirements and contractual limitations and, in the case of public works contracts, subjec to the local laws concerning the use of subcontractors, the general contractor is normally free to purchase materials from any source he wishes, and to schedule work in any manner that he sees fit in the absence of any contractual provisions to the contrary.

SETTLEMENT OF DISPUTES BY ARBITRATION

Business Disputes

In the world of business, disputes are inevitable. One person may understand his rights and obligations differently from another no matter how carefully a contract is written.

This could lead to delayed shipments, complaints about the quality of the work, claims of nonperformance of the terms of the contract, and similar misunderstandings. And, even with the best of intentions, parties often perform less than they promise.

Such controversies seldom involve great legal issues. On the contrary, they generally deal with the same facts and interpretation of contract terms that owners and contractors are used to dealing with every day. Therefore, when disputes arise out of day-to-day activities, the parties frequently like to settle them privately and informally. This is what commercial arbitration is for.

What is Arbitration?

Arbitration is the voluntary submission of a dispute to one or more impartial persons for final and binding determination. It is private and informal, and is designed for quick, practical, and inexpensive settlements. But at the same time arbitration is an *orderly* proceeding, governed by the rules of procedure and standards of conduct that are prescribed by law. The most commonly used arbitration procedures these days are those administered by the American Arbitration Association. The AIA, the NSPE, and the ASCE/AGC General Conditions all call for arbitration under the Construction Industry Arbitration Rules of the American Arbitration Association. The Association does not act as arbitrator. Its function is to *administer* arbitrations in accordance with the agreement of the parties and to maintain panels from which arbitrators may be chosen.

The arbitrators are quasi-judicial officers. Their decisions represent their judgments of the rights of the parties to a dispute. One significant difference between the rules that govern civil action in court and an arbitration proceeding is that in arbitration the strict rules of evidence do not apply. The arbitrator's guiding principle is to hear *all* the evidence that may be material and to hear *no* arguments or evidence from one side that the other has no opportunity to comment upon or rebut.

The arbitrator is the final judge of matters brought before him. His decision will not be reviewed on its merits where procedures were fair and impartial. More than a hundred years ago in 1854, the United States Supreme Court said:

> If an award is within the submission, and contains the honest decision of the arbitrators, after a full and fair hearing of the parties, a court of equity will not set it aside for error, either in law or in fact. A contrary course would be a substitute of the judgement [sic] of the chancellor in place of the judges chosen by the parties, and would make an award the commencement, not the end, of litigation.

Most arbitration cases are heard by a panel of three arbitrators, each usually representing a different field of specialization. Unless the agreement of the parties requires a unanimous decision, the arbitrators are governed by majority rule, both in procedural decisions and in rendering the award. In some cases, usually those in which the amount in question is relatively small, a single arbitrator may serve if desired by the parties. It is customary, when three-man boards are used, for one of the arbitrators to serve as a chairman. His powers, however, are exactly the same as the other two.

Authority of the Arbitrator

The arbitrator has broad powers to determine matters of fact, law, and procedure. This decision-making authority must be exercised by the arbitrator alone to the best of his ability, and it may not be delegated to others. It would render his award subject to attack in court if, for example, the arbitrator sought clarification of a point of law by outside consultation.

The award, under the rules of arbitration, must be in writing, and it must represent the judgment of at least the majority of the board unless the contract of the parties requires a unanimous decision. He must word the award clearly and definitely. The arbitrator must answer all the questions before him, but he may not deal with any matter not submitted to arbitration. The relief granted in his judgment must be consistent with the contract, and may include specific performance as well as monetary damages. Arbitrators are not required to write opinions explaining the reasons for their decisions. As a general rule, their awards consist of a brief direction to the parties on a single sheet of paper. There are a number of reasons for this. One is that written opinions might open avenues for attack on the award by the losing party.

As stated earlier, arbitrators are the final judges of all matters of both fact and law before them. Courts will not review their decisions on the merits of the case even when the arbitrators have come to a conclusion that is different than that which the court might have reached. In particular, courts are concerned only with the face of the award itself, not any additional explanatory matter.

The members of the National Panel of Arbitrators of the American Arbitration Association volunteer their time and talent without any fee, although on hearings that last for more than two days some payment is made. There is an administrative fee that must be paid to the American Arbitration Association for handling claims; however, the amount is relatively small. The American Arbitration Association was founded in 1926 as a private, nonprofit organization "to foster the study of arbitration, to perfect its techniques and procedures under arbitration law, and to advance generally the science of arbitration."

Arbitration Agreements Regulated by Law

Commercial arbitration agreements today are recognized by statute by the United States Arbitration Act and in all but three states. However, the extent to which these agreements are enforceable differs widely. In overruling common law, many states distinguish between agreements to submit present disputes to arbitration and agreements to arbitrate unknown dispues that might arise in the future. The most modern arbitration laws provide that all agreements to arbitrate, whether of present or future controversies, are valid, irrevocable, and enforceable. In some other states, the laws merely provide that present and known disputes are arbitrable when the parties agreed by contract to arbitrate them. In cases of present disputes, however, many statutes require that the arbitration agreement be made a rule of court before it becomes irrevocable and enforceable.

Some confusion has been caused by some writers who state that in some of these older laws, agreements to arbitrate future disputes are void. In most states such agreements are valid in the sense that it is permissible to enter into such agreements. The only problem that remains is the one of enforcing it.

For the basis of comparison, the various arbitration laws of the different states will be divided into three groups. The breakdown will be based upon those states that have by statute or judicial law changed the common law rule of revocability that permitted either party to an arbitration agreement to terminate it at his will at any time prior to the rendition of an award.

Group I—Statutes Allowing Arbitration of Present and Future Disputes

The first group of states will be those in which there is specific authority by statute or judicial ruling that holds that an arbitration clause in a commercial contract is valid, irrevocable, and enforceable. The first 23 states listed, as well as the federal government, have statutes that conform to or embody features that are essentially similar to "modern arbitration law" in which all written agreements to arbitrate, whether present controversies or future controversies between the contracting parties, are valid, irrevocable, and enforceable. Virginia, while not having a modern arbitration law, has amended its arbitration statute to make arbitration agreements binding upon the parties. In addition, there are court decisions from Colorado and Nevada that declare that agreements to arbitrate future disputes are valid and enforceable without the aid of any special statutes.

The 26 states and federal law in Group I are shown below:

1. Alaska	15. New Jersey
2. Arizona	16. New York
3. California	17. Ohio
4. Connecticut	18. Oregon
5. Florida	19. Pennsylvania
6. Hawaii	20. Rhode Island
7. Illinois	21. Virginia
8. Louisiana	22. Washington
9. Maine	23. Wisconsin
10. Maryland	24. Wyoming
11. Massachusetts	25. Colorado
12. Michigan	26. Nevada
13. Minnesota	27. United States Code, Title 9 Sec. 1–2
14. New Hampshire	28. District of Columbia

Group II—Statutes Allowing Arbitration of Present Disputes Only

The following 21 states have statutes that provide essentially that agreements to arbitrate *present* controversies are valid. It should be noted that although Texas passed a modern arbitration act in 1966, the law contains a unique provision that excludes *construction,* labor, and insurance agreements.

The following list indicates those states in Group II in which arbitration statutes exist, but they contain varying restrictions that could affect the application of a future arbitration clause in the General Conditions of a construction contract:

1. Alabama	11. Missouri
2. Arkansas	12. Montana
3. Delaware	13. Nebraska
4. Georgia	14. New Mexico
5. Idaho	15. North Carolina
6. Indiana	16. North Dakota
7. Iowa	17. South Carolina
8. Kansas	18. Tennessee
9. Kentucky	19. Texas
10. Mississippi	20. Utah
	21. West Virginia

Group III—States with No Arbitration Statutes

In the third group there are three states that have *no* statutes on commercial arbitration. Despite the lack of an applicable statute, it is probable that these states would apply common law principles to arbitration law. Under this, a pending suit could be submitted to arbitration.

The three states in Group III are:

1. Oklahoma
2. South Dakota
3. Vermont

Bibliography

Construction Manual, State of California, Department of Transportation, Section 2–70 Protests, Potential Claims, and Claims; issued by the Division of Construction and Research, Office of Construction, Sacramento, California, 1975.

A Businessman's Guide to Commercial Arbitration and *A Manual for Commercial Arbitrators* and *Construction Industry Arbitration Rules,* published by the American Arbitration Association, New York.

Gerald Asken, "Resolving Construction Contract Disputes Through Arbitration," from *Delays and Disputes in Building Construction,* published by the American Arbitration Association, New York.

18
PROJECT CLOSEOUT

ACCEPTANCE OF THE WORK

At first it would seem that all that would be necessary to close out a project would be to inspect it, accept it for the owner, and see that the contractor receives his final payment. But, what about all the guarantees, operating instructions for equipment, keying schedule, record drawings, bonds, and similar items that must be accounted for first? What about liens that may have been filed against the property by subcontractors? Each of these items will require careful handling to assure the owner of a quality product that is free of encumbrances, and that will be backed up by the guarantees that were called for in the original documents.

Acceptance of the work and final payment to the contractor must proceed in accordance with the terms of the construction contract documents. Although the methods may vary somewhat from job to job, they basically all begin with a request from the contractor to make a final inspection of the work. Generally, there may be two inspections required to close out the project. The first will establish those areas still requiring correction or other remedial work, and the final inspection will be a check-off to assure that all work is substantially complete and that all corrections have been made.

The check-off list or ''punch list'' as it is normally called, is a detailed list made near the end of the project, showing all items still requiring completion or correction before the work can be accepted and a Certificate of Substantial Completion issued. Before acceptance, all workmanship must meet specified standards, all work must be installed and complete, and all equipment must be tested and operational.

In some cases it is possible to accept a project as being "substantially complete" if only minor items remain to be finished. This simply means that the project is close enough to being completed so that it can be put to use for the purpose it was intended, and that all remaining incomplete work is comprised of relatively minor items that the contractor agrees to correct while the structure is occupied—for example, maybe the wrong wall switch plates were installed. In this case the owner could use the building while he was waiting for the contractor to receive the proper wall plates and replace them.

If a "Certificate of Substantial Completion" is filed, and written on the certificate is a complete list of all work remaining to be done to complete the project, anything that is not indicated on the list of deficiencies requiring correction on the Certificate of Substantial Completion is considered as being satisfactory as-is. Often, final payment to the contractor is held for 35 to 45 days after completion and is not released until correction of all remaining deficiencies. Final payment involves the release of all retainage held during the project, which generally amounts to about 5 to 10 percent of the total cost of the project.

WARRANTY PERIOD

Generally, the work covered in a construction contract includes a stated guarantee period, which is frequently one or two years. In some cases the overall project may be guaranteed for only one year, although certain portions of the work may be covered by supplementary guarantees for longer periods. Normally, there is no need to withhold payment from the contractor for the purpose of assuring performance during the stated guarantee period, as the performance bond may be written to cover this period. While some contracts call for 100 percent of the performance bond to be continued in force during the entire guarantee period (a costly arrangement for the contractor) many contracts allow for a reduced portion of the performance bond to cover any defects noted during the guarantee period. After all, if the project is 100 percent complete, there is little reason to believe that it will *all* fail. Thus, many such bonds are reduced to 10 percent or some other reduced percentage of the performance bond during the guarantee period. This seems quite reasonable, because frankly, if a significant percentage of failures were noted in the first year following completion, it would certainly appear to cast doubt over the quality of the inspection that was provided.

The contractor's warranty does not imply, however, that he is liable for the adequacy of the plans and specifications unless he prepared them himself, or unless he agreed to guarantee their adequacy. A contractor is only required to construct in accordance with the terms of the contract documents, and when he does so, he cannot ordinarily be held to guarantee that the architect's or engineer's design will be free from defects or that the completed job will accomplish the purpose intended. He is responsible only for the quality of the workmanship, the quality of the materials used, and for performance of the contract. It should be kept in mind that in the evaluation of the adequacy of the contractor's work, the standard of comparison is not to be based upon the previous experience of the inspector as to what he considers inferior work, but rather upon specific or substantial conformance with the terms set forth in the contract documents. The contractor can only be obligated to perform that which he specifically agreed to do in the written contract; anything required of him that is beyond this would be valid grounds for a claim for additional compensation.

In Wisconsin, a court ruled that a contractor does not absolutely guarantee his work against defects or losses prior to the owner's final acceptance [*E. D. Wesley Co. vs. City of New Berlin,* 215 N.W. 2d 657 (1974)]. The case involved a problem with a booster pump and the owner withheld the contractor's final payment. The city maintained that since *it had not yet accepted the work,* the contractor was absolutely liable for all repair costs. The court found that the damage was not caused either by a defect in the pump or by the contractor in his installation. Therefore, the court ruled that the damage was not within the scope of the contractor's liability either before or after acceptance of the work.

CONTRACT TIME

Most contracts are quite specific as regards the amount of construction time allowed to complete the work, and many provide for the payment of "liquidated damages" by the contractor to the owner for failure to complete on time. It should be noted, however, that in the absence of a provision establishing "time as the essence of the contract," neither the beginning date nor the date of completion can be considered as creating an absolute schedule for the purpose of imposing the provisions of a liquidated damages clause for exceeding the specified completion dates. According to a ruling by the Supreme Court of Nebraska, time is not of the essence in a construction contract unless specifically stated in the contract documents. [Kingery Construction Co. v. Scherbarth Welding, Inc., 185 N.W. 2d 857 (1971)]. If a contractor's failure to complete a project on schedule was the result of delays that occurred because of the owner's action, however, a North Carolina Court of Appeals has ruled that the contractor would not be liable for liquidated damages [*Dickerson, Inc., vs. Bd. of Transportation,* Court of Appeals of North Carolina, June 18, 1975].

When computing contract time, particular attention should be paid to the contract wording—is it "calendar days" or "working days"? If it is working days, particular care will have to be taken in determining the definition of a working day. Generally, this will have to be resolved by checking the master labor agreement for the area involved to see what is considered as a holiday and what is not. The easiest time to compute is *calendar* days, as this method includes all days, including Saturdays, Sundays, and holidays.

Normally, construction time is computed from the date on the written Notice to Proceed given to the contractor at the beginning of the job (Fig. 9.7). If no such notice was issued, the determination of the actual contract period may be indefinite. Preferably, a Notice to Proceed should be issued at the beginning of each project to assure a complete understanding as to the actual date construction work was authorized to begin. This document should not be confused with a Notice of Award (Fig. 9.6)—that document simply establishes the identity of the contractor who will be given the contract to do the work and obligates the owner to sign the contract. It does not establish the date of starting construction. Once a contract has been signed, however, most specifications require that the contractor begin work within 10 or 15 days after the signing of the agreement. If this takes the place of a formal Notice to Proceed, then to compute the completion date, you will have to automatically allow the contractor an additional 10 or 15 days added to the contract term to allow for the latest date at which time he could begin the work. As stated before, unless time is stated as the "essence of the contract" in the contract documents, there is always the possibility that a contractor may be reasonably secure from charges of liquidated damages for relatively minor time overruns.

The establishment of the date of completion of a project, in the absence of a formal document that specifically identifies the date upon which all work was completed may be more difficult. It is in the owner's best interests to file a formal certificate of completion upon completing his project. This should be filed as early as possible before the release of the contractor's final payment and retention money. The filing and recording of such notice generally sets the lien law "time" running in the owner's favor. Sufficient holding time should be provided in the specifications to enable the owner to retain the contractor's final payment until a waiver of claims or final payment of all subcontractors and material suppliers has been made; otherwise the contractor will have received his final payment and all of his retainage money, and the owner will be encumbered with liens on his property. Of course, the owner has legal recourse to recover from the general contractor, but that could be a long and costly process. Meanwhile, the owner would be obligated to pay the liens filed by the subcontractors and suppliers in order to clear title to his own property (see "Final Payment to the Contractor" in Chapter 14).

CLEANUP

In addition to the requirement that the contractor keep the jobsite clean during the progress of the work, he is similarly obligated to thoroughly clean up the construction site at the end of the job before the work can be accepted. The final cleanup is of significantly greater proportions than previous cleanup work, since all of the various items of demobilization rightfully are included under the cleanup category. This includes removal of temporary utilities, haul roads, temporary fences, field offices, detours, stockpiles, surplus materials, scrap, replacement of landscaping where temporarily removed, street cleaning, and the obtaining of releases from the various city, county, or other governmental authorities having jurisdiction.

The contractor is obligated to clean up the site of his own operations as well as all areas under the control of the owner that may have been used by the contractor in connection with the work on the project. He should be required to remove all temporary construction, equipment, waste, and surplus material of every nature unless the owner has approved otherwise in writing. Final acceptance of the work should be withheld until the contractor has satisfactorily complied with all of the requirements for final cleanup of the project site. This includes cleanup of city streets as well, where dirt or other deposits have accumulated as a result of his operations.

Disposal of all waste and refuse should be at the contractor's expense. No waste or rubbish of any nature should be allowed to be buried or otherwise disposed of at the site except upon receipt of written approval of the owner.

CLOSING OUT THE PROJECT

Contrary to the layman's belief, the inspector's job is not finished when the contractor completes the work at the site and a Certificate of Completion is executed. It is only then that the work of closing out the project *really* begins. The field staff must be reduced to the minimum number of persons necessary to complete the closeout activities; all office equipment must be returned to the office that supplied it; telephone and utility services must be terminated; radio paging devices or similar communications equipment must be returned and their contracts terminated; project records must be transferred into the office of the inspector's employer; and a copy of a complete field office inventory should precede the return of all supplies and equipment and records of the field office.

Notices of address change should be sent to all parties who were previously addressing correspondence to the field office, and a closing schedule should be sent to the design firm and the owner so that appropriate plans can be made for the smooth transition of field personnel being released from the closing project into another assignment. Generally, the closeout will be accomplished by one or two persons; namely, the resident project representative and, if the work load warrants, a field clerk-typist.

The closeout period may actually begin several weeks to a month before the contractor completes the work on the project and can often extend for a month after completion of the work. In many cases the inspector will be required to assure that all data have been posted on a copy of the plans showing the actual manner and location of all work as actually completed. These are referred to as ''record drawings'' and they are normally in the form of red pencil marks on a set of prints of the contractor's. These are often required to be turned over to the architect or engineer or owner when completed, and from these the architect or engineer or owner may be required to have his draftsmen revise the original tracings to reflect recorded field information.

A summary of the principal closeout activities for a medium to large size project is shown in the following list. Although some of the items may vary from job to job and the order may vary somewhat, the tasks do not vary significantly:

1. Receive notification from the contractor that he has substantially completed the work and is ready for a walk-through inspection.
2. Prepare a complete project check list possibly as early as three to four weeks before the closing date in the schedule. Note on the check list all those items that require special operational testing prior to acceptance.
3. Schedule and conduct an inspection of all items on the check list. The inspection party should include representatives of the contractor and his CQC representative (if applicable), the architect, the civil, structural, mechanical, and electrical engineers (as applicable), the resident project representative, and the owner. Careful

PRELIMINARY PUNCH LIST - JULY 28, 1976

North Base Office Complex   Project No. 1553-07

UNCOMPLETED WORK

1. Installation of Fire Alarm System in Building No. 4400.
2. Installation of shelter over relocated transformer at rear of hangar (Modification).
3. Installation of road signs (Modification).
4. Operation and Maintenance Manuals.
5. Fire Detection System, Office Complex, including pull-boxes.
6. Repair of roof (Modification).
7. Paint doors in Annex (Modification).
8. Balance Air Conditioning System.

OUTSTANDING DEFICIENCIES

Exterior Trailer Complex

1. Final grading and clean-up.
2. Grout light pole - install cover.

Roof of Office Complex

3. Install 4 by 4 under ductwork lets as required.
4. Insulate around register boxes.
5. Clean-up.
6. Close opening in plywood decking used for electrical poles.
7. Additional support leg required.
8. Electrical cover plates (Fire Detection).
9. Intall door stops.
10. Exit lights.
11. Office lights checkout.
12. Operation of A/C system including thermostat.

Specific Items

13. Cut doors for clearance, Rooms 8, 9 and 10.
14. Finish carpet and install topset base in Rooms 2, 62, 63, 67, 50, 57, and 72.
15. In women's sanitary facility, touch up paint, complete topset base and floor, install chrome strip on leg of partition.
16. In Room 65, patch conduit openings and connect heater. Operation of water heater.
17. Finish painting in Rooms 66, 76, 77, and 78.

Figure 18.1   A project ''punch list''

notes should be kept by each inspector in his diary or log book of all corrective, remedial, or extra work required to meet acceptance standards, and this data should be used to develop a preliminary "punch list" of all items still requiring completion or correction before acceptance of the work. The contractor must make corrections before the final inspection date.

4. Begin a partial reduction of field office inspection staff if project is large enough to require several full-time inspectors in addition to the resident inspector.

5. Begin an inventory of all architect/engineer or owner property in the field office. List separately all office equipment, records and reports, supplies, field inspection and testing equipment, vehicles, cameras and photographic supplies, office furniture, and other property.

6. Complete final reduction of the field office inspection staff to the minimum number of persons necessary to complete the closeout administrative activities.

7. Using the preliminary punch list, conduct a final inspection of all work on the project approximately one week before the closing date if possible. The final inspection team should include the same persons who participated in the initial check list inspection. All items indicated as requiring correction on the preliminary punch list should be reinspected, and all tests that were originally unsatisfactory should be conducted again. Tests should not only include run-up of motors, pumps, air conditioning systems, fire protection systems, communications systems, and similar installed work, but should include the testing of fail-safe devices, switches, controls, and other emergency devices. In addition, all doors should be operated, all locksets operated, and any other moving parts operated to assure that they will function properly before acceptance of the work. A final punch list should be developed for any outstanding deficiencies still requiring correction.

8. The contractor's record drawing set should be checked to see that he has marked all changes and variations from the original contract drawings on the set of prints or tracings that he may be required to submit under the terms of the contract. If properly completed, these should be turned over to the resident project representative for transmittal to the architect/engineer or owner.

9. Prior to acceptance of the work, the resident project representative should obtain the following items from the contractor if required under the contract:
   Guarantees
   Certificates of inspection
   Operating manuals and instructions for equipment items
   Keying schedule
   Maintenance stock items; spare parts; special tools
   Record drawings
   Bonds (roof bonds, maintenance bonds, guarantee bonds, etc.)
   Certificates of inspection and compliance by local agencies
   Releases of liens (varies from state to state)

10. If all work has been substantially completed and all punch list items satisfactorily accomplished to the satisfaction of the inspecting team, a *Certificate of Substantial Completion* (Figs. 18.2 and 18.3) should be prepared. On a Certificate of Substantial Completion all remaining remedial work required to be done, as noted on the final punch list, should be listed on the appropriate place on the form. A *Certificate of Completion* should not be executed if *any* tasks remain to be done. Execution of a *completion* notice constitutes acceptance by the owner of the work *as is*—the presumption being that it is totally complete. Under such conditions the contractor has no further obligations under the contract except possibly to satisfy any claims made under the provisions of the guarantees.

   An owner who unqualifiedly accepts the work and makes final payment on a construction contract without taking exception to any part of the work has been held by the Montana Supreme Court to waive the owner's right to demand correction or get damages for defects in the work that are known at the time. Furthermore, such flaws do not fall under the coverage of the guarantee clause [*Grass*

CERTIFICATE OF SUBSTANTIAL COMPLETION

OWNER ☐
ARCHITECT ☐
CONTRACTOR ☐
FIELD
OTHER

AIA DOCUMENT G704

PROJECT:
(name, address)

ARCHITECT:

ARCHITECT'S PROJECT NUMBER:

TO (Owner)

CONTRACTOR:
CONTRACT FOR:

CONTRACT DATE:

DATE OF ISSUANCE:

PROJECT OR DESIGNATED AREA SHALL INCLUDE:

The Work performed under this Contract has been reviewed and found to be substantially complete. The Date of Substantial Completion is hereby established as
which is also the date of commencement of all warranties and guarantees required by the Contract Documents.

DEFINITION OF DATE OF SUBSTANTIAL COMPLETION

The Date of Substantial Completion of the Work or designated portion thereof is the Date certified by the Architect when construction is sufficiently complete, in accordance with the Contract Documents, so the Owner may occupy the Work or designated portion thereof for the use for which it is intended.

A list of items to be completed or corrected, prepared by the Contractor and verified and amended by the Architect, is appended hereto. The failure to include any items on such list does not alter the responsibility of the Contractor to complete all Work in accordance with the Contract Documents.

ARCHITECT _____ BY _____ DATE _____

The Contractor will complete or correct the Work on the list of items appended hereto within _____ days from the above Date of Substantial Completion.

CONTRACTOR _____ BY _____ DATE _____

The Owner accepts the Work or designated portion thereof as substantially complete and will assume full possession thereof at _____ (time) on _____ (date).

OWNER _____ BY _____ DATE _____

The responsibilities of the Owner and the Contractor for maintenance, heat, utilities and insurance shall be as follows:
(NOTE — Owner's and Contractor's legal and insurance counsel should determine and review insurance requirements and coverage)

Figure 18.2 AIA Certificate of Substantial Completion

CERTIFICATE OF SUBSTANTIAL COMPLETION

Owner's Project No. ....   Engineer's Project No. ....

Project ....

Contractor ....   Contract Date ....

Contract For ....

Project or Specified Part Shall Include ....

....

....

DEFINITION OF SUBSTANTIAL COMPLETION

The date of Substantial Completion of a Project or specified part of a Project is the date when the construction is sufficiently completed, in accordance with the Contract Documents, so that the Project or specified part of the Project can be utilized for the purpose for which it was intended.

To ....
(Owner)

And To ....
(Contractor)

Date of Substantial Completion ....

The Work performed under this contract has been inspected by authorized representatives of the Owner, Contractor and Engineer, and the Project (or specified part of the Project, as indicated above) is hereby declared to be substantially completed on the above date.

A tentative list of items to be completed or corrected is appended hereto. This list may not be exhaustive, and the failure to include an item on it does not alter the responsibility of the Contractor to complete all the Work in accordance with the contract documents. These items shall be completed by the Contractor within .... days of Substantial Completion.

NSPE 1910–8–D (1970 Edition)

Page 1 of .... pages

Figure 18.3 NSPE Certificate of Substantial Completion

The date of Substantial Completion is the date upon which all guarantees and warranties begin, except as noted below.

The responsibilities between the Owner and the Contractor for maintenance, heat, and utilities shall be as set forth below.

---   ---
      ENGINEER   **AUTHORIZED REPRESENTATIVE**   date

The Contractor accepts the above Certificate of Substantial Completion and agrees to complete and correct the items on the tentative list within the time indicated.

---   ---
      CONTRACTOR   **AUTHORIZED REPRESENTATIVE**   date

RESPONSIBILITIES: (For heat, maintenance, utilities, etc.)

    OWNER:

   CONTRACTOR:

EXCEPTIONS AS TO GUARANTEES AND WARRANTIES:

ENCLOSURES (*identify and attach*):

Page .... of .... pages

Figure 18.3 (continued)

Range High School District No. 27 vs. Wallace Diteman, Inc., Supreme Court of Montana, 465 P. 2d 814 (1970)].

11. Receive the contractor's request for his final progress payment. This does *not* include a release of his retainage money, however.
12. Check all work quantities and the value of the work completed from the punch list, retaining funds for those portions of the work named as still required to be done on the Certificate of Substantial Completion.
13. Submit contractor's payment request to the owner through the design or construction management firm with recommendation to pay, if warranted, less the retainage specified in the contract.
14. Obtain signatures of the architect/engineer, the contractor, and the owner or their authorized representatives on the Certificate of Completion or Certificate of Substantial Completion, then file the certificate for recording in the Office of the County Recorder where it serves as a public record and puts all potential lien holders on notice that their lien filing period has begun.
15. Notify owner, through the architect/engineer, that the building or other project is ready for occupancy or beneficial use, subject to completion of pickup work during occupancy.
16. If using a contractor-furnished field office, terminate any architect/engineer or owner obligations for telephone or other utility services to the field office. Transfer all records, supplies, equipment, and all other items on the inventory to the architect/engineer's or owner's office. Move into other quarters during the final administrative functions involved in the termination of all owner/contractor obligations.
17. If final completion of all pickup work noted on the Certificate of Substantial Completion has been accomplished, and if no liens have been filed during the holding period specified in the contract for making final payment, the architect/engineer may recommend to the owner that the retainage funds be released. The making of final payment will normally constitute a waiver of all claims by the owner except those arising from:

   a. Unsettled liens.
   b. Faulty or defective work appearing after substantial completion.
   c. Failure of the work to comply with the requirements of the contract documents.
   d. Terms of special guarantees required by the contract documents.

The making of final payment will also constitute a waiver of all claims by the contractor except those previously made and still unsettled.

SUBSTANTIAL COMPLETION AND PARTIAL UTILIZATION

Substantial completion and partial utilization are based upon the owner being able to use the project or the portion that is substantially complete for the purposes intended, and that the remaining activity of the contractor will not interfere with such use. The definitions of

AIA and NSPE vary slightly in their definition as to what "substantial completion" actually is; the AIA definition states:

> The date of substantial completion of a project or specified area of a project is the date when the construction is sufficiently completed, in accordance with the contract documents, *as modified by any change orders agreed to by the parties,* so that the *owner can occupy the* project or specified *area* of the project for the *use* for which it was intended.

Particular note should be made of the term "occupy," for in the construction of buildings this is the factor that determines whether a project is usable or not. The NSPE definition of substantial completion varies slightly:

> The date of substantial completion of a project or specified part of a project is the date when the construction is sufficiently completed, in accordance with the contract documents, so that the project or specified *part* of the project *can be utilized* for the *purpose* for which it was intended.

Certain facts are worthy of consideration before executing a Notice of Substantial Completion. If the contractor is to be excluded from the area involved except to the extent necessary for him to have access to correct or complete the pickup work items on the "punch list," it will be necessary for the architect/engineer or owner to indicate who will have the responsibility for maintenance, heat, and utilities for the area involved. Under the NSPE position on substantial completion the owner is not asked to sign the document, as he may not wish to accept a project that is only substantially complete, when in all fairness to the contractor he should do so. The extent to which the issuance of a Certificate of Substantial Completion will affect the insurable interest of the owner and the contractor in the project should be discussed with an insurance counselor.

The date of substantial completion has legal significance in many respects. The architect/engineer or owner and his resident project representative exercise great caution to be certain that the condition of the project meets the definition of being *substantially* complete before issuing such a certificate. In some states the date of substantial completion is the date on which the statute of limitations commences to run in the contractor's favor. Where liquidated damages are provided for in the specifications, the date of substantial completion may be used to indicate when such damages start to accrue.

The signing of a Certificate of Completion releases the contractor of all responsibility and obligation for further maintenance of the work, and ownership of the project passes to the owner. It is important to see that the owner is fully aware of the significance of this document in terms of his added responsibility. In the case of a Certificate of Substantial Completion, however, there seems to be some question as to whether the terms of the guarantees and the insurance begin at the time of substantial completion or after final acceptance upon completing all the remaining pickup work that was listed on the certificate. Normally, a certificate of substantial completion seems to relieve the contractor of the hazards of liquidated damages for any work performed subsequent to its execution. Thus it certainly seems to be in the contractor's best interest to obtain such a certificate as early as possible. As for a deficiency noted on the punch list that required the replacement of a piece of defective equipment, it would seem within reason that the guarantee period for the affected equipment should begin after the receipt of the replacement equipment and conclusion of a satisfactory operational test.

Index